JOURNAL FOR THE STUDY OF THE NEW TESTAMENT
SUPPLEMENT SERIES
174

Executive Editor
Stanley E. Porter

Editorial Board
David Catchpole, R. Alan Culpepper, Margaret Davies,
James D.G. Dunn, Craig A. Evans, Stephen Fowl, Robert Fowler,
Robert Jewett, Elizabeth Struthers Malbon, Robert W. Wall

Sheffield Academic Press

Academic Constraints in Rhetorical Criticism of the New Testament

An Introduction to a Rhetoric of Power

J. David Hester Amador

Journal for the Study of the New Testament
Supplement Series 174

Copyright © 1999 Sheffield Academic Press

Published by Sheffield Academic Press Ltd
Mansion House
19 Kingfield Road
Sheffield S11 9AS
England

Printed on acid-free paper in Great Britain
by Biddles Ltd
Guildford, Surrey

British Library Cataloguing in Publication Data

A catalogue record for this book is available
from the British Library

ISBN 1-85075-923-5

CONTENTS

PREFACE

There comes a time in the life of a project when it must simply be let go. After all the editing and feedback, after all the tinkering and toying, after all the hard work to make it the best argument one can invent and offer, it must be allowed to live the wild life of being read by anyone, anywhere, anytime. I have usually formulated a standard by which to judge when that time has come: when I no longer exactly agree with what is being said. When that point is reached, I know I have learned something, something which leads me to the next book to read, the next conversation to engage in, the next project to embark upon.

My favorite words are 'yes, but...' That's what I feel like saying at this point to this work: There is so much more to 'reality' than what my little mind can conceive, and it all exists in the beauty of a chaos which refuses to let anyone rule over it for very long (if at all).

A friend and colleague in mathematics once chided me: 'You humanities types never really contribute anything new; you just quote everybody else.' He's right, of course, but there often comes something quite new out of the mixture. I hope I have succeeded in at least offering a perspective that, while not new, may spark an unexpected thought or idea in others. That is all a rhetor can hope for.

MISCELLANY

Style

Parentheses
Asides intended to flesh out an idea, but due to restrictions of the material medium of codex-writing, and due to questionable relevancy regarding the immediate topic, the parenthetical text is inserted rather than allowed to participate in the immediate discourse.

Brackets
Additional authorial reflections; often commentary upon the parenthetical comments in the text. In direct citations of sources they represent editorial expansions.

Footnotes
Full citations of sources are given once per chapter, then abbreviated throughout that chapter.

Occasional Oddities
I often play with words, breaking them up, adding parenthetical pre/suf/in-fixes, and many other odd habits not often encountered in academented works. These habits extend, fortunately or unfortunately, to the disruptive and fragmentary at the level of sentence, paragraph, even chapter.

One habit in particular should be mentioned: I use the now acceptable American English spellings of 'womon' and 'womyn' out of deeply held philosophical convictions not immediately relevant to this tome, but having to do with issues of power and freedom.

I hope the reader will indulge me these little quirks.

Acknowledgments

First and foremost, I must thank my family, whose love and support, whose availability to bounce off ideas and share new insights, whose driving love of learning and teaching have provided me the kind of environment guaranteed to give me the chance, if and when I was willing to take it, to thrive. I have found no greater colleague than my father, Dr James D. Hester, to support me, to question and dis/cover new philosophies and theories of rhetoric. I have found no more formidable supporter and instigator of research, writing and completion of this work than my mother, Darilyn Hester. My brother, Dr D. Micah Hester, and his wife, Kelly Shermon, continued to offer me the insight, direction, instigation, research and support to complete(?) this work.

I must also thank Dr Paul Danove [Villanova University] and Eric Thompson [Santa Rosa Junior College], colleagues and friends during the writing of this work at the Graduate Theological Union who are both off in the world leaving their marks on it. Without their constant infusions of laughter, dancing and Scotch, none of us would have been [in]sane enough to survive the rough and tumble of the socialization into academentia. The only reason I am (reasonably) [mal]adjusted is due in great part to them.

I also had the good fortune of receiving the generous assistance of a number of individuals who set aside their time and energy to read drafts of various portions of this manuscript: Dr Thomas Olbricht, formerly of Pepperdine University, offered thoughtful insights on Chapter 2, which at the time was a mess of scattered summaries; he helped me to see the necessity of bringing the material into a more argumentatively driven form. Dr Wilhelm Wuellner graciously read and commented on Chapter 3; his ability to question every conclusion, elaborate every potential, and disconcert every certainty has provided me with a Mentor more able than Athena herself to steer me through the difficult choices I have had to make not only in this chapter, but more importantly throughout my career. Additionally, Dr Elisabeth Schüssler Fiorenza read through that portion of Chapter 4 which focused upon her work and sat down with me in Chicago to work through some questions that were raised, as did Dr Vernon Robbins, who read through that portion of the same chapter which focused upon his work. All of these people contributed greatly to the strength of this tome, but the responsibility for its final shape, arguments and conclusions must rest firmly on my shoulders.

Additionally, I must thank Dr Stanley Porter, who as a colleague in rhetoric has had to put up with a great deal of my idiosyncracies and foibles over the years as I presented admittedly strange papers and made incessant and infuriating comments during many public discussions and presentations. He has, along with the people at Sheffield Academic Press, my deepest gratitude for being willing to risk the publication of this rather untraditional and atypical tome on rhetoric and the New Testament.

Pride of place must be granted to Dr Herman Waetjen who has stuck by me through fierce political battles, encouraged me to explore the fringes of disciplinarity, grounded me by challenging me to offer the best critical arguments I could invent, and has given me the comfort found only among those committed to the ideals of learning and teaching—to provide an environment of safety and excitement.

Finally, I dedicate this work to Cassiel Asherah Amador: Any dreams you dare to imagine will never be denied you.

Chapter 1

INTRODUCTION: 'ARE ALL SALES FINAL, OR CAN I RETURN THIS BOOK?'

Scrutinizing performances of rhetorical criticism yields a twofold contribution to knowledge. We learn, first, what critics reveal to us about the architectonics of reality-defining discourse, i.e., about the strategic constructions that organize our lives. We are reminded, second, of the reflexivity of critical practice, i.e., that critics deliberately construct knowledge of rhetorical practice; they design the discernible to achieve certain objectives. Given that the strategic architecture of criticism authorizes knowledge claims, its implementation in any given case cannot reliably serve the purposes of anyone who would mistake the outcome for disinterested insight. Thus, we must critique critical performance from the strategic perspective of vested interest—adopting, revising, and rejecting knowledge claims according to the personal and institutional ends they promote. As critics of criticism, moreover, we cannot afford to assume the immutability, or fail to examine the rhetoricity, of situated interests. By engaging in a calculated consumption of rhetorical scholarship, we complete the cycle of reflexive reconstructions, which keeps us alert to the interplay of motives in each performance of criticism.

'Scrutinizing Performances of Rhetorical Criticism'
Robert L. Ivie

Introduction

One of the most significant recent trends in biblical criticism is the reinvigoration, if not reinvention, of rhetoric as a tool for the critical analysis of discourse. Reintroduced to biblical studies around the time of Muilenburg's presidential address to the Society of Biblical Literature,[1] rhetoric as a means of investigation and interpretation of the biblical

1. James Muilenburg, 'After Form Criticism What?', *Journal of Biblical Literature* 88 (1969), pp. 1-18.

text has generated an enormous amount of interest. Currently we are witness to the application of rhetorical methods upon both Old[2] and New Testament[3] texts. We see an interest upon both the chronological history of rhetorical tradition in European education,[4] as well as a synchronic approach to the systematic and non-systematic rhetoric of the discourse of many cultures and traditions, both ancient and modern.[5]

As many scholars have noted, this resurgence of interest in rhetorical method and theory is a significant development within the history of rhetorical education and biblical interpretation. For 1500 years throughout the west, rhetoric's prominence in exegesis was secured through its role in education and the *trivium* (grammar, logic/dialectic/philosophy, rhetoric)[6] and through its relationship with hermeneutics.[7] Rhetoric was the standard exegetical approach for hundreds of years,[8] from Origen to

2.   For a sample of recent articles on rhetoric of and in the Old Testament, cf. Bibliographies, Biblical Studies and Rhetoric: Old Testament.

3.   For a sample of recent journal articles on rhetorical criticism of and in the New Testament, cf. Bibliographies, Biblical Studies and Rhetoric: New Testament.

4.   For a sample of recent articles focusing on this issue, cf. Bibliographies, Rhetoric and the West: Medieval through Nineteenth Century.

5.   For a select sample of vernacular rhetorics, both ancient and modern, and focusing particularly on rhetoric of the Far East, cf. Bibliographies, Vernacular Rhetorics.

6.   See James Murphy, *Rhetoric in the Middle Ages: A History of Rhetorical Theory from St. Augustine to the Renaissance* (Berkeley: University of California Press, 1974).

7.   Cf. Wilhelm Wuellner, *Hermeneutics and Rhetorics: From 'Truth and Method' to Truth and Power* (Stellenbosch, RSA: Centre for Hermeneutical Studies, 1989).

Cf. also K. Eden, 'Hermeneutics and the Ancient Rhetorical Tradition', *Rhetorica* 5.1 (1987), pp. 59-86. G.R. Evans, *Old Arts and New Theology: The Beginnings of Theology as an Academic Discipline* (Oxford: Clarendon Press, 1980); G.R. Evans, *The Language and Logic of the Bible: The Earlier Middle Ages* (Cambridge: Cambridge University Press, 1984); G.R. Evans, *The Language and Logic of the Bible: The Road to Reformation* (Cambridge: Cambridge University Press, 1985); M.J. Hyde and C.R. Smith, 'Hermeneutics and Rhetoric: A Seen but Unobserved Relationship', *Quarterly Journal of Speech* 65.4 (1979), pp. 347-63; H.P. Rickman, 'Rhetoric and Hermeneutic', *Philosophy & Rhetoric* 14.1 (1981), pp. 100-11. S. Mailloux, 'Rhetorical Hermeneutics', *Critical Inquiry* 11 (1985), pp. 620-41; G. Mosdt, 'Rhetorik und Hermeneutik: Zur Konstitution der Neuzeitlichkeit', *Antike und Abendland* 30 (1984), pp. 62-79; T. Todorov, 'Rhetorique et Hermeneutique', *Poetique* 23 (1975), pp. 289-415.

8.   It is important to note, however, that at no point during this history could we

Augustine during the Second Sophistic, through the Middle Ages and into the early period of the Reformation.[9] With the advent of both religious and educational reformations of the sixteenth century, rhetoric's decline was signaled with the Ramist constriction of rhetoric's prescriptive and classical tradition to concerns of only elocution and style, a restriction which distinguishes rhetoric from hermeneutics'/dialectics' focus on reasoning, invention and logic.[10] Ramus's was the culmination of centuries of development of rhetorical theory. Although initially the sixteenth and seventeenth centuries saw a rise of works on rhetoric and

identify a 'standard' rhetoric; cf. Wilhelm Wuellner, 'Death and Rebirth of Rhetoric in Late Twentieth Century Biblical Exegesis', in Tord Fornberg and David Hellholm (eds.), *Texts and Contexts: Biblical Texts in their Textual and Situational Contexts* (Festschrift Lars Hartman; Oslo: Scandinavian University Press, 1995), pp. 917-30; Wilhelm Wuellner, 'Rhetorical Criticism and its Theory in Culture-Critical Perspective: The Narrative Rhetoric of John 11', in P.J. Hartin and J.H. Petzer (eds.), *Text and Interpretation: New Approaches in the Criticism of the New Testament* (Leiden: E.J. Brill, 1991), pp. 167-81. Cf. also the diversity of theories and practices of rhetoric in classical and late antiquity as described by Thomas Conley, *Rhetoric in the European Tradition* (White Plains, NY: Longman, 1990), pp. 1-71. While rhetoric was taught as a closed system of rules (based primarily upon Ciceronian, then later Quintilian models), in both theory and practice it reflected a wide variety of influences, from both western and non-western cultures, Greek, Latin, Hebrew and Arab traditions, vernacular movements of the late Middle Ages, and the experience of alternative theories and practices arising from colonial and missionary expansion.

For further reflection upon the impact Jewish rhetoric may have made upon Greco-Roman theory and practices, the role of the rabbinic houses in developing an alternative discourse of critique to the dominant Greco-Roman milieu, cf. Wilhelm Wuellner, 'Der vorchristliche Paulus und die Rhetorik', in Simon Lauer and Hanspeter Ernst (eds.), *Tempelkult und Tempelzerstörung (70 n.Chr.)* (Bern: Peter Lang, 1995), pp. 133-65.

9. For a review of this history, and of the relationship between hermeneutics and rhetoric during this period, see Wuellner, *Hermeneutics and Rhetorics*, pp. 2-24. Cf. also G.A. Kennedy, *Classical Rhetoric and its Christian and Secular Tradition from Ancient to Modern Times* (Chapel Hill: University of North Carolina Press, 1980); Wilhelm Wuellner, 'Where Is Rhetorical Criticism Taking Us?', *Catholic Biblical Quarterly* 49.3 (1987), pp. 448-63 (450-54).

10. Rhetoric was also impacted upon by the rise of vernacular literature, the advent of print technology, and its relationship with the new Protestant hermeneutics which emphasized the grammatical and socio-historical context of semantic meaning and interpretation. Cf. Wuellner, *Hermeneutics and Rhetorics*, pp. 5-10.

its influence upon biblical interpretation,[11] by the eighteenth and nineteenth centuries we witness the demise of rhetoric in academented theology, a demise which coincided with the rise of historical scientism
and the fragmentation of exegesis into sub-topics of specialization (text
criticism, philology, literary criticism, historical and theological interpretation).[12] [I would also attribute rhetoric's demise to the growing
impact of print technology upon the consciousness of the western mind,
particularly within academented fields of inquiry; more on that later
(non-Chapter 4e).] It is with this history in mind that we may well be
astonished by the resurgence of rhetoric [we should not be], but clearly
throughout the history of biblical exegesis in the west rhetoric has
played an important role and should *not* be considered 'a comparative
newcomer to the field of biblical studies'.[13]

This movement, however, is more than a modern revival of traditional rhetorical theories and practices. It is, as Terry Eagleton suggests,
a reinvention of rhetoric[14] whose impact can be seen and felt beyond
biblical studies in areas such as: philosophy, literary theory and theories
of reading and reception, postmodern hermeneutics, ideology criticism,
even science.[15] The essence of this reinvented rhetoric goes beyond
its communicative purposes to focus instead upon the 'discursive practices' of a 'text', 'grasping [them] as forms of power and performance'
and 'as forms of activities inseparable from the wider social relations
between writers and readers'.[16] Modern rhetorical theories emphasize

11. See Wuellner, *Hermeneutics and Rhetorics*, pp. 11-19, and 'Rhetorical Criticism and its Theory', p. 3.

12. Cf. Wuellner, 'Rhetorical Criticism and its Theory', pp. 2-3, and 'Death and
Rebirth', pp. 1-2, where he lists further influences which came to effect the demise
of rhetoric: The rise of vernacular movements and the concomitant awareness of
alternative rhetorical theories and practices; the missionary movements beyond cultures of the west; post-Romanticism's disdain of rhetoric; the identification of rhetorics and poetics/stylistics. On the exegetical side, we must also note the growing
awareness of the rhetorical traits of *individual* biblical authors and books, and the
division between secular and sacred hermeneutics. Cf. also *Hermeneutics and
Rhetorics*, pp. 19-22.

13. Martin Wárner, *Philosophical Finesse: Studies in the Art of Rational Persuasion* (New York: Oxford University Press, 1989), p. 3.

14. Terry Eagleton, *Literary Theory: An Introduction* (Minneapolis: University
of Minnesota Press, 1983), pp. 205-206.

15. Cf. Wuellner, *Hermeneutics and Rhetorics*, pp. 26-28.

16. Eagleton, *Literary Theory*, p. 206.

the 'means by which a text establishes its relationship to its audience in order to achieve a particular effect'[17] in *every* form of discourse: 'written or spoken, poetic or ordinary language, indeed in all use of signs, as forms and functions of living discourse—not just once when first uttered, but retaining in its textuality [read: materiality] the text's [read: media's and message's] power for future readers [read: audiences]'.[18] The power both *in* and *of*[19] a 'text' is not just limited to readers and audiences as producers of 'text', but extends as well to the producer and reader of theories about 'textual' power.[20] This is J. Hillis Miller's concept of rhetorical reading, which concentrates upon the *materiality* of a 'text', by which he means not just the medium through which the communicative act is enabled, but also considers its authoritative status in a given community (canonicity), its genre and 'intertextual' context; its social, political, institutional context of production and interpretation; and the context of each individual act of 'reading'; all of which serves to show 'that an apparently abstract, purely "theoretical" issue may have decisive institutional and political consequences'.[21] [Here we note the *durative* aspects of the conventions informing reading both *prior to*, *during* and *after* the activity of the 'textual' encounter,[22] i.e. their productive and reductive roles in the regulation and control of 'texts' and their commentary.] Modern rhetoric overcomes hermeneutics' hegemony of 'truth and method' to consider 'truth and power' in *all* its dimensions.[23]

17. Dale Patrick and Allen Scult, *Rhetoric and Biblical Interpretation* (Bible and Literature Series; Sheffield: Almond Press, 1990), p. 12.

18. Wuellner, 'Death and Rebirth', p. 3.

19. The rhetoric *in* the text is defined by Wuellner, 'Rhetorical Criticism and its Theory', p. 4, as 'the overt and discernible intentionality and appeal of the text, regardless of the text type or literary genre'. The rhetoric *of* the text is further defined as that approach 'where rhetoric stands for that aspect of the text as a whole, or text as an integral act of communication and appeal to action'.

20. Wuellner, 'Death and Rebirth', p. 3. Cf. also Wuellner, 'Rhetorical Criticism and its Theory', p. 6.

21. J. Hillis Miller, 'The Triumph of Theory, the Resistance to Reading, and the Question of the Material Base', *Publications of the Modern Language Association* 101.3 (1987), pp. 281-91 (288).

22. Cf. Peter J. Rabinowitz, *Before Reading: Narrative Conventions and the Politics of Interpretation* (Ithaca, NY: Cornell University Press, 1987).

23. Cf. also Wuellner, 'Rhetorical Criticism and its Theory', p. 5, where he distinguishes between modern and postmodern rhetorical criticism: 'In most traditional

Rhetoric's modern return to the field of biblical studies [for, as we shall see, rhetorical approaches to the Bible are hardly new] was signaled by James Muilenburg's presidential address to the Society for Biblical Literature in 1968, entitled, 'After Form Criticism What?' Muilenburg's suggestion was a concept of rhetoric [*that's* 'what'!] which was primarily literary and stylistic, concerned with identifying narrative and poetic structures (chiasms, parallelisms, etc.) in the Hebrew text. A number of scholars picked up his proposal and ran with it, but soon encountered a growing sense of displacement, a feeling that too much of what constituted rhetorical analysis of the Hebrew text was done intuitively, without the benefit of careful work on developing a shared theoretical basis and methodology.

In New Testament, the most important initial contributions came from the Seminar on Paul of the late 1970s, out of which a number of important articles and monographs were produced, the most well known perhaps being Hans Dieter Betz's work on Galatians. Since then, the number of journal articles, monographs, Festschriften and dissertations which purport to adopt a rhetorical-critical approach to the New Testament has increased exponentially, especially in the last 15 to 20 years. There seems to be no end in sight for this renascence, and the future of rhetoric scholars of the Bible looks generally bright—except to a few of us who are beginning to ponder the ramifications of some of the methodological and critical assumptions which are all too often made in rhetorical-critical analyses of biblical texts. For the more such analyses are produced, the more one becomes aware of a predilection on the part of rhetorical-critical scholarship (esp. of the New Testament) to produce what others have termed a 'rhetoric restrained'. Far too frequently analyses have been focused upon issues of style (*topoi*, figures) or attempt to identify (in rigid fashion) a given unit's arrangement or structure [as though identification of the parts of a speech is supposed to help us understand its rhetorical impact]. Assumptions are frequently made concerning the relationship of a speech to its rhetor and its audience, an almost 'causalist' notion of argumentation being adopted in order to reconstruct what 'must have been' the text's initial effects (hence, the rhetor's 'intention'). And, in almost every case, the whole

and modern rhetorics, texts merely express and transmit knowledge, social relations, and the self in contrast to the postmodern notion of texts by which knowledge, social relations and the self get *constituted.*'

of the rhetorical interpretive enterprise has been set within a historical-critical paradigm [the *defining* feature of biblical interpretation] and its hermeneutical center: the reconstructed 'original' 'meaning'.

What makes this questionable is not that historical reconstructions of a given text's effects are foreign to rhetorical-critical analyses [for they are not], nor that such reconstructions are necessarily 'wrong' for a rhetorical critic to pursue [though it may be a bit more problematical than assumed]. It is that there is so much more that rhetoric can bring to the field of biblical interpretation, *if* it were allowed to make the kind of impact which it is beginning to make on other fields. The qualitative contrast of research and analysis presented in journals from the field of rhetoric [*Pre/Text, Quarterly Journal of Speech, Communications, Communications Monograph, Philosophy & Rhetoric*, etc.], the plethora of philosophical and theoretical musings, the myriad of interpretive and critical approaches found therein, and the comparatively monolithic results produced by rhetorical critics of the Bible, is striking. By 'monolithic' is meant simply this: not only a predominance of ancient rhetorical treatises as the basis of rhetorical-critical work, but also consistently *exegetical* direction of the analyses, that is, rhetoric as a means for reconstructing social, cultural and historical circumstances of utterance which are then used as a basis for determining the 'original' 'meaning' of the text under consideration. It is a consistently historicist approach which absorbs a number of assumptions, and predetermines the direction of the inquiry and its 'appropriate' methodological tools and theoretical bases. The result is a startling consistency, with minimal variation, in rhetorical-critical analyses [not of conclusions or results, but of *approach*] of the biblical material.

One is, however, initially enheartened to see some biblical rhetorical scholars showing interest in exploring further ramifications that might be brought about if one ponders the implications of approaching the biblical text in terms of its persuasion. Each one of the four scholars on whom I shall direct our attention in this tome (Burton Mack, Vernon Robbins, Elisabeth Schüssler Fiorenza, Antoinette Wire) has explicitly addressed this question. They offer a variety of insights which ensue therefrom: that since audiences have a determining impact upon the kinds of persuasion pursued, 'we' may be able to trace carefully through the various stages of the tradition the social make-up of groups as represented by their argumentative and persuasive discourse; that 'we' may be able to reconstruct the 'other side of the conversation' not directly recorded in the tradition, but which the tradition nevertheless addressed; that all this bespeaks a dynamism of instruction which adapted to the changing circumstances of the community; that therefore biblical authority be reconsidered in light of its rhetorical tradition of adaptation and its changes in persuasive discourse practices, rather than be approached as a monolithic dogmatic authority over the community; that 'rhetoric' necessarily means a respect for the authority of the audience to reject or accept the argument presented, its appeals to 'reason' and not to force, and thereby granting to the audience the freedom to determine what expressions best represent its convictions; that indeed forms of persuasion embraced at certain stages of the tradition now be questioned in light of the precedence they have set in Christian discourse, their impact upon Christian faith and practice, and the damage that has ensued therefrom on the world and on the people with whom Christians have come into contact.

These are important insights which hold within them the seeds for a radical transformation of authority and power in Christian faith and tradition. The question I shall ask in this tome will be, however, whether this transformation is as complete as these scholars are hoping for. It is my belief that it is not, and the reason is because none of them crucially challenges the exegetical enterprise of biblical interpretation and the centers of power generated by a historicist hermeneutics.

How Did 'I' Get Here?

It may be necessary at this point to 'contextualize' the impetus and foundations of the argument to be explored in this tome. After all, the implications of the statements so far offered seem troubling, if not arrogant. They seem to suggest a fundamental challenge not only to rhetorical critics who continue to perpetuate the historical-critical paradigm, but also to undermine the paradigm itself and question its disciplinary formation. What are the intentions of this work, and how can they be justified?

To begin, it is my intention to develop a limited strategic critique for the disruption of certain important disciplinary assumptions and practices. This critique takes its inspiration from a *rhetorical* hermeneutic which understands all epistemological and hermeneutical theorizing as strategies of argumentation dedicated to a given purpose, legitimated according to those specific aims. As such, the critique approaches a historicist hermeneutic not only on the basis of the rejection of certain

a priori assumptions regarding the nature of language/meaning/inter-
pretation, but also with the view to exposing the particular strategic
purposes and systemic networks of disciplinary power which such a
herme-neutic serves to legitimate, and which in turn serve to legitimate
it.

The rhetorical hermeneutic informing this tome was initially inspired
by Bakhtin's critique of Saussurian linguistics.[24] Saussure distinguishes
three aspects of language: *langage* ('speech' as the totality of physical,
physiological and psychological linguistic expression), *langue* ('language') and *parole* ('utterance'). He goes on first to reject altogether
the importance of *langage* from linguistics because of its complexity
and heterogeneity. In contrast, *langue* is a self-contained whole, an
assemblage of stable and autonomous forms which is the normative
basis for all other manifestations of speech. On this basis, *parole*, too,
is rejected as the object of linguistic study, since it is an individual act
of will, accessory and random in contrast to the essential, the social, the
stable.

This *synchronic linguistics* Bakhtin rejects as historically untenable,
arising from a discourse on language which seeks to abstract language
from its history and concrete manifestations. At no point could such a
synchronic system be said to exist in any point in time. Furthermore,
Bakhtin also rejects the description of the relationship between the
individual speaker and linguistic norms: according to the approach to
the philosophy of language represented by Saussure, language is set
apart from the individual as an inviolable, incontestable set of forms.
The individual, on her/his part, learns to operate according to these
forms. An act of communication is only recognized as such by recognizing its compliance with this abstract system of language. Under such
a system, the consciousness of speakers seems to become concerned
primarily with linguistic forms and language as such. Bakhtin suggests
instead that what the speaker is in fact concerned with is not a language

---

24. Cf. Pam Morris (ed.), *The Bakhtin Reader: Selected Writings of Bakhtin,
Medvedev and Voloshinov* (London: Edward Arnold, 1994), pp. 26-37, and
excerpts from V.N. Voloshinov, *Marxism and the Philosophy of Language* (trans.
L. Matejka and I.R. Titunik; Cambridge, MA: Harvard University Press). See also
Mikhail M. Bakhtin, *Speech Genres and Other Late Essays* (ed. V.W. McGee;
trans. C. Emerson and M. Holquist; Austin, TX: University of Texas Press, 1986);
and Mikhail M. Bakhtin, *The Dialogic Imagination: Four Essays* (ed. M. Holquist;
trans. M. Holquist and C. Emerson; Austin, TX: University of Texas Press, 1981).

system per se, but with concrete utterances set in specific, material and ideological contexts. Language, in its practical application, has both form and content, and acts upon us behaviorally and ideologically. It cannot be divorced from this immediate circumstance, and it is of this concrete historical dimension which any philosophy of language must take account.

'Meaning' itself arises from such concrete circumstances. That is, rather than locating 'meaning' in a monologic, isolated form (in an 'abstract, objective' space), it arises from the *dialogic* interaction between speaker and listener, writer and reader. For Bakhtin, to 'understand' another person's utterance is to orient oneself with respect to it, to put it in a 'proper' context, indeed to fashion a response, a 'counter word'. There is no reason to suggest that 'meaning' belongs to a word as such, but is realized only in the word's 'position between speakers'.

How is this supposed to shed light on exegesis and current rhetorical-critical practices? First, we must take from Bakhtin his notion of 'meaning' as engendered in the dialogical encounter of two or more 'intention-alities' set within 'contexts' reverberating with social and ideological implications. Then we expand this notion by reference to the *materiality* of a discourse's medium. That is, both reception theory and Marshall McLuhan show that *heteroglossia* isn't something limited to the immediate context of utterance and/or production of a text. Rather, the dialogical encounter is enacted every time a text (as a material medium) is picked up, every time a performance is enacted before an audience. And each time it does so, new ideological assumptions and socio-cultural 'contexts' arise to effect the 'meaning' taken away/ brought to the encounter.

'Dialogics' as an active understanding between a speaker and her/his audience, a notion which Perelman and Olbrechts-Tyteca pick up on when they speak of the 'audience as a product of the speaker' and the 'speaker as a product of the audience'.[25] This notion must be expanded to take into account new material forms of communication and its production/distribution. That is why in this work the word 'text' will be found in quotations, to signal the fact there is a material dimension to communication which must be considered.

---

25. Chaim Perelman and Lucie Olbrechts-Tyteca, *The New Rhetoric: A Treatise on Argumentation* (Notre Dame, IN: University of Notre Dame Press, 1969), pp. 19-26.

'Text' is a very bad word for the object of interpretive inquiry of biblical scholars, since so often by this term 'we' also mean not just the written documents, but the oral traditions behind them. Indeed, I would suggest that 'we' treat even the written documents as though they were oral performances, insofar as so much of what 'we' do as exegetes is an attempt to recover the 'original' 'intentions', 'meanings' or 'effects' of the 'text' as though 'we' are an audience at its performance, that is, as a unique event. Speeches, never written down and eventually forgotten, are entirely unique experiences. Texts, however, go on to encounter new audiences in new circumstances and at different points in time. They do, that is, if they survive. Manuscripts survive their context of production, and hence are highly problematic in their interpretation. [We shall leave aside the new difficulties and potentialities which are generated through electronic communication, e.g. audio tape recording, video recordings, virtual reality, etc., each of which brings about new dynamics in communicative exchanges precisely because the specific form of communication brings with it unique implications concerning its reception.]

Hermeneutics, in a fashion similar to Saussure's structuralist linguistics, made a profound disciplinary shift when it became a general theory of 'understanding', thereby generating theories of 'knowledge', 'meaning' and 'Being-in-the-world' without reference to the specific and the concrete. It has tried to become a general, abstract theory about such questions, one which purports to describe how we *all* come to 'be' and 'know'. In contrast, rhetoric, as a dialogical model of persuasion, is interested in the consequences of such a shift. First, it is clear that any general hermeneutics takes place within specific discourse practices which limit the kinds of reasoning and which advocate a particular constellation of argumentative forms (and even styles). That is, it is unavoidable for hermeneutics to pursue its inquiry without engaging in processes of selection of 'data' (texts, argumentative traditions, etc.), adaptation to an audience, without making presumptions regarding the way people and the world work, judgments concerning 'right' from 'wrong', 'good' from 'bad' reasoning, without engaging in assumptions regarding 'truths' and 'facts' (which are, after all, contingent upon the agreement of the rhetor and audience concerning their constitution), without participating in argumentation and trying to shift adherence from known and accepted values to those the hermeneut wishes to advocate, without appeals to particular, universal and elite audiences.

Indeed, all of these constitute the very foundation of rhetoric. It would be interesting to note the kinds of rhetorical practices in which hermeneutics engages, in an effort not only to learn more about its argumentative traditions and assumptions, but also to find the limits imposed by such assumptions.

More important to the immediate issue of this tome, however, are the consequences that ensue when adapting one hermeneutical theory over another. Specifically, as a rhetorician I am interested in the consequences of assuming that the most authoritative understanding of a 'text' is with reference to its 'original' 'context'. That is, arising from rhetoric's incessant concern with the social aspects of argumentation, (the role of shared values, judgments, what constitutes 'truth' and 'fact', what are the acceptable forms of generating a *liaison* between premises and conclusion) it is possible to approach interpretive moments and their foundationalist assumptions as argumentative acts socially located in and by rules of inquiry. In contrast to every other New Testament scholar employing rhetorical approaches to the Bible, rather than using rhetoric as a discourse analytical tool for interpreting the Bible this tome will use rhetoric to analyze the discourse practices of rhetorical criticism *itself* as informed by a particular [foundationalist hermeneutic] understanding of historical-critical inquiry. Such typical rhetorical approaches ['naturalistically', ideologically] make use of argumentative strategies based on shared values, 'data', fundamental conceptions of 'Truth', hermeneutical assumptions, traditions of acceptable scholarly argumentation, and so on. The intention of this work is to explore the ways in which the dominant historicist hermeneutic shapes rhetorical analysis in ways subtle and deeply immersed in disciplinary power, in order to offer potential insights into the places where alternative practices can shape the future not only of rhetorical criticism, but perhaps of biblical studies itself.

Some Relief: A Map of the Terrain Ahead

How shall I clarify this? Perhaps as follows, in as specific a fashion as possible regarding the strategic outline of this work.

The argument of this tome proceeds in four phases: the first phase seeks to show that rhetorical criticism of the Bible is a discourse practice dominated by a neo-Aristotelian paradigm which assumes an antiquarian turn [refers only to ancient rhetorical treatises] in a synthesist fashion [ignoring the significant differences of these various treatises in favor of a 'universal' rhetorical paradigm], applies the model taxonomically [mere identification of rhetorical parts, a 'neo-form criticism'], and on the basis of a causalist understanding of rhetorical language [an argument 'fits' its audience situation, hence the situation can be determined by the argument], then reconstructs the 'original' 'intention' and/ or 'effect' of the discourse upon its immediate audience [a historical hermeneutic]. This is found in Chapter 2, and its 'purpose' is to awaken a sense of the broader disciplinary terrain of rhetorical criticism, and the potential it could hold for introducing a much greater variety of theoretical and methodological approaches to the rhetorical-critical analysis of the Bible.

The second phase develops an alternative philosophical, theoretical and methodological approach which I have termed a 'rhetoric of power'. The 'purpose' of Chapter 3 is not to develop a methodological toolbox for mechanistic application, but to suggest a wholly alternative approach to what it means to engage in a 'rhetorical reading' of a 'text', and to offer the theoretical and philosophical foundations for such an approach.

The third phase immerses into the 'rhetoric of power' [in a move similar to what is now called a 'critical rhetoric of inquiry'] four important rhetorical scholars of the Bible, all of whom see in rhetoric the potential for a profound transformation of the relationship between the 'text' and the community of believers. Unfortunately, as I shall show, they themselves are caught up in disciplinary systems of power that restrain their discourse practices, eventually subverting/undermining any shift of power away from the community of believers and into their own hands. The rhetoric of power is not a 'history of ideas, theories and methods', but looks to the academented-institutional and religio-political 'contexts' of biblical studies in an effort to trace the 'origins' of its specific discourse practices and disciplinary self-understanding. The 'purpose' of Chapter 4 and non-Chapter 4e is to expose the systems of power at work that secure them a place at the center of authoritative biblical interpretations.

The fourth and final phase begins to explore the kinds of directions that rhetorical analysis and theory could take, thus considering the ways in which rhetoric, if freed from the disciplinary restrictions we have been considering, could affect the discipline of biblical studies. The 'purpose' of Chapter 5 is to begin a dialogue/polylogue that could shape the future not just of rhetorical criticism, but of 'biblical studies' itself.

Whether 'I' subscribe to these 'purposes', or whether such 'purposes' are successfully achieved, is ultimately irrelevant. It is not my intention to control the reading of this tome through this outline, nor at any time throughout the reading of this tome. It is simply enough to toss the rock into the waters and watch the surface begin to refract.

Chapter 2

'WHAT IS THE LAY OF THE LAND?'
OR
'WHY SHOULD I CARE?'

We'll have to wait
'til Yesterday is here...
                                        Frank's Wild Years
                                        Tom Waits

Rhetorical Criticism of the Bible

The question that confronts us, a question of immediate importance, is
the question of context: What is the current situation confronting an
individual who wishes to engage in rhetorical interpretation of the
Bible? The recent explosion of interest in rhetorical theory and criticism in the humanities, not to mention its plethora of methods and philosophical foundations, would suggest a healthy, vibrant and variable ex-
ploratory framework within which a rhetorical critic of the Bible could
operate. Even a cursory glance at introductory surveys of rhetorical
criticism shows a dizzying variety of methods and materials available
to the critic who would wish to approach the biblical texts and traditions with the intention of pursuing such analyses. A rhetorical critic
of the Bible, it would initially seem, would be blessed by an embar-
rassment of methodological riches, and we would expect to see a variety of articles and monographs employing a wide range of approaches
to the 'text' in an effort to describe and enliven the Bible's rhetorical
power.

Alas, this is not the case. Instead, we find a monotonous/monolithic
dominance of a particular constellation of methodological assumptions
governing nearly the entire production of rhetorical-critical activity,
particularly with respect to the New Testament. We can bring this constellation into focus by tracing current practices back to the stage-setting

accomplished by the influential works coming out of the Seminar on Paul [hosted by the Society of Biblical Literature in the late 1970s and whose (since more prominent) members included such advocates of rhetorical criticism as Hans Dieter Betz, Robert Jewett, Wilhelm Wuellner and James Hester]. What has resulted from these powerful contributors was an assumption, now laid at the foundation of the (new) rhetorical critical effort, of ancient rhetorical models as being the [only? normative?] appropriate methodological tools for interpretation [what I shall term the **antiquarian turn**], an assumption which continues to haunt the field, as reflections from Stanley Porter's introduction to the important new collection of materials from the 1992 Heidelberg Conference suggests.[1] These models were initially constructed with reference, in particular, to Lausberg's formidable works, *Elemente der literarischen Rhetorik* and *Handbuch der literarischen Rhetorik*,[2] both of which established the unfortunate precedence of a **synthesist turn** in the field, especially focusing upon Greco-Roman preceptive traditions. Ever since, reconstructions of ancient rhetoric, drawing from not only Aristotle, Quintilian, Cicero, but also Hermagoras, Hermogenes, to a lesser extent Dionysius of Halicarnassus, 'Longinus', the *Rhetorica ad Herrenium*, the *Rhetorica ad Alexandrum*, but now also including the long-neglected handbooks and *progymnasmata*, were totalizing efforts at developing a sense of 'common', 'universal' and 'expected' discourse practices as taught in the schools or theorized in the literature. George Kennedy's enticement to participate in and his eventual contribution to the field only gave sanction to this effort from one of America's most prestigious historians of rhetoric.[3]

---

1.   E.g. his comments on the theoretical essays of the collection: how Jeffrey A. Crafton's use of Kenneth Burke's rhetorical model is a departure 'from the *normally* defined rhetorical categories', and how, in general, it is in the reflections of methodology and theory that 'the contributors depart in varying ways and to varying degrees from the *norms* of rhetorical criticism, at least as it is traditionally and usually understood'. The 'norms' to which he is referring are, of course, ancient models of rhetoric. Cf. Stanley E. Porter and Thomas H. Olbricht (eds.), *Rhetoric and the New Testament: Essays from the 1992 Heidelberg Conference* (*Journal for the Study of the New Testament*, Supplement Series, 90; Sheffield: Sheffield Academic Press, 1993), pp. 24, 25.

2.   Heinrich Lausberg, *Elemente der literarischen Rhetorik* (Munich: Max Hueber Verlag, 1967); and *idem, Handbuch der literarischen Rhetorik* (2 vols.; repr.; Stuttgart: Franz Steiner, 1990).

3.   George A. Kennedy, *New Testament Interpretation through Rhetorical*

Another tendency, directly related to this synthesist turn, was the imposition of taxonomies: (1) Aristotelian genres (*epideictic, forensic, deliberative*), (2) arrangement as described by both Cicero and Quintilian with respect to legal argumentation (*exordium, narratio, partitio, amplificatio, refutatio,* [*digressio*], *peroratio*), (3) Hermagorean theory of *stasis* (*coniecturalis, definitiva, qualitas, translatio*) and (4) stylistic features (esp. figures of thought, figures of speech, and tropes). The result of this taxonomic turn was not only the identification and elaboration of the rhetorical structure [predominantly in the form of an outline of the unit], 'the' central issue and intention of the argument, but also an odd [boring] assumption that identification was enough: by indicating these features, the enterprise of rhetorical criticism was thought essentially to be complete.

The next step would then be the reconstruction of historical effect or authorial [argumentative] 'intention', a step founded upon the identification of the rhetorical features and genre and a **causalist** assumption regarding the circumstances to which such an argument would be 'fit'. Among the theoretical justifications offered for this assumed correspondence between argumentative 'text' and its 'context' is the rather favored work of Lloyd Bitzer and his theory of the 'rhetorical situation'. Offered in a now famous article which introduced the journal *Philosophy & Rhetoric* to the scholarly public,[4] Bitzer proposed a pragmatist understanding of language and rhetoric in order to identify the characteristics that give rise to rhetorical discourse (as opposed to other types of discourse, say, poetic or scientific), thereby shifting the focus of rhetorical-critical inquiry away from issues of persuasion and argumentative intention and directing it toward the analysis of situations. As he proposes:

> Hence, to say that rhetoric is situation means: (1) rhetorical discourse comes into existence as a response to situation, in the same sense that an answer comes into existence in response to a question, or a solution in response to a problem; (2) a speech is given rhetorical significance by the situation, just as a unit of discourse is given significance as answer or as solution by the question or problem; (3) a rhetorical situation must

Criticism (Chapel Hill: University of North Carolina Press, 1984). In the study of Pauline letters, the synthesist turn was anticipated by research into ancient epistolographic theory and examples.

4. Lloyd F. Bitzer, 'The Rhetorical Situation', *Philosophy & Rhetoric* 1.1 (1968), pp. 1-14.

exist as a necessary condition of rhetorical discourse, just as a question must exist as a necessary condition of an answer; (4) many questions go unanswered and many problems remain unsolved; similarly, many rhetorical situations mature and decay without giving birth to rhetorical utterance; (5) a situation is rhetorical insofar as it needs and invites discourse capable of participating with situation and thereby altering its reality; (6) discourse is rhetorical insofar as it functions (or seeks to function) as a fitting response to a situation which needs and invites it. (7) Finally, the situation controls the rhetorical response in the same sense that the question controls the answer and the problem controls the solution. Not the rhetor and not persuasive intent, but the situation is the source and ground of rhetorical activity—and, I should add, of rhetorical criticism.[5]

A 'rhetorical situation' thereby becomes defined, and frequently referred to among biblical scholars, as

> a complex of persons, events, objects and relations presenting an actual or potential exigence which can be completely or partially removed if discourse, introduced into the situation, can so constrain human decision or action as to bring about the significant modification of the exigence.[6]

There are three constituents of any rhetorical situation: an *exigence* ('an imperfection marked by an urgency' and which can be modified only or primarily through the intervention of discourse),[7] an *audience* ('capable of being influenced by discourse and of being mediators of change'),[8] and *constraints* ('made up of persons, events, objects, and relations which are parts of the situation because they have the power to constrain decision and action needed to modify the exigence').[9] Rhetorical discourse is called into existence by situation; the situation which the rhetor perceives amounts to an 'invitation' to create and present discourse. It invites a *fitting* response, not just any response, which therefore means the situation somehow *prescribes* the response that fits. The exigence and constraints that generate rhetorical discourse are 'objective and publicly observable historical facts in the world we experience, are therefore available for scrutiny by an observer or critic who attends to them. To say the situation is objective, publicly observable, and

5.   Bitzer, 'The Rhetorical Situation', pp. 5-6.
6.   Bitzer, 'The Rhetorical Situation', p. 6.
7.   Cf. Bitzer, 'The Rhetorical Situation', pp. 6-7.
8.   Bitzer, 'The Rhetorical Situation', p. 8.
9.   Bitzer, 'The Rhetorical Situation', p. 8.

historic means that it is real or genuine.'[10] Finally, rhetorical situations come into existence, mature and decay, or mature and persist, but in any case, to speak of a situation as maturing means that it 'evolve[s] to just the time when a rhetorical discourse would be most fitting'.[11]

The responses to Bitzer's formulation were numerous, and a debate was begun which lasted well over ten years. While some pondered (both negatively and positively) the implications of this theory upon disciplinary boundaries,[12] the primary struggle was centered around the empiricist and objectivist epistemology [the emphasis upon 'facts', 'reality', 'objectively observable'], the causalist historical assumptions [situations 'determine' and 'invite' 'fitting' responses], and the implicit neo-Platonic metaphysics at work behind this formulation. The greatest single critique was offered by Richard Vatz in his now [in]famous article, 'The Myth of the Rhetorical Situation',[13] wherein he overturns every statement made by Bitzer regarding the relationship between discourse and situation:

> I would not say 'rhetoric is situational', but situations are rhetorical; not '. . . exigence strongly invites utterance', but utterance strongly invites exigence; not 'the situation controls the rhetorical response', but rhetoric controls the situational response; not '. . . rhetorical discourse . . . does obtain its character-as-rhetorical from the situation which generates it', but situations obtain their character from the rhetoric which surrounds them or creates them.[14]

Vatz rejected the objectivity and causality [and its implicit alleviation of ethical responsibility on the part of the rhetor][15] inherent in Bitzer's

---

10. Bitzer, 'The Rhetorical Situation', p. 11.

11. Bitzer, 'The Rhetorical Situation', p. 13.

12. Against: K.E. Wilkerson, 'On Evaluating Theories of Rhetoric', *Philosophy & Rhetoric* 3.1 (1970), pp. 82-96. For: Richard L. Larson, 'Lloyd Bitzer's "Rhetorical Situation" and the Classification of Discourse: Problems and Implications', *Philosophy & Rhetoric* 3.3 (1970), pp. 165-68.

13. *Philosophy & Rhetoric* 6.3 (1973), pp. 154-61.

14. Vatz, 'The Myth of the Rhetorical Situation', p. 158.

15. Note Vatz, 'The Myth of the Rhetorical Situation', p. 156: '[Bitzer] states, "any exigence is an imperfection marked by urgency; it is a defect, an obstacle, something waiting to be done, a thing that is other than it should be". Not only is a "waiting to be done" now existing in the event, but we also learn that it contains an ethical imperative supposedly independent of its interpreters. Bitzer adds that the situation is rhetorical only if something *can* be done, but apparently it is only rhetorical also if something *should* be done.'

program and asserted the agency of the rhetor in helping not only to give shape to exigences at work in the situation, but to determine the situation itself. Bitzer's blatant naiveté[16] throughout his article regarding the interaction between situation and discourse could not withstand Vatz's pointed assaults which took their cue from Perelman's understanding of the function of 'presence' and the inventional quality of the choice and presentation of 'facts' and 'evidence' in argumentation[17] [hence the *active* role of rhetor in developing and determining a situation and her/his audience]. It was a blow from which situation theory struggled to recover and could only do so by radically reformulating itself away from its descriptive implications [empiricism and causation] and toward, instead, a *prescriptive* theory of invention.[18]

What is bizarre is that this debate makes *absolutely no appearance whatsoever* in the discourse of biblical critical application of situation theory. If Bitzer's theory, with respect in particular to the 'fittedness' of discourse, is in fact *prescriptive*; if at least it makes room for the perception of the individual regarding the exigences and constraints, the situation and its solution; if a speaker can fail due not only to her/his misreading of the situation, nor only to the poor performance of her/his discourse, but also to her/his having misread the situation's timing

---

16. Cf. Vatz, 'The Myth of the Rhetorical Situation', p. 156: 'Bitzer seems to imply that the "positive modification" needed for an exigence is clear... We learn, for example, that the obvious "positive modification" of pollution of our air is "reduction of pollution". One wonders what the obvious "positive modification" of the military-industrial complex is.'

17. Cf. Vatz, 'The Myth of the Rhetorical Situation', p. 157.

18. Alan Brinton, 'Situation in the Theory of Rhetoric', *Philosophy & Rhetoric* 14.4 (1981), pp. 234-48. Cf. Scott Consigny, 'Rhetoric and its Situations', *Philosophy & Rhetoric* 7.3 (1974), pp. 175-86, rejecting Bitzer as too determinate and Vatz as too creative, tries to offer a mediating position by suggesting that a rhetorical situation is indeterminate, but given shape through recourse to inventional use of *topoi*. John Patton, 'Causation and Creativity in Rhetorical Situations: Distinctions and Implications', *Quarterly Journal of Speech* 65.1 (1979), pp. 36-55, tries to suggest that the understanding of causation which Vatz and others have seen in Bitzer's article in fact isn't there and instead there lurks behind it another kind of causation which allows for the perception of the rhetor to determine the situation. Bitzer, 'Functional Communication: A Situational Perspective', in Eugene E. White (ed.), *Rhetoric in Transition: Studies in the Nature and Uses of Rhetoric* (University Park, PA: Pennsylvania State University Press, 1980), pp. 21-38, tries to pick up on this, but continues to embrace an empiricist and objectivist epistemology and a neo-Platonist metaphysics.

['maturation' or 'decay']; if pragmatic discourse isn't strictly causalist: there is little to no evidence of these important corrections and caveats upon those who make use of situation theory for New Testament interpretation. Rather, they continue to operate a rule-governed, strict-causalist conception of the relationship between rhetorical performance and the context to which, and the immediate audience to whom, it was addressed.

They do so because such a conception of the relationship between speech and context allows them, through the rules of argumentation (e.g. enthymemes) and identification of genre *telos*, to reconstruct the circumstances which such a performance is perceived to 'fit' best. This critical achievement is often seen as the end of the analytical effort, whose energy is thereby directed to one or more of three possible avenues: a reconstruction of the (implied) author's argumentative intentions; a reconstruction of the specific exigences, constraints and circumstances to which the argumentation was directed; and/or a reconstruction of its (intended) effects upon the audience. This is the **historical hermeneutic turn** which transforms rhetorical analysis into a tool for cleaning the text-as-window.[19]

Oddly, the result of this latter turn is a criticism which often avoids judgment or critique concerning the text's rhetorical power or performance. In other words, biblical rhetorical interpretation becomes a criticism that is often arrested before it fulfills its *critical* task. This is, perhaps, the most important of all the previously mentioned characteristics, as it leaves intact certain disciplinary discursive practices as a hegemonic, totalizing and restrictive paradigm under which rhetorical-critical interpretation is performed: namely rhetorical interpretation restricts its notion of persuasion and power to the immediate context of historical performance, and thereby becomes a means for something *other* than rhetoric. It becomes a means for furthering historical inquiry and reconstruction. Indeed, by the time many of these articles are finished being read, one wonders whether they haven't defeated the whole purpose of pursuing an interpretation through a *rhetorical* approach.

---

19. Cf. D. Jasper's critique of the historical hermeneutic informing rhetorical criticism, 'Reflections on the London Conference on the Rhetorical Analysis of Scripture', in Stanley Porter and Thomas Olbricht (eds.), *The Rhetorical Analysis of Scripture: Essays from the 1995 London Conference* (*Journal for the Study of the New Testament*, Supplement Series, 146; Sheffield: Sheffield Academic Press, 1997), pp. 476-82 (476).

Examples in which most or all of these characteristics (esp. the latter) can be found are, unfortunately, ready to hand. To begin, it is rather easy to spot the perpetuation of these assumptions in the works of those students affiliated with the members of the Seminar on Paul: Margaret Mitchell (a student of Hans Dieter Betz), Frank Witt Hughes (a student of Robert Jewett), and Duane Watson (affiliated with George Kennedy [who was not, of course, a member of the Seminar]). All are living proof that 'a student is not above her/his teacher', but that 'it is enough for a student to be like her/his teacher'.

For example, Mitchell's analysis of 1 Corinthians[20] draws its examples of rhetorical theory and practice exclusively from ancient sources (including not only the rhetorical treatises of Aristotle, Quintilian and Cicero, but also various handbooks, as well as examples of speeches from antiquity culled from the histories and several ancient Greek letters) in a synthesist effort of deriving general characteristics of the deliberative genre. She does so in order to argue for the identification of 1 Corinthians as a unified letter containing deliberative rhetoric that is directed at the issues of factionalism and unity. After a careful and thorough taxonomic identification and description of the arrangement of the argument and the presence of *topoi* appropriate to this genre, Mitchell then draws certain conclusions regarding both Paul's rhetoric (that it approached practical ecclesial problems by viewing the church as a political body to whom he appealed for unity through traditionally deliberative argumentation, and as such was probably a failure in light of 2 Corinthians) and her own particular approach to rhetorical criticism: that it is an 'overt' attempt to keep rhetorical criticism under the auspices of historical criticism in order to read an ancient text 'on its own terms'. While no effort is made at pursuing a reconstruction of the historical situation, and while she notes the continuing presence (in spite of its initial failure) of the letter and its argumentative appeal to unity throughout Christian history, her critical effort essentially ends with genre identification determined by classical models and the reconstruction of original (historical) argumentative intent.

---

20. Margaret Mitchell, 'Paul and the Rhetoric of Reconciliation: An Exegetical Investigation of the Language and Composition of I Corinthians' (PhD Dissertation; Chicago: University of Chicago, 1990), also published in the Hermeneutische Untersuchungen zur Theologie Series, 28 (Tübingen: J.C.B. Mohr, 1991).

Frank Witt Hughes's excursion into ancient epistolary rhetoric endeavors to identify 2 Thessalonians[21] as an example of a Greco-Roman deliberative letter exhibiting features similar to Demosthenes's *Epistle 1*. Once again, after a synthesis of ancient treatments of genre and arrangement, he also offers a thorough outline of the letter identifying the specific role of each verse in the parts (exordium, *partitio*, *probatio*, *peroratio*, exhortation and epistolary postscript). Rather than stopping there, however, Hughes goes on to pursue a reconstruction of historical events leading up to the production of this letter by a 'late first-century', 'traditionally minded' Pauline Christian who was 'outraged by the authoritative claims of his adversaries' and sat down to write, on the basis of 1 Thessalonians, 'a powerful, well-argued reply, full of apocalyptic fire and yet chillingly cold, but clearly a polished piece of religious rhetoric'.[22] Hughes understands the contribution of rhetorical criticism to be that which can help us to diversify 'our' understanding of the development of Pauline Christianity after the death of Paul, to refuse to blunt the sharp rhetorical edges of these letters in order to fit them into a perspective of early Christianity as a 'golden age', or in order to perpetuate 'the myth of Pauline theology as a fundamentally unified or uniform phenomenon which could serve as a sort of "canon within the canon"'.[23] Indeed, not only is rhetoric helpful for historical reconstruction, it also helps to appreciate the doctrinal and theological character and integrity of the deutero-Pauline and Pastoral letters, to suggest perhaps an authority (or at least a similarity in creativity and approach) to Paul himself.

Duane Watson focuses upon invention, arrangement and style in Jude and 2 Peter.[24] Set within Kennedy's model, he develops another grand synthesis of ancient rhetorical theories, drawing once again from Aristotle, Cicero and Quintilian, but also noting the contribution of Longinus, Demetrius and Hermogenes to the theories of style. He

---

21. Frank Witt Hughes, *Early Christian Rhetoric and 2 Thessalonians* (*Journal for the Study of the New Testament*, Supplement Series, 30; Sheffield: Sheffield Academic Press, 1989).

22. Hughes, *Early Christian Rhetoric*, p. 95.

23. Hughes, *Early Christian Rhetoric*, p. 103.

24. Duane F. Watson, *Invention, Arrangement and Style: Rhetorical Criticism of Jude and 2 Peter* (Society of Biblical Literature Dissertation Series, 104; Atlanta: Scholars Press, 1988).

makes an explicit (and causalist) use of Bitzer to determine the originating 'rhetorical situation', secures identification of genre and stasis, and proceeds to make a careful analysis of argumentation within classical theory of arrangement. He completes the analysis of each letter with an evaluation that judges them according to their adherence to conventional rhetorical principles of invention and arrangement, then turns to identification of style (low, middle, high and forceful), and then finally judges the argumentative effect given the reconstructed situation of audience and the rhetor's intention with respect to exigence. Finally, he identifies the contribution of rhetoric in terms of literary coherence and dependence. In other words, rhetorical criticism helps further analysis of source and particularly redaction criticism (although, in this instance, not very successfully).[25]

None of these really tests the disciplinary boundaries and discursive practices established by Betz/Kennedy, but simply perpetuates the methodology of rhetorical criticism as a tool for the historian. And recent trends in dissertations embracing New Testament rhetorical analysis show only a glimmer of hope for a different possible future: of the 31 dissertations of the past 10 years (1985 to 1994) in North America that purport to offer a rhetorical-critical interpretation of the New Testament,[26] 24 continue to perpetuate the methodological and/or philosophical status quo we have been exploring here.[27] Furthermore, perhaps the best representative example of the current 'state of the Art' in recent years is the collection of essays from the Heidelberg conference[28] which was attended by some of the world's most important scholars in rhetorical criticism (and not just *biblical* rhetorical

---

25. Cf. his conclusions in Watson, *Invention, Arrangement and Style*, p. 189.

26. According to a keyword search in the 1994 American Theological Library Association Dissertation Abstracts database.

27. Cf. Bibliographies, Dissertations (1985–94).

28. Stanley E. Porter and Thomas H. Olbricht (eds.), *Rhetoric and the New Testament: Essays from the 1992 Heidelberg Conference* (*Journal for the Study of the New Testament*, Supplement Series, 90; Sheffield: Sheffield Academic Press, 1993). Note the slow advent of alternative voices and the development of methodological plurality in the essays collected by Stanley E. Porter and Thomas H. Olbricht (eds.), *The Rhetorical Analysis of Scripture: Essays from the 1995 London Conference* (*Journal for the Study of the New Testament*, Supplement Series, 146; Sheffield: Sheffield Academic Press, 1997).

criticism). Even here, however, we must note how 9[29] of the 19 articles in Part 1, 'Rhetoric and New Testament Interpretation', are *still* engaged in some combination of the use of synthesist classical models, taxonomic identification of argumentative structures presupposing inherent critical understanding of their persuasive function and effect, and the historical hermeneutic center of 'intention', 'circumstance' and 'effect'. Fortunately, however, this collection is beginning to show the cracks in the paradigmatic wall: four other articles in Part 1[30] argue for a more judicious use of Greco-Roman models (of rhetoric and/or epistolography), although they choose to remain within its discursive practices; and seven[31] of the final eight essays of Part 2, 'Rhetoric and Questions of Method', make enormous advances in the critical assumptions of doing rhetorical-critical inquiry, as modern methods and hermeneutical issues are engaged and thereby take seriously the tone of the editor's

29. Frank W. Hughes, 'The Parable of the Rich Man and Lazarus (Luke 16.19-31) and Graeco-Roman Rhetoric' (pp. 29-41); Folker Siegert, 'Mass Communication and Prose Rhythm in Luke–Acts' (pp. 42-58); Daniel Marguerat, 'The End of Acts (28.16-31) and the Rhetoric of Silence' (pp. 74-89); David Hellholm, 'Amplificatio in the Macro-Structure of Romans' (pp. 123-51); Joop Smit, 'Argument and Genre of 1 Corinthians 12–14' (pp. 211-30); Duane F. Watson, 'Paul's Rhetorical Strategy in 1 Corinthians 15' (pp. 231-49); A.N. Snyman, 'Persuasion in Philippians 4.1-20' (pp. 325-37); Claudio Basevi and Juan Chapa, 'Philippians 2.6-11: The Rhetorical Function of a Pauline "Hymn"' p. 338-56); and John W. Marshall, 'Paul's Ethical Appeal in Philippians' (pp. 357-74).

30. Stanley E. Porter, 'The Theoretical Justification for Application of Rhetorical Categories to Pauline Epistolary Literature' (pp. 100-22); C. Joachim Classen, 'St Paul's Epistles and Ancient Greek and Roman Rhetoric' (pp. 265-91); Jeffrey T. Reed, 'Using Ancient Rhetorical Categories to Interpret Paul's Letters: A Question of Genre' (pp. 292-324); and Thomas H. Olbricht, 'Hebrews as Amplification' (pp. 375-87).

31. Klaus Berger, 'Rhetorical Criticism, New Form Criticism and New Testament Hermeneutics' (pp. 390-96); Bernard Lategan, 'Textual Space as Rhetorical Device' (pp. 397-408); Pieter J.J. Botha, 'The Verbal Art of the Pauline Letters: Rhetoric, Performance and Presence' (pp. 409-28); Jeffrey A. Crafton, 'The Dancing of an Attitude: Burkean Rhetorical Criticism and the Biblical Interpreter' (pp. 429-42); Lauri Thurén, 'On Studying Ethical Argumentation and Persuasion in the New Testament' (pp. 464-78); Angelico-Salvatore Di Marco, 'Rhetoric and Hermeneutic—On a Rhetorical Pattern: Chiasmus and Circularity' (pp. 479-91); and Wilhelm Wuellner, 'Biblical Exegesis in the Light of the History and Historicity of Rhetoric and the Nature of the Rhetoric of Religion' (pp. 492-513).

call for 'the need and the relevant place for self-criticism in rhetorical studies'.[32]

So, where did this particular accumulation of assumptions come from? How do they relate to other methodological movements in the recent history of American 'speech criticism'? Interestingly, the closest parallel to be found is that which was once identified as neo-Aristotelian criticism, now currently revived (and revised) under the term 'neo-classical criticism'. Let's look at the history of this movement more closely to see what biblical studies can learn from it.

Neo-Aristotelian criticism[33] received its most influential formulation in a famous essay by Herbert Wichelns published in 1925,[34] an essay whose impact sent reverberations throughout the field of rhetorical criticism which were still echoing 40 years later. In this essay he laid out a program of criticism, fleshed out in much greater critical detail and application by Thonssen and Baird in *Speech Criticism*,[35] in which could be found one of the most encompassing syntheses ever offered of classical Greco-Roman rhetorical treatises for the sake of critical analysis (similarities with biblical rhetorical criticism noted in italics and elucidate in comments between brackets):

> The scheme of a rhetorical study includes the *element of the speaker's personality* as a conditioning factor; it includes also the public character of the man—not what he was, but what he was thought to be [ethos and persona]. It requires a *description of the speaker's audience* [reconstruction of historical context] and of the *leading ideas with which he plied his hearers*—his topics, the motives to which he appealed, the nature of the proofs he offered [taxonomy]... Attention must be paid, too, to the *relation of the surviving texts to what was actually uttered* [source and redaction criticism]: in case the nature of the changes is known,

---

32. Stanley E. Porter, 'Introduction', pp. 21-26 (26).

33. The following draws from historical surveys found in B.L. Brock, R.L. Scott and J.W. Chesebro (eds.), *Methods of Rhetorical Criticism: A Twentieth Century Perspective* (Detroit: Wayne State University Press, 2nd rev. edn, 1980), pp. 24-31; and Edwin Black, *Rhetorical Criticism: A Study in Method* (Madison, WI: University of Wisconsin Press, 2nd edn, 1978), pp. 10-35.

34. Herbert A. Wichelns, 'The Literary Criticism of Oratory', in Bernard Brock, Robert Scott and J.W. Chesebro (eds.), *Methods of Rhetorical Criticism: A Twentieth Century Perspective* (Detroit: Wayne State University Press, 2nd rev. edn, 1980), pp. 40-73.

35. Lester Thonssen and A. Craig Baird, *Speech Criticism* (New York: Ronald, 1948).

there may be occasion to consider adaptation to two audiences—that which heard and that which read. Nor can rhetorical criticism omit the speaker's *mode of arrangement and mode of his expression* [taxonomy] nor his habit of preparation and his manner of delivery from the platform; though the last two are perhaps less significant. 'Style'—in the sense which corresponds to diction and sentence movement—must receive attention, but only as one among various means that secure for the speaker ready access to the minds of his auditors. Finally *the effect of discourse on its immediate hearers* [historical reconstruction of originary 'meaning' and 'effect'] is not to be ignored, either in the testimony of witnesses, nor in the record of events. And throughout such a study one must conceive of the public man as influencing the men of *his own times* by the power of his discourse.[36]

This spawned a whole barrage of works which came to dominate the field of speech criticism, eventually producing an important three-volume series sponsored by the Speech Association of America (later known as the Speech Communication Association) entitled *A History and Criticism of American Public Address*.[37] The identifying characteristics of the neo-Aristotelian movement included

...the classification of rhetorical discourses into forensic, deliberative and epideictic; the classification of 'proofs' or 'means of persuasion' into logical, pathetic, and ethical; the assessment of discourse in the categories of invention, arrangement, delivery, and style; and the evaluation of rhetorical discourse in terms of its effects on its immediate audience.[38]

Its analytical focus and critical purpose was to explicate through classical rhetorical principles the rhetorical features of the text under consideration by reference to its historical situation, the perspectives and goals of the rhetor in addressing that situation, and the effect her/his performance had upon its outcome. The analog with biblical studies, I hope, is hereby quite obvious.

36. Thonssen and Baird, *Speech Criticism*, p. 23.

37. W. Norwood Brigance (ed.), *A History and Criticism of American Public Address* (2 vols.; New York: McGraw–Hill, 1943); Marie Hochmut Nichols (ed.), *A History and Criticism of American Public Address*, III (London: Longmans, Green, 1955).

38. Black, *Rhetorical Criticism*, p. 31.

Its success was formidable, but even during its 'halcyon days' of McKeon and Crane's school of 'Chicago Formalists' (1940s and 1950s)[39] grumblings were beginning to be heard: under its formulation it was inevitable that the discipline be dominated by the pursuit of rhetorical history at the expense of other theoretical and critical pursuits. As Loren Reid saw it, rhetorical critics operating under neo-Aristotelian principles were actually generating 'second-rate history'[40] rather than rhetorical criticism.[41] There was a growing sense that there was more to rhetoric than describing the circumstances and events surrounding a particular performance, and this sense eventually erupted into a full-scale and devastating attack by Edwin Black in his famous *Rhetorical Criticism.*

The attack, while informed by premises concerning the nature and function of criticism which may well be questioned,[42] is of some interest to us here, since it is so remarkably relevant to the current situation of biblical rhetorical criticism: for neo-Aristotelianism, like biblical rhetorical criticism, 'the discovery of historical context is especially

39. As noted by Stephen E. Lucas, 'The Schism in Rhetorical Scholarship', in James R. Andrews (ed.), *The Practice of Rhetorical Criticism* (New York: Longman, 1990), pp. 303-23. Cf., esp., Loren Reid, 'The Perils of Rhetorical Criticism', *Quarterly Journal of Speech* 30.4 (1944), pp. 416-22.

40. Reid, 'The Perils of Rhetorical Criticism', p. 419.

41. This 'split' between 'history' and 'criticism' continues to be assumed, as seen in the editors' introduction to 'Traditional Criticism' in Brock, Scott and Chesebro (eds.), *Methods of Rhetorical Criticism*, pp. 24-31. It can also be seen, perhaps, in the directions which neo-Aristotelianism took after its fall: on the one hand, 'criticism' became translated into issues addressing the pragmatics of the pedagogical difficulties faced by speech and composition departments (and their relationship to English departments); here we note the influence of scholars such as Wayne Booth, Richard Weaver, Richard Hughes, and Edward P.J. Corbett. On the other hand, a number of rhetoricians began to retrace the history of rhetoric in the West, focusing particularly upon recovering the works and educational impacts of rhetorical theorists since the time of Quintilian; here we note the works of Michael Leff, Thomas Conley, and George Kennedy. (This is not to suggest, however, that neo-Aristotelianism, now known as neo-classical criticism, does not have its adherents today who perform a similar historical-exegetical approach to speeches.)

42. Even Edwin Black suggests that his book be 'buried', having done what it needed to do, but no longer sufficiently representative of his current understanding of the philosophy of rhetoric to warrant his assent. Cf. his introduction to *Rhetorical Questions: Studies of Public Discourse* (Chicago: University of Chicago Press, 1992).

important…because of [the] penchant for appraising the discourse as a response to a particular occasion'.[43] These critics take a remarkably restricted view of the concept of 'context', 'their tendency being to comprehend the rhetorical discourse as tactically designed to achieve certain results with a specific audience on a specific occasion'.[44] The problem Black has with this is that it is a critically arbitrary delimitation of the notion of rhetorical and argumentative 'intention' or 'purpose'. Even if, for example, 'we' were to continue to pursue a historical approach to rhetorical interpretation of, say, 1 Corinthians, the reconstitution of the context must take into account (but never seems to take seriously) the idea that Paul was writing not only to the 'church of god which is in Corinth', but also 'to those sanctified in christ Jesus called to be saints *together with all those who in every place* call on the name of our lord Jesus christ'. The same could be said for any [of the canonical (and non-canonical)] literature: to reconstruct the rhetorical interpretation, 'intention', 'impact' of the text in terms of the immediate performance is simply an arbitrary, *a priori* delimitation assumed by the critic without respect to the text's materiality, the rhetor's oeuvre, or the notion that audiences other than the immediate and empirical may be in mind [here are the roles of Perelman and Olbrechts-Tyteca's 'intended' audiences which must also include the 'particular', 'universal' and 'elite'].

Furthermore, as Black noted the inability of neo-Aristotelians to fulfill the general critical task of 're-creation' because of this emphasis upon the immediate audience and immediate situation,[45] so too can we attribute this same penchant on the part of biblical rhetorical scholars to uncritically adopt 'the unique perspective imposed by such a critical position rather than rhetorical discourse itself'.[46] When Black states that 'we have too many examples of rhetorical discourses that retain their doctrinal vitality' and that 'the neo-Aristotelian critic's focus on the immediate issues of a discourse does not necessarily exhaust the discourse',[47] he could have found no better example than that of biblical literature and its historicity, materiality and power, on the one hand,

---

43. Black, *Rhetorical Criticism*, p. 38.
44. Black, *Rhetorical Criticism*, p. 39.
45. Black, *Rhetorical Criticism*, pp. 42-60, cf. 36-37.
46. Black, *Rhetorical Criticism*, p. 47.
47. Black, *Rhetorical Criticism*, p. 59.

and biblical rhetorical exegesis and historical hermeneutical reconstruction, on the other. A 'text' has a much more complicated relationship to
history than the immediate context of composition and utterance (setting aside the difficulty of determining and delimiting that particular
'context'), but can continue to have an impact through a variety of contexts generated by a myriad of social, historical, cultural, technological
and analytic circumstances. We can have no better example of this than
the Bible's reception history. But according to biblical critics, the only
authoritative and hermeneutical foundation upon which to build its interpretation is with respect to a single [and I would argue, irretrievable]
'context' (of utterance)—rhetorical criticism does not stop 'here' (and
now), but way back 'there' (and then).

Finally, as we have noted earlier, Black points out the inability (or at
least the reticence) of neo-Aristotelian scholarship to engage in any
kind of judgment without engaging in the question of its 'effectiveness'. The difficulty the neo-Aristotelian confronts, however, arises
from her/his focus which is limited to the 'effect' the performance is
said to have upon the immediate audience. This makes it difficult to
determine on just what basis a speech could be said to be 'rhetorically
good', and yet nevertheless fail,[48] which seems to have been the case
with, for example, 1 Thessalonians and 1 Corinthians. It also puts the
critic in the awkward position of judging 'effect' solely from the basis
of the rhetor's argumentative intent—did s/he succeed in 'convincing'
the audience of her/his point of view—thereby eliminating any ability
to make a moral judgment on the purpose of the speech or text itself,[49]
a judgment rarely engaged by biblical rhetorical critics [assuming the
authority of the text and/or rhetor's perspective regarding the 'rhetorical situation']. Finally, it completely ignores the fact that 'effectiveness' can also be defined in broader terms: a critic can

> ...interest himself [*sic*] not alone in the short-range effect of a discourse
> on its immediate audience, but also in its effect on later audiences and its
> indirect effects to the extent that all of these audiences, under the influ-
> ence of the discourse, themselves exert influence in speaking, writing
> and acting. He [*sic*] can inquire into the effects of the arguments, the
> message of the discourse, and the effects of its ways of arguing—its rhe-
> torical techniques, which may have consequences quite distinct from its

---

48. Black, *Rhetorical Criticism*, pp. 66-67.
49. Black, *Rhetorical Criticism*, pp. 77-78.

arguments. He [*sic*] can legitimately investigate the effects of the discourse on the rhetor, on those of other rhetors on the same subject, on those of other rhetors on other subjects, and its effects on the memory and influence of previous rhetors and discourses as they are reappraised by audiences and by the critic himself [*sic*] in the light of a new rhetorical event. The critic can, in short, assess all the differences a rhetorical discourse has made in the world and will make, and how the differences are made and why.[50]

This is precisely the kind of breadth of rhetorical criticism that will be envisioned in Chapter 3, and one that has yet to be pondered with any serious consideration by biblical rhetorical critics who continue to operate at the level of historical reconstruction of rhetorical 'effects'.

On the other hand, the critical pursuit of judgment as suggested by Wichelns (and Black) highlights one of the major differences between neo-Aristotelian criticism and biblical rhetorical studies: whereas neo-Aristotelian criticism analyzes texts recent enough to have at least *some* accompanying documentation regarding the circumstances of the performance and its reception,[51] biblical scholars have *no* independent reports of the situations surrounding them. All conclusions regarding argumentative intention, historical situation and rhetorical effect are based on extrapolations from either roughly contemporaneous historical sources, literary, social-scientific and cultural-anthropological analysis of these sources, some archaeological data, and, much more frequently, from the text itself under the rhetorical-critical gaze. While recent calls for taking advantage of as many disciplinary sources and models as possible when pursuing a rhetorical-critical analysis[52] have the merit of developing a broad 'data'base from which to draw conclusions, and a variety of alternative means of verification by which they might be tested, any reconstruction of the 'effectiveness' of the rhetor's 'intention' with respect to its original audience is still, at best, a guess. Herein, biblical interpretation according to the collections of assumptions we have been considering here is at a severe disadvantage regard-

50. Black, *Rhetorical Criticism*, p. 74.
51. Cf., e.g., Parts 2 and 3 of Andrews (ed.), *The Practice of Rhetorical Criticism*, which explore critical case studies of Lincoln's 'Second Inaugural Address' and Nixon's 'Address to the Nation on the War in Vietnam', as well as speeches by Eisenhower, Reagan and others.
52. Cf. Vernon K. Robbins, *Exploring the Texture of Texts: A Guide to Socio-Rhetorical Interpretations* (Valley Forge, PA: Trinity Press International, 1996).

ing the critical aim it sets out to achieve when engaging in rhetorical critique.[53]

Furthermore, even if 'we' let 'our' minds wander into dementia and allow for the future possibility of uncovering and verifying the authenticity of eyewitness testimonies of an original performance of a particular Gospel or letter reading from which 'we' can judge 'our' conclusions, the question that 'we' must face is: just exactly why is this important? As historians of rhetoric, it would be 'important' insofar as what 'we' would be doing is seeing rhetorical practice in play. But that is not what 'we' are doing as biblical exegetes. 'We' are in fact asserting a hermeneutical authority for an arbitrary interpretive move on 'our' part: the move to identify the 'original intention' of Jesus, or the various communities behind the oral traditions, or Paul, or the Gospel authors, or the authors of deutero-Pauline and pseudo-Petrine letters, etc. It is the belief that if somehow 'we' can get back to that pristine moment, 'we' have an authoritative basis upon which to judge any tradition, ethic, instruction or interpretation that might use this text for justification. But, would this moment be enough to explain all 'we' might want it to explain: how it related to other controversies and discussions going on around it; how it impacted future discussions; how it was used in debates which its 'author(s)' could never have foreseen; how it came to be part of the tradition; how it came to impact the cultures and people in times and places the 'author(s)' simply could not have imagined; by what implicit and subtle ways it has been absorbed into cultures and systems of social relations; how it may have inspired people to great or ignoble feats of action, of contemplation, of proclamation and witness, of revelation and insight? 'We' both do and do not ignore these expanded 'effects', multivalent 'intentions' and multiple audiences and conception/perceptions regarding the 'author(s)': 'we' *do*, insofar as biblical rhetorical critics choose to delimit their hermeneutic center [the original historical context of invention, performance, and response]; 'we' *do not* insofar as 'our' results are intended to impact and control further interpretive use of the texts 'we' analyze [unless, of course, 'we' are only in it as 'historians', which is not the objective and innocent task of description it is often meant to be].

53. This is not to suggest that rhetorical historians can avoid the epistemological and hermeneutic problems shared with biblical studies; only that they have at least some advantage in fulfilling the task of discerning immediate effect, insofar as there is available *some* contemporaneous evidence regarding it.

Finally, Black continues by exploring the effects of the philosophy of rhetoric adopted by neo-Aristotelians and its effects on their conception of the nature of discourse, as well as on the kinds of interpretive results [limitations] that ensue therefrom. The most interesting of these for current purposes is to note, along with Black, that with respect to the use of ancient rhetorical treatises as tools for analysis, the 'very application itself is probably alien to the conceptions of Aristotle [or Cicero, or Quintilian, or Hermogenes], since there is no evidence in the *Rhetoric* [or *De Oratore,* or *Institutio Oratoria,* etc.] that its generalizations were intended for the appraisal of rhetorical discourses'.[54] This is not to say that as heuristic tools these treatises are inappropriate or fruitless for us; it is simply to undermine the immediate assumptions that they were meant to be critical tools at all. And if they were not 'meant' to be used as such, then the appropriateness of their use is governed, in fact, by the fruitfulness of the criticism they help to generate. This, in turn, is limited by the ways each of them adopts a given notion of what constitutes the field of rhetoric [not to mention the 'blind spots' inherent in the canon comprising the classical tradition, that is, the 'blind spot' to vernacular rhetorics (e.g. the varieties of rabbinic literature), to gender rhetorics, etc.]. Whether it constitutes 'the art of speaking well' or of discovering 'all the available means of persuasion'; whether it concerns the public spheres of the court, the assembly or the games; whether it explores the effects of plain, grand, elegant or forceful styles on audiences: how each understands 'rhetoric' is going to effect what the critic

---

54. Black, *Rhetorical Criticism,* p. 92. Cf. Stanley Porter, 'The Theoretical Justification for Application of Rhetorical Categories to Pauline Epistolary Literature', in Porter and Olbricht (eds.), *Rhetoric and the New Testament,* pp. 100-22 (110): 'The support by Betz and Kennedy for their positions, however, gives the impression that the ancients themselves would have recognized the kind of analysis being performed by modern interpreters of the Pauline epistles. There is something inherently satisfactory in thinking that the kind of analysis being performed has some basis in the analysis in which the ancients themselves were engaged. But do the ancients give any credence to such a supposition? How would one go about finding such support? How would one formulate a theoretical justification for analysis of the Pauline epistles by means of the formal categories of ancient rhetoric? The fact that there has been some apparent success in this procedure (for example, in the works of Betz, Jewett, Watson and others) is a proof that this kind of thing can be done from the standpoint of modern interpretation; it is not a proof that the ancients would have had any recognition of this procedure.'

will achieve when adopting one, or all, of these treatises for her/his ana-lytical foundation.

The same, however, can be said regarding the adoption of modern rhetorical theories. But if this is the case, then there is no good reason for excluding *a priori* any rhetorical theory as potentially useful [a con-cept (pre?-)determined by the critic him/herself] for analysis of these ancient texts.[55]

Black's criticisms of neo-Aristotelianism came at an important mo-ment in the history of rhetorical criticism in American speech and communication departments. It gave voice to a growing disease in the discipline that something somewhere had gone wrong. While his cri-tique was instrumental for the ensuing transformation of the discussion in America regarding philosophy of rhetoric and the development of new rhetorical theories, it did not, however, spell the doom of neo-Aristotelianism, which mutated into several different forms: on the one hand, there developed the pursuit of the reconstruction of the history of (western) rhetoric, rhetorical praxis and education;[56] on the other hand, a counter-reform movement attempted to rescue the classical tradition by appealing to the utility of the application of classical rhetorical trea-tises to issues confronting invention and arrangement in modern courses of composition.[57] Indeed, recently neo-classicism has enjoyed a revival

55. Note C. Joachim Classen, 'St. Paul's Epistles and Ancient Greek and Roman Rhetoric', in Porter and Olbricht (eds.), *Rhetoric and the New Testament*, pp. 265-91 (290): '[t]here is no reason why one should restrict oneself to the rhetoric of the ancients in interpreting texts from antiquity, and not avail oneself of the discoveries and achievements of more recent times.'

56. Cf. Bibliographies, Rhetoric and the West: Medieval through Nineteenth Century (Selected Materials).

57. By far the best example of this movement in composition theory is the col-lection of essays dedicated to Edward P.J. Corbett: Robert J. Connors, Lisa S. Ede and Andrea A. Lunsford (eds.), *Essays on Classical Rhetoric and Modern Dis-course* (Carbondale, IL: Southern Illinois University Press, 1984). Cf. also Edward P.J. Corbett, *Classical Rhetoric for the Modern Student* (New York: Oxford Uni-versity Press, 1965), as well as a bibliography of his works included in Connors, Ede and Lunsford (eds.), *Essays on Classical Rhetoric and Modern Discourse*, pp. 250-57.

Cf. also, e.g., Lloyd Bitzer and Edwin Black (eds.), *The Prospect of Rhetoric* (Englewood Cliffs, NJ: Prentice–Hall, 1971); Charles Cooper and Lee Odell (eds.), *Research on Composing* (Urbana, IL: National Council of Teachers of English, 1978); James J. Murphy (ed.), *The Rhetorical Tradition and Modern Writing* (New York: Modern Language Association, 1982).

of the method, now perhaps better informed by some of the lessons learned from its near-exile.[58] There may be a number of reasons for its tenacity: perhaps out of sheer habit, the impact throughout western educational history of particularly Ciceronian, but also eventually resurgent Aristotelian (not to mention Platonic) rhetoric being undeniable and unavoidable—or perhaps the useful insights which ancient treatises continue [when stretched] to generate with respect to both criticism and composition. But the most important function might be the ancients' emphasis upon the understanding of rhetorical activity as grounded in the 'civic' life, in history, that is, in the material, in the pragmatic and political effects of discourse. Neo-Aristotelian (neo-classical) criticism, if it does nothing else, at least brings to the forefront the concept of discourse as an *activity* which can and does have profound effects in the lives and history of people. [Perhaps this is nothing but a 'deep-cover' humanism which the American dream/nightmare refuses to let vanish.]

To that end, biblical studies would do well to continue to ground its efforts at rhetorical interpretation within the circumstances of the human, the practical, the everyday give-and-take of people wrestling with ideas, testing hypotheses, experimenting in persuasion. However, biblical studies would find itself in a much better position to do this if it were to broaden its critical scope with respect to theoretical assumptions, methodological approaches, interpretive goals and objects of its analysis. As it currently stands, its antiquarian and synthesist construction of rhetorical theory, its dominantly taxonomic explication of argumentation, its causalist assumptions regarding the relationship between discourse and context [theory and practice], and the dominance, over all this, of its historical hermeneutics makes it terribly vulnerable to the same kind of critique raised 30 years ago to its counterpart, neo-Aristotelianism. We must take seriously the claim long since asserted and

---

58. Cf., e.g., Andrews, *The Practice of Rhetorical Criticism*; Michael C. Leff and Fred J. Kauffeld (eds.), *Text in Context: Critical Dialogues on Significant Episodes in American Political Rhetoric* (Davis, CA: Hermagoras Press, 1989); Michael C. Leff, 'Lincoln at Cooper Union: A Rationale for Neo-Classical Criticism', in Andrews, *The Practice of Rhetorical Criticism*, pp. 347-56; William A. Linsley (ed.), *Speech Criticism: Methods and Materials* (Dubuque, IA: Wm C. Brown, 1968); Robert T. Oliver, *History of Public Speaking in America* (Boston: Allyn & Bacon, 1965). The journal, *Rhetorica*, put out by the International Society for the History of Rhetoric (Berkeley: University of California Press), predominantly features articles representing this neoclassical approach.

explored that there is more to rhetorical criticism than rhetorical history: not only must one re-envision the key methodological assumptions regarding history and historicity of 'texts',[59] but one must be available to the insights and ideas of developing approaches and theories, not to mention confronting the tenacity of 'texts' to 'mean' and 'effect' circumstance far beyond their moment of composition and original performance.

What Lies Ahead

Rhetoric is a broad and growing discipline, taking on the potential of interdisciplinary and transdisciplinary dimensions and extending them beyond traditional concerns with 'discourse' *per se* to include ideology, epistemology, ontology and materiality. Given the range and future possibilities of rhetoric (as an epistemological, ontological and linguistic 'principle'), it is rather disappointing that biblical studies has chosen to limit its participation 'intentionally' ['motivistically'] to a methodological perspective guaranteed to subsume rhetoric to historical-critical interests. It is disappointing, but not necessarily surprising.

Why it is not surprising will be the focus of the rest of this effort [a(rtifa)ct, argument]. In order to proceed, however, it is 'necessary' [traditional, incumbent, expected, *demanded*] that we next consider a philosophical, theoretical and methodological foundation for the inquiry I wish to pursue herein. This is where the proposed 'rhetoric of power' will come in: rather than perpetuating the disciplinary *pouvoir/ savoir* of biblical rhetorical criticism by remaining within its dominant paradigm, I will propose a method (and its philosophical and theoretical principles) that will achieve [advocate] (at least) three important precedents: it will endeavor to generate a new methodological alternative that embraces at least certain aspects of modern rhetorical theories (without claiming to be a totalizing theory [although any and every theory demands such loyalty, often resulting in the implication of totalization {fascism is, perhaps, unavoidable in theorizing}]). It will also

---

59. Cf. Wilhelm Wuellner, 'Biblical Exegesis in the Light of the History and Historicity of Rhetoric and the Nature of the Rhetoric of Religion', in Stanley E. Porter and Thomas H Olbricht (eds.), *Rhetoric and the New Testament: Essays from the 1992 Heidelberg Conference* (*Journal for the Study of the New Testament*, Supplement Series, 90; Sheffield; Sheffield Academic Press, 1993), pp. 492-512 (esp. 501-11).

seek to build in a reflective mechanism in the activity of theorizing and critique. Finally, it will attempt to break open new vistas of rhetorical-hermeneutical relevance regarding 'text' and 'meaning', so as to transform [or not: we shall see] the discipline of biblical studies through the introduction of a much more flexible [not quite; perhaps 'intentionally deconstructive'] philosophy of rhetorical readings (as *opposed* to exegesis).

But it would be much too easy simply to develop a new theory and use it to interpret a biblical text rhetorically ['easy' = simplistic, non-critical, false-consciously and ideologically submissive]. In order to experience the fullness of this theory in interpretive action [not 'fullness' as in 'totality', but 'fullness' as in 'precedence for further mimetic (no, more like 'playfully inspired', 'randomly associational') inquiry in all sorts of directions otherwise unanticipated], I will in fact concentrate *not* on the [mundane, banal] task of interpreting a biblical text, but of interpreting biblical rhetorical criticism. And to make the task even more subtle and difficult, I will eschew any sitting-duck targets, such as those explored in this chapter, for those rhetorical-critical efforts that seem to suggest a broader agenda: the scholars whose work we will herein explore all suggest that the resurgence of a rhetorical approach to the biblical text has important ramifications for biblical interpretation, whether they include the undermining of biblical-theological authority for modern faithing Christians, the transformation of biblical interpretation into an interdisciplinary effort, the means by which interpreters can retrieve the silenced voices from the past, or the justification of a hermeneutic of liberation grounded in an activist community. It will be the test of a 'rhetoric of power' to find the ideological limitations of the *pouvoir/savoir* of biblical studies as a discursive formation with respect to these rather 'radical' biblical rhetorical critics; for the intention of (this particular application of) a 'rhetoric of power' is to find the *loci* of power that continue to dominate and govern biblical interpretive practices. Once these 'blinders' have been exposed [taken off?], it will be up to us to suggest a potentially fundamental revision of the discipline which would/could be made possible by the incursion of other rhetorical-theoretical and philosophical paradigmata.

Chapter 3

TOWARD A DEFINITION
OF A RHETORIC OF POWER

It is the nature of a hypothesis, when once a man has conceived it, that it
assimilates every thing to itself, as proper nourishment; and, from the
first moment of your begetting it, it generally grows the stronger by
everything you see, hear, read, or understand. This is of great use.

The Life and Opinions of Tristram Shandy
Laurence Sterne

The purpose of this chapter is to develop a critical approach based upon
a rhetorical theory whose focus is upon 'truth and power' in every act
of signification. This theory embraces a concept of 'meaningfulness' of
an act/event/circumstance which by its very attribution of 'meaning' is
more or less *selective* and *persuasive*, hence is more or less engaged in
power. The philosophy of rhetoric informing such a theory is a *non*-
mechanistic approach that embraces a trinitarian complex of values/
perceptions governing every rhetorical analytical, critical and performative act, even this very act of theorizing itself.

It is non-mechanistic, insofar as it rejects rigidly formalist and causalist assumptions regarding methodology in criticism: the assumptions an
audience of scholars brings to a discussion of methodology are only
fulfilled when analytical 'tools' and their appropriate 'functions' are
presented and then 'put to work' on canonically prescribed texts/events
in such a way that not only is their 'application' clarified, but also the
results are 'reduplicative'. In this way, 'objectivity', or at least intersubjective accessibility, is ensured such that *any* scholar could take
the same methodological tools and using similar raw materials could
achieve similar results. This, of course, smacks of an industrialist conception of the production and consumption of knowledge, one important effect of which is a concentration upon the *means* and *results* of

knowledge productivity *to the express exclusion of* the individual who contributes to this end result. It is a 'factory model' of knowledge with a fascinating parallel to industrial and corporate ideological degradation of the individual worker (who can be replaced at any time) and exaltation of productivity/profitability 'for the sake of the company' (in academentia: 'for the sake of the pursuit of knowledge' [read: 'discipline']).[1] The origin/cause (= 'intention') of this model (which must also include the impact of technological developments in communication, esp. the printing press) is not of as much interest as the advent [better: blatant exposure of latent philosophical underpinnings] of capitalist consumerist ideology [declared (by capitalists) the historical 'winner' over communism] now dominating the discourse of American philosophy of education and its current praxis: not only is greater productivity demanded from scholars and professors as heavier workloads are assigned and more research/publishing expected, but also higher education is being called upon to make up for the failure of public education in providing the country with an immediately employable workforce. The commodification of knowledge and education as a facet of a mechanistic approach to critical analysis has relationships to contexts of power in need of further analysis.

Furthermore, a mechanistic approach to theory and method smacks of a positivist and empiricist approach to 'reality' whose mechanistic foundation of 'cause and effect' lends them to be generalized into 'laws' that help the scholar to anticipate and precipitate certain results given certain circumstances/events. Unfortunately, such a perspective regarding *discourse, communication* and *persuasion* is not only irrelevant, but the dominance of this paradigm has resulted in the near eclipsing of the importance of the liberal arts in education in America. It exacts a standard of certitude from the humanities which can be neither defended nor achieved. The imposition of its standards of knowledge (through definitional presumptions-turned-normative-basis of *all* analytical pursuits and their expected results) could be easily understood as fascistic, as they work toward the autocratic elimination of alternative viewpoints and perspectives of research methods and goals for the sake of maintaining a dominant perspective on scholarly pursuit. Indeed, not only is such a standard inimical to the humanities, but it should itself become

1. For an interesting example of a rhetorical theory thoroughly embedded within corporate/capitalist discourse, cf. Herbert W. Simons, 'Toward a New Rhetoric', *Pennsylvania Speech Annual* 26.1 (1967), pp. 7-20.

the target of the humanities' critical gaze in an effort to expose the ideological assumptions and reject as exclusivist its understanding of the world. Here, too, the systems and contexts of power need to be explored.

With respect to rhetoric in particular, the imposition of mechanist presumptions upon its critical and analytical pursuit(s) is particularly damaging. On the one hand, it too often results either in discussions governed by efforts at identification, classification and summary presentation of traditional argumentative genres, canons, divisions, figures (of thought and speech), tropes and/or colors,[2] or in critical metamorphosis of modern efforts at metaphor, argumentation, dramatist, narrative, fantasy-theme, feminist, etc., theories into mechanistic 'methods' of critical analysis,[3] or in attempts at limiting, defining and distinguishing *rhetorical* discourse from other 'non-rhetorical' forms of discourse (philosophical, poetic, etc.).[4] The issue is not with the appropriateness of their respective *foci* per se, nor with the elaboration of critical approaches as perspectives from which to analyze and compose communicative activities, but with the ideology of mechanism that informs their application, an ideology that gives shape to their discourse in ways that present their results as 'certain', 'objective' or 'reduplicatable'—take a 'text', run it through a method, and present a 'result' as 'the' (intended) effect or 'the' (intended) meaning. Typically, such mechanist ideology eliminates certain aspects of discourse dynamics as irrelevant (or ignores them as outside of its purview) in order for the method to work effectively. It also approaches the *dynamic*

---

2. Cf. Kathleen Welch's critique of the Heritage School of rhetorical approaches embracing the classical traditions in: *The Contemporary Reception of Classical Rhetoric: Appropriations of Ancient Discourse* (Hillsdale, NJ: Lawrence Erlbaum, 1990).

3. Cf. Sonja K. Foss's otherwise exceptional collection of rhetorical-critical methods, *Rhetorical Criticism: Exploration and Practice* (Prospect Heights, IL: Waveland Press, 1989).

4. The early works of Henry W. Johnstone, Jr, saw him make strident efforts at separating rhetoric from philosophy; see his articles, 'Some Reflections on Argumentation', 'A New Theory of Philosophical Argumentation' and 'Persuasion and Validity in Philosophy', in Maurice Natanson and Henry W. Johnstone, Jr (eds.), *Philosophy, Rhetoric and Argumentation* (University Park, PA: Pennsylvania State University Press, 1965); see also his translation of Olivier Reboul, 'Can There Be Non-Rhetorical Argumentation?', *Philosophy & Rhetoric* 21.3 (1988), pp. 220-33.

of communication as though it were an artifact, an object whose en-
livenment is only generated *through the method itself*.[5] Rather than
seen as heuristic approaches highlighting perspectives and dynamics of
persuasive 'discourse' (including its own as rhetorical activity), mechanist approaches of rhetorical theory and method deaden discourse in
order to control analytical results, especially concerning its rhetorical
effectiveness and its hermeneutical 'meaning' which are only brought
to light (shown at work) through the critical and interpretive act.

On the other hand, mechanistic presumptions regarding the application of rhetorical theories to rhetorical activities force philosophical
explorations into the causality inherent in discourse situations, reducing
persuasive dynamics to that of pragmatics.[6] Arguing that 'exigencies'
and 'rhetorical situations' generate and constrain responses, this approach highlights to the exclusion of alternative perspectives the *pragmatic* foundation of rhetorical communication.[7] But what is described
in causalist terms is in fact individual [alas, not necessarily 'free']
choice regarding audience expectations, sociolinguistic conventions,
cultural traditions to which rhetors and their audiences in varying
degrees adhere. It is this fact that has caused a shift from seeing situation theory as descriptive (causalist, mechanist) to *prescriptive*.[8]

5. Cf. David Berlo, 'A Model of the Communication Process', in Jane Blankenship and Robert Wihoit (eds.), *Selective Readings in Public Speaking* (Belmont,
CA: Dickenson Press, 1966), p. 8, the study of rhetoric must '*arrest the dynamics
of the process* in the same way that we arrest motion when we take a still picture
with a camera'. Emphasis mine.

6. Lloyd Bitzer, 'The Rhetorical Situation', *Philosophy & Rhetoric* 1.1 (1968),
pp. 1-14.

7. Cf. Lloyd Bitzer, 'Functional Communication: A Situational Perspective',
in Eugene E. White (ed.), *Rhetoric in Transition: Studies in the Nature and Uses of
Rhetoric* (University Park, PA: Pennsylvania State University Press, 1980), pp. 21-
38.

8. Cf. the rejection of Bitzer's theory offered most devastatingly by Richard
Vatz, 'The Myth of the Rhetorical Situation', *Philosophy & Rhetoric* 6.3 (1973),
pp. 154-61; also by K.E. Wilkerson, 'On Evaluating Theories of Rhetoric',
Philosophy & Rhetoric 3.1 (1970), pp. 82-96. Others have tried to adjust Bitzer's
theory in light of these critiques, including Richard Larson, 'Lloyd Bitzer's "Rhetor-
ical Situation" and the Classification of Discourse: Problems and Implications',
Philosophy & Rhetoric 3.1 (1970), pp. 165-68; Scott Consigny, 'Rhetoric and its
Situations', *Philosophy & Rhetoric* 7.3 (1974), pp. 175-86; John Patton, 'Causation
and Creativity in Rhetorical Situations: Distinctions and Implications', *Quarterly
Journal of Speech* 65.1 (1979), pp. 36-55; and, finally, its reformulation into a

Because what is at issue is not mechanistic restraint of rhetorical activity, but in fact the role of accident, experiment, choice, opportunity, accessibility, selectivity and ability. Indeed, perhaps the fundamental philosophical basis for a non-mechanistic approach to rhetorical theory and praxis is a certain concept of freedom [although, certainly *not* an Enlightenment concept of individual freedom outside of systems of power, but the freedom to continually pester, bother, question, interrupt, disrupt].

Instead of a mechanistic approach, I here present a philosophy of rhetoric that embraces a *symbiotic, symphonic* and *museful* approach to rhetoric. This approach is organic in perspective, conceiving of rhetorical theory and critical practice as environmental, taking shape and form according to [but also with the potential to take shape 'contrary' to] the circumstances in which they arise, without the strict confines of causality, but within the fluidity and dynamism of the interrelationship of freedom and restraint. Or, better, this philosophy conceives of rhetoric as experimental, but not experimental for its own sake: its purpose is to bring into the mixture of rhetorical models, methods, theories and histories the multiplicity engendered through awareness and rejection of the hegemony of the single sense, of 'point of view', of the reductionism of dialectical 'thesis–antithesis–synthesis'. Indeed, its ultimate driving impulse is toward the Outside, the 'outlaw', the *hysterical,*[9] to point out continually the 'almost, but not quite' and the 'that *still* isn't right' of any and every interpretive, argumentative, communicative act.[10] Such a philosophy of rhetoric, while initially caught in

prescriptive theory offered by Alan Brinton, 'Situation in the Theory of Rhetoric', *Philosophy & Rhetoric* 14.4 (1981), pp. 234-48.

9. For a brilliant discussion of the (lack of) contours to a 'pararhetorics' of the hysterical, see, the works of Victor J. Vitanza, esp. 'An Open Letter to my "Colligs": On Paraethics, Pararhetorics, and The Hysterical Turn', *Pre/Text* 11.3–4 (1990), pp. 238-87 (287). Further works include Victor Vitanza, 'Cackling with Tears in my Eyes; or, Some Responses to "The Gang of Three" Scott–Leff–Kennedy', *Rhetoric Review* 7.1 (1988), pp. 214-18; Vitanza, 'Critical Sub/Versions of the History of Philosophical Rhetoric', *Rhetoric Review* 6.1 (1987), pp. 41-66; Vitanza, ' "Notes" Towards Historiographies of Rhetoric; or, Rhetorics of the Histories of Rhetorics: Traditional, Revisionary, and Sub/Versive', *Pre/Text* 8.1–2 (1987), pp. 63-125; Vitanza, ' "Some More" Notes, Towards a "Third Sophistic" ', *Argumentation* 5.5 (1991), pp. 117-39.

10. This idea comes from Julia Kristeva, 'Woman Can Never Be Defined', in

its own hegemony of the printed 'word-made-idol' (text, not hyper-text)[11] and academented assumption of arrogant interpretive activity, sees itself as organistic (ever adaptive, ever growing/dying) *contra*band which, in the end, will still not 'agree' with its own interpretive acts, but will simultaneously be 'against' and 'alongside' ('contra') every effort at subverting grand narratives. [That's close, but still not it!]

A *symbiotic* approach to rhetorical activity and analysis emphasizes the fluid historicity of an act, the multiple intentionalities at work in every performance, including the performance of analysis. An act (its meaning-effect) does not exist alone, apart from rhetor, form, audience or context, but interacts with all of these [and certainly *beyond* all three of these]. Intentions are found not only in the selection of values, per-spectives, conclusions, argumentative strategies and presentation on the part of the rhetor; not only in the situation that governs and is governed by the *medium* (form, artifacticity) of communication, the social con-straints, the restraints of legality, time, space, money, broadcast access and publication/distribution; but also on the part of the receivers who themselves have certain intentions in 'hearing' what one has to say. In particular, it is this emphasis upon including both 'text' (as media-arti-fact), 'context' (with historicity, *through* time and space), and 'audi-ence' (who are active participants in shaping discourse both prior to, during and after reception, are not necessarily homogenous in social, cultural, religious, ethical or chronological origins[12] and may not nec-essarily be friendly) that gives rhetorical activity its *symbiotic* and con-tinuing character. All of these participants in communicative activities

Elaine Marks and Isabelle de Courtivron (eds.), *New French Feminisms: An An-thology* (New York: Schocken Books, 1981), pp. 137-41.

11. Cf. Robert M. Fowler, 'How the Secondary Orality of the Electronic Age Can Awaken Us to the Primary Orality of Antiquity—or—What Hypertext Can Teach Us about the Bible', presented at the Annual Meeting of the Eastern Great Lakes Biblical Society, April 1994. Cf. also Richard Lanham, *The Electronic Word: Democracy, Technology and the Arts* (Chicago: University of Chicago Press, 1993); Jay David Bolter, *Writing Space: The Computer, Hypertext and the History of Writing* (Hillsdale, NJ: Lawrence Erlbaum, 1991); and George Landow, *Hypertext: The Convergence of Contemporary Critical Theory and Technology* (Baltimore: The Johns Hopkins University Press, 1992).

12. Cf. Donald P. Cushman and Phillip K. Tompkins, 'A Theory of Rhetoric for Contemporary Society', *Philosophy & Rhetoric* 13.1 (1980), pp. 43-67, who emphasize the need to take into account the diversity of audience composition in modern rhetorical theory due to the advent of mass media.

are essential aspects to *persuasion* [but more: disclosure, disruption, perhaps even attack and counterattack], demanding a recognition of their dynamic interactivity in the development of any rhetorical theory and critical method. But this is not enough: The symbiotic dimension of theorizing must also come to recognize the disruptive tendency of all and every form of intentionality in all these contexts to *speak at cross-purposes, to mean more and other than it can say/do through the act of saying and doing*, to deny access to others/Others who are silenced, and by that silencing, are guaranteed a presence. This is the disruptive actualization of all communicative activity, the escapability of language and persuasion due to the multiplicity of forces, contexts, meanings, powers, (sub)consciousnesses and 'intentions'. All rhetorical analysis must keep in mind this totality of communication-as-organism-of-[attempts at]-'persuasion', not in an effort to control it, nor to understand/arrest it, but to actualize its further chaos for an increasing multiplicity of participant voices.

A *symphonic* approach requires the recognition of multiplicity of critical approaches and perspectives regarding both the presentation and analysis of the a(rtifa)ct. This is the interdisciplinary nature of rhetorical theory which can and must draw from a myriad of other disciplinary (and other) sources for both analysis, inspiration and composition. Rhetoric is no longer simply about *text* analysis, speech and/or written composition or linguistic communication, but about the 'persuasive' dimension of the whole social semiotic activity, a dimension that requires both rhetor and analyst to take into account the potential contributions and insights offered by other disciplines—literary, social, media, psychological, scientific, artistic, etc. Each disciplinary analysis concentrates upon a theme present in the total *symphonic* composition, a 'voice' in the 'orchestral' arrangement. As such, it heuristically highlights aspects of 'persuasive' performance(s) whose significance can be argued for, from which certain disciplinary conclusions can be presented as contributing to the understanding of the nature of the 'persuasive' act and to 'persuasion' as a whole. But each discipline is only a partial performance, as though only one instrument or section in an orchestral piece were to play its part alone; the experience of the total performance, when analyzed through the lens of critical methods, *can never be achieved.* Nevertheless, a *symphonic* approach to rhetoric will engender an environment in rhetorical theory and analytical praxis that provides an important corrective against singular methodological approaches, and embraces the need for a multiplicity of perspectives and critical methods.

It should *not*, however, be assumed that this multiplicity will work in harmony, but could and perhaps should be set to use and to create cacophony, undermining potential hegemony of synthesized visions of 'one world, one vision'. Indeed, the metaphor of 'orchestra', with its implicit potential analog to be taken 'under direction', is thoroughly problematic. Since the destruction and transformation of music from Schoenberg to Cage, a symphonic approach must be understood to be disruptive. The metaphor should be seen more as an 'orchestrated' action of terror(-ism), a maximalist assault of polyphony, an eclectic and willful manipulation of methods, even those working at cross-purposes. The intention is not to integrate further into some monolithic 'interdiscipline', but to break apart disciplinary constraints/restraints into a free-floating space of continual polymorophous adaptation.

Finally, a *museful* approach to rhetorical theory and analysis is one that turns to the Sophistic (Gorgianic) ethic[13] which denies an ontology of 'truth' and embraces the *dynamis* (power) of words (not Logos, Rationality, but multiplicities, irrationalities). Rhetorical activity is ongoing, participating in the auto- and inter-didactic processes of experimentation, comprehending *'persuasivity'* as both temporal and ephemeral [as both impositional and freeing], as participating in the exchanges of values and ideas that are a part of fluid human culture [and exiled apart from human culture]. Rhetoric undermines appeals to universal validity by viewing 'texts' as examples 'of purposes pursued, targets hit or missed, practices illuminated for the sake not of pure knowledge, but of further (and improved) practice'.[14] Such 'texts' must also include those that indulge in theorizing, philosophizing, constructing methods and offering analyzes as part of the tradition of [and, through disciplinary practices, set apart from] rhetoric. Hence, rhetoric as *museful* not only embraces the playful, the emotive, the tentative, the forceful, the moving, the unsuccessful, the repressed, the silenced, the

---

13. Cf. in particular the important work done by Susan C. Jarratt, *Rereading the Sophists: Classical Rhetoric Refigured* (Carbondale, IL: Southern Illinois University Press, 1991). Cf. also Conley, *Rhetoric in the European Tradition*, in which he traces throughout the history of rhetoric in the west the continuing presence of four major philosophies, including the Isocratean-Gorgianic.

14. Wayne Booth, *The Rhetoric of Fiction* (Chicago: University of Chicago Press, 2nd edn, 1983), p. 441.

ignored, the violent, the dominant in communicative and 'meaningful' events/a(rtifa)cts, but also sees these in the very activities of developing and presenting rhetorical theories, rhetorical critical methods, rhetorical analytical praxis. Rhetoric must approach *'persuasivity'* within an organic [and hence, I can't stress enough, messy] process of self-reflection and improvement [with the ever-present question, 'to what ends and against what purposes?'], a process at work in every communicative a(rtifa)ct. A *museful* approach to analysis is both thoughtful [-less] and thought[-less]-provoking, both insightful and experimental; it conceives of itself as part of the greater chaotic dynamic of attempts successful and failed for ever More [and more and more].

But its *museful* pursuit is not to be approached for the sake of theorizing itself, nor is it to take place exclusively within rhetoric's traditions. It is to be grounded in the historical, the contingent, the 'contextual'-pragmatic spheres of the relationship between persuasion and action. This grounds rhetorical theory and praxis within the cultural traditions within which they arise. While I would not go so far as to suggest that rhetoric be 'subordinated' to the history of consciousness,[15] the consequences suggested by Black are worth noting for a philosophy of rhetoric which is *museful*:

> First, 'would be to promote a rigorously contextual view of rhetorical theories of the past—to understand them as time-bound. That perspective...would oblige us...to reserve the possibility that a theory of rhetoric may speak for its time, that it may retrieve for us a *mentalité*, long vanished, that it faithfully [or not] reflects. A second consequence...would be to render rhetorical theory a product of rhetorical criticism...So conceived, a rhetorical theory would not then be an abstract or ideal model of a rhetorical transaction. Rather, it would be a generated *interpretation* of a body of rhetorical transactions that had actually occurred [including those transactions of theorizing *itself*]'.[16]

This philosophy of rhetoric provides the environment within which theories of rhetoric should be developed. The opportunity exists within such an environment to occasion/demand a wide variety of theoretical models which should not be perceived as exclusive of one another, but as part of a necessary and disharmonious *symphony* of perspectives, whose very diversity helps to foster a stronger dynamic toward disciplinary chaos. Within such an environment, theories could be developed which concentrate upon the pragmatic tradition of rhetoric: *for whom and against whom* 'prescriptive' rules for composition and presentation [better: disruption and re/presentation] are generated. Other theories could be developed as part of the critical and analytical tradition of rhetoric [but to what 'end'? I suggest the 'end' of theoretical, analytical, structural and systemic hegemonic violence, the attempt to categorize and maintain a 'point of view']. In every case, each theory stands to return to/for the Others *musefully* in an organic [messy, perhaps violent] *symbiosis*.

The particular theory I would like to explore in this tome is an analytical and critical theory that focuses upon 'texts' and 'contexts' of power. I use the term 'power' loosely, heuristically, stretching it to encompass a disparate variety of reflections on [both repressive *and* productive] incarnations of violence and control. One such advent would include the power of and in belief systems, whether they be philosophical, ethical, religious, scientific, political, economic, or the fundamental assumptions cohering the constellation of these systems around concepts of gender role and essences; whether they be rendered through systematic presentation, or left assumed and inherent; but in every case, their uses in discourse and activities are to reinforce certain values over others in an effort to maintain adherence, secure beliefs, and affect (conscious and unconscious) activity *in the interest* of their adherents to help them secure a position of prestige, wealth, control, and/or strength in society and 'the world'.

  Another aspect of power would include the presence of structures that are generated out of belief systems, and in turn help reinforce their hegemony, whether these structures are explicitly mandated, voluntarily agreed upon and ceremoniously sanctioned, [and/]or are promulgated by terror and raw force; whether they are assumed as shared and unquestioned practices reinforced through socialization and myth-making, or are intentionally given shape and form through (semi-) public rules and constitutions; whether they are political structures, economic systems, religious governing bodies, academented institutional structures or perhaps voluntary associations. Structures of power and their mechanisms of enforcement (police, military, judicial; peer reviews, tenure reviews, editorial boards, professional societies; paramilitary organizations, vigilante groups; church 'leaders', encyclicals, etc.) serve to secure the adherence to belief to shared/assumed values through manipulation [from implicit threat to oversacralizing] of behavior.

One other epiphany of power that should be considered is the power in and of persuasion *itself*. It can be described in terms of the degrees of choice and freedom in which both rhetor and audience participate, with which they affect one another; in terms of the inscribed value or ethos granted to a person, a tradition, or an artifact; in terms of the emotive, inspirational and affective influence seen to inhere in a person or a(rtifa)ct; in terms of the accessibility to persuasive discourse granted an individual or group.[17] [But more than this: There is an element of violence in 'persuasion' as an activity of imposing one's own 'point of view' upon another.]

The most insidious extreme of power would take the form of the suppression of discourse, the elimination of free discourse exchange, the exclusive and enforced hegemony of (any)one perspective/tradition/belief, and most importantly the eradication and torture of participants in the discourse who have been stigmatized/demonized as outcasts and pariahs. The most beneficent extreme would be the embracing of plurality and freedom of individuals, cultures, ideas, values and experiences; the assurance of free discourse exchange, opportunities for sharing perspectives; the fundamental guarantee for basic human and nature survivability, indeed *thrive*ability; the participation of (once) marginalized people and their voices; a position that is a continual alternative to all forms of power, working against every attempt at developing a hegemonic grand narrative.

It is to power in all its implicit and explicit forms [including others not mentioned here] that my rhetorical theory concentrates upon as only *part* of the *total* 'persuasive' experience. A rhetoric of power, then, chooses to emphasize this dimension of communicative exchange, and does so with the explicit commitment to search out and question the 'powerful' within the presumptions, values, judgments, 'truths', 'facts'

17. In particular, note the issue of gender as a means of restriction and access; cf. Karlyn Kohrs Campbell, *Man Cannot Speak for Her* (2 vols.; New York: Greenwood Press, 1989). In this regard, too, note the gender role assumptions which help reinforce the hegemony of male scholarly discourse as explored in psychoanalytic theory by Martha Noel Evans, 'Hysteria and the Seduction of Theory', in Dianne Hunter (ed.), *Seduction and Theory: Readings of Gender, Representation and Rhetoric* (Urbana, IL: University of Illinois Press, 1989), pp. 73-85.

and beliefs at work in every rhetorical a(rtifa)ct; the systems perpetrat-
ing and legitimating the 'powerful'; and, finally, the 'powerful' as
given form in the a(rtifa)ct itself [and its repressed, oppressed Other].
Hence, a rhetoric of power approach to the biblical text would note not
only the *symbiosis* of ecclesiastical, ethical, social systems and assumptions governing biblical distribution, content, form, presentation and
interpretation; nor only the *symphonic* voices of traditions performing
thematic developments both in history and through the Bible's historicity; nor only the *museful* dimensions of biblical analysis, interpretation
and methodological self-reflection; but also the 'goadings of mystery'
inherent in [assigned to] *religious* texts as texts whose effect and persuasion reach beyond the simple temporal/spatial here-and-now, but
also the spiritual and eternal dimensions at work outside/within physical existence. It would explore the *violence* at work when religion and
the Bible are set to work for sociopolitical agendas of either Right or
Left [as though religion and the Bible are themselves neutral 'tools' for
oppression? That is *precisely* what I *do not* mean to imply].

The critical means for exploring this dimension of power will be
derived from three principal sources. The first is the work of Perelman
and Olbrechts-Tyteca which helped to introduce the New Rhetoric. It is
in particular the inventional system they develop in their theory of argumentation from which I will draw. This inventional system is founded
upon the [First and Third] Sophistic rejection of the pursuit and attain-
ment of 'ultimate' 'truth'. Hence, it focuses upon the role audiences
play in the strategic development and presentation of arguments for
securing adherence to beliefs, as well as the role values play in persuasive and convincing discourse. [Question: Just how important should
audiences *be* for invention? The 'tyranny of audiences'...] The second
source is the elaboration of the implications of this system which has
been proposed in the recent works of Wilhelm Wuellner. Such a choice
is quite propitious, as his efforts are not only driven by the interest to
expand rhetorical theory and (analytical) praxis to include (social-)
semiotic, literary, narrative, materialist, feminist and ideological-critical
theories, but to do so within the context of biblical studies itself. The
third [and for now, final] source is the work of Steven Mailloux who
argues for an awareness of the institutional origins (and *telos*) of the
rhetoric of a critical discipline and its impact upon the kinds of hermeneutical argumentative strategies sanctioned for use in critical analysis
when attempting to secure an authoritative interpretation of a given

work. Drawing from these sources, a rhetoric of power can begin to address *symbiotically*, *symphonically* and *musefully* the question of the function of rhetorical criticism in New Testament exegesis.

Perelman and Olbrechts-Tyteca

The Polish-born, naturalized-Belgian philosopher Chaim Perelman was professor of logic, ethics and metaphysics at the University of Brussels when he began his exploration in 1947 into the means whereby people secure adherence to values through reasoned discourse. Having first studied law, he then turned to philosophy and did his thesis on the German logician Gottlob Frege. He later met his associate Lucie Olbrechts-Tyteca, a student of Eugéne Dupréel and a reader of social science and economics. Together they spent 11 years doing research on rhetoric and argumentation theory, first presenting their proposal in 1949 at the Institut des Hautes Etudes de Belgique, and after a series of intermittent articles, presenting their findings in the seminal and impressive work, *La nouvelle rhétorique: Traité de l'argumentation*, published in 1958.

As Perelman describes it, his interest in rhetoric arose out of his exploration into the role of value judgments in the concept of justice.[18] Coming out of a school of logical positivism emphasizing self-evidential truth and analytic reasoning,[19] he found that in order to write scientifically and rationally about the application of justice, values had to be ignored or discarded as irrelevantly subjective and emotional

18. Perelman explores the question of justice and the role of values in argumentation in his earlier work, 'Concerning Justice', in *The Idea of Justice and the Problem of Argumentation* (London: Routledge & Kegan Paul, 1963), first published as *De la Justice* (Brussels: Offices de Publicité, 1945). He also reviews the application of the rule of formal justice in §52 'The Rule of Justice', in C. Perelman and L. Olbrechts-Tyteca, *The New Rhetoric: A Treatise on Argumentation* (Notre Dame, IN: University of Notre Dame Press, 1969), pp. 218-20. For a brief synopsis of his own personal exploration into philosophy and law which led him to rhetoric, see 'Introduction', in James L. Golden and Joseph J. Pilotta (eds.), *Practical Reasoning in Human Affairs: Studies in Honor of Chaim Perelman* (Dordrecht: D. Reidel Publishing Company, 1986), pp. 1-4.

19. For an exploration into the role of self-evidence in proof, and its inherently *rhetorical* aspect, see 'Self–Evidence and Proof', in Perelman, *The Idea of Justice*, pp. 102-24.

expressions. Was this possible? Could justice be sought and made manifest without the appeal to values? Reviewing six principles of just distribution, such as

1. to everyone the same thing,
2. to everyone according to his merits,
3. to each according to his work,
4. to everyone according to his needs,
5. to each according to his rank,
6. to each according to his legal entitlement,

it becomes obvious that these *indeed* are concerned with values, with a particular concept of the world. What about his own proposed concept of *formal* justice, the equal treatment of persons under similar circumstances? Could appeal to and application of this rule avoid judgments based upon values? Certainly and clearly not, for as soon as one sets out to determine the similarity of different circumstances, and from there to determine comparatively similar treatment of individuals, one embarks upon questions of values. It appears that the move from *formal* justice to *material* justice *necessarily* introduces questions of value judgment. It therefore appears that logical empiricism leaves no way to describe how values function to secure 'reasonable decisions', and must thereby regard these decisions as having no 'rational' basis.[20]

And yet, people *do* reason about values and make efforts at providing justifications for their decisions. If one discards as irrational any effort made at reasoning based upon values, then the only other alternative to offering explanations, to engaging with others in a process of persuasion, is violence. In between the two extremes of logical positivism and violence lies the so-called 'irrational', and yet it is precisely between these two extremes that people everyday, everywhere encounter one another with arguments seeking to justify actions, to adhere to beliefs, to adopt certain behavior. The whole realm of human life, society, language and culture is sold off by logical positivists in a gigantic effort of willful ignorance.

The issue is not whether people *can* reason within the daily life of values and beliefs, since they already *do*, but *how* people do so, and *how* one makes a better choice based upon reasoning concerning values. It is in pursuit of an answer to these questions that Perelman and

20. For his rejection of absolutism in empiricism and philosophy, cf. 'Opinions and Truth', in Perelman, *The Idea of Justice*, pp. 125-33.

Olbrechts-Tyteca then embarked upon a massive survey of literature of areas in which value judgments are prevalent: ethics, law, philosophy, politics and aesthetics. What they came to discover was that people *justify* theses regarding values through the rational activity of *argumentation*, which stands distinct from, but complementary to, formal logic and *demonstration.*[21] And it is the realm of *argumentation*, the realm of the everyday effort at offering 'good' reasons for making certain decisions, that is the realm of rhetoric.

Thus, Perelman and Olbrechts-Tyteca distinguish between analytical reasoning (such as that found in Aristotle's *Prior Analytics*, and later in modern formal logic, mathematics and the empirical sciences) and rhetoric (collapsing in the latter term Aristotle's notion of both dialectics, as explored his *Topics*, and rhetoric).[22] This is an important contribution to the theory of rhetoric, for if one distinguishes instead between *dialectics* and *rhetoric*, as Ramus did, rhetoric devolves into concerns of eloquence and style, with dialectics seen as a separate operation of inventional and logical strategies. On the other hand, if one emphasizes too much the distinction between *analytics* and *dialectics*, as Kant and the mathematical logicians did, then there is no ready means available by which one can explore the non-demonstrative reasonings that take place in natural language, the traditional domain of dialectics and rhetoric.[23] Rhetoric, thus broadly conceived, thereby fills

21. Hence, Perelman and Olbrechts-Tyteca represent a movement that has come to be known as the 'good reasons' movement (represented also by Booth, Toulmin, Gottlieb and Wallace) which seeks to describe the role of value judgments in decision making. Cf. an excellent survey and assessment by Walter Fisher, 'Toward a Logic of Good Reasons', *Quarterly Journal of Speech* 64.4 (1978), pp. 376-84.

22. Aristotle defined dialectics and rhetoric in terms of audience: The former concerned itself with argumentation and reasoning between two individuals, while rhetoric dealt with the means by which one presents ideas to larger audiences who lacked specialized knowledge and the ability to follow long chains of reasoning. See Aristotle, *Rhet.* 1357a.

For a critique of the relationship between dialectic and rhetoric as represented in the theoretical writings of the 'good reasons movement', cf. Timothy Crusius, 'A Case for Kenneth Burke's Dialectic and Rhetoric', *Philosophy & Rhetoric* 19.1 (1986), pp. 23-37, and an insightful response by Paul Bator, 'The "Good Reasons Movement": A "Confounding" of Dialectic and Rhetoric?', *Philosophy & Rhetoric* 21.1 (1988), pp. 38-47.

23. Chaim Perelman, *The Realm of Rhetoric* (Notre Dame, IN: University of Notre Dame Press, 1982), pp. 2-4. Cf. also Perelman, 'Logic, Language and Communication', in *idem, The Idea of Justice*, pp. 143-53.

in the gap left when the domains of the empirical sciences, mathematics and formal logic restrict the concept of rationality to demonstrative proofs by means of axioms, appeals to self-evidence, reduplicatable experimentation, closed language systems, and determined rules of reasoning conclusions from premises.[24] Perelman and Olbrechts-Tyteca's theory of argumentation seeks to describe the various methods people, through natural language,[25] persuade and convince in an effort to gain the adherence of any audience to particular values.[26]

For Perelman and Olbrechts-Tyteca, argumentation presupposes a 'meeting of minds', the presence of a whole set of conditions without which argumentation cannot take place: the sharing of a common language, an occasion on which presentation may take place [in any medium: film, oral, dramatic presentation, etc.], the publication of the presentation [distribution of books, film; performance of work; distribution of printed or electronic material, the use of devices for amplification of visual and audible communication]. Often these conditions are prescribed by law or tradition: set occasions of state, of a culture, of academented institutions; religious and social gatherings; significant events in the life of individuals, or of a community or nation. Often these prescriptions work against the desire to affect an exchange: there are parliamentary rules to be followed; rallies are sometimes forced to disperse; social standing or the reputation of an individual or group may not be important or desirable enough to warrant interaction; class, race and gender roles may place certain restrictions regarding certain behavior and social interaction; commercial distribution channels may monopolize, hinder or exclude rivals. There may also be topics that are seen, on given occasions, as inappropriate. But by the very fact that an individual wishes to engage another in argumentation, it shows the desire for mutual respect and concern for the other: s/he is not disregarded, nor disrespected, as an object to ignore or upon which one inflicts harm through subjugation and force. For Perelman and Olbrechts-Tyteca, argumentation implies a context of egalitarianism and freedom. The meeting of minds seeks to gain 'convictions or dispositions through

24. Perelman and Olbrechts-Tyteca, *The New Rhetoric*, pp. 13-14.
25. Cf. 'Logic, Language and Communication', in Perelman, *The Idea of Justice*, pp. 143-53.
26. Perelman, *The Realm of Rhetoric*, p. 5. Cf. 'The New Rhetoric', in Perelman, *The Idea of Justice*, pp. 134-42.

discourse...instead of imposing [one's] will through constraint or conditioning'.[27]

This anti-fascist *Weltanschauung* (world-view) arises particularly from Perelman's immediate experiences of World War II and the Nazi occupation of Belgium. It explicitly and unavoidably establishes the persuasive intent of argumentation within an ontology of 'free will', and hence gives rhetoric an *ethical* foundation.[28] Rhetoric as a theory of argumentation, for Perelman and Olbrechts-Tyteca, has as its foundation the free exchange of values and ideas, and has as its focus the *rationality* and *reasonability* of discourse. Rhetoric thereby avoids reduction to concerns of effectiveness alone as determinative for rhetorical 'success'.[29]

Curiously, this philosophy of rhetoric *restricts* rhetoric's purview, eliminating as it does the persuasive elements of *non-discursive* social semiotic practices, such as the exchange of goods and currency, the use of the threat of force or violence, and the unstated social structures that govern discourse. Perelman and Olbrechts-Tyteca chose to develop a theory of argumentation and to discern therefrom the rationality and reasonability of *discursive* communication alone. [I shall set aside the very important assumption that discursive communication is not violent, but rather subsumes violence under rationality, which is itself the antithesis to violence.] One of the most important reasons for this

27. Perelman, *The Realm of Rhetoric*, p. 11.

28. This political background comes to light again in his distinction between education and propaganda: Education is the means whereby a free society conservatively reinforces the values shared within a society (we note later its connection with epideictic rhetoric) as presented by one who 'has been commissioned by a community to be the spokesman for the values it recognizes, and, as such, enjoys the prestige attaching to his office'. Propaganda, on the other hand, is involved with controversial values, and a propagandist must first seek out the respect and adherence of the audience to the values being discussed, and will do so through any available means. Cf. Perelman and Olbrechts-Tyteca, *The New Rhetoric*, pp. 51-54.

29. Contra the critique offered by F.H. van Eemeren, R. Grootendorst and T. Kruiger, *Handbook of Argumentation Theory: A Critical Survey of Classical Backgrounds and Modern Studies* (Dordrecht: Floris Publications, 1987), pp. 213, 258. See also Ralph T. Eubanks, 'An Axiological Analysis of Chaim Perelman's Theory of Practical Reasoning', in James L. Golden and Joseph J. Pilotta (eds.), *Practical Reasoning in Human Affairs: Studies in Honor of Chaim Perelman* (Dordrecht: D. Reidel Publishing Company, 1986), pp. 69-83; Walter Fisher, 'Judging the Quality of Audiences and Narrative Rationality', in Golden and Pilotta (eds.), *Practical Reasoning in Human Affairs*, pp. 85-104.

particular emphasis was Perelman's legal, academented and philosophical background, which will come to play an important role throughout
the treatise. As such, it is essentially a convenient and familiar limitation that overlooks the important ideological and inherently *propa-
gandistic* dimension of education, philosophy and jurisprudence in
maintaining structures of power. This is the first important corrective to
their theory which I would like to offer: rhetoric, as a rhetoric of *power*,
and extended to include any form of communication (social semiotics),
can be used to analyze the 'meeting of minds', *and the 'exclusion of
Other minds'*, which takes place through *non*-discursive means, exposing the underlying 'unspoken' constrictions, constraints and dynamics
affecting every 'communicative' act. Furthermore, rhetorical acts can
and do take place outside of these structures of validation, and are often
directed at exposing the violence and rejecting their [manifest and
latent] hegemony. A rhetoric of power must be formulated so as to
advocate and nurture precisely *this* impetus: to expose the means of
limitation and exclusion, to undermine discursive and non-discursive
hegemonies.

Thus, when Perelman and Olbrechts-Tyteca go on to define rhetoric
as discourse that seeks to incite action, or at least the disposition to
action,[30] they restrict their focus to the *discursive* means of both written
and oral communication. Nevertheless, within this self-imposed limitation they render some very important and expansive reformations of
traditional philosophies of rhetoric. Rejecting ancient and persistent
divisions of inventional strategies that conceive of rhetoric as directing
itself to various and distinct 'faculties' of the individual (will, mind,
emotion),[31] Perelman and Olbrechts-Tyteca insist on approaching
rhetoric as an appeal to the whole person.[32] Therefore, depending upon
the circumstances of location, time, situation and disposition of the
audience, the rhetor will choose from different styles, topics, values and
approaches in order to secure adherence, create a *liaison* and bring the
audience along to the point (hopefully) to which the rhetor wishes them
to commit. Perelman and Olbrechts-Tyteca emphasize the different
discursive, reasonable and argumentative means available to enable the

---

30. Perelman, *The Realm of Rhetoric*, p. 12.
31. Cf. Bacon's famous definition: 'The duty and office of rhetoric is to apply
reason to imagination for the better moving of the will', *Advancement of Learning*,
2.18.2. Thus is implied the presence of Aristotle's *logos, pathos* and *ethos*.
32. Perelman and Olbrechts-Tyteca, *The New Rhetoric*, pp. 45-47.

speaker to appeal to the whole person, to shift the *adherence* from premises to conclusion, and to convince the audience to act or contemplate action.

It must be noted, however, that while this is an important shift from the typical divisions and isolating classifications of traditional rhetorical concepts to a more *symbiotic* perspective of the discursive means of persuasion, there are nevertheless far more media available that can contribute to persuasive effectiveness through appeal to other sensory channels. Perelman and Olbrechts-Tyteca, while aware of the power of non-discursive media to influence audiences, simply do not explore their function. As technological extensions of the body, particularly channels of mass communication employ both audio and visual (as well as, perhaps, tactile) means to immerse an audience in a more *totalizing* experience. These means may not readily appeal to 'reason' as traditionally conceived, hence may not be readily available to analysis along the lines employed by Perelman and Olbrechts-Tyteca, but they cannot be excluded from rhetorical exploration: each extension and its use in communicative experiences/expressions has its own 'reasons' and 'rules', its own unique contribution to make in the maintenance of values and the function of power. This is where both a *symphonic* and a *symbiotic* approach to rhetoric can help us break out of the hegemony of the 'Word' when pondering the elements of persuasion, truly embracing the 'whole' of the person.

Any medium of communication 'must' also adapt itself to the settings as deemed appropriate to the occasion and intended audience, as determined by the communicator. Every medium carries within it an 'intention' and meaning-effect which contributes to the message in a way that makes it unique from a performance in any other medium. Indeed, as Marshall McLuhan has studied the social and cultural consequences of the shift from oral to cheirographic to print technologies, so too has Walter Ong studied the epistemic effects in these same shifts in media. What a rhetoric of power must do is not only be accessible to pondering these (social and epistemic) consequences of various communicative media, but also consider the particular (rhetorical-hermeneutic) effect of choosing one medium over another in a given rhetorical performance. For example, what are the consequences upon rhetorical criticism of the New Testament that these texts are mass-produced through the print medium? This is an important aspect for exploration which

Perelman and Olbrechts-Tyteca leave aside to concentrate on the discursive means of argumentation.

Perelman and Olbrechts-Tyteca *do*, however, appropriately note the impact upon inventional theory, occasioned by the inherent complexity of mass communication, in determining the role of 'audience' in argumentation. Argumentation, in both modern and ancient western rhetoric,[33] traditionally seeks to adapt itself to the needs and assumptions of the audience. In ancient times, the audience was typically conceived of as a body of people gathered for a specific occasion or event, of limited number and generally sharing similar values and beliefs.[34] Hence, rhetoric developed models of speech writing appropriate for these occasions: for the legal system (forensic), for the political system (deliberative), or for the socio-religious system (epideictic). In modern times, both occasions and audiences have been transformed beyond all prior conception due to advances in communicative technology and important social (religious, scientific, ethical) developments. But the conception of this complexity does not stop at the issue of dissemination and heterodoxy; for Perelman and Olbrechts-Tyteca it also embraces the whole dynamic of 'real' (empirical) and 'fictive' (constructed) audiences and their *active* roles in shaping argumentation. [The question, of course, that should continually be kept in mind is whether these audiences *ought* to be allowed such roles in the first place. Here is where an inventional strategy must be embraced not so much for its prescriptive usefulness for a rhetoric of power, but for its descriptive insight into the assumed/presumed/presumptuous 'mob rule' of audiences and the fascist proclivity to 'give them what they want'. (But also and also and again: not only into the assumption of the tyranny of audiences regarding their 'positive' composition, but with respect to those they exclude, ignore, silence.)]

33. For a contrasting view on the deliberate rejection of audience assumptions found in the rhetoric of the Ch'an Buddhist masters, cf. Dale S. Wright, 'The Discourse of Awakening: Rhetorical Practice in Classical Ch'an Buddhism', *Journal of the American Academy of Religion* 61.1 (1993), pp. 23-40.

34. See Edwin Black, 'The Mutability of Rhetoric', in Black, *Rhetorical Questions*, pp. 171-86. This is a rewrite of the same article by the same title found in: Eugene E. White (ed.), *Rhetoric in Transition: Studies in the Nature and Uses of Rhetoric* (University Park, PA: Pennsylvania State University Press, 1980), pp. 71-85.

Perelman and Olbrechts-Tyteca understand the relationship between rhetor and audience as one of *dialectical* interaction and impact. On the one hand, they point out that *the audience is a construction of the rhetor*, 'the ensemble of those whom the speaker wishes to influence by his [*sic*] argumentation'.[35] Given the impact of mass communication, the number and variety of audiences is nearly infinite, making this selection an important and necessary, though highly complex, ingredient in developing the argument. Often, the composite quality of audiences requires the speaker to construct an audience in such a way that it does not exclude or insult one or more groups that may compose the empirical audience (those who actually listen). Once argumentation is engaged, the view of the audience as brought about through the presentation of the argument may cause any number of reactions: if the argument is persuasive, some may accept the role(s) they are expected to play in the argumentation [this is the role of the 'spellbinding' quality of communication], others may reject some or all of them, still others may find themselves feeling 'lost' or incompetent [the 'stupid', the 'insane'] or bored. Certain members of the audience will suspend disbelief for the sake of 'hearing the argument through to the end', and will discuss and contemplate later whether they found it persuasive. The danger, however, is always lurking that the selection of the audience, its ensuing portrait developed through the argumentation, the roles it is expected to play during the discourse, will be so unacceptable that people will 'walk away', or even rebel and keep the rhetor from continuing.[36]

Once s/he has made this selection, the rhetor 'must' then construct her/his argumentative appeals with this audience in mind. In order for argumentation to take place at all, much less be effective, s/he 'must' adapt him/herself to the audience whom s/he has selected. In other words, *the rhetor becomes a construction of the audience*. If a rhetor

35. Perelman and Olbrechts-Tyteca, *The New Rhetoric*, pp. 19-23 (19).

36. Although often, it must be noted, this audience has already been selected beforehand for her/his social and cultural norms of interaction, legal restrictions, particular settings such as schools, convocations, rallies, formal gatherings, parliamentary and political debates, meetings of learned societies, etc. All these forces limit beforehand the scope (and nature) of the audience to be engaged in and through argumentation, although often one can use these forums for occasions in which to speak to an audience which is broader than, or other than, those constituting the empirical audience at the moment of presentation.

refuses to acknowledge the important starting points of contact between him/herself and the audience, to employ the implicit values and ideals, the means of reasoning and the world-view of the audience s/he has selected, s/he may not even be given the chance to be 'heard'. 'In argumentation, the important thing is not knowing what the speaker regards as true or important, but knowing the views of those he [*sic*] is addressing'.[37] Adaptation to the audience secures both the chance to be heard and provides the standards by which the argument is judged to be valid: 'Arguments that in substance and form are appropriate to certain circumstances may appear ridiculous in others'.[38]

Argumentation is also shaped according to the aims determined by the rhetor. For example, the rhetor who is concerned with obtaining immediate and tangible results will seek to *persuade* by employing argumentation which 'claims validity for a particular audience'.[39] This is the connection often seen between *persuasion* and *action*. Such argumentation works within the limited field of values, presumptions, 'truths' and 'facts' to which a limited audience adheres, without seeking justification or validation which members of other audiences would find persuasive. It attempts to address the immediate circumstances, situations and perspectives of a particular audience in an effort to get them to act, to effect a change, to make a decision.[40]

In contrast to *persuasive* argumentation, it is often the case that a speaker is concerned 'with the rational character of adherence to an argument' and thereby seeks to *convince* her/his audience through 'argumentation that presumes to gain the adherence of every rational being'.[41] This is the connection often made between *conviction* and *intelligence*. *Convincing* argumentation seeks to provide justification, 'valid' and 'good' reasons for the action(s) being advocated, for the conclusion(s) being offered, for the decision(s) being made. It seeks to

---

37. Perelman and Olbrechts-Tyteca, *The New Rhetoric*, pp. 23-24.
38. Perelman and Olbrechts-Tyteca, *The New Rhetoric*, p. 25.
39. Perelman and Olbrechts-Tyteca, *The New Rhetoric*, p. 28.
40. This is the pragmatic dimension of discourse to which situation theory addresses itself. Cf. Bitzer, 'The Rhetorical Situation', pp. 1-14; John Patton, 'Causation and Creativity in Rhetorical Situations: Distinctions and Implications', *Quarterly Journal of Speech* 65.1 (1979), pp. 36-55; and Brinton, 'Situation in the Theory of Rhetoric', pp. 234-48.
41. Perelman and Olbrechts-Tyteca, *The New Rhetoric*, pp. 27, 28.

overcome the conflicting interests and 'particularity' of limited audiences by appealing to 'universal' values and by reasoning through strategies with which 'everyone' would agree. As Perelman and Olbrechts-Tyteca explain, 'Every person believes in a set of facts, of truths, which he [*sic*] thinks must be accepted by every "normal" person, because they are valid for every rational being'.[42]

The embodiment of these values, the people for whom these arguments would be convincing, Perelman and Olbrechts-Tyteca term the 'universal' audience. The role of this 'universal' audience in argumentation is *normative*, and adherence of the 'universal' audience to the precepts and conclusions proposed is a matter of *right*, not of *fact*.[43] The difficulty lies in the fact that the particular qualities of 'universality' that are chosen [assumed!] depend not only on the individual perspectives of the rhetor, but on the social, cultural and historical 'context' in which both rhetor and argumentation are embedded [and which may be shared across space/time contexts].[44]

Every audience which is 'universal' to some may be 'particular' to others. Once the charge of 'particularity' arises, it undermines the authority (not just the validity) of the argument. There is only one form of defense against such a charge: to eliminate from the discussion the individual or group who is raising it. This is done either by recourse to 'disqualifying the recalcitrant' as insane or incompetent, or by appealing to an 'elite' audience 'endowed with exceptional and infallible means of insight'.[45] [The role of the 'expert' as arrogant assumption of power.]

Perelman and Olbrechts-Tyteca, when they focus their attention upon the role of the audience within and upon argumentation, are simply continuing a tradition prominent throughout rhetoric's history. Aristotle, in his *Rhetoric*, considers the character of audiences in an effort to explore the various passions and emotions which the orator might effectively excite. When considering the typical occasions for oratory in his day, he limits the roles of the audience to specific practices and contexts: in forensic oratory, the audience is asked to judge rightness or wrongness of a past act, and the guilt or innocence of an individual. In deliberative oratory, the audience becomes a judge of future action, and

42. Perelman and Olbrechts-Tyteca, *The New Rhetoric*, p. 28.
43. Perelman and Olbrechts-Tyteca, *The New Rhetoric*, p. 31.
44. Perelman and Olbrechts-Tyteca, *The New Rhetoric*, p. 33.
45. Perelman and Olbrechts-Tyteca, *The New Rhetoric*, p. 33.

is advised or dissuaded concerning things deemed most useful. In epideictic, an audience considers the speaker him/herself as s/he speaks on common values, as s/he praises or blames individuals or groups according to their adherence to these standards. In this final instance, the occasion was typically that of the games, wherein the audience was asked to judge the quality of oration. Epideictic thereby became known as a degenerate kind of eloquence, whose aim was simply to please the audience, to consider uncontroversial and unprovocative ideals, facts or values.[46] Indeed, it was considered more nearly related to literature than argumentation.

In contrast, one of the most significant contributions Perelman and Olbrechts-Tyteca make to argumentation theory is the reconceptualizing of epideictic as *central* to argumentation: 'Its role is to intensify adherence to values, adherence without which discourses that aim at provoking action cannot find the lever to move or to inspire their listeners.'[47] Epideictic, therefore, sets about to enable the 'meeting of minds', to provide the common ground speaker and audience share, in order to bring them to action. 'The epideictic discourse normally belongs to the edifying genre because it seeks to create a feeling or disposition to act at the appropriate moment, rather than to act immediately... The goal is always to strengthen a consensus around certain values which one wants to see prevail and which should orient action in

46. Cf., however, Lawrence W. Rosenfield, 'The Practical Celebration of Epideictic', in White, *Rhetoric in Transition*, pp. 131-55, where he argues against this traditional description of epideictic as 'degenerate', and instead suggests that Aristotle's typology was meant to distinguish a particular type of speech activity whose goal was to elicit the 'excellence-in-itself' of an object/person/ideal for the sake of praise. Epideictic was never self-display (which was known as panegyric or diatribe) nor non-controversial, ceremonial speech (which was known as *laudatio*).

47. Perelman, *The Realm of Rhetoric*, p. 19. This should not in any way lead one to consider epideictic as primarily interested in maintaining socially conservative values and structures. The aim of epideictic discourse is 'to increase the intensity of certain values, which might not be contested when considered on their own but may nevertheless not prevail against other values that might come into conflict with them' (p. 51). Thus, epideictic will serve equally well a conservative Catholic and/or Protestant's protestation regarding abortion, an ethnically and sexually oppressed group's demands for full equality under the law, businesswo/man's advocacy of free enterprise, the PLO's demands for recognition under international standards of human rights, etc.

the future.'[48] Hence, the connection between education and epideictic [the connection between socialization/hegemony and epideictic], and the overwhelming presence of epideictic in religious discourse [*the* ideology-legitimizing form]. Not all discourse is epideictic, since the intended goals of argumentation are multiple: adherence, deliberation, decision, contemplation and reasoning, justification.[49] But at the heart of convincing argumentation, of any speech wherein the presuppositions cannot be taken for granted or assumed, or in which particular values require *presence* in order to become accessible and effective (the vast majority of discourse, in fact), epideictic seeks to secure the ground upon which is founded the disposition to action.[50]

In order for argumentation to be effective, indeed in order for it to take place at all, a 'contact of minds' needs to be established between rhetor and audience. This can only[?] evolve if the rhetor 'choose[s] as his [*sic*] points of departure only the theses accepted by those he addresses'.[51] The aim of argumentation is not to demonstrate the truth of a proposition, but to gain the *adherence* of an audience to its conclusions. In this respect, it is vital that the rhetor first seeks out those premises to which the audience already commits itself, and to transfer that *adherence* through argumentation to the conclusion s/he wishes them to reach.[52] When this transfer does not take place, it is likelier that the

48. Perelman, *Realm of Rhetoric*, p. 20.

49. Perelman and Olbrechts-Tyteca, *The New Rhetoric*, pp. 45-47. Note, Donald C. Bryant, 'Rhetoric: Its Function and Scope', *Quarterly Journal of Speech* 39.1 (1953), pp. 405-406, while not building specifically upon Perelman and Olbrechts-Tyteca's definition, also recognizes and celebrates the breadth and complexity of discourse which could be understood as 'epideictic', a category he defines as 'catch-all'.

50. For an alternative definition of 'epideictic' informed by speech-act theory and developed into a more systematic and specific typology, a definition inspired by and empathetic with Perelman and Olbrechts-Tyteca, see Walter H. Beale, 'Rhetorical Performative Discourse: A New Theory of Epideictic', *Philosophy & Rhetoric* 11.4 (1978), pp. 221-45.

51. Perelman, *Realm of Rhetoric*, p. 21.

52. From a practical point of view this is an extremely important aspect of rhetorical invention, but it is also made increasingly difficult with the particularly modern awareness (fostered through mass communication and information systems) of the plurality of cultures and complexity of audiences. Donald P. Cushman and Philip K. Tompkins, in an essay entitled, 'A Theory of Rhetoric for Contemporary Society', *Philosophy & Rhetoric* 13.1 (1980), pp. 43-67, offer a prescriptive inventional strategy in an effort to address the problem of how one chooses *which*

audience will reconsider and dismiss one or more of the premises than to accept an odious conclusion. This is an example, in argumentation, of the fallacy *reductio ad absurdum*: in demonstration, a false conclusion leads one to reject a premise as false; in argumentation, an unacceptable conclusion leads one to reject a premise as unacceptable. *Reductio ad absurdum* is also the reason why people cannot 'talk across paradigms' [without first undermining the legitimacy of one paradigm to the point where the advantages of another become more present/ apparent].

Therefore, to be unconcerned with the audience's *adherence* to certain premises is to commit a grievous error in argumentation, the error of *petitio principii*, 'begging the question'.[53] This fallacy has traditionally been seen as a logical error in demonstration 'which consists in postulating what one seeks to prove'.[54] But in logic, every demonstration implies its own proof. Indeed, such a concept is fundamental logical law: it is the principle of identity [exclusion].[55] If approached from the perspective of argumentation, however, 'begging the question' is a miscalculation, because if a speaker is concerned with obtaining *adherence* to a particular conclusion, s/he can't afford to assume its acceptance by the audience. 'To adapt to an audience is, above all, to choose as premises [not conclusions] of argumentation theses the audience already hold.'[56]

Perelman and Olbrechts-Tyteca identify two major categories of agreements from which a rhetor may draw: (1) Agreements concerning the real, which are assumptions concerning 'facts', 'truths' and 'presumptions'; and (2) agreements concerning the preferable, which are assumptions concerning 'values', 'hierarchies' and the 'loci of the preferable'.

1. In a theory of argumentation, 'facts' and 'truths' cannot be considered without concern for the attitude of the audience regarding them. In some cases, 'facts' and 'truths' are granted an objective, verifiable

---

values as being those fundamental to and shared by an audience when it may be composed of members with extremely divergent cultural, social and ideological perspectives and values.

53. Perelman, *The Realm of Rhetoric*, pp. 21-22; Perelman and Olbrechts-Tyteca, *The New Rhetoric*, pp. 110-14.

54. Perelman and Olbrechts-Tyteca, *The New Rhetoric*, p. 112.

55. Perelman, *The Realm of Rhetoric*, p. 22.

56. Perelman, *The Realm of Rhetoric*, p. 23. Emphasis mine.

status, and thus are granted a stability and certainty that relieves the rhetor of the necessity of reinforcing the *adherence* of an audience to them. In other cases, however, something considered a 'fact' by the rhetor may be contested, in which case s/he cannot rely upon it as 'fact' without answering the charge(s). S/he may do this either by offering proof, thereby rejecting the charge(s) directly, or s/he may call into question the authority, status and reasonability of the individual in leveling them. Without the guarantee of an infallible and incontestable authority to which we may refer in an effort to establish their certainty, 'facts' and 'truths' are always open to question. [This is the call of postmodernity and critical rhetorics.] In order to question a 'fact' or 'truth', one often resorts to other 'facts' and 'truths' that have more authority and with which they are incompatible. However, some 'facts' and 'truths' may hold enough sway, enough general acceptance, that to disregard them or dispute them is to be put at risk of being labeled a 'fool'[57] [or worse, much, much worse].

'Presumptions' refer to the way individuals conceive of reality, what normally happens based on common experience and common sense. These include, for example,

> the presumption that the quality of an act reveals the quality of the person responsible for it; the presumption of natural trustfulness by which our first reaction is to accept what someone tells us as being true; the presumption of interest leading us to conclude that any statement brought to our knowledge is supposed to be of interest to us ... the existence, for each category of facts, and particularly for each category of behavior, of an aspect regarded as normal and capable of serving as a basis for reasoning.[58]

Presumptions are based on the idea that what happens is 'normal'. The problem is, the concept of normality is notoriously variable according to context, and often people argue concerning which presumptions are acceptable given 'the facts of the case'. A rhetor 'must' take care to appeal to those presumptions most fitting in the eyes of the audience, but when these are contested, the burden of proof rests upon the one who wishes to argue otherwise.

---

57. Perelman, *The Realm of Rhetoric*, pp. 23-24; Perelman and Olbrechts-Tyteca, *The New Rhetoric*, pp. 67-70.

58. Perelman and Olbrechts-Tyteca, *The New Rhetoric*, pp. 70-71.

2. In contrast with theses that refer to 'a known or presumed reality', there are those that 'express a preference (values or hierarchies) or which indicate what is preferable (the *loci* of the preferable)'. 'Values' play a role in every argumentation, and are used to 'induce the hearer to make certain choices above others and, most of all, to justify those choices so that they may be accepted and approved by others'.[59] 'Universal' values, such as Truth, Good, Beautiful, Just, help the rhetor to find common ground with the audience precisely through their *lack* of specific content. Once given content, this helps to identify the distinct concepts of individual groups and/or perspectives, but also just as readily the specificity leads to conflict with other alternative groups.[60] [It might be worth pondering the 'identity' of 'universal' values shared by supposedly 'disparate' groups such as the neo-Right and the liberal humanist Left which allows for the kind of centrist synthesis Zero (middle) to reign in American politics.]

'Hierarchies' refer to the argumentative means whereby one value is given greater authority than another. Indeed, most audiences can be characterized less by reference to the values they hold, than to the way in which they categorize them, the degree to which they adhere to certain principles that help them to make a decision when important values come into conflict with each other. [But both fascists and communists 'share' the belief in sacrifice of the individual to the cause, whether that sacrifice is 'willing'/'voluntary' or scapegoated (Dachau, gulag, San Quentin).]

Finally, when a rhetor seeks to gain adherence to certain values or hierarchies, s/he may also resort to the '*loci* of the preferable', the general argumentative means that are 'affirmations about what is presumed to be of higher value in any circumstances whatsoever...'[61] For example, the *locus* of quantity is used when one argues for 'the greatest good for the greatest many'.[62] The *locus* of quality argues for the superiority of the unique, the singular, the timely, the precarious.[63] The *locus* of

---

59. All quotes from Perelman and Olbrechts-Tyteca, *The New Rhetoric*, p. 75.

60. In this regard, also see Perelman's very difficult distinction between 'abstract' and 'concrete' values, *The New Rhetoric*, pp. 77-80 and *The Realm of Rhetoric*, pp. 27-28.

61. Perelman, *The Realm of Rhetoric*, p. 29; Perelman and Olbrechts-Tyteca, *The New Rhetoric*, pp. 83-85.

62. Perelman and Olbrechts-Tyteca, *The New Rhetoric*, pp. 85-89.

63. Perelman and Olbrechts-Tyteca, *The New Rhetoric*, pp. 89-93.

order emphasizes superiority of cause over effect.[64] The *locus* of the existent argues for the real over the possible.[65] The *locus* of essence argues for the superiority of somebody insofar as they embody the essence of a category.[66] These *loci*, for Perelman and Olbrechts-Tyteca, are not strategies of argumentation, but are the assumed structures of reality upon which certain argumentative strategies are based, are the *implicit* justifications of value hierarchies and presumptions.[67]

These agreements, both of the real and the preferable, 'must' be understood and secured in every individual and specific act of argumentation according to the circumstances and contexts of the presentation. They provide the basis whereby the rhetor secures and deepens *communion*[68] with her/his audience, and secure both the foundation upon which, and the appropriate avenues by which *adherence* may be transferred from and through them to the conclusions desired. They are the assumptions that need to be regarded as the rules within which argumentation proceeds. It is also with respect to them that the connection between research concerning the social dimension of discourse and communication (sociology of knowledge, social and cultural anthropology, social semiotics, feminism, ideological criticism, etc.[69]) and rhetoric can be established.

Furthermore, and more importantly, they provide the mass of available premises accepted by the audience from which the rhetor makes her/his choice. They help to govern the selection of relevant evidence, the interpretation of data, and the presentation of the 'facts' and issues whereby their significance and *presence* are made known to the audience. But it is up to the rhetor to make the choice among these premises: unlike demonstration, in which every step is carefully detailed and explicated, argumentation allows the speaker to leave implicit certain

---

64. Perelman and Olbrechts-Tyteca, *The New Rhetoric*, p. 93.
65. Perelman and Olbrechts-Tyteca, *The New Rhetoric*, p. 94.
66. Perelman and Olbrechts-Tyteca, *The New Rhetoric*, p. 94.
67. Perelman and Olbrechts-Tyteca, *The New Rhetoric*, p. 88.
68. Cf. Perelman and Olbrechts-Tyteca, *The New Rhetoric*, pp. 163-67, concerning the means by which, through various figures in discourse, communion is sought between speaker and audience.
69. Perelman, 'The Social Contexts of Argumentation', in Perelman, *The Idea of Justice*, pp. 154-60.

assumptions (cf. Aristotle's distinction between syllogism and enthymeme), and to dwell on others.[70] 'Choosing to single out certain things for presentation in a speech draws the attention of the audience to them and thereby gives them a *presence* that prevents them from being neglected.'[71] One can, for example, offer physical evidence of an act, or offer a recreation of events, or display visual or audible effects in an effort to lend importance to an event, situation or scenario. Traditionally, however, rhetoric has focused upon discursive means by which a rhetor might evoke 'realities that are distant in time and space', which traditionally have included figures of thought and speech.[72] In either

---

70. Perelman, *The Realm of Rhetoric*, p. 37. The 'subjective' dimension of choice lies, with respect to argumentation, in the acceptance or rejection of those premises and data held up by the rhetor for the consideration of the audience: 'Choice of elements, of a mode of description and presentation, judgments of value or importance—all these elements are considered all the more justifiably as exhibiting a partiality when one sees more clearly what other choice, what other presentation, what other value judgment could oppose them' [Perelman, *The Realm of Rhetoric*, p. 34]. Objectivity, best described as the acceptance of a value, datum, or presumption by the universal audience, is never secure, but must be constantly renewed: 'If disagreement with another, equally well-qualified person underscores the subjectivity of our opinion, or at least the fact that it is not accepted by everyone, the agreement of another is not sufficient to guarantee objectivity or even universality, because it may be only an opinion common to a milieu or a given epoch.' However much agreement there may be on an issue, that does not secure its status as ontologically necessary or obvious. Cf. Perelman, *The Realm of Rhetoric*, p. 35.

71. Perelman, *The Realm of Rhetoric*, p. 35. For a detailed exploration into the notion of *presence* and its implications for the theory of knowledge informing Perelman and Olbrechts-Tyteca's rhetorical theory, cf. Louise Karon, 'Presence in *The New Rhetoric*', *Philosophy & Rhetoric* 9.2 (1976), pp. 96-110.

72. Perelman, *The Realm of Rhetoric*, pp. 37-40, and Perelman and Olbrechts-Tyteca, *The New Rhetoric,* pp. 167-79, list a number of figures which they define not according to the form of discourse alone, but according to argumentative intent and effect. E.g. repetition, accumulation of detail, accentuation, amplification, aggregation, *synonymy* (use of different ways of saying the 'same' thing), *enallage* (substitution of gender, person, tense, etc., for another), *hypotyposis* (vivid description of an action or event), *prolepsis* (applying an attribute now that will happen in the future) can all serve the argumentative purpose of presence, communion. Certain figures attempt to secure the status or value of an object or idea: values can become 'facts' (transforming 'liar' into 'person having a tendency to mislead deliberately'), and facts can become 'values' (reduction of the conclusions of various authors on a given topic to mere 'opinions' or 'theories'). As Perelman

case, however, the emphasis is not upon generating a simple awareness, the 'presence' of an event or fact 'to the consciousness', but to generate a sense of *importance* in the audience concerning them.

This is not to suggest, however, that there is an ontological position of neutrality concerning 'facts' from which to judge 'distortions' concerning their 'presentation'. In natural language, there is no such neutrality [Richards's language-as-metaphor, but also more than and different than this], for 'ordinary and common language is a manifestation of the agreement of a community in the same way as are traditional ideas and commonplaces. Agreement on the manner of presenting certain facts—or at least the lack of reserve regarding them—can facilitate the audience's agreement on the substance of a problem.'[73] The argumentative dimension to the selection of qualifiers,[74] the reference to and use of notions,[75] the function of modals[76] in discourse all show that the concept of 'neutrality' is highly context-specific to the audience and circumstances of the presentation. Certain elements of interpretation may strike one as highly specious and value-laden, while others may pass by unnoticed.[77] In argumentation, identification of 'interpretation' (over against 'datum') is dependent upon the degree of agreement concerning the way in which something is described or signified: 'As long as the multiplicity of possible interpretations is not taken into account and the interpretation given has no rival, there is no inclination to dissociate the data from the construct. The distinction appears only where a controversy is raised by a divergence of interpretation.'[78]

goes on to argue: 'A figure is argumentative if its use, leading to a change in perspective, seems normal in relation to the new situation thus suggested. But if the discourse does not gain the audience's adherence, the figure will be perceived as an ornament, a figure of style, ineffective as a means of persuasion.' This is perhaps one of the most important contributions Perelman and Olbrechts-Tyteca have made to rhetorical theory: the transformation of rhetorical figures from stylistic concerns to argumentative strategies, and the exploration of the contexts in which such a transformation takes place in discourse.

73. Perelman, *The Realm of Rhetoric*, p. 40.

74. Perelman and Olbrechts-Tyteca, *The New Rhetoric*, pp. 126-29.

75. Perelman and Olbrechts-Tyteca, *The New Rhetoric*, pp. 130-41.

76. Perelman and Olbrechts-Tyteca, *The New Rhetoric*, pp. 154-63.

77. Perelman and Olbrechts-Tyteca, *The New Rhetoric*, pp. 149-54.

78. Perelman, *The Realm of Rhetoric*, p. 42.

This phenomenon is particularly acute in the interpretation of texts and other forms of communicative exchange that are not artificial language constructs seeking to eliminate ambiguity (e.g. mathematics). In natural languages, signification and interpretation must remain fluid, in that both their history and their continuing development perpetually adapt signifiers to changing contexts, thereby ensuring the possibility of multiple interpretations.[79] Although certain factors can be taken into account in an effort to reduce the number of possible interpretations (textual, intertextual and extratextual context of performance), or can be legislated as necessary conditions of interpretation (legal prescriptions), the normal use of a language introduces a number of means whereby signification and interpretation can multiply: choice of *epithets* (Orestes as 'murderer of his mother' or 'avenger of his father'), coordination or subordination of propositions by use of conjunctions (Jesus *and* Marx; everyone *except*…; in spite of…), positive and negative implication, selection of metaphors and symbols, etc. It is particularly to the *argumentative* function of the use of figures of signification in language that Perelman and Olbrechts-Tyteca wish to draw our attention: even common, and hence 'value-neutral/objective' labels or interpretations only remain so as long as they are accepted as such by the audience. As soon as another perspective becomes present, the inherent 'subjectivity' of 'objective' language is exposed for consideration. In which case, the choice of what is significant in the selection and presentation of data itself becomes argumentative.

Thus, for a 'meeting of the minds' to take place, for argumentative discourse to both take place and meet with success, the premises (concerning both what is real and what is preferable) 'must' be agreed upon explicitly or implicitly by both the rhetor and her/his audience. This agreement need not be met with by explicit reference to shared values, but can be left as unstated, implicit starting points of argumentation. It could also be achieved through explicit, but ironic reference to opposing or unacceptable premises. It could be made crediting the audience

---

79. Even the interpretation regarding what are *signs* (those things that attempt communication: a word, a token) and what are *indices* (those that simply indicate something: footprints, precipitate from a chemical reaction) remains unclear until we consider the audience receiving them: To some, the stars in the sky *indicate* the presence of distant suns (astronomy); to others, they *signify* important means by which people can determine their fate (astrology). Cf. Perelman and Olbrechts-Tyteca, *The New Rhetoric*, pp. 122-23.

directly with these values as arising from themselves, not on the part of the speaker nor through the discourse. There are various and multiple means by which the 'meeting of minds' might be achieved.

Nevertheless, in any and every case, and by whatever means, whether seeking to convince or persuade, the rhetor 'must' keep in mind the *adherence* of her/his audience to particular premises upon which to enter into discussion, in order to seek the appropriate argumentative means by which to translate that *adherence* to the conclusion s/he wishes to offer them. If there is disagreement about either the *status* of the premises (e.g. the rhetor 'begs the question' concerning certain values), the *choice* of the premises (e.g. the audience considers certain 'facts' or values alluded to as irrelevant), or the *presentation* of the premises (e.g. the audience agrees about the relevance of the 'facts' presented, but does not accept their signification, or interpretation), then the discourse 'must' review, reconsider and re-present these premises in a more acceptable fashion, else its success will be jeopardized.

Turning now to the techniques of argumentation, the greatest bulk of Perelman and Olbrechts-Tyteca's effort is found in exploring the means by which discourse seeks to create *liaisons* between concepts, or seeks to distinguish and separate connections already presumed. They develop a typology based upon observations of the ways in which people seek to convince or persuade one another. This typology comprises a survey of general argumentative schemata that can be used in argumentation, but whose selection and application is determined by intention of the rhetor, and whose interpretation and acceptance is determined by the audience to whom it is addressed. 'Since argumentation concerns theses to which different audiences adhere with variable intensity, the status of elements which enter into argumentation cannot be fixed as it would be in a formal system: this status depends on the real or presumed adherence of the audiences.'[80] Theses are accepted or rejected based upon the perceived strength of the reasons and arguments offered on their behalf. Arguments interact with one another in varying ways, often supporting each other and providing a 'strong' and 'persuasive' case, but just as often conflicting with each other, weakening in totality the strength each alone might have in convincing the audience. There are no guarantees: unlike demonstration, with its fixed rules and unambiguous symbol systems, argumentation depends upon a

---

80. Perelman, *Realm of Rhetoric*, p. 48.

loose corpus of premises from which to draw, premises to which various audiences might adhere with varying intensity.

The intention of this typology is to provide the necessary tools and vocabulary by which one may analyze the use and role of argumentative strategies.[81] Perelman and Olbrechts-Tyteca divide these strategies into two broad categories: 'Arguments are sometimes given in the form of a *liaison* which allows for the transference to the conclusion of the adherence accorded the premises, and at other times in the form of a *dissociation*, which aims at separating elements which language or a recognized tradition have previously tied together.'[82] Included under the former category, Perelman and Olbrechts-Tyteca group arguments according to whether they are *quasi-logical*,[83] *appeal to the structure of reality*[84] or *seek to establish the structure of reality*.[85] Under the latter category, Perelman and Olbrechts-Tyteca explore the use of philosophical pairs (appearance/reality) and their function as *dissociative argumentation*,[86] and which are distinct from antithetical pairs (good/ evil), and classificatory pairs (north/south). We will not explore these categories in any great detail, instead referring the reader to the much more developed presentation found in *The New Rhetoric*, as well as the concise summary found in *The Realm of Rhetoric*.

Finally, Perelman and Olbrechts-Tyteca turn to consider the issues of argumenative fullness, strength and interaction, amplitude, and order,[87]

81. It must be carefully noted that while Perelman and Olbrechts-Tyteca draw their examples from the discourse of numerous cultures (including Japanese) and various ages (from ancient to modern), this typology is not an attempt at complete classification. A thorough study of one's own culture or group, or of a particular era, could reveal techniques of argumentation not addressed in Perelman and Olbrechts-Tyteca's study. Furthermore, their emphasis upon the *reception* and *perception* on the part of the audience concerning argumentative schemata indicates an important perspective regarding the use of these classifications: they are intended as heuristic devices, not as rigid formulations, whose ultimate purpose is to explore the totality of strategies, presumptions and possible effects. They are tools to help us identify common techniques used to supply support for a position in order to expose the dynamic interaction of argumentative strategies.

82. Perelman, *The Realm of Rhetoric*, p. 49.

83. Perelman and Olbrechts-Tyteca, *The New Rhetoric*, pp. 193-60.

84. Perelman and Olbrechts-Tyteca, *The New Rhetoric*, pp. 261-49.

85. Perelman and Olbrechts-Tyteca, *The New Rhetoric*, pp. 350-10.

86. Perelman and Olbrechts-Tyteca, *The New Rhetoric*, pp. 411-59.

87. Perelman and Olbrechts-Tyteca, *The New Rhetoric*, pp. 460-508.

where their observations continue to focus upon the profound impact that audiences have upon argumentative dynamics and structure. Perhaps the most important insight that Perelman and Olbrechts-Tyteca bring to the rhetorical canon of arrangement is their notion of the *argumentative situation*, or 'the influence of earlier stages of the discussion on the argumentative possibilities open to the speaker'.[88] It is this situation that makes its impact upon argumentative composition and effect, a situation that is continuously fluid, fed by the audience's response throughout the developing presentation of proofs, examples; by the presence or absence of alternative positions, rebuttals, objections; by the varying levels of attraction to implicit and explicit premises; by the reaction of the audience as it comes to awareness of the discourse itself, its structure and order, and begins discussion concerning it; by the contextual factors of rules to be followed, attention span, broadcast and physical deterrents to optimal reception; by contextual factors of economics (manufacture and distribution of communicative materials), politics (laws governing acceptable speech and circumstances), rules of order (debates, time limitations, order and types of evidence, response, etc.). It is the *argumentative situation* [***not!!*** Bitzer's 'rhetorical situation'] that helps to determine the appropriate means of persuasion, the expectations regarding what is understood as effective. However, as the argumentative situation 'is capable of extension, depending on the fields taken into consideration... [and] shifts each moment as argumentation proceeds',[89] there is no one objective standard by which an argument's strength, number or order can be determined. But in every case, both the number of proofs offered in support of a thesis and the strength of both individual and cumulative argumentation are issues determined by constellation of circumstances surrounding the production and presentation of an idea that one wishes an audience to accept and embrace.

In summary, the theory of argumentation propounded by Perelman and Olbrechts-Tyteca is one that focuses upon the persuasive power of discourse from the perspective of the means by which people *reason* concerning values and judgments that have no self-evident means of securing certainty and adherence. Indeed, the purview of their theory extends to include virtually all forms of communication through natural language. Only the artificial communicative systems of mathematics,

88. Perelman and Olbrechts-Tyteca, *The New Rhetoric*, p. 491.
89. Perelman and Olbrechts-Tyteca, *The New Rhetoric*, p. 460.

logic and science are excluded, as demonstration does not require concern with securing adherence to premises (which are assumed) nor transferring *adherence* to the thesis (which is accepted if the methodology is orthodox, the reasoning logical and the measurement accurate). Yet, even here the role of the audience, the most important aspect of argumentation emphasized by Perelman and Olbrechts-Tyteca, breaks open scientific discourse to rhetorical analysis: every presentation of mathematical and scientific theory is based upon premises accepted by the audience, but if the conclusion appears to undermine the status quo, even if valid by all means of experimentation and measurement, it will often go unheeded, rejected or misunderstood until verified through independent examination.[90] Furthermore, it is often the case that individuals not recognized by the guild will not be granted a hearing, nor will any valid observations on their part be taken seriously if not presented in the form expected and demanded.

It appears, then, that *all* argumentation is fully dependent on its success upon the values, expectations, regulations, reactions and opportunities regulated by the demands of the audience. The implications inherent in a theory of argumentation based upon these observations are profound, and offered boldly by Perelman and Olbrechts-Tyteca:

Rejection of Irreconcilable Opposites
The complexity of values and judgments, the contextuality of perception, motive and perspective demand the recognition of the potential for the exchange of ideas. Rhetoric is the discursive means by which such oppositions can be bridged, by appeals to common and shared values that allow for the meeting of minds.

> We combat uncompromising and irreducible philosophical oppositions presented by all kinds of absolutism: dualisms of reason and imagination, of knowledge and opinion, of irrefutable self-evidence and deceptive will, of a 'universally' accepted objectivity and an incommunicable subjectivity, of a reality binding on everybody and values that are purely individual.[91]

90. Cf., of course, Thomas Kuhn, *The Structure of Scientific Revolutions* (Chicago: University of Chicago Press, 2nd edn, 1970). Cf. also Herbert W. Simons, 'Are Scientists Rhetors in Disguise? An Analysis of Discursive Processes Within Scientific Communities', in White, *Rhetoric in Transition*, pp. 115-30.

91. Perelman and Olbrechts-Tyteca, *The New Rhetoric*, p. 510.

Rejection of Irrefutable Certitude

Rhetoric recognizes the changeable character of values and judgments through time and among cultures and contexts. No conclusions can be reached without appeal to these values, if at the very least as premises to which a group of people adhere.

> We do not believe in definitive, unalterable revelations, whatever their nature or their origin. And we exclude from our philosophic arsenal all immediate, absolute data, be they termed sensations, rational self-evidence, or mystical intuitions. This rejection does not, of course, imply that we deny the effect of experience or reasoning on our opinions, but we will stay clear of that exorbitant pretension which would enthrone certain elements of knowledge as definitively clear and solid data, and would hold these elements to be identical in all normally constituted minds, independently of social and historical contingencies, the foundation of necessary and eternal truths.[92]

Rejection of Empiricism as the Standard, Exclusive Means of Judgment

> Those who hold facts and truths to be the sole norms for guiding opinions will endeavor to attach their convictions to some form of evidence that is indubitable and beyond discussion…With these self-evident things as starting point, proof will take the form of a calculation or of resort to experiment. The increased confidence thus brought about in the procedures and results of the mathematical and natural sciences went hand in hand with the casting aside of all the other means of proof, which were considered devoid of scientific value…But if essential problems involving questions of a moral, social, political, philosophical, or religious order by their very nature elude the methods of the mathematical and natural sciences, it does not seem reasonable to scorn and reject all the techniques of reasoning characteristic of deliberation and discussion—in a word, of argumentation…The assertion that whatever is not objectively and indisputably valid belongs to the realm of the arbitrary and subjective creates an unbridgeable gulf between theoretical knowledge, which alone is rational, and action, for which motivations would be wholly irrational.[93]

It also ignores the inherent motivational aspect of theoretical knowledge.

---

92. Perelman and Olbrechts-Tyteca, *The New Rhetoric*, p. 510.
93. Perelman and Olbrechts-Tyteca, *The New Rhetoric*, pp. 511-12.

Rejection of Distinction between Value Judgments and Judgments of Reality

This distinction is itself based upon implicit agreements concerning ontology and epistemology. The criteria upon which someone determines value judgments from empirical observation must not only be agreed upon, but also be free from ambiguity. 'There would have to be an agreement about the linguistic elements without which no judgment can be formulated.' But this is untenable, as it would require a theory of language which sees it 'either as a reflection of reality or as an arbitrary creation of an individual', which would 'forget an essential element, the social aspect of language, which is an instrument of communication and influence on others. All language is the language of a community... The terms used, their meaning, their definition, can only be understood in the context of the habits, ways of thought, methods, external circumstances, and traditions known to the users of those terms.' Any agreement concerning reality and a vision of the world, 'even though it may not be disputed, is not indisputable; it is linked to a social and historical situation which fundamentally conditions any distinction that one might wish to draw between judgments of reality and value judgments'.[94]

Perelman and Olbrechts-Tyteca have broken open the discussion of how people reason with one another over concerns about which there is no certainty. Indeed, they begin with the assumption that 'men [*sic*] and groups of men [*sic*] adhere to opinions of all sorts with a variable intensity, which we can only know by putting it to the test. These beliefs are not always self-evident, and they rarely deal with clear and distinct ideas.'[95] A theory of argumentation attempts to provide a means whereby we can describe the 'possibility of a human community in the sphere of action' which is not and cannot be based upon reality or objective truth. Perelman and Olbrechts-Tyteca are fighting a battle against the hegemony of an ideology of scientific reasoning in which objectivity becomes the only standard of rationality.

One important result of Perelman's and Olbrechts-Tyteca's efforts [in particular for *our* understanding] is that we come to recognize the presence of power in all forms of discourse, 'power' understood as the assumptions governing and controlling the opportunity for and structure

---

94. All quotes from Perelman and Olbrechts-Tyteca, *The New Rhetoric*, p. 513.

95. Perelman and Olbrechts-Tyteca, *The New Rhetoric*, p. 511.

of the exchange of ideas and values, reinforced by rules, pre-under-standing, social, political and historical contexts, tradition, individual and group experience. Once someone seeks to engage another in a dis-cussion in an effort to influence their thoughts, behavior and/or future action, they are engaged in rhetoric. In order to be effective, in order to secure *adherence* to the convictions espoused, appeal 'must' be made to the shared implicit premises governing the meeting of minds. Power is at play in every exchange, in every attempt at persuasion: even 'objective' and 'neutral' sciences presuppose a *Weltanschauung* and methodology within which it is necessary to work in order to present results.

The *argumentative* dimension of persuasion allows for us to see the means by which people appeal to values, judgments, experiences, per-spectives (i.e. to structures of ideology and power) in their efforts to connect with and have influence over others. The regeneration of rhetoric into a study of argumentation is both a rejection of the traditional concentration upon style and figures, as well as a recognition of the motivational aspect of all discourse. Theories regarding argu-mentation can themselves become the object of study and interpretation [which themselves can become further objects of study]. The contex-tuality not only of the argumentative situation of the discourse, but of the discussion of the discourse, forces recognition of the presence of power at every stage, and of the implicitly and explicitly accepted values upon which all motivated communication is based.

Rhetoric becomes a tool by which we can describe how people attempt to persuade, interpret, justify, defend, laud and condemn. It *prescribes* no single set of normative rules [though it may offer advice], but instead offers an example of how one can *describe* the normative rules governing discourse contexts.

With respect to rhetorical criticism of biblical texts, this would indi-cate not only the chance to consider the persuasive strategies of the biblical texts themselves, but the continuing interpretation and appli-cation of them to the changing contexts of community and history. Perelman and Olbrechts-Tyteca offer the chance to consider the con-texts of power that brought the various canons into existence, that secured the varying acceptable means of interpretation, the argumen-tative dynamics and motivations at stake in religious discourse and its analysis. The awareness of the impact of audiences upon the argumen-tative situation breaks open the question of authority of *both* biblical texts *and* exegesis/theology by giving us the means whereby we may analyze the implicit and explicit values appealed to, the (ideological) structures of power within which all such discussion takes place. By emphasizing not only *production* and *reception* of argumentative discourse found in the biblical texts (from smallest rhetorical unit up to canons and canons-within-canons), but also the premises and agreements met with in the *analysis* of these texts and their reception, Perelman and Olbrechts-Tyteca open the door to the contexts of persuasion and power at all levels: Bible, preaching, hermeneutics, exegesis, theology. Here is where the *living* [but, for many, the *dying*] quality of 'the word' in all its ideological dimensions could be encountered.

Wilhelm Wuellner

Wilhelm Wuellner's interest in rhetorical method and theory is informed by a wide experience of exploration into such fields as history of hermeneutics, non-western rhetorics, classical rhetoric, postmodern literary theory and hermeneutics, structuralism, materiality of discourse, semiotics, reader-response, narrative poetics, speech-act theory, feminism, and ideological criticism, to name just a few. Over 20 published articles, 70 lectures and 40 books (authored, co-authored, edited and co-edited) concern themselves with the *continuing* relevancy of biblical exegesis, hermeneutics and interpretation for the modern reader and/or believer. This is his central concern: how can we rescue the Bible from the hegemony of academented specialists and their exclusivist tendencies which arrest the power of the text at a frozen moment in time, accessible only through the methods of an elite, but ever more irrelevant group of scholars?

With respect to rhetoric in particular, Wuellner is seeking to develop a theory of argumentation that can describe the 'context' and performance of power *within* the biblical text and beyond it, a 'context' that includes academented *and* theological interpretations, canons and methods. It is Wuellner's purpose and goal to correct the degeneration and limitation of rhetorical theory and criticism to the extremes of literary/ communication theory on the one hand and social description on the other. It is his endeavor to generate and develop a rhetorical theory and practice that is distinctly *rhetorical*, that is, which can create, analyze and evaluate the power of persuasion in the performance of, reaction to, and critique of [particularly biblical and critical] discourse in any and all its forms.

His own exploration into rhetoric develops within the framework of the theory of argumentation as proposed by Perelman and Olbrechts-Tyteca. At first, his rhetorical analyzes of the biblical text were heavily influenced by the interests of scholars who focused upon historical re-search into so-called 'classical' rhetorical theory and practice.[96] Soon, however, the limitations of this latter approach caused him slowly to turn to a model of analysis that uses as its foundation the New Rhetoric, into which certain aspects of classical rhetorical theory were selectively integrated.[97] It is the New Rhetoric's focus upon argumentation and the connection made between persuasion and action that brings to the fore the dynamics of power at work both in 'texts' and their 'contexts'. These insights provided Wuellner with a foundation upon which he began to build a model of rhetorical analysis that considers the *materiality* of both 'text' and 'context' informed by theories of intentionality ('author') [better: Burkean 'motivation' on the part of both 'author/rhetor' *and* 'reader'] and action ('reader') [better: 'action' of both 'author/rhetor' *and* 'reader/audience', as well as 'analyst/consumer'] which can describe 'historical' (i.e. 'material', 'continual', 'ideological') features of argumentation,[98] how 'text', 'author', 'context' and

---

96. Wilhelm Wuellner, 'Paul's Rhetoric of Argumentation in Romans: An Alternative to the Donfried-Karris Debate over Romans', *Catholic Biblical Quarterly* 38 (1976), pp. 330-51. Written in response to K.P. Donfried, 'False Presuppositions in the Study of Romans', *Catholic Biblical Quarterly* 36 (1974), pp. 332-55, with a response by R.J. Karris in the same volume, pp. 356-58. In Wuellner's article, he argues for recognition of the importance of the insights offered by the New Rhetoric of Perelman and Olbrechts-Tyteca, but his own rhetorical analysis depends heavily upon H. Lausberg, *Handbuch der literarischen Rhetorik* (2 vols.; repr.; Stuttgart: Franz Steiner, 1990), as does Hans Dieter Betz's model first presented in 'The Literary Composition and Function of Paul's Letter to the Galatians', *New Testament Studies* 21 (1975), pp. 353-79.

97. Wilhelm Wuellner, 'Greek Rhetoric and Pauline Argumentation', in William R. Schoedel and Robert L. Wilken (eds.), *Early Christian Literature and the Classical Intellectual Tradition: In honorem Robert M. Grant* (Théologie Historique, 53; Paris: Beauchesne, 1979), pp. 177-88. See also Wilhelm Wuellner, 'Paul as Pastor: The Function of Rhetorical Questions in First Corinthians', in A. Vanhoye (ed.), *L'Apôtre Paul: Personnalité, style et conception du ministère* (Leuven: Leuven University Press, 1986), pp. 49-77.

98. Wilhelm Wuellner, 'Where Is Rhetorical Criticism Taking Us?', *Catholic Biblical Quarterly* 49.3 (1987), pp. 448-63.

'reader' each exhibit intentionalities ('motives') that impact upon, and complement each other in the activity of 'reading'. Wuellner's model avoids the unfortunate tendency of most rhetorical-critical scholarship to focus upon one of two extremes: an emphasis upon the 'text' or 'author' (figures, structure, style; psychology, intention) at the expense of 'context' (a focus that cannot explain 'power', 'persuasion'); or an emphasis upon the 'context' or 'audience' (socio-historical reconstruction; historical impact, reception) at the expense of 'text' (a focus that makes rhetoric a mere 'tool' for historical-critical scholarship). The result of Wuellner's effort is a theory of rhetoric that can describe the power inherent not only in the Bible (from verse to canon), but in the uses to which the Bible is/was put and the effect it continues to have upon faith, (institutions of) religion, and (academented, homiletic, contemplative) interpretation.

Wuellner identifies important aspects of the recent developments in philosophy of rhetoric that characterize current research, relating these to critical approaches to the biblical text: first is rhetoric's (Perelmanian) emphasis on the rationality of argumentation. This impacts all critical analysis by focusing upon textual strategies in terms of argumentative effect and intention, over against traditional efforts at designating narrative, topical and/or stylistic features.[99] Stylistic techniques in particular are no longer considered formal and decorative features, but are understood as part of the argumentation's structure, disposition and coherence. They are the 'modalities of literary expression'[100] now seen as functioning to secure *adherence*, to persuade and convince.

Such is an important development within rhetorical theory in particular, as it represents an attempt to define 'rhetoric' away from the 'typical' and all-too-traditional analysis found in the history of rhetoric which consists of 'listing and labeling the rhetorical figures of speech and figures of thought'. We need to be careful of the fact that many prevailing theories of rhetoric are victims of a tendency, 'so tenaciously enduring into our own days', of a 'rhetoric restrained', 'i.e., victims of the fateful reduction of rhetorics to stylistics, and of stylistics in turn to

99. Wilhelm Wuellner, 'Rhetorical Criticism and its Theory in Culture-Critical Perspective: The Narrative Rhetoric of John II', in P.J. Hartin and J.H. Petzer (eds.), *Text and Interpretation: New Approaches in the Criticism of the New Testament* (Leiden: E.J. Brill, 1991), pp. 167-81 (3, 4).

100, Wuellner, 'Rhetorical Criticism and its Theory', p. 4.

the rhetorical tropes or figures'.[101] It is by means of (re-)turning to classical rhetoric's focus upon *invention* and incorporating the New Rhetoric's focus upon *argumentation* that rhetorical criticism *could* be pulled away from this predominant emphasis upon disposition and style. Then criticism would be governed not only by a concern with the *effect* of discourse on an audience, but will also see both discourse and analysis as practice and 'activity inseparable from the wider social relations between writers and readers'.[102] Here we can also note the future and not-quite-fully-discerned impact of modern linguistics, social semiotics and deconstruction (postmodernism) upon rhetorical theory [an impact that *must* be more fully explored and, perhaps, championed].[103]

For biblical critics, modern rhetorical criticism can therefore highlight the *argumentative*, not just stylistic and artistic dimensions inherent within the biblical text.[104] Biblical narrative is now understood to be *rhetorical* narrative, not only with respect to *intent*, but also in terms of *communion, commitment* and *action*. We have come to realize that 'religion is by nature persuasive; the study of the rhetoric of religion is a study in persuasiveness and motives. Not only are God's actions in history said to have a rhetorical purpose, but even biblical poetry is experienced/read as "poetry with a purpose".'[105] It will be the purpose of a rhetoric of power to explore this purpose and to critique the nature and intent of biblical communion, commitment and action.

Second, Wuellner sees 'one of the main features of modern rhetoric [to be] its focus on practical intentions, or practical force with motivating action, as constitutive of rhetorical discourse. This is the concern for the text's "rhetorical situation" or its intentionality or exigency.'[106]

---

101. Wuellner, 'Where Is Rhetorical Criticism Taking Us?', pp. 450-51.

102. Terry Eagleton, *Literary Theory: An Introduction* (Minneapolis: University of Minnesota Press, 1983), p. 206.

103. Wuellner, 'Where Is Rhetorical Criticism Taking Us?', p. 454. Cf. 'Rhetorical Criticism', in Elizabeth Castelli, Stephen Moore, Gary Phillips and Regina Schwartz (eds.), *The Postmodern Bible* (New Haven: Yale University Press, 1995), pp. 149-86.

104. George Kennedy, *New Testament Interpretation through Rhetorical Criticism* (Chapel Hill: University of North Carolina Press, 1984), p. 159.

105. Wilhelm Wuellner, 'Rhetorical Criticism [2]' (Manuscript Draft 1992), p. 2; the quotation, 'poetry with a purpose' is from Harold Fisch, *Poetry with a Purpose: Biblical Poetics and Interpretation* (Bloomington: Indiana University Press, 1988).

106. Wuellner, 'Rhetorical Criticism and its Theory', p. 3.

Here we note the *pragmatic* concern with rhetoric's emphasis upon the connection between persuasion and power, between conviction and action. It is also this pragmatic concern that must continually ground rhetorical theory, lest theorizing discourse (including methodology and critical analysis) become autonomous and lose its relevancy for the practical application of rhetorical prescriptive tradition.[107] As Berlin so forcefully noted,

> At the most obvious level, those of us who are concerned especially with the relations of rhetoric and text production in schools and colleges are simply ignored by those who regard rhetoric as a theoretical pursuit that must remain free of the taint of practice. As I have already indicated, the fact that most of the great rhetorics of the West were written by teachers who were as concerned with practice as with theory goes unnoticed. Rhetoric thus tends to reinscribe the binary oppositions of literary studies, valorizing theory over practice, contemplation over action, the sacred theoretical over the practical profane, the priestly class of theorists over the menial class of teachers, truth over utility, and consumption over production.[108]

Rhetoric, as both theory and praxis, must remain contextual, and its *museful* quality must continually return to the notion that persuasive activity is *symbiotic*, grounded in the circumstances of performance: rhetoric is founded upon a life of *action*.[109]

Here in particular can be noted the contribution of feminist rhetorical theories and their emphasis upon the contextuality of theorizing. Recent works by feminist rhetoricians are noting the ideological similarities between philosophy's rejection of rhetoric and the social marginalization of womyn: rejecting the 'metaphysical tradition of Western

---

107. This is an important point made throughout the collection of essays edited by Brian Vickers, *Rhetoric Revalued: Papers from the International Society for the History of Rhetoric* (Medieval and Renaissance Texts and Studies, 19; Brighampton, NY: Center for Medieval and Early Renaissance Studies, 1982). Cf., e.g., Vickers, 'Introduction', pp. 13-35; Michael Leff, 'The Material of the Art in the Latin Handbooks of the Fourth Century A.D', pp. 71-76; etc.

108. James Berlin, 'Postmodernism, Politics and Histories of Rhetoric', *Pre/Text* 11.3-4 (1990), pp. 170-87 (185).

109. Cf. Brian Vickers, 'Territorial Disputes: Philosophy *versus* Rhetoric', in Vickers (ed.), *Rhetoric Revalued*, pp. 247-66 (259-60) on the roots and expressions of pragmatics in the rhetoric used in defense of rhetoric against philosophy.

philosophy' and the 'hierarchical epistemological structures it engenders',[110] these scholars are calling for a return to the 'materialist anthropology' of the early Sophistic tradition and its emphasis upon the 'provisional codes (habits or customs) of social and political behavior, socially constructed and historically (even geographically) specific'.[111] The recognition of the relation shown to exist between rhetoric of feminist theoretical discourse and Sophistic rhetorics results not only in an expansion of the canon of rhetorical literature and the advent of what is now termed a Third Sophistic in rhetorical theory, but in a reappraisal of rhetorical history which would also require us 'to study ideology, or the interconnecting system of values and beliefs that informs attitudes and behaviors'.[112] However, the pragmatics of such studies is shown in the demand that it not be pursued for the sake of benefiting theory-in-and-of-itself, but in order 'to improve the effectiveness of communication—to generate ideas about how we and others may communicate more effectively'.[113] This practical approach to 'communication' breaks open the field of analysis, forces the analyst and theorist to address not only fellow rhetoricians, but 'everybody' in an effort to describe the persuasive effects and uses of symbols [this is the shift from speaking *for* to speaking *to*], to become aware of the underlying values and presumptions at work when we attempt to communicate effectively, and to see critical and analytical discourse itself as perpetuating and participating in the systems, structures and 'contexts' of power in which we do our work.

For biblical critics, this perspective shifts the understanding of the biblical text away from eternal dogmatic-theological proclamation, away from static 'word' of eternal 'truth'. Instead, a rhetorical approach emphasizes the Bible's generation, compilation and interpretive tradition as having arisen (and continually arising) in response to *practical* circumstances and situations. These are yielded up in particular when viewing the 'social, cultural, ideological values imbedded in the arguments' premises, *topoi* and hierarchies (e.g. old and wise as superior to

110. Susan C. Jarratt, 'The First Sophists and Feminism: Discourses of the "Other"', *Hypatia* 5.1 (1990), pp. 27-41. Cf. also Susan C. Jarratt, *Rereading the Sophists: Classical Rhetoric Refigured* (Carbondale, IL: Southern Illinois University Press, 1991).

111. Jarratt, 'The First Sophists and Feminism', p. 35.

112. Welch, *The Contemporary Reception of Classical Rhetoric*, pp. 158-59.

113. Foss, *Rhetorical Criticism*, p. 7.

young and foolish; civilized versus primitive; culture versus nature; maleness as strong and rational versus femaleness as weak and emotional, etc.)'.[114] The analysis of these premises, *topoi* and hierarchies are not limited to those *in* the Bible, but also those assumed when arguing *about* and *with* (both 'against' and 'by means of') the Bible. All religious discourse takes part in shifting contexts of power, in the debate that gives shape to the 'first rough draft of living',[115] and participates in the *for*-or-*against* that is part of persuasion. A rhetoric of power must bring out *this* perspective and its continuing persistence throughout history of interpretation [and its relationship to politics] in an effort to undermine the fascistic revisionism of monolithic 'one truth' proclaimed by fundamentalisms [of *all* types, particularly, but not limited to, Christianity].

It is therefore not surprising to see Wuellner suggesting that the modern rhetorical-critical engagement of a text's meaning and impact, that is, the theoretical encounter of a text as praxis, 'is perceived as taking place within a *plurality* of interpretive communities: religious, academic, political, ethnic, gender and communities in struggle for justice and freedom'.[116] The authority of a text and its objectivist interpretation are now understood as limited to specific contexts of power and rhetorical stratagems: as Eagleton has so directly put it, 'The claim that knowledge should be "value-free" is itself a value judgment'.[117]

But the issue here is not only the rhetorical *exposure* of ideologies as though they were simply methodological assumptions regarding some analytical approach to life, assumptions whose exposure, like upturning a rock and watching the bugs scatter, somehow dissipates their persuasivity. Nor should the issue be limited to ideological confession on the part of analyst-as-rhetor (or rhetor-as-social-critic), who is then somehow absolved of the responsibility of the limitations of her/his arguments [cf. 12-step program(matic)s]. What must be kept in mind is the *pragmatic* relationship that rhetoric has asserted as existing between commitment and action, between speech and power. The issue is the

---

114. Wuellner, 'Rhetorical Criticism and its Theory', p. 4.

115. Edmund Burke, 'Art—and the First Rough Draft of Living', *Modern Age* 8 (1964).

116. Wuellner, 'Rhetorical Criticism [2]', p. 4. Emphasis mine.

117. Eagleton, *Literary Theory*, p. 14.

connection between ideas and the relationship they have 'to the main-tenance and reproduction of social power'[118] which finds its incarnation in various structures, including academented/disciplinary institutions that 'appear in the cultural conversation as strategic arguments and rhetorical figures [read: inventional strategies]'.[119] As Steven Mailloux has argued, rhetoric's emphasis on the plurality and limitation of critical engagement embraces

> ...a skepticism toward foundational accounts of interpretation in general and an attraction to narratives surrounding specific rhetorical acts and their particular sociopolitical contexts. Such attempts place theory, criticism, and literature [including biblical] itself within a cultural conversation, the dramatic, unending conversation of history which is the 'primal scene of rhetoric'.[120]

Critics who are engaged in ideological criticism employ rhetoric as a means of critiquing a text's (and its interpretation's) power, if it is used 'in the service of sexism, racism, social injustice, or pedagogical/physical abuse in society's betrayal of the child or the like'.[121]

But it is not just power located in the 'text' or its interpretation that perpetrates these structural abuses: here, again, we can find important contributions being made by feminist rhetorical theorists who are beginning to make us aware of the physical and mental toll exacted upon womyn through social structures legitimizing and legitimized by gender role idea(l)s. In particular, they focus upon the function of gender concepts to *preclude/exclude* voices (and their reception/availability to audiences) from social (political, ecclesial, academented) discourse altogether. Recent works of feminist rhetoricians are approaching the question of how people who are forbidden from speaking (as opposed to overlooked and ignored) attempt to engage a hostile audience in order to persuade it to act in the interest of those other than themselves (indeed, those whom they would rather *not* help).[122] This not only once again breaks open the rhetorical canon, but also may impact upon the very notion of persuasive techniques (argumentation, approach, stylis-

118. Eagleton, *Literary Theory*, p. 15.

119. Steven Mailloux, *Rhetorical Power* (Ithaca, NY: Cornell University Press, 1989), p. 60.

120. Mailloux, *Rhetorical Power*, p. 18.

121. Wuellner, 'Rhetorical Criticism [2]', p. 4.

122. Cf. the work of Karlyn Kohrs Campbell, *Man Cannot Speak for Her* (2 vols.; New York: Greenwood Press, 1989), esp. vol. 1.

tics, etc.) which since Quintilian's *vir bonum* (good man) has been almost exclusively determined by reference to *public* forums that deter (even violently) womyn's presence. Feminist rhetorical theorists are showing us the importance of other (ignored, degraded) discourse forms as areas for evaluation of persuasivity, as certain features of the rhetoric of marginalized groups can become identified through descriptive analysis. But description is not enough: it is the 'context' in which such discourse takes place, the 'context' of repression and silencing that becomes the *telic* interest of rhetorical-critical analysis, for this 'context' limits not only acceptable discourse forms (those that perpetuate the systems of power), but also the responses (critique, evaluation, *action*) to such discourse.[123] It is the purpose of feminist rhetorics not only to develop a history of womyn's rhetoric, nor only to generate a 'gendered' rhetorics,[124] but to develop an awareness of the repressive and violent aspects of any 'cultural performance' of *all* socially contrived behaviors and systems of power (sex, gender, race, age, etc.).

One important area for critical interpretation of power is that concerned with biblical authority: while the biblical text may be the 'archetypal example of how power [is] constituted by discourse',[125] the rhetorical critic, as cultural critic, 'will use this method to call into question prevailing cultural norms informed by conventional uses of

123. As Gabriele Schwab, 'Seduced by Witches: Nathaniel Hawthorne's *The Scarlet Letter* in the Context of New England Witchcraft Fictions', in Dianne Hunter (ed.), *Seduction and Theory: Readings of Gender, Representation and Rhetoric* (Urbana: University of Illinois Press, 1989), pp. 170-91 (173), pointed out, these 'contexts' can replace discourse with maiming and torture as *telic* 'readings' of victims' bodies: 'The body became the medium of an interaction, enacting a spectacle of seduction where the gestures devalued the spoken word, that is, the affirmations of innocence. The culturally institutionalized body-language became a visual (dis)play which split off from and devalued spoken language.'

124. Cf. Susan C. Jarratt, 'Speaking to the Past: Feminist Historiography in Rhetoric', *Pre/Text* 11.3-4 (1990), pp. 190-209, who speaks of the need for 'a history conceived in terms of gender as an analytic [which would differ] from "women's history" in that it investigates the ways social categories are constituted around or in the absence of each other. With [Joan Wallach] Scott, I feel we should be asking not only "Who are the neglected women rhetoricians?" but also "How does gender give meaning to the organization and perception of historical knowledge?"' (p. 193).

125. Dale Patrick and Allen Scult, *Rhetoric and Biblical Interpretation* (Bible and Literature Series, 26; Sheffield: Almond Press, 1990), p. 27.

Scripture, rather than perpetuating cultural norms in the name of allegedly objective, hence neutral hermeneutical or rhetorical science'.[126] This is not an entirely exceptional understanding of the rhetorical function of biblical texts, as the historical Judaic and Christian religious critique of the dominant Greco-Roman cultural milieu, not to mention the reform movements of medieval and modern Christianity, clearly show.[127] How the Bible functions rhetorically in social discourse, how power functions in biblical interpretation, to what end such interpretation is directed, are important frontiers for rhetorical critical engagement. The question is: how will this 'frontier' be 'settled'? [explored!]

Unfortunately, it is precisely these areas that are ignored by biblical exegetes who are advocating a rhetorical approach to the Bible. Rhetoric as tool for critical analysis of biblical texts has tended to focus upon a limited textual and temporal dimension of reading: on the one hand, close attention has been paid to the text's stylistic and argumentative dynamics *during* (i.e. at the arrested moment of) the act of reading. Here we see a concern for the text's structure, coherence, imagery, syntax, color, repetition, convention, genre, style, devices and techniques. The persuasive intentionality secures the text's 'integrity, coherence, and textual constraints as a rhetorical unit, with a discernible beginning and ending, connected by some action or argument'.[128] Rhetoric can, in this way, help to 'control' reading by providing the means whereby weak or wrong readings can be singled out.[129] Nevertheless, rhetoric can also thereby be susceptible to 'the idolatry of the single sense', especially those models of criticism that emphasize pure description of linguistic and semantic features of the text.[130]

---

126. Wuellner, 'Rhetorical Criticism [2]', p. 5; cf. also 'Rhetorical Criticism and its Theory', p. 4: 'It is in this area that rhetorical criticism operates truly as criticism, whether as imaginative criticism, practical criticism, or ideological criticism (e.g. gender role).'

127. Wuellner, 'Rhetorical Criticism and its Theory', p. 2. It is, I would argue, a new trend in rhetorical theory itself to see rhetoric as a tool for deconstructing authoritative monopolies of power, as Conley has argued. Indeed, it is a trend whose exceptionality must be noted against the traditional pedagogical function of rhetoric to secure the social status quo and to fulfill the administrative needs of governments (religious hierarchies) throughout the history of the west.

128. Wuellner, 'Rhetorical Criticism and its Theory', p. 5.

129. Cf. Robert Alter, *The Pleasures of Reading in an Ideological Age* (New York: Simon & Schuster, 1989), p. 223.

130. Wuellner, 'Rhetorical Criticism [2]', p. 27.

On the other hand, this 'idolatry of the single sense' need not be limited to those whose interest are strictly linguistic and semantic: socio-historical critics of the Bible also limit the temporal dimension of the act of reading when using rhetoric within a hermeneutic that locates the act of reading in the reconstructed, originating performance. It is in particular this limited concept of 'context' that Wuellner attacks, arguing instead that rhetoric breaks open the concept of 'context' to mean 'more than historical context or literary tradition or genre or the generic *Sitz im Leben*'.[131] 'Context' includes theories of intentionality, argumentative situation, the 'attitudinizing conventions, precepts that condition (both the writer's *and* the reader's) stance toward experience, knowledge, tradition, language, and other people'.[132] Rather than subsuming rhetoric to the historian's interest in social description, rhetoric must regard

> 'the texts it studies not as isolated and timeless artifacts [or revelations of timeless truths], but as products of a time of writing *and* of a time of reading'. With the significance of the text changing as cultural conditions and beliefs change...the discipline of rhetorical criticism will emerge as 'a dynamic process'...[of] imaginative criticism, a criticism of the dialogical imagination which is cognizant of the Bible as 'ideological literature' and of biblical hermeneutics as part of the 'politics of interpretation'.[133]

It is this *dynamic* aspect of 'context' which Wuellner explicitly explores by combining the insights of the New Rhetoric of Perelman and Olbrechts-Tyteca with theories of intentionality [which I argue is best discarded for Burkean 'motivation'] and action in a model to which we can now turn.[134] This particular model should itself be approached 'contextually', as its focus upon 'context' was driven [somewhat] by the circumstances of its production: a seminar on the 'context' of

131. Wuellner, 'Where Is Rhetorical Criticism Taking Us?', p. 450.

132. T. Sloan, 'Rhetoric: Rhetoric in Literature', *New Encyclopedia Britannica*, XV (London: Encyclopedia Britannica, 15th edn, 1975), pp. 802-803, quoted in Wuellner, 'Where Is Rhetorical Criticism Taking Us?', p. 450.

133. Wueller, 'Where Is Rhetorical Criticism Taking Us?', p. 463. quoting R.M. Fowler, *Linguistic Criticism* (Oxford: Oxford University Press, 1986). Emphasis by Wuellner.

134. Wuellner, 'Reading Romans in Context', unpublished paper presented to the Seminar on Reader Criticism, Society for New Testament Studies meeting held at the University of Göttingen, 25–27 August 1987, p. 1.

biblical texts. While this model will therefore be viewed as an instanciation of Wuellner's theory, its relationship to both prior and subsequent works allows it to become a good illustration of his critical approach.

Given this, in his model 'context' is delimited (defined) in terms of

(1)   the context in the text, which is explored through the theory of intentionality and its relationship to a theory of action. Here Wuellner focuses upon the *intra*textual features of modality, indices, and proper names, each of which 'show author and reader in relation to *inter*-textual, con-textual components'.[135] Wuellner then considers...

(2)   ...the context *of* the text that is discerned through the rhetorical features of the text addressing *inter*textual and (socially, historically, ethically based) contextual factors of both (real and implied) author and (real and implied) audience, factors that are 'essential for the pragmatic, performative part associated with reading [religiously]: with personally and collectively (socially, communally, culturally) responsive reading' *through* time and *in* time.[136]

Both the context *of* and the context *in* the text are inseparable aspects of communication and discourse, as are the intertextual and intratextual features; their separation for the sake of theoretical reflection does not and cannot undermine their fundamental unity in the text's creation, material production/distribution, and reception.

The function of this model in analytical application emphasizes the complementary *duality* found in three fundamental areas:

(1)   The duality of the actual and implied contexts of the text *producer*: the contexts for the real author's and the implied author's thinking by writing; the contexts for generating written texts over time and in time.

(2)   The duality of the actual and implied contexts of the very *materiality* of written texts, whether cheirographic, typographic, or other forms of the technical, material aspects of the product (for both author/producer and reader/consumer) and the distribution of the text as product over time.

135. Wuellner, 'Reading Romans in Context', p. 2. Emphases mine.
136. Wuellner, 'Reading Romans in Context', p. 1.

(3)   The duality of the actual and implied contexts of the text *user*:
      the contexts for the real reader's and the implied reader's
      thinking by reading; the contexts for generating read texts
      over time and in time.[137]

Both unique event and continuing events of writing, production and
reading (including spontaneous commentary) are inseparable aspects of
communication. The result of this fundamental expansion of the concept of 'context' is a model of rhetoric that rescues the text *from* history
for histor(icit)y.

Wuellner uses this concept of 'context' to introduce important expansions into Perelman and Olbrechts-Tyteca. The **framework of argumentation** helps us to understand the social and political 'contexts'
facilitating (or hindering) the 'meeting of the minds', including 'both
customs or habits, and detailed rules for achieving this contact...'
(membership in the same class, exchange of visits, etc.),[138] as well as
'symbolic universes' (myths, narrative traditions, aesthetic traditions)
shared between rhetor and audience. These include not only systems of
contact at work at the time of writing, but also at work both during and
after writing, reception, and transmission.

In linguistic-based discourse, one aspect of this 'meeting of minds'
includes the complex role of audience upon the shape of the discourse,
an audience constituted not simply by the person(s) addressed (empirical) but also by any one of 'the ensemble of those whom the speaker
wishes to influence by his argumentation', including the various
'universal' audience constructs ('elite/ideal', single interlocutor, self-
deliberator). The 'context' of and generated by these various concepts
of audience are explored by Wuellner.

For example, the 'universal' audience, to whom convincing argumentation is directed, while conceived of as an 'ideal' audience, is always
and only grounded in a historically, socially, culturally, and even sexually [gender as social construction and performance] determined 'context': 'Each individual, each culture, has...its own conception of the
universal audience.'[139] This primarily *ideological* conception of 'universal' reasonability is an important entry into 'the text's context, the

137. Wuellner, 'Reading Romans in Context', p. 1.

138. Wuellner, 'Reading Romans in Context', p. 2; cf. Perelman and Olbrechts-
Tyteca, *The New Rhetoric*, pp. 14-17.

139. Perelman and Olbrechts-Tyteca, *The New Rhetoric*, p. 33.

world outside the text, or better: presupposed by the text as argumentation, the "social grounds of knowledge" involved in every argumentation'.[140]

One important embodiment of the 'universal' audience is the 'elite' audience, which is 'regarded as a model to which [persons or groups] should conform in order to be worthy of the name: in other words, the elite audience sets the norm for everybody. In this case, the elite is the vanguard all will follow and conform to... [it] embodies the universal audience only for those who acknowledge this role of vanguard and model.'[141] This particular construct helps us to see that the various audiences conceptualized in argumentation are not empirical individuals or groups whose social roles can be determined by a simple reading of their argumentative role. Indeed, two very important observations need to be made regarding the relationship between empirical audiences (of any time and place) and the fictive audiences embodied in the various 'universal' audience constructs: on the one hand, 'particular concrete audiences are capable of validating a concept of the universal audience which characterizes them. On the other hand... the undefined universal audience [can be] invoked to pass judgment on what is the concept of the universal audience appropriate to such a concrete audience... *audiences pass judgment on one another.*'[142]

This helps us to see an important difference between historical situation and *argumentative* situation in the notion of 'context'. It also breaks open the incredible complexity of 'audience' when considering the 'context' of any performance: any historicist reading must take into account the judgmental and dynamic interaction between 'universal' and 'elite' audiences and avoid making naive assumptions regarding role of the empirical audience in argumentation.

It also remains to be explored how audiences give shape to other forms of communication, including fundamental issues of spatial and chronological limitations (and expansions!) engendered by mass reproduction technologies and how these impact upon concepts of 'audience': the issue is not the identification, even *reduction* of these communicative forms to analogies with linguistic discourse, but the

140. Wuellner, 'Reading Romans in Context', p. 4.
141. Wuellner, 'Reading Romans in Context', p. 4, quoting Perelman and Olbrechts-Tyteca, *The New Rhetoric*, p. 34.
142. Wuellner, 'Reading Romans in Context', p. 5, quoting Perelman and Olbrechts-Tyteca, *The New Rhetoric*, p. 35. Emphasis mine.

generation of sensitivity to the unique roles expected from audiences and their impact upon performance as a result of the *materiality* of the communicative form itself, not to mention the inherent requirements of performance and reception that are part of choosing one communicative form over (or in conjunction with) another. Are there, for instance, comparable 'universal' or 'elite' audiences in virtual reality holography? What roles do audiences play in film and television, in drama, newsreports, documentaries, etc., which are performed again and again, all over the world? What is the 'framework' governing generation and reception of various musical genres, video, cyberspace, dance, sculpture and hypertext? How is this framework altered by the communicative and reproductive technology? What ideological issues of power are at stake when a government sends into exile poets and classical musicians, but sponsors modern rock musicians?[143] What ideological issues are at stake when a country explicitly identifies and labels offensive musical performances, issues warnings concerning unsuitable material presented through the medium of television and film, but declines similar activity with respect to books? These are questions concerning the 'framework of argumentation' that can only begin to be developed when once a sensitivity to the unique persuasive aspects of communicative forms other than textual and linguistic is developed in rhetorical theory and criticism.

The **starting points of argumentation** which focus upon the premises, presumptions, values, hierarchies, 'facts', 'truths' and *loci* of argumentation, provide a rich store of information regarding the text's 'context'. 'What premises are chosen and adapted for argumentation may be as indicative of a text's context as the presentation of the premises…'[144] Aside from these presumptions, we note the 'context' inherent in the values expressed through the *presentation* of the premises: here modality and indexicalities play an important role in determining and reflecting a 'context' for a 'text'.

Modalities 'modify the reality, the certainty or the importance' of an argument and its components. Modal systems operate not only as part of the text's intentionality, and hence presumably express the author's intentionality, but are also operative in the reader or user.[145] Within the

143. This was the policy of the communist government in Czechoslovakia during the first decades of their coup.

144. Wuellner, 'Reading Romans in Context', p. 5.

145. Wuellner, 'Reading Romans in Context', p. 13. For more information on

text one finds 'that modalities of meaning are preferably expressed by particular grammatical forms, but that these forms can also serve to express other modalities'.[146] One not only notes the various use of verbal moods and tenses, but considers the argumentative function of conjunctions (coordinative, subordinative), pronouns, articles, demonstratives, adverbs, explicit and implied negatives, even the epistemic 'certitude' implied in declaratives: 'All these forms of presentation have an influence on what the logicians regard as modalities: certainty, possibility, and necessity of a proposition'.[147]

The relationship between modalities and **indices**[148] is a complementary one: concentration upon modals considers the role of 'certainty' and 'possibility' as expressed by the argumentation and presumably shared [or developed and considered, perhaps even forced] between rhetor and audience, while concentration upon indices concerns the posturing effect between rhetor and audience made in and by the discourse. Obviously there is some overlapping: modality is often expressed through the various personal, intonational, spatial and temporal deixes. But it is the overall effect of the argumentation regarding the assumptions shared between rhetor and audience that Wuellner considers in his analysis of modality.

Deixis 'refers to the orientation of the content of a sentence in relation to time, place, and personal participants. The spatial, temporal, and interpersonal orientation of a sentence is expressed by deictic indicators. Moreover, deictic... features of a language are used... to construct contexts of utterance and of reference'[149] which relate both reader and

English modes and modalities, cf. J. Coates, *The Semantics of Modal Auxiliaries* (London: Croom Helm, 1984); M. Ehrman, *The Meaning of Modals in Present-Day American English* (The Hague: Mouton, 1966); D. Kastovsky and A. Szwedek (eds.), *Linguistics across Historical and Geographical Boundaries: In Honour of Jacek Fisiak* (The Hague: Mouton, de Greute, 1986); T. Givón, 'Evidentiality and Epistemic Space', *Studies in Language* 4 (1982), pp. 23-49; M.A.K. Halliday, 'Functional Diversity in Language as Seen from a Consideration of Mood and Modality in English', *Foundation of Language* 4 (1970), pp. 225-42; F.R. Palmer, *Modality and English Modals* (London: Longman, 1979) and *idem, Mood and Modality* (Cambridge: Cambridge University Press, 1986).

146. Perelman and Olbrechts-Tyteca, *The New Rhetoric*, p. 154.

147. Perelman and Olbrechts-Tyteca, *The New Rhetoric*, p. 163.

148. Cf. R.J. Jarvella *et al.*, *Speech, Place and Action: Studies in Deixis and Related Topics* (New York: Wiley, 1982).

149. Wuellner, 'Reading Romans in Context', p. 14.

text to the social, historical, cultural 'contexts' reflected in language. In the act of reading the utterance, these contexts are 'the context[s] of *reading*, not writing; the context[s] of use, not production'.[150] These indices are noted not merely for the syntactic, affective, or semiotic function and form in discourse, but primarily for their argumentative. The identification of 'what they are' must be wrought under the concern of 'what they do'.

Such indices [they are not meant to be approached as empirical objects with definitive content, but heuristic categories soliciting potentially relational experiences generated in reading and analysis] include, for example:

- *Personal deixis* 'which includes the use of personal and demonstrative pronouns, and, of course, also the use of personal names'.[151] Here we note the argumentative function of the various fictive and empirical audiences which can be addressed with argumentative distinction, though sharing the same personal pronoun: 'you' can be the 'universal' audience addressed directly, addressed to particular forms of 'elite' audiences, etc. 'You' can also, of course, be directed to the empirical audience(s), the actual addressees. Furthermore, one should also note the argumentative and ideological significance of the personal pronoun 'his' 'to index the context/content of a given reference as "divine" rather than human'.[152]

- *Proper Names* are closely related to personal deixis, and disclose an intentionality beyond mere reference to individuals or groups. Argumentatively, named individuals can become references to elite groups, to models or anti-models for emulation or rejection.[153]

- *Intonational deixis* which can also include modalities that express emotion of greater or lesser degree. 'Expressive' intonation and intentionality, however, is not merely concerned with the affective and emotive dimensions of discourse, but with the argumentative. Here we note the *evaluative* dimension

150. Wuellner, 'Reading Romans in Context', p. 14.
151 Wuellner, 'Reading Romans in Context', p. 14.
152 Wuellner, 'Reading Romans in Context', p. 15.
153. Wuellner, 'Reading Romans in Context', p. 16.

of discourse and the potential for critique or praise inherent in intonation.[154]

- *Spatial deixis* involves not only here/there, but coming/going, out/in, specific or general locations, and considers the argumentative importance of distance.[155]

- *Temporal deixis* includes the argumentative effect of then/now, old/new and the values and norms, postures and hierarchies set into effect through this labeling.[156]

Set within a theory of argumentation, a careful consideration of indices and their function in (both narrative and argumentative) discourse can help us better understand the 'context' of intentionality, the posturing generated by the discourse, and create an awareness of how 'intentionality' of text/author/reader interact and affect one another in the production of activity. [Of course, such close textual analysis should not be the primary or even major operative means of rhetorical analysis. Instead, it should be viewed as a methodological 'voice' in the *symphonic* array of choices that can be made by an analyst, this one perhaps particularly apt at heuristically discerning ('invent'-ing?) 'textual' and (implied *and* real) 'authorial' intention/intonation, which must also be set against/within 'audience' and 'contextual' intention/intonation.]

This ['intentional'] activity is further 'contextualized' by the argumentative situation implied by the function of the discourse as demonstrative, defensive/accusational or deliberative, each of these genres defined in classical rhetorical theory according to the 'context' in which they took place (at 'games', in courts, or at legislative session, respectively). While genre and setting are not causally related, this connection nevertheless serves to emphasize the connection between argumentation and action/commitment. An analysis of the 'situation' will not focus on the content or consequences of the intended effect, but upon its intensity.[157]

---

154. Wuellner, 'Reading Romans in Context', p. 15.
155. Wuellner, 'Reading Romans in Context', p. 15.
156. Wuellner, 'Reading Romans in Context', p. 15.
157. Wuellner, 'Reading Romans in Context', p. 22, where he quotes Mark Jordan, 'Ancient Philosophical Protreptic and the Problem of Persuasive Genres', *Rhetorica* 4.3 (1986), pp. 309-33 (331), whom I paraphrase here.

If there is a corrective which herein needs to be offered [and there certainly is!], it would be that Wuellner's interest in semiotics and language creates a myopic concentration upon text-as-discourse which should be balanced by an awareness of 'modalities' and 'indexicalities' present in other communicative media and forms. In filmic representations, for example, the additional dimensions of point of view, color, lighting, perspective, editing, special visual effects, not to mention sounds and background music, are all part of the communicative effects that 'modify the reality, its certainty or importance' and which 'orient the content of the performance in relation to time, place, and personal participants'. New computer technology, with the multimedia ability to present not only traditional texts for consumption, but which also allows for an interactive participation in their development, not to mention their aural presentation and supplementation, will also have a profound impact upon our awareness of the 'starting points of argumentation'. Music itself, through its modal performance, will provide an important element in orientation; the relationship between music and rhetoric has long been recognized,[158] but what has only recently begun to be appreciated is the reproducibility of performances and their interpretive manipulation through other media forms and mass consumption. It is not only the larger cultural and epistemological implications generated by the advent of computer and electronic technologies which should be kept in mind [the impact of *form*], but the impact upon rhetorical terminology, typology, analytical approaches, objects of criticism, and so on [the unique representation of *content* inherent in each *form*]. What is desperately needed is the advent of rhetorical criticisms which can begin to describe the rhetorical features of the incredible and immediate variety of communicative forms, forms whose uniqueness lie in the reduplication, but now also active participant-manipulation, of performance: rhetoric of film, rhetoric of video, rhetoric of computer technology, rhetoric of television, etc. These forms profoundly impact the 'context' of communication, argumentation, persuasion, action and the ways in which we approach not only their 'starting points', but also the 'techniques'.

Wuellner next considers the 'context' revealed through the **techniques of argumentation**. Here Wuellner's critical effort is directed at maintaining the *descriptive* tradition of rhetoric re-initiated by Perelman

---

158. Cf. Brian Vickers, 'Introduction', in Vickers (ed.), *Rhetoric Revalued*, pp. 19-20. See Bibliographies, Music and Rhetoric.

and Olbrechts-Tyteca in their research approach to argumentative techniques for securing adherence to values. While the *museful* quality of rhetoric requires that we use the results of observation and descriptive analysis as part of the continuing *prescriptive* tradition, it is the descriptive tradition that must act as the foundation for rhetorical composition and the return of the *technē*, otherwise we will witness the return to the tendency (so prevalent in the history of the western and Byzantine rhetorics) to *impose* standards of 'proper' performance and composition. This imposition not only overlooks, downplays or outright rejects any interest in the rhetoric of the discourse of the everyday, of the vernacular or of other cultures, but always serves the interest of socio-cultural power systems. The return to description as the foundation for rhetorical models helps us to see that societies which may not have much of a history of 'rhetorical theory' as expressed in systematic rules of invention and disposition we come to expect (as a result of Greco-Roman tradition) nevertheless adhere to presumed 'rules' and 'standards' by which individuals or groups attempt to argue reasonably. Thus we can begin to ask about the rhetoric of China, India, Japan, Korea, Africa, Native North and South Americans, and of subcultures and groups (including gender-role categories) in each of these broad geographical areas and cultures.

We can further begin to ask about the impact of 'rhetorical' rules of discourse at work influencing both the authors and the readers of the first- and second-century Christian writings, and it is *this* question that seeks to undermine the trend in biblical rhetorical criticism that turns to a general, 'unified' Greco-Roman model as the presumed standard by which to judge early Christian discourse. Wuellner's research into the rhetoric of Jewish biblical interpretation (discussions, debates, exegesis, homiletics, etc.) not only muddies the [*artificially* clear] waters, but effectively decenters this whole historical enterprise: the recognition of the pluralism of Greco-Roman and (Hellenistic and Palestinian) Jewish rhetorical theories undermines the authority of the prescriptive tradition, breaking open the analysis of these texts to a multitude of models made available through a descriptive approach.

Finally, the **order and interaction of argumentation** are dictated by adaptation to the audience and the developing argumentative (not rhetorical) situation. Wuellner explains this adaptation to 'context' and 'exigence' by reference to 'intentionality' of the argument and the *social* dynamics inherent in this concept, rather than the specific historical situation of production. 'Context' for both writing and reading is thereby determined by and through the sequence of argumentation informed by the argumentative situation 'which has to be met *the first time and every time the text gets used'*.[159] This is rhetoric's concern with the *performance* of a text, one which turns the encounter with the text, even the most critical, into a 'dialogic relation [requiring] two consciousnesses and two subjects', if not more.[160] Here Wuellner explores the relationship between the theory of intentionality with the theory of action in the question of what constitutes 'context', and the complementary relationship they both have to Perelman and Olbrechts-Tyteca's theory of argumentation: not only does the theory of intentionality explore 'modality' and 'indexicality' (explored above), but the theory of action also finds common cause with Perelman and Olbrechts-Tyteca's understanding of argumentation as discourse which seeks to create or intensify commitment to action.

Intentionality 'covers the whole range of mental states on the sides of *both* author *and* reader…These mental states have their propositional content, and their appropriate action, whether as intention *preceding* action…or *in* the action.'[161] Intentionality is analyzed in terms of complexity (from lesser to greater), and whether it is fixed or open.[162] One of the ways in which intentionality is given expression is through the particular forms of modality and indices found in the performance of (an argumentative) discourse-act. It must be noted, however, that intentionality is typically analyzed and reviewed in a rather limited focus, either by reduction of 'mental states and structures of action to the materiality of biological bodies [of authors or readers] on the one hand' or by reduction of 'materiality of texts and contexts… to economics and sociology' on the other.[163] These two emphases distort and eliminate other important 'contextual' factors of reading, and are ultimately unable to explain motivational (i.e. Burke's notion of identification and transformation), affective (i.e. Kennedy's notion of

---

159. Wuellner, 'Reading Romans in Context', p. 12. Emphasis mine.
160. Wuellner, 'Rhetorical Criticism [2]', p. 23, quoting Mikhail M. Bakhtin, *The Dialogic Imagination: Four Essays* (ed. Michael Holquist; trans. Caryl Emerson and Michael Holquist; Austin, TX: University of Texas Press, 1981), p. 125.
161. Wuellner, 'Reading Romans in Context', p. 12. Emphasis mine.
162. Wuellner, 'Reading Romans in Context', p. 12.
163. Wuellner, 'Reading Romans in Context', p. 18.

the ontological basis of 'rhetoric'), and ideological dimensions of rhetoric.[164]

Intentionality must be informed by a **theory of action** [language as performative event] which views reading as a form of *activity* set within a *material* 'context' and medium [which must also include the 'materiality' not only of the text as final product, but also of the processes engaged in the production of the text, including the 'materiality' of authors, editors, copyists, etc.]. As an *act*, reading encompasses characteristics of human behavior, whether individual, social or individual within social. As an activity within *history*, reading requires time and space for execution. *Reflection* upon the act of reading makes us realize 'the principles by which we identify and explain action', principles which are themselves 'part of the actions, that is, they are partly *constitutive* of actions'.[165] One important factor for consideration which arises from the theory of action is the awareness of the impact of materiality upon discourse and communication. 'Materiality' is not just limited to the 'medium' of communication, but also to the entire holistic background of human culture and ideology which controls and shapes both form and content of discourse (its production), as well as its 'context' of reception. The theory of intentionality must be complemented by the awareness of the ideological dimensions of literature *itself* as a material product of human culture,[166] an awareness which is generated through the theory of action.

As a '*context*', reading confronts two distinct materialities:

(1)   The 'context' 'from within and out of which the original writer once wrote, which includes the contexts of the materiality of the produced text for the user/reader'.

Even here, however, as we have noted above, rhetoric requires that we avoid the common fallacy of exegesis which

164. Cf. George Kennedy, 'A Hoot in the Dark: The Evolution of General Rhetoric', *Philosophy & Rhetoric* 25.1 (1992), pp. 1-21.

165. Wuellner, 'Reading Romans in Context', p. 16; quotation from John R. Searle, *Minds, Brains and Science* (Cambridge, MA: Harvard University Press, 1984), p. 59.

166. For an exploration into the relationship of 'materiality' in critical rhetoric and the recovery of the 'subject self', cf. Raymie E. McKerrow, 'Critical Rhetoric and the Possibility of the Subject', in Ian Angus and Lenore Langsdorf (eds.), *The Critical Turn: Rhetoric and Philosophy in Postmodern Discourse* (Carbondale, IL: Southern Illinois University Press, 1993), pp. 51-67.

considers a hermeneutic of only one consciousness. '[Reading] deals with not one but *two* intentionalities; with not one but *two* relevances...'[167]

Furthermore, reading must also conceive of the text not as formal definition, but contextual meaning, as 'integrated meaning that relates to value—to truth, beauty, and so forth—and requires a *responsive* understanding, one that includes evaluation'.[168]

Finally, we have to be careful to distinguish between an author writing to a reader and an author writing to an audience. ' "Readership" is not a collective noun. It is an abstraction in a way that "audience" is not.'[169]

(2) The 'context' of 'the cultural and technological changes affecting the text's materiality'.[170] This includes shifts within cheirographic culture which began to identify texts with names and began to include punctuation, paragraphing, chapter and verse markings, even ornamentation and iconographic signs. Of course, it doesn't stop there: 'New contexts are generated by technology of print, let alone the latest electronic technologies, each one, in its own ways, materially/technically embodying what Bakhtin calls "contextual meaning" inviting reader, viewer, user to interaction as "*responsive* understanding" '.[171] Just as print technology generated the concept of sequential-as-causal reasoning, as well as the 'hot' medium of 'texts' which allow for no interaction between producer and receiver (other than economic), so electric technology has returned us to forms of communication which are 'synesthetic', as whole 'contexts' become the constellations of total participation within which discourse (in all its media) takes place (cyberspace, virtual reality, interactive technologies, etc.).[172] Indeed, the advent of hypertexts (interactive reading

---

167. Wuellner, 'Reading Romans in Context', p. 17.

168. Wuellner, 'Reading Romans in Context', p. 17.

169. Wuellner, 'Reading Romans in Context', p. 17; quotation from Walter Ong, *20th Century Literary Theory* (Albany: SUNY Press, 1987), p. 404.

170. Wuellner, 'Reading Romans in Context', p. 17.

171. Wuellner, 'Reading Romans in Context', p. 17.

172. Cf. Marshall McLuhan, *Understanding Media: The Extensions of Man* (New York: Signet/McGraw–Hill, 1964).

wherein the reader chooses the destiny and experience of the text, hence writes the text) suggests a whole new dimension to the concept of 'reading', one which has never been confronted by the print-centered culture: the concept of actively *shaping the very content and final [?] form of discourse through interactive selectivity*; in other words, in hypertext, the hegemony of 'author-ship/-ity' is set on the path of extinction.

However, it is clear that '[a]ll of this is conceivable even if, as is progressively unlikely, we were to look at any document...as an individual, isolated, material text'. Another important aspect of materiality as part of human culture is the 'context' of religious canon: 'When [a text's] materiality gets preserved in a sacred canon, it acquires a contextuality that goes beyond the intertextuality indigenous to every linguistic entity.'[173]

'Intentionality', so informed by the theory of action, is expressed through the modalities and indices of a discourse that comprises the 'context' *in* the text. This 'context' includes two components: (1) the propositional or intentional 'content' of the discourse, and (2) the social forms enabling the conditions that make it possible for particular expressions of intentionality to take place. Both of these components include not only the notion of 'intentionality' on the part of historical readers/authors/texts, nor only 'intentionality' on the part of 'implied authors' and 'implied readers', but also extend to include an 'entire network of subsidiary intentions' which form the background 'context' of every act of production and reception of discourse.[174] [Not to mention 'motivations' which are 'beneath' intentions: the sub-conscious, the unconscious.] Especially with respect to religious texts whose claims upon divine intentionality give them certain weight within a cultural context, this 'intentionality' or background must also be seen to include not only the 'co-author' of every *bona fide* religious author, god or spirit of god, but also the mythic/religious co-texts and traditions both preceding and following (whether as commentary or independent from, but nevertheless recognized as part of the same canon) the production of the text.

173. Wuellner, 'Reading Romans in Context', p. 17.
174. Wuellner, 'Reading Romans in Context', p. 14.

Not once, not ever since its very first reading has [a religious text, e.g. the Bible in various canonical forms, Koran, Baghavad Gita, I Ching, Tao De Ching] been read without background or context, nor could it be read without such. But different times and cultures could, and did, generate backgrounds or contexts other than the one prevailing at the time the text was first generated.[175]

A theory of 'intentionality', when complemented by a theory of action [and elaborated to include *un*'intended' acts] allows us to consider the full complexity of 'contexts' (both *in* and *around* 'texts') in which the order and strengths of argumentation can be received and analyzed.

In sum, Wuellner understands the 'context' *of* a 'text' as the argumentative context in which the [mis-]use and [re-]reading of the 'text' occurs in time and place every time the 'text' is picked up. However, complementarity of the concepts of 'context' *of* and 'context' *in* a 'text' must be kept in the forefront of any analysis of the argumentation, as it is here that the multiplicity of [un]intentionalities is located. It is clear that 'context' not only includes the historical moment of production, but is materially informed as part of the culture in which 'texts' *continue* to be produced artifactually (books, films, audio tapes), intellectually (reading, discussion) and ideologically (controlling the means of production, access, expectations, methods and theories, point of view). Reading is a function of two [or more: author, reader, text] [un]intentions, of two [or more: production, reproduction, reception] activities. Argumentation is a function of rhetor (real and implied), 'text' (including medium) and audience (real and implied).

Wuellner embraces the theory of argumentation in order to explore not only communicative products (texts, speeches, performances, music, art, books, articles), but also the systems in which they take place, the ideological background informing production and reproduction in the first place, and the 'context' of 'audiences' who *do* things with 'texts'. Rhetoric will not guarantee a particular reading over another, but can inform us of the reasons *why one reading has been chosen over another*. It can help us discern the function of 'power' in the production, reception, interpretation and discussion of 'texts', especially the form of 'power' which is the essence of sacred literature: the 'monstrous', the 'rhetoric of the sublime', the 'goadings of mystery', all of which are perhaps *best* brought to light [exposed] through rhetoric [which itself

---

175. Wuellner, 'Reading Romans in Context', p. 13.

then needs to have its 'mysteries' exposed].[176] Rhetorical criticism is 'rhetorico-political activity' which concerns not only the rhetoric in and of a 'text' [e.g. the Bible], but the theories and philosophies of critical approaches (even rhetorical-critical approaches) themselves. It breaks open our awareness of the ideology of and in 'texts' and methods, and makes us 'careful to look for and find...instruments of persuasion embodying principles of development and change—in Burke's terms, "identification and transformation"'.[177] For Wuellner, Perelman and Olbrechts-Tyteca have opened up rhetorical analysis not only to the dimensions of argumentation *in* discourse, but *of* the function and use of discourse. And, I would argue, by so doing he has not stretched the boundaries of the theory of argumentation beyond that which was inherent in its formulation to begin with, but has managed to offer us a glimpse into the depths and potential of its ability to transform not just biblical criticism, but the whole [irrelevant] structure of specialist 'textual' interpretation.[178]

Steven Mailloux

It isn't enough, however, simply to *assert* this potential impact of rhetoric upon the fields of biblical criticism and specialist 'textual' interpretation. We must provide the means by which this impact can be assessed, that is, we must consider more explicitly the institutional dynamics of power which gave rise to and continue to sanction the current methodological and hermeneutical assumptions at work in historical-critical exegesis. In other words, a rhetoric of power must also look at the rhetorical strategies and assumptions of a discipline and assess their relationship to the greater *academented* systems and structures of power in all their forms. It is a move away from the hegemony of the wor(l)d of the 'text' [which has dominated the discussion so far] to the wor(l)d of [academented and religious] politics. It is here, in particular, that Steven Mailloux will make his contribution to our

176. Cf. Wilhelm Wuellner, 'Death and Rebirth in Late Twentieth Century Exegesis', in Tord Fornberg and David Hellholm (eds.), *Texts and Contexts: Biblical Texts in their Textual and Situational Contexts* (Festschrift Lars Hartman; Oslo: Scandinavian University Press, 1995), pp. 917-30.

177. Wuellner, 'Where Is Rhetorical Criticism Taking Us?', p. 462.

178. Wuellner, 'Where Is Rhetorical Criticism Taking Us?', pp. 462-63.

exploration by offering important insights which arise from his presentation and defense of 'rhetorical hermeneutics'.

Mailloux begins by rejecting the pursuit of hermeneutical Theory as incapable of securing the kinds of effects for which it strives, namely, to provide 'binding prescriptions' (based on general observations of reading practices) for critical practice which are developed and applied in the effort to assure 'correct' readings.[179] Instead, he rightly suggests that such pursuits at Theory are (1) *rhetorical* attempts at persuasion which (2) take place within specific historical contexts, and which (3) address *institutional* concerns of a critical discipline.

1. Such pursuits at Theory are rhetorical attempts, insofar as they seek to secure prominence within the critical workings of a discipline by means of argumentation, even though the ultimate goal of Theory is to secure a foolproof means by which verifiable results of interpretation can be objectively (or at least intersubjectively) secured. In other words, Theory's goal is to transcend the limitation of the immediate context of argumentation concerning Theory in order to provide a 'universally' recognized means of proving interpretational validity.

2. Such pursuits at Theory are historically limited, insofar as the rhetorical practices (as well as assumptions) of hermeneutical Theory, and their resulting systems, change their dynamics over time, accepting and rejecting arguments according to the empirical audience's own values and assumptions.

3. Such pursuits are institutional, insofar as they are pursued for the sake of providing a critical basis and justification for a discipline's analytical efforts, without which basis 'an institutionalized discipline has no way of grounding its production of new knowledge'.[180] Mailloux embraces the anti-Theorist stance of recent scholars that the pursuit of Theory, based on 'establishing principles for explicating texts best derived from an account of how interpretation works in general',[181] is simply doomed to failure, and hence irrelevant. There is simply no Archimedian standpoint beyond which we can judge the truth claims of a given Theory; Theory can't do what it claims to do. [Aha! This is nothing other than one more entry in the continuing debate over the 'epistemic' nature of rhetoric.]

179. Steven Mailloux, 'Rhetorical Hermeneutics', *Critical Inquiry* 11 (1985), pp. 620-41 (621).

180. Mailloux, 'Rhetorical Hermeneutics', p. 622.

181. Mailloux, 'Rhetorical Hermeneutics', p. 621.

At this point, however, his argument differs from Stanley Fish's or Steven Knapp's and Walter Michaels' rejection of Theory as 'inconsequential'.[182] For Mailloux, while it may be the case that having a 'correct' or 'incorrect' account of interpretation ultimately neither 'enables nor disables the critic in doing interpretation', it is nevertheless the case that 'having *this* rather than *that* hermeneutic account does affect the *kind* of interpretation'.[183] The pragmatic effect such efforts have on a discipline can be found in the methods and pursuits resulting from sanctioning one Theory rather than another: 'The *attempt* to do the impossible (to have a correct Theory that guarantees valid interpretations because it is correct) does have consequences for practice that directly follow from the theoretical attempt, consequences such as critics talking about the author's mind or becoming preoccupied with biography [or pursuing readerly effects or reconstituting socio-historical contexts, etc.]'.[184]

It is precisely on these effects that Mailloux wishes to focus critical attention by ceasing any further effort at developing a foundationalist Epistemology and instead embracing a *rhetorical hermeneutics* which 'continues theorizing about interpretation only therapeutically, exposing the problems with foundationalism and explaining the attraction of realist [text-centered] and idealist [reader-oriented] positions'.[185] Such a hermeneutics 'would not view shared interpretive strategies as the creative origin of texts...but, rather, as historical sets of topics, arguments, tropes, ideologies, and so forth, that determine how texts are established as meaningful through rhetorical exchanges. In this view, communities of interpreters neither discover nor create meaningful texts. Such communities are actually *synonymous* with the [historical, social, political, economic, gender, ethical] conditions in which acts of persuasion about texts take place.'[186]

---

182. Cf., for an in-depth discussion of Knapp's and Michaels' argument for 'inconsequentiality', as well as Fish's anti- 'Anti-professionalism' argument, Mailloux, *Rhetorical Power*, pp. 150-66.

183. Mailloux, 'Rhetorical Hermeneutics', pp. 628-29. Emphasis his.

184. Mailloux, 'Rhetorical Hermeneutics', pp. 628-29. Emphasis his.

185. Mailloux, 'Rhetorical Hermeneutics', p. 631.

186. Mailloux, 'Rhetorical Hermeneutics', p. 629. Emphasis mine.

It is therefore of no surprise that for Mailloux a rhetorical hermeneutics must inevitably turn to the pragmatic[187] ground, that is, become rhetorical history: rhetorical hermeneutics must provide the contexts in which 'particular theoretical and critical discourses have evolved... [since] acts of persuasion always take place against an ever-changing background of shared and disputed assumptions, questions, assertions, and so forth. Any full rhetorical analysis of interpretation must therefore describe this tradition of discursive practices in which acts of interpretive persuasion are embedded.'[188] Here we see one dimension to the assertion he makes when defining rhetorical hermeneutics as an analytical approach which 'uses rhetoric to practice theory by doing history'.[189] Mailloux goes on to provide historical-critical analyses of the interpretive debates of particular documents (the reception history of *Huckleberry Finn* in late nineteenth-century American debates over slavery and the 'bad-boy boom';[190] biblical interpretation in pro- and anti-slavery argumentation and the reception of *Narrative of the Life of Frederick Douglass, an American Slave, Written by Himself*;[191] the Anti-Ballistic Missile Treaty dispute set off by the Reagan administration's 1982 reinterpretation of 'peaceful purposes' clause),[192] setting these debates within the context of greater social, cultural and political issues[193] in which interpretations take place in order 'to describe and explain past and present configurations of rhetorical practices as they affect each other and as they extend and manipulate the social practices, political structures, and material circumstances in which they are

187. Cf. Steven Mailloux, 'Rhetorical Hermeneutics Revisited', *Text and Performance Quarterly* 11 (1991), pp. 233-48 (235-38), where he appeals to Rorty's neo-pragmatic argument against foundationalist epistemology. Cf. also Mailloux, *Rhetorical Power*, pp. 144-47.

188. Mailloux, 'Rhetorical Hermeneutics', p. 631.

189. Mailloux, 'Rhetorical Hermeneutics Revisited', p. 233.

190. Mailloux, *Rhetorical Power*, esp. Part 3: 'Cultural History and *Huckleberry Finn*'.

191. Mailloux, 'Rhetorical Hermeneutics Revisited', pp. 244-46. Cf. also Steven Mailloux, 'Misreading as a Historical Act: Cultural Rhetoric, Bible Politics, and Fuller's 1845 Review of Douglass's *Narrative*', in James L. Machor (ed.), *Readers in History: Nineteenth-Century American Literature and the Contexts of Response* (Baltimore: The Johns Hopkins University Press, 1993), pp. 2-31.

192. Mailloux, *Rhetorical Power*, 'Conclusion: The ABM Treat Interpretation Dispute'.

193. Cf. Mailloux, 'Misreading as a Historical Act', pp. 4-5.

embedded at particular historical moments'.[194] Specifically, Mailloux argues for a concept of rhetorical hermeneutics which situates it within the growing emphasis on 'culture studies' in American universities,[195] turning his critical and analytical eye on the 'political effectivity of trope and argument in culture'.[196]

Here it must be noted that his own deliberative and apologetic strategies are embedded within the particular experiences of modern literary studies in America which underwent a profound transformation due to New Criticism's impact upon the field in the 1940s and 1950s. Rhetorical hermeneutics attempts to balance literary studies' post-New Critical focus upon 'close reading' (context-less reading of 'textual' dynamics and structures) by developing

> critical analyses and stories of reading [which are] open to a range of factors usually ignored in most [post-New Critical and post-structuralist readings], factors constituted by social, political, and economic categories including race, age, gender, ethnicity, nationality, religion, sexuality, and class. This talk about historical acts of reading was strongly encouraged by changes within related institutional practices: the turn to history within theoretical accounts of textual interpretation and the attention to politics within historical analyses of intertextuality.[197]

Literary theory and literary studies in America are experiencing profound transformations, coming to realize what was denied and suppressed by New Criticism's agenda: '[H]ow reading is historically contingent, politically situated, institutionally embedded, and materially conditioned...how reading any text, literary or nonliterary, relates to larger cultural politics that goes well beyond some hypothetical private interaction between an autonomous reader and an independent text; and...how our particular views of reading relate to the liberatory potential of literacy and the transformative [*sic*] power of education'.[198]

It is in particular these latter insights that give voice to another harmonic resonance within his concept of rhetorical hermeneutics as 'doing history': the *historicity* of a 'text' and its 'context', including 'texts' which endeavor to define trans-historical theories of reading and

---

194. Mailloux, 'Rhetorical Hermeneutics Revisited', p. 234.
195. Mailloux, 'Rhetorical Hermeneutics Revisited', pp. 233-34.
196. Mailloux, *Rhetorical Power*, p. xii.
197. Mailloux, 'Misreading as a Historical Act', p. 5.
198. Mailloux, 'Misreading as a Historical Act', p. 5. See his defense of this latter position on pp. 239-44.

interpretation.[199] Rhetorical hermeneutics grounds *all* theory and interpretation in histor(icit)y, even its own theoretical position and analytical application and results, which it sees as 'a specific piece of
rhetorically pragmatic theorizing about interpretation'.[200] There is no
escape either from rhetoric or histor(icit)y into some transcendental
realm from which standards of correct interpretation can be discerned
and prescribed: such standards are part of the traditions for argumentative appeal 'accepted within particular communities, disciplines, discourses, and so on, but these are local, contingent, rhetorical constructs,
which have all the force of such construct, which is all the force needed
for interpretive debate and knowledge production to take place'.[201]

His efforts at describing the particular rhetorical practices at work in
shaping American literary studies before, during, and after New Criticism's hegemony will have some value to our effort at describing the
function of rhetorical criticism in New Testament exegesis. His emphasis upon the histor(icit)y of interpretation, interpretive models and
hermeneutical theory, and the social, cultural, political and economic
contexts in which they operate will also be important to our work. Of
great interest to us at this point, however, is the very important emphasis he gives to the kinds of rhetorical activity which takes place when
institutionalized disciplines seek to maintain their place in academentia.
In contrast with others who have emphasized the impact of political and
economic forces upon academented disciplines and the resulting shape
these give to the disciplines' codes and analytical *teloi*,[202] Mailloux
suggests that their establishment, maintenance and development in
universities can only be *partially* explained through analysis of factors
outside these institutions, since once an institutional space has been
carved out, 'the specific interpretive work and rhetorical practices

199. Cf. Mailloux, *Rhetorical Power,* pp. 134-35.
200. Mailloux, 'Rhetorical Hermeneutics Revisited', p. 238; cf. Mailloux, *Rhetorical Power*, p. 135.
201. Mailloux, 'Rhetorical Hermeneutics Revisited', p. 244. Mailloux, *Rhetorical Power*, p. 180: '[I]t has been the argument of this chapter and of the entire
book that textual interpretation and rhetorical politics can *never* be separated'.
Emphasis his.
202. E.g. Richard Ohmann, *English in America: A Radical View of the Profession* (New York: Oxford University Press, 1976); John Fekete, *The Critical
Twilight: Explorations in the Ideology of Anglo-American Literary Theory from
Eliot to McLuhan* (London: Routledge & Kegan Paul, 1977); Eagleton, *Literary
Theory*.

within this space seem only crudely affected by extrainstitutional
factors'.[203]

It will be our starting point to determine the *intra*institutional factors
at work in rhetorical criticism of the New Testament: in contrast to
literary studies, for example, biblical studies has been profoundly aware
of the 'history' of the 'text'. It has not, however, explored (to the point
of methodological impact) the *historicity* of the biblical text, choosing
to limit its focus to historical-critical inquiry into the socio-, religio-
and theologico-historical aspects of the original or generative performance which is the determinative hermeneutical event [all other interpretations or uses of the biblical text are judged against this antiquarian
'context']. We shall explore the implicit assumptions regarding the
nature of 'text' and 'context' in rhetorical criticism and their impact
upon the ways in which rhetorical criticism is applied to the New Testament. And we shall do so in order to expose explicitly the institutional hegemony of a particular concept of biblical interpretation that
continues to haunt these scholars in spite of their best efforts. [In other
words, we shall do so, because we can thereby explore *power*.]

We shall also consider the *inter*institutional forces which give/gave
shape to the domain which biblical studies carved out for itself within
both academentia and ecclesial structures. However, it is also important
to emphasize that questions concerning these *inter*institutional forces
must not be limited to a 'history of ideas', to method, to *Forschungs-
berichte* (report on previous studies) and *-auslegungen* (explanation of
approach). As a materialist and historicist theory, a rhetoric of power
must also note the means of production and distribution (peer review
committees, journals, academented societies and their relationship to
publishing houses, grant committees, etc.) by which such efforts at
sanctioning and marginalization of methods and research take place. It
is the entire complex of academented and disciplinary systems of
power which we must include in a rhetoric of power.

Finally, we shall also ponder the *extra*disciplinary forces, insofar as
they impact upon the analysis offered by the scholars we choose as
examples of rhetorical criticism of the New Testament. Here we shall
consider the relationship between biblical studies and the broader cultural issues to which these scholars are seeking to address the research.
We shall note therefrom not only the traditional cultural rhetoric in

203. Mailloux, 'Rhetorical Hermeneutics', p. 632.

which they are participating, but also the limitations of their field to address these issues, the struggles they undergo (but do not necessarily succeed) to become relevant to the sociopolitical and cultural-religious conversation in which they wish to participate.

It is all of these factors, pursued *symphonically* (not necessarily structurally independent of each other, not 'chronologically' or 'logically'), which will help us *musefully* to explore potential new directions of rhetorical theory being systematically marginalized by the discipline of biblical studies as traditionally conceived and currently practiced. The contours for revolutionary reconstitution of the discipline [perhaps even paradigm *destruction*] will begin to show their potential shape from this exploration.

Summary

What *is* a rhetoric of power? It is an [incomplete and far-too-coherent attempt at] rhetorical theory which approaches communicative exchanges from the multiple complexes of intentionality and action which take place within, are shaped by and have impact upon contexts of power. As a theory, it is a highly complex and *symphonic* accumulation of insights from a variety of disciplines and fields of critical inquiry into the nature and effect of communication, society, aesthetics and technology. It sees every communicative exchange, every event of 'meaning' [= persuasion][204] as a *symbiotic* relation of multiple intentionalities not only on the part of rhetor and audience, but also engendered through the dynamic impact of communicative form itself. A rhetoric of power is also *museful*, insofar as its analytical, critical and compositional aspects are embedded within a process of continuing creativity, reflection, evaluation and the recognition that 'truth' is relative to the 'contexts' of persuasion in which 'truth' asserts its hegemony, 'contexts' which demand to be understood [not 'uncanny'].

However, an important [and fair] question to ask at this point would be: are there lacunae, blind spots in the theory as we have so far developed it? I believe so, and the first to come to mind is the emphasis on *invention* and *arrangement* shown in recent theories of rhetoric to the near exclusion of other important aspects of communicative exchange. This results in an important distortion which should be corrected: since

204. Kenneth Burke, *A Rhetoric of Motives* (Berkeley: University of California Press, 1950), p. 696.

its inception, rhetoric also included concerns of *style, memorization* and *delivery*. While these additional canons were the result of the particular form in which rhetorical performance was primarily engaged at the time, and while arguably the emphasis upon concerns of *elocution* and *style* have been problematic throughout the history of rhetoric,[205] I nevertheless herein wish to embrace at least the tendencies which they embody: a concern with the standards of rhetorical performance as dictated by the communicative form in which a persuasive act takes place. To turn to Aristotle: as we have so far explored rhetoric in the works of New Testament rhetorical-critical scholars, we have sacrificed rhetoric on the altar to the God of *logos*, whereas a great deal of rhetoric (as both performance and analysis) may have to deal with *ethos* and *pathos*. [No, not quite.] The forms of power are manifold, and it is often not only rational appeal, but emotional (mythic) and authoritative appeal that helps to secure conviction (and perhaps more importantly: persuasion). [Better; continue.] Part of a rhetor's power may just lie in her/his style (both personal appearance and comportment, as well as selection of discursive tropes and figures), in her/his delivery (including settings and communicative forms selected for publication and presentation),[206] even in memorization (one of the most important *ethos* elements of the power of speakers is the command they show of their subject). [Still too 'text' centered.] One suspects that a great deal of the wariness that modern rhetorical theory shows toward elocution is due, in part, to the prominence of the *written* material medium in the academemented circles in which such theorizing takes place. Here, written material dominates critical attention as both means of production and object of analysis. Additionally, one suspects that the wariness toward elocution is grounded in the fear of the re-emergence of the *technē* tradition in which rules of performance became the dominant concern of rhetoric instruction (as it now is with the advent of 'composition studies' as the major forum of rhetorical research and application in America) [which is *not* meant to be a criticism from a superior 'theorist' position]. This is an amazing turn of events for elocution, which Antonio Capmany once called 'such an absolute necessity to the orator that without it he

205. Cf. Ian Thompson, 'Rhetoric and the Passions, 1760–1800', in Vickers (ed.), *Rhetoric Revalued*, pp. 143-47.

206. See the fascinating Gorgianic understanding of rhetoric and the inherent *violence* in elocution and language by Roger Moss, 'The Case for Sophistry', in Vickers (ed.), *Rhetoric Revalued*, pp. 207-24.

is incapable of producing his ideas, and all his other talents, however great they may be, are entirely useless'.[207] As one scholar has put it, 'modern disapproval of stylistic rhetoric…is wholly unhistorical. If you cannot pick up a list of the figures and read it through avidly, thinking of all the instances of their application and re-creation in Petrarch or Racine or Shakespeare or Milton, *then you ought not to be studying rhetoric.*'[208]

Perelman and Olbrechts-Tyteca are in fact aware of the impact of questions of style and delivery on argumentation when they discuss not only the argumentative use of figures and the role of modalities, but also the selection and presentation of data.[209] Wuellner, too, in spite of his vociferous condemnation of stylistics and the *technē* tradition as the tenacious presence of 'rhetoric restrained'[210] recognizes the role of elocution (through his interest in semiotics, perhaps even his interest in materiality) in a theory of rhetoric which views modalities and indices in the context of power and argumentation. The exploration of style and delivery could become an important component in the analysis of the function of power in various discourse forms, *if and only if* it returns to argumentation and persuasion as the 'context' in which to analyze and critique its presence. In particular, by concentrating on the *materiality* of the 'text', we can begin to note some functionally powerful factors in the form and content of social discourse: the advent of electronic multimedia and its reduction, indeed almost *elimination* of complex narrative development in favor of rapid and encompassing imaging. Here one could seek to describe the ideological function not only of the content, but of the impact-stylistic rapid-editing features and its non-linear (hence anti-rationalist) imaging within a context of consumerist culture, for example. One could also note the (un)'intentional' psychological effects of visual imaging and stylistics: the relationship between 'psy-

207. Antonio de Capmany, *Filosofia de la eloquencia* (Madrid, 1777), p. 30, translated by and quoted in Don Abbot, 'Antonio de Capmany's Theory of Human Nature', in Vickers (ed.), *Rhetoric Revalued*, pp. 149-56 (152).

208. Brian Vickers, 'On the Practicalities of Renaissance Rhetoric', in Vickers (ed.), *Rhetoric Revalued*, pp. 133-41 (137). Emphasis mine.

209. Perelman and Olbrechts-Tyteca, *The New Rhetoric*, § 2, Parts 2 and 3, pp. 115-83.

210. Wuellner, 'Where Is Rhetorical Criticism Taking Us?' pp. 450-51.

chology' and rhetoric has long been noted[211] and with modern emphasis upon the social origins of repression one can advocate the connection of particularly (also Marxist) psychoanalytic literary criticism[212] with a rhetoric of power. There is an important potential field of exploration to be pondered here rhetorically through stylistic analysis (but not exclusively so).

But perhaps the most important lacuna isn't so much the absence of certain theoretical issues of rhetorical interest (though this is important), as it is perhaps the relative lack of direction so far shown in this exploration: as a theory of rhetorical analysis, critique and performance, we have explored a vast array of potential issues confronting a critic who wishes to concern him/herself with the function of power in the rhetoric of 'discourse'. Hence, the necessity of exploring the wide variety of analytical *foci*, approaches and perspectives which multiply exponentially the realms for analysis. The theory, as we have so far outlined it, is *musefully* presented in its broadest form in order to display the full potential of individual applications in critical encounter. If it had been done in any other way, this rhetoric of power would not have been a *symphonic* theory. In part, the *[un]intentionality* of this lack of direction should and could be carried on to further and more [il]legitimate extremes, of denying the attempts at rationalizing reality, which is but one more imposition of violence upon 'the groundlessness of everyday life'. The effort so far directed, in spite of its inherent proclivity, has not been hysterical enough: it still resists exploration into and explication of 'the uncanny—that is, the nonrational desire-in-language'.[213] It is partly this to which Ernesto Grassi refers when he demands that all philosophy be understood as grounded in the 'vulgar', the 'inverted world' of irony and the joke, the metaphorical, the 'passionate' and

211. Cf. the brief survey in Brian Vickers, 'On the Practicalities of Renaissance Rhetoric', in Vickers (ed.), *Rhetoric Revalued*, pp. 133-41.

212. See Eagleton, *Literary Theory*, pp. 151-93; the collection of essays in Hunter (ed.), *Seduction and Theory*; but also the demand for the advent of the hysterical and uncanny in any rhetorical and ethical theorizing and historicizing by Vitanza, 'Open Letter'. Cf. also 'Psychoanalytic Criticism', in Castelli *et al.*, *Postmodern Bible*, pp. 187-224.

213. Vitanza, 'Open Letter', p. 257.

'tragic' of language-existence, instead of pursuing rationalist (acontextual, ahistorical) attempts at discerning Being.[214] The point is to let the chaos of the repressed and suppressed be given a chance to be expressed; to *musefully* celebrate/cerebrate the fact that if you try to organize totally, 'you end up paradoxically with the equivalent of chance'.[215]

Unfortunately, the immediate demands of institutional power and discourse practices will continue to limit and restrict such musings [for now]. Here is one more example of P.J. Rabinowitz's theory of 'objectivity' and 'canonization': not only are there conventions that are instituted 'before' my reading of the following four scholars (hence, there are 'wrong' and 'right' ways of reading), but part of these conventions are constituted around and help to constitute concepts of 'canonical' forms of analysis and interpretation; but, as he states, 'canonization is, in large part, a matter of misapplication'.[216]

Hence, the more immediate issue is to begin to concentrate our gaze on the particular issue at hand. And, indeed, a rhetoric of power must look for guides governing the application and insights of the several rhetorical issues we have been exploring within the 'context' of its application: each application is *symbiotically* and *symphonically* related to institutional expectations (previous rhetorical performances; audience values, institutional structures), objects of analysis (both their form and content; their 'canonicity' and inter-'text'uality), explicit goals of the analyst (not just ideological location, but the explicit limitation and direction intentionally adapted), and form of analysis (= rhetorical performance). In particular, a rhetoric of power uses these 'contextual' boundaries not as limitations constraining analytical focus and direction, but as springboards for *museful* participation in their critical *demise*: all scholarship is 'interested' scholarship, and it is the purpose of a rhetoric of power not only to expose the ideological basis for a given institutional (not just academemented institutions, but political, social, economic and religious as well) praxis, but also to note its concrete structural and *rhetorical* form. Any critique of power has to be

---

214. Cf. Ernesto Grassi, 'Why Rhetoric Is Philosophy', *Philosophy & Rhetoric* 20.2 (1987), pp. 68-78.

215. P.J. Rabinowitz, *Before Reading: Narrative Conventions and the Politics of Interpretation* (Ithaca, NY: Cornell University Press, 1987), p. 50.

216. Rabinowitz, *Before Reading*, p. 43.

located in the systems of power that perpetrate and perpetuate the dissemination of the ideology which acts as its foundation. Philosophies, ideologies rarely, if ever, perpetrate themselves by ephemeral, supernatural means (although they may be ascribed to the supernatural). They are set in place by forces both disseminated and incarnated in social systems, and the structures which are extensions of these systems can and must be identified, their characteristic workings analyzed, and the impacts they have upon discourse explored and noted. Along with Mailloux, we note in a rhetoric of power that one important entry into the analysis of structural and systemic power is in the assumed values, presumptions, 'truths', 'facts' and argumentative strategies sanctioned as the 'appropriate' means of pursuing persuasion.

Our particular effort to this end is the question of power as manifested in rhetorical-critical efforts of interpretation of the Bible. It is particularly with respect to the advent of new philosophies of rhetoric and their *lack* of impact in biblical exegetical discourse embracing rhetorical criticism that I wish to direct our attention: even among those scholars whose advocacy of decentralizing and destabilizing modern, American conservative interpretation and hermeneutics of the Bible, and who see in rhetorical criticism the means for this end, nevertheless *arrest* interpretive authority to a singular historical act which becomes the authoritative touchstone for biblical interpretation. I want to explore *how* such claims are made (by exploring the hermeneutical limitation of the 'meaningful' interaction of 'texts' and their 'contexts') and then begin to reflect upon the *institutional* and '*environmental*' factors that govern this rhetorical praxis (and which are in turn supported through such rhetorical praxis). In the end, I will ponder the de(con)structive implications of biblical interpretation noticed with the insights garnered here through our exploration of a rhetoric of power. The *demise* of the discipline is paradoxically necessary for its survival as a *lack* of discipline which conspires to overthrow [like Jericho, like Babel] biblical exegesis.

Chapter 4

THE (NEW) RHETORICAL CRITICISM(S)
AND
NEW TESTAMENT EXEGESIS

'I must thank you for your hospitality, Comrade Wooster,' [old Row-
botham] said.

'Oh, not at all! Only too glad—'

'Hospitality!' snorted the man Butt, going off in my ear like a depth-
charge. 'I wonder the food didn't turn to ashes in our mouths! Eggs!
Muffins! Sardines! All wrung from the bleeding lips of the starving
poor!'

'Oh, I say! What a beastly idea!'

'I will send you some literature on the subject of the Cause,' said old
Rowbotham. 'And soon, I hope, we shall see you at one of our little
meetings.'

Jeeves came in to clear away, and found me sitting among the ruins. It
was all very well for Comrade Butt to knock the food, but he had pretty
well finished the ham; and if you had shoved the remainder of the jam
into the bleeding lips of the starving poor it would hardly have made
them sticky.

'Comrade Bingo'
P.G. Wodehouse

As we turn now to the application of this proposed rhetoric of power,
we keep in mind [I shall continue to assert these points, like a map, like
a guide to the lengthy terrain ahead, to keep our bearings] the tension
between the application of rhetorical theory as a tool of critical analytics, and the insight of such application upon further theoretical
development. The purpose of this chapter, then, is not simply to critique the function of rhetorical criticism of the New Testament. It is
also to provide the foundation for further analysis which will seek to
explicate and elaborate systems and contexts of power (non-Chapter
4e) contexts which will provide insight for reflection upon the theory of

power itself and its [de(con)structive] impact upon biblical criticism [and itself!] (Chapter 5). This is the *museful* function of rhetorical theory: a necessary, self-reflecting mechanism wherein the contextuality and historicity of a rhetoric of power is given a means for ideological location and (self-) evaluation.

But this is not all. Indeed, keeping in mind the emphasis appropriately made by Kathleen Welch,[1] theoretical development for analysis cannot be the *telos* of rhetorical analytics, but must be grounded in the pragmatic tradition of rhetoric. Rhetoric has always shared a prescriptive tradition of composition, providing the means whereby persuasive presentation (traditionally, *discourse*) could be invented, arranged and performed. This is not *exactly* a tradition in which we shall participate; that is, the kinds of prescriptions *we* shall make will not necessarily help to further the institutional goals of composition courses and fields. It is, however, to the *pragmatic* effects that we shall constantly be turning, to the institutional implications of our analysis upon both biblical studies, rhetorical criticism *and* to our rhetoric of power. These implications will, indeed, be impactful.

We shall begin by pondering the rhetorical assumptions of biblical exegetical scholarship [is there any other?] with the help of Perelman and Olbrechts-Tyteca: in biblical studies both the framework and starting points of argumentation have been governed by the traditional and restrictive 'needs' of the academented institutionalization (definition) of the discipline. These 'needs' have caused the field to experience a ghetto-ization both from the academented world and from the ecclesiastical systems [not to mention from the even more nebulous concept/ activity of religiously based 'values'] of American society. In order best to understand this development, and hence to point to possible new directions (institutional definitions) for the discipline which modern rhetoric (both theories and critical methods) can offer as a pragmatic [de(con)structive] response to this context, it is necessary first to consider how the recent advent of rhetorical criticism [the latest methodological fad] makes its manifestation in the current guild of New Testament exegesis.

It is my intention here to focus upon the work of four critics whose work applies this (new) method called 'rhetorical criticism'. I do so in order to identify the hermeneutical authority granted by the discipline's

---

1.   Kathleen E. Welch, *The Contemporary Reception of Classical Rhetoric: Appropriations of Ancient Discourse* (Hillsdale, NJ: Lawrence Erlbaum, 1990).

rhetorical discourse to historical-critical interpretation. What I hope to make present here in this chapter is that every rhetorical critic we shall encounter [and these four are among the most vocal advocates of the impact of rhetoric upon the discipline of biblical exegesis] restricts the critical function of rhetoric to a methodological tool that continues to operate within, and indeed reinforce and solidify the hegemony of, the tradition-discursive frameworks of the discipline. Rhetoric, in the variety of ways in which it is used, in the variety of perspectives with which it is engaged, simply serves [either 'intentionally' or 'logically'] to shore up disciplinary boundaries and the hermeneutical hegemony of historical reconstruction. This is a new twist on the concept of a 'rhetoric restrained', one whose function strikes me as particularly odd given the explicit interpretive goal of these scholars to make *more relevant* the function and (ab)use of the biblical text within contemporary systems of repressive power, that is, the call for greater accessibility and disciplinary 'democratization' [even if not un-limitation].

To put it differently: what sets these scholars apart from those whom we have surveyed (Chapter 2) is their understanding of the potential for rhetoric to extend [to the breaking point] the disciplinary boundaries of biblical interpretation, that is, they embrace a *critical* turn, based on the insights of modern rhetorical theory, which not only concerns the biblical text itself, but the disciplinary practices regarding its interpretation: each of them considers the potential of power generated by and generating systems of 'entextualization' and physical control [church dogma, church structure, academented systems of credentialling, but also legal and social imposition of biblical ethics] within both the academented and ecclesial pursuit of biblical interpretation. Each acknowledges the need for biblical studies' reassessment of its role in both society and academnia. In other words, each of them speaks of the potential for rhetoric to fulfill its task as a tradition dedicated to the exploration into (and performance of) persuasion, argumentation, conviction, dissuasion, power, etc.

Nevertheless, as we shall see, they cannot shake off the shackles of the discursive practices which have defined the discipline of 'biblical studies'. They continue to reinforce disciplinary assumptions [and their own position within its structures] by focusing upon the centrality of historical reconstruction to the interpretive moment. This will culminate in two rather interesting results: (1) through the (new) rhetorical criticism(s) they will stake claim to an authoritative liberal ethic at the foundation of Christian social formation and discourse practices; and (2) methodological and hermeneutical access to such interpretation perpetuates, indeed *shores up*, traditional biblical studies institutional practice [as we shall explore in greater detail in non-Chapter 4e].

An awareness of hermeneutic authority granted to biblical exegetical institutional interests and the academented pursuit of antiquarian historiography, and its limitation of the hermeneutical concept of 'context' and 'text' in the generation of authoritative meaning, will become an important starting point for delimiting the analysis of the (new) rhetorical criticism(s) through a rhetoric of power.

a. *Burton Mack*

For Mack, the development of thought regarding the question of 'text' and 'context' in his exegetical endeavor will be explored not chronologically, but thematically. His pursuit for a new proposal for the reconstruction of Christian origins is introduced and outlined in his article, 'Gilgamesh and the Wizard of Oz'. It is given theoretical and methodological justification in *Rhetoric and the New Testament*. His method is further employed and conclusions explored in *Patterns of Persuasion in the Gospel*, co-authored with Dr Vernon Robbins. His conclusions are then given full expression in *Myth of Innocence*, and later elaborated [and somewhat emended, at least in tone and emphasis] in *The Lost Gospel*.

Survey of Methodology and Results
'Gilgamesh and the Wizard of Oz'[2] is a programmatic essay by Burton Mack in which he presents the direction of, and the reasons for, his particular interest in the social history of early Christianity. Written as a reflection upon the first *Jesus Seminar*, held March 1985, it ponders both the nature of historical-critical inquiry within biblical studies and how to present its findings to the public (a stated goal of the *Jesus Seminar*). My interest in this essay lies in its fascinating portrayal, and critique, of biblical critical scholarship as a quest for origins, as a hero's journey and return. Born out of the Enlightenment's call for reason and

---

2.   *Forum* 1.2 (1985), pp. 3-29.

scientific method, New Testament scholars have set out 'to study critically the foundational documents of Christianity, to assess the beginnings, to define the message, isolate the event, uncover the moment
when it started...' The goal is nothing short of determining 'the origins
behind and beneath the surface of the text...'[3]

Mack here surveys the history of achievement of this quest, pointing
to the need/desire of biblical scholars to determine the unique character,
that decisively transformative event that marked the mysterious origins
of Christianity. This extremely difficult goal was thought to have been
reached on numerous occasions, with several theories achieving prominence only later to be discounted. Scholars have looked to Jesus'
personality and ethical teaching, to apocalyptic, to Paul's preaching, to
the experience of the presence of the resurrected Lord in the community's liturgy, to the *kerygma*, to the passion narrative and most recently
to the parables. In every case, though, once it was found that those
distinctive qualities of Christian origins were not so distinctive after all,
they lost their attraction to scholars.[4]

It is the quality of uniqueness that drives biblical scholarship, regardless of the terms, methods and disciplines applied. 'It is a mysterious,
miraculous event of radical inversion, understood to be creative of
something brand new, that New Testament scholars want to determine.'[5] It is precisely this event and its quest that is mythic to begin
with, derived from the very Christian myth it seeks to anchor. And it is
here that Mack most lucidly summarizes the thesis he will spend the
next several years developing and refining.

He locates the mysterious event within the Christian myth-ritual function of the Gospel, as first formulated by Mark. Although this Gospel
was not perhaps intended for liturgical use, its myth-ritual combination
functioned as such.[6] Construction of churches at those locations depicted in the Gospel, with liturgies and rituals developed and cycled in
order to remember the events traditionally said to have taken place at
those locations, helped to foster and reinforce the notion of the Gospel

3.   Mack, 'Gilgamesh and the Wizard of Oz', p. 9.
4.   Mack, 'Gilgamesh and the Wizard of Oz', pp. 9-10.
5.   Mack, 'Gilgamesh and the Wizard of Oz', p. 14.
6.   Mack, 'Gilgamesh and the Wizard of Oz', p. 15. The following is a summary of a series of lectures delivered by Jonathan Z. Smith entitled, 'To Take
Place: Jerusalem as a Focus of Ritual', at Brown University, Providence, Rhode
Island, in March 1985.

as story of origins. The pilgrimage became the means of reliving the christ-event as originary moment.[7] Once Palestine fell to the Persian/ Islamic Empire, the church itself (i.e. both Rome and cathedral) took on the role of pilgrimage center, with liturgies, rituals and new symbolic structures substituting as re-enactments of mythic origins and events. When the Reformation replaced these traditions with the Bible, however, the pilgrimage was transformed from one of symbolic re-enactment to one of historical reconstruction. The notion of Gospel as myth of origins remained intact, but was now transformed through the Enlightenment as the object of scientific and historical research.[8]

Mack suggests that the Christian pilgrimage (events of origin) was read into the ancient epic of the hero's quest, now [mis-]understood as a quest for pristine beginnings.[9] The impact of this interpretation upon the scholarly imagination has been profound.

> As the Enlightenment dawned, and the questions about religion, culture, ethnos, language, history and scientific evolution emerged, it was the Christian epic that provided the outline for classifying everything in terms of a development of stages from a single point of origination …Thus the illusion of critical research into the origins and history of cultures was born. Biblical scholarship was also born in this mix. One myth (Christian epic) set the pattern and agenda. Another (hero quest) guided the critical imagination back to nail things down.[10]

Unfortunately, there is simply no evidence, no data for a 'crucial, unique, radically transformative moment of origination for Christianity—neither a person, word, vision, miracle or event. All designations referring to such an origination (e.g. Easter) merely demonstrate its mythic status. New Testament scholarship has been devoted to an impossible task, the critical determination of the historical reality of a myth.'[11]

What Mack calls for instead is a recognition of the importance of the discoveries made so far, but ignored and devalued as irrelevant to the quest. What scholars have found in the New Testament texts, that is, 'the literary forms, symbols, images, fantasies, polemics, poetics, pronouncements, rites, rules, practices, liturgical texts, threats, expression

---

7. Mack, 'Gilgamesh and the Wizard of Oz', p. 16.
8. Mack, 'Gilgamesh and the Wizard of Oz', p. 15.
9. Mack, 'Gilgamesh and the Wizard of Oz', p. 16.
10. Mack, 'Gilgamesh and the Wizard of Oz', p. 16.
11. Mack, 'Gilgamesh and the Wizard of Oz', p. 20.

of desire, and projections of ideals',[12] is an amazing collection of evidence concerning the struggle for identification and existence in a formative period of social history.

It is here that Mack formulates specifically his driving theoretical interest: the description of the social history of the Jesus and christ movements which eventually led to the formulation of the myth of a single point of origins. 'Instead of trying to relate all of our logia and traditions (from Jesus to the gospel) to a single mysterious moment, we should try to relate them to the many human social movements.'[13] The situation was highly complex, born of concerns both constructive and polemical, reflecting a great variety of traditions which were selected, rearranged and given specific purpose at specific junctures of the social history of these many groups. To reduce this complexity to a single point of origins is simply not possible. To discover these manifold social junctures, however, is not only possible, but may even help both biblical scholars *and* others outside the field to recognize the presence, impact and function of the Christian myth within our society.[14]

But how are 'we' to recognize the role of myth in these developing traditions? Mack assures 'us' that 'we' have all the tools necessary to bring this about. New Testament critics have traditionally been interested in analysis at the level of 'ideas, imagination, rhetoric, discourse and literature'.[15] Nevertheless, these have not been adequately grounded at the level of human social history.[16] By exploring the incongruity of the relationship between what people say they are after and are doing, on the one hand (social), and how they rationalize it, on the other (ideological), 'we' may be in a position to explain the developing social conflicts, the plural movements, the manifold struggles for authority which constitute the tradition.[17] *Thus, textual rhetoric firmly embedded within social history will not only help 'us' to discern the trajectory of the developing traditions, but will also help 'us' to describe the contexts (important social junctures) from which they originated and by which they may have been altered in order to continue to be relevant.*

12. Mack, 'Gilgamesh and the Wizard of Oz', p. 20.
13. Mack, 'Gilgamesh and the Wizard of Oz', p. 21.
14. Mack, 'Gilgamesh and the Wizard of Oz', pp. 23, 27.
15. Mack, 'Gilgamesh and the Wizard of Oz', p. 22.
16. Mack, 'Gilgamesh and the Wizard of Oz', pp. 22, 24.
17. Mack, 'Gilgamesh and the Wizard of Oz', pp. 21-22.

This is a multifaceted project for Mack, a *traditionsgeschichtliche* (tradition-history) enterprise which includes a reduction of a saying or tradition to a core and an explanation of social contexts that can account for every stage of the performance until it reaches the form found in the Gospel setting. The example given here is the saying about the physician in Mk 2.17a.[18] It is only the knowledge of social context and the history of social formation around and from Jesus that would help 'us' to see that as a historical remembrance certain features are problematic: the presence of the Pharisees, the question being posed to the disciples, the language about sinners. If 'we' strip the story of these features, 'we' reduce it to a *chreia* with features very similar to those found attributed to Cynics: a situation leads to an accusation concerning a violation of social conventions on Jesus' part. His response is pointed and clever, appearing to admit to the terms of the charge, but twisting them in such a way that he turns it into a critique of these same conventions and norms. There is no great ideological battle here, no defensive apology, no prophetic announcement. It is simply a question of what constitutes table fellowship. What social context would generate this story? Can 'we' work out a social trajectory of meal sharing that would help 'us' locate this story at some formative juncture of a group's history? Could this go back to Jesus, to Jesus movements, to the Hellenistic christ cult? What impact would this have upon 'our' understanding of the history of these groups? Where would this fit into the development of their social formation? Or could this story have been created, complete with Pharisees, disciples, righteous and sinners? If not, what would the circumstances have been that would have brought about this later elaboration? 'The point must be clear. Our texts need *social* contexts. If some can be reconstructed, a very tellable story of the difference Jesus made, of how the gospel came to be, and what it has to do with real people might be possible.'[19]

Here we see the formative stages of a process fleshed out in later works: knowledge of textual dynamics (rhetoric, intertextuality within contemporary history, etc.) helps 'us' to discern layers of tradition.[20]

18. The following is a summary of the discussion in Mack, 'Gilgamesh and the Wizard of Oz', pp. 24-26.

19. Mack, 'Gilgamesh and the Wizard of Oz', p. 27.

20. This is not exactly correct, as at this stage there is a lot of 'social formation' history informing his discussion. While an explicit justification for this methodological move does not seem to be forthcoming, he will develop this aspect of his

Each layer or performance reflects a stage of social formation. The text becomes a means whereby 'we' can reconstruct a plausible social setting, that is, a setting which would help 'us' to understand why such a performance was necessary. The result would be a description of the complex history of social development of the many groups whose traditions are brought together in the Gospels.

Perhaps we can best understand the important theoretical justification for his move from 'text' to 'context' by reviewing his work, ***Rhetoric and the New Testament***. It is in particular the redefinition and reinvention of rhetoric brought about by the publication [and English translation] of Perelman and Olbrechts-Tyteca's *The New Rhetoric* that becomes the foundation of a method which is interested in 'text' as social, historical and cultural phenomenon. According to Mack, these authors provided the theoretical basis for a method attempting to bridge the New Critical and structuralist gap between 'text' and historical 'context'. They did so by emphasizing three aspects of communication as approached through rhetorical theory.

- They defined rhetoric itself as a theory of argumentation. This ran contrary to nearly 2000 years of development that emphasized rhetoric as style and ornamentation, a phenomenon that arose during the Second Sophistic out of the impact upon civic institutions by the rise of imperial Rome,[21] was given further impetus by the encroaching dominance of grammar in medieval education,[22] and culminated in the Ramist educational

model more thoroughly with reference to ancient rhetorical systems, especially concentrating upon the *progymnasmata* and *chreia* elaboration exercises prevalent at the time and location of the developing traditions. This in and of itself, without worrying about the circularity involved when discerning textual traditions in order to find periods of social formation by reference to these periods of social formation, is a problematic move.

21. See James J. Murphy, *Rhetoric in the Middle Ages: A History of Rhetorical Theory from St. Augustine to the Renaissance* (Berkeley: University of California Press, 1974), pp. 35-41. With the elimination of the civic forum as a place for deliberative debate, one of rhetoric's major social occasions was lost. Furthermore, the courtroom setting soon became the domain of legal specialists. This left rhetoric only those settings for encomiastic speeches (funeral orations, speech competitions, etc.), and soon the practice of declamation, or discourse upon a stated theme, became dominant in rhetorical education and practice.

22. For an in-depth survey of the development of prescriptive grammar in medieval educational tradition, which soon took over not only instruction in syntax, but

reforms which eliminated from rhetoric's purview the system of invention. In contrast, by emphasizing argumentation Perelman and Olbrechts-Tyteca revived the traditional classification of rhetoric as the 'art of persuasion', and revived the centrality of invention to rhetorical theory and practice.

- Perelman and Olbrechts-Tyteca emphasized the impact of an audience upon argumentative dynamic and effectiveness. They worked out the various factors that impinge upon the speaker–audience relationship in terms that describe and distinguish socio-historical circumstances. According to Mack, this is done particularly in the discussion of the rhetorical situation [Bitzer! *not* Perelman and Olbrechts-Tyteca], that specific constellation of argumentative circumstances giving impetus to persuasive discourse. Once the central argumentative issue is identified, the impact of both speaker and audience upon the strategy of persuasion can be assessed. The effect of an audience to influence argumentation is not limited to the position taken by the speaker upon a given issue, but includes the dynamics of the explicit argumentative appeals, the examples chosen, the premises left unstated, the universal appeals to reason, the use of commonplaces and rhetorical figures. All of these, and many other aspects of the rhetoric in and of the performance, reflect the speaker's assessment of persuasive strategies needed to move the audience, the socio-historical context from and to which the argument is addressed, thereby immersing 'the study of speech events in social situations'.[23]

- The ability to reconstruct the impact of social setting upon communication opens a door which had hitherto remained a locked barrier between literary and social theories. Within New Testament scholarship, it revives the interest in understanding the text's *Sitz im Leben* and its effect upon textual meaning. [(A)*musingly* interesting to ponder the return of the *Sitz im Leben* concept of form criticism, and the nearly identical form-critical turn which much of rhetorical scholarship

metrics, rhythmics and even rhetorical disposition, see the discussion in Murphy, *Rhetoric in the Middle Ages*, pp. 135-93.

23. B. Mack, *Rhetoric and the New Testament* (Minneapolis: Fortress Press, 1990), p. 15.

has taken in its focus upon arrangement and style.] It also furthers the interest of those who wished to study the text as a means of reconstructing the social history of its context.[24] [Text as window; rhetoric as tool to be used and discarded.]

- By combining within the concept of persuasion both argumentative and contextual factors Perelman and Olbrechts-Tyteca succeeded in emphasizing the rhetorical nature of all communication. Rhetoric is now 'at the center of a social theory of language'.[25] It becomes a description of the rules of social discourse, of the language games we enact when interacting with one another. 'Rhetorical theory defines the stakes as nothing less than the negotiation of our lives together. A criticism based upon such a theory of rhetoric might hope to get to the heart of the human matter.'[26]

In fact, the emphasis upon argumentation as espoused by the New Rhetoric is very similar to the perspective taken by ancient rhetoric on the nature of social discourse. Old rhetoric was also a treatise on argumentation developed by careful observation of the means of persuasion used by those in the public forum. Distillation of practice brought forth prescriptive rules which were tested and fine-tuned in the circumstances of discussion, debate and display. Soon a discipline was formed which sought to instruct people in the art of speaking persuasively. Handbooks were created which contained lessons in mimicry, in argumentative strategy, in elaboration, in presentation. Syllabuses prescribing the full dimension of the education of an orator were produced, an education which soon took on nearly mythical proportions [esp. in Quintilian]: since rhetorical skill could be used in any topic at almost any time and in front of any audience, the orator needed to learn not only the basics of language and skills in presentation, but was also required to be well versed in mathematics, government, astronomy, law, ethics, philosophy. Ancient rhetoric, like its modern parallel, sought to describe the persuasive dimension of social discourse and prescribe rules for effective argumentation, and saw its domain extending to every communicative exchange.

24. Mack, *Rhetoric and the New Testament*, p. 15.
25. Mack, *Rhetoric and the New Testament*, p. 16.
26. Mack, *Rhetoric and the New Testament*, p. 16.

It is this last point, that in the New Rhetoric 'we' have a method very close to that which flourished during the time of the developing Jesus and christ movements, that provides the theoretical justification for the move Mack makes from rhetorical assessment to social reconstruction of discourse of Christianity. If the New Rhetoric's emphasis upon invention and argumentation is a rearticulation of ancient rhetorical theory and practice, then 'a modern criticism commends itself that is curiously appropriate to the culture of context within which the literature under investigation was written'. This allows the biblical scholar interested in historiography to resuscitate ancient preceptive rhetoric as descriptions of discourse in a 'society conscious of its culture',[27] hence as social histories. [It also gives the scholar a weighty justification for exploring the texts with this particular methodological tool.]

Therefore, according to Mack, Perelman and Olbrechts-Tyteca have provided a theoretical basis for discussing the *social* dynamic of language by reviving the ancient rhetorical notion of persuasive discourse. Ancient *prescription* regarding effectiveness of persuasive strategy becomes for Mack, through its affiliation with modern rhetorical theory, *description* regarding social context of argumentative exchange. Rhetoric provides the means whereby texts are turned into the data necessary for describing the developing social issues of early Christianity.

To do so requires knowledge and appreciation of the standards of argumentative exchange as described in the rhetorical handbooks and treatises extant at the time of writing of the New Testament. By being able to compare and contrast[!] the strategies of persuasion used within the biblical traditions with those dominant in the culture, 'we' not only discover argumentative structures in the writings of the New Testament heretofore overlooked, but can discern the unique[!] qualities of the developing Christian *paideia*. Mack therefore sets out (1) to describe [argumentatively] the history of the theory and practice of rhetoric in an effort to show how its pervasive impact upon culture could effect the traditions of the New Testament; and (2) to distill from rhetorical handbooks a common, if not standard, core of rhetorical theory[28] covering

27. Mack, *Rhetoric and the New Testament*, p. 17.
28. George Kennedy, *Classical Rhetoric and its Christian and Secular Tradition from Ancient to Modern Times* (Chapel Hill: University of North Carolina Press, 1980), p. 89, concludes: 'Theophrastus' work on style and delivery, the study of figures and periods by writers like Demetrius, and Hermagoras' contributions,

the methods, genres and argumentative patterns in order to show the presence of rhetorical composition and the particular forms of argumentative strategy present in the New Testament. The definitive point upon which his analysis of social origins hangs is that there was a standard Greco-Roman preceptive rhetorical practice recognizable throughout the various Hellenistic cultures whose normative function allows him to contrast the particular features of early Christian rhetoric. *If this was the case, and if 'we' can therefrom find unique argumentative features in the rhetoric of the New Testament, then 'we' can extract unique social issues facing the Christian communities as they wrestled and argued among themselves and with other social groups.* This is the heart, the justification and foundation for all the further socio-historical elaboration of early Christianity he will explore.

When he sets out to describe the history and development of ancient rhetoric, it is therefore not surprising that he depicts a monolithic view of both rhetoric and Greco-Roman culture: ancient rhetoric emerged in the sixth and fifth centuries BCE among the Greek city-states as a result of their new democratic governing and social structures. Oligarchies and citizen councils provided contexts for debate over state policies and litigation, while civic-religious festivals were occasions for celebratory speeches. By the beginning of the fourth century BCE, an awareness of successful speaking techniques had grown to the point that rhetorical theory and practice began to flourish.[29]

---

including stasis theory, largely complete technical rhetoric. Throughout the rest of antiquity the same basic body of theory, accompanied by exercises in composition and declamation, was taught to Greek and Roman boys. There are variations in emphasis, terminology, and a very few new theories favored by some authorities. Most rhetorical handbooks seem to have set forth the complete system, but there were separate works on aspects of style, important for the history of literary rhetoric. This standard theory of classical rhetoric, as taught from around 150 BC to the end of antiquity [s]ome moderns call Ciceronian rhetoric, since it was known in Western Europe largely through writings of Cicero, but it was also known in the East, and not from Cicero.'

See also the thorough discussion in Stanley Bonner, *Education in Ancient Rome: From the Elder Cato to the Younger Pliny* (Berkeley: University of California Press, 1977), esp. Chapter 18.

29. For greater exploration into the three distinctive traditions (sophistical, philosophical and technical) and their impact upon one another throughout antiquity, cf. Kennedy, *Classical Rhetoric*, esp. pp. 18-119.

The public forum in which rhetoric had up to this point thrived, how-ever, saw tremendous changes as a result of the rise of Alexander and his aggressive campaign of Hellenism which took place throughout the conquered lands of the eastern Mediterranean. The Greek cities which were established as the primary means of the dissemination of Greek culture were no longer independent city-states, but were under imperial control. The new political structures created subtle shifts in the con-texts of judicial, deliberative and epideictic discourse which resulted in changes within rhetorical theory and practice. Greater emphasis was placed upon style and oratorical finesse, found in a new speech form known as 'declamation', a rehearsed speech used in a situation calling for rhetorical display. Deliberative rhetoric was now constrained to classroom and debate, since the circumstances of democratic discussion of governing policy were severely restricted. Judicial proceedings were complicated by question of jurisdiction and the option of appeal.[30] As the political circumstances of the Greek, then Roman, Empires altered the context and nature of the traditional domains of rhetoric, theory and practice were inexorably domesticated to sustain and strengthen impe-rial culture.[31] What had once been a thriving exploration into the many forms of oratorical persuasion in contexts of free debate and display [in a particular culture and society] had now been called into the service of conservation of that culture. The theories of persuasion now empha-sized the use of appeals to traditional values, cultural and social history, and canonized literary sources in the very construction of argumen-tative strategy.[32] *As this strategy became a standard technique, rhetoric was reduced to the theory and practice of persuasion within and for the sake of conserving imperial culture.*

The significance of such a development in rhetorical theory for the cultural context of the New Testament traditions becomes clear only when 'we' keep in mind the influence of Greek culture and education throughout the Mediterranean. The efforts by Alexander for the dis-semination of Hellenism were highly successful even throughout Palestine. While it has traditionally been thought that the main centers for education and culture were located in important imperial cities such as Athens, Alexandria, Antioch, Rhodes, etc., it would not be accurate

---

30. Mack, *Rhetoric and the New Testament*, pp. 28-29.
31. Mack, *Rhetoric and the New Testament*, p. 29.
32. Mack, *Rhetoric and the New Testament*, pp. 43-47.

to limit the impact of Hellenism strictly to these cities and their immediate surroundings. As Mack points out, the recognition by the ancients
of significant scholars and philosophers from smaller Hellenistic cities
such as Gadara[33] suggests that the influence of Greek culture was pervasive throughout the many regions of the eastern Mediterranean.[34]

Furthermore, Greek culture (*paideia*) was disseminated by Greek
education (*paideia*), whose structures became standard and included at
the secondary level a rudimentary introduction to rhetoric. If rhetoric at
this time developed a standard structure and approach to argumentation, then knowledge of rhetorical theory and practice was standardized
through Greek educational systems. [There were other educational systems, however, i.e. the rabbinic 'houses' and the synagogues throughout the Diaspora come quickly to mind.] In addition, both Greek education and rhetorical discourse were decidedly public affairs, taking
place in marketplace and on street corners [of cities]. Thus, not only the
well educated and professional, but anyone going to market, walking

33. Mack, *Rhetoric and the New Testament*, p. 29.

34. Contra the conclusions of Sean Freyne, *Galilee: From Alexander the Great
to Hadrian* (Wilmington, DE: Michael Glazier; Notre Dame, IN: University of
Notre Dame Press, 1980), esp. pp. 22-200, which argue for a social, economic and
political stratification of the Galilean population throughout this era which would
have hindered a great deal of the impact of Greco-Roman influence upon significant
agrarian segments of the population. The point is not to dispute the power and
influence of Hellenism in the region, but simply to complicate the picture a bit.
Certain segments of the population may implicitly have understood and appreciated
Greco-Roman rhetorical discourse, but not necessarily all of the population. Nor
would this discourse have become the only form of debate or instruction in the
region.

See also Martin Hengel, *Jews, Greeks and Barbarians: Aspects of the
Hellenization of Judaism in the Pre-Christian Period* (Philadelphia: Fortress Press,
1980). Hellenization would have affected various classes and locales differently,
but was not entirely successful at integrating Jewish thought, and apostasy among
Jews was very rare. Educational systems, language, philosophical *Weltanschauung*,
economic and political systems made significant inroads, particularly in Egyptian
and other Diaspora communities (see pp. 93-109), but in Palestine as well (see
pp. 110-26) particularly after the Roman conquest of the region (see pp. 53, 61, 66,
74). Nevertheless, before painting Palestine as a colony successfully integrated into
Greco-Roman culture and values, one has to keep in mind the variety of impact
such cultural imperialism made upon the many different sectors of the population,
and the fact that Judaism continued to maintain its religious and cultural identity
throughout the Mediterranean (see, e.g., pp. 80, 100, 107-108).

the streets, interacting in public became immersed in the techniques of persuasion.[35] It could not be avoided, as speeches by traveling dignitaries, the debates between rhetorical schools, the clever workings of the Sophists, or the public oratorical displays at festivals and games filled the air. People grew to accept and expect (if not explicitly, then implicitly) standard structures of speech forms, debates, and displays.[36]

35. For a thorough discussion on the increase of illiteracy in the Roman Imperium, see William V. Harris, *Ancient Literacy* (Cambridge, MA: Harvard University Press, 1989).

A.S. Wilkins, *Roman Education* (Cambridge: Cambridge University Press, 1905), emphasizes throughout his work an important point regarding the lack of standardization in education, even for those financially able to attend all levels, in the ancient world. See particularly pp. 29, 90. Unfortunately, he is virtually alone in this respect. Indeed, it is typical in treatises concerning education in the ancient world to systematize and consolidate into a standard curriculum the total educational opportunity (primary, grammar and professional schools), available in fact only to a very few, and in particular to emphasize *rhetorical* education. Cf., e.g., Bonner, *Education in Ancient Rome*, who, once hitting upon higher educational stages, focuses exclusively upon rhetorical education and pedagogy; Donald L. Clark, *Rhetoric in Greco-Roman Education* (Morningside Heights, NY: Columbia University Press, 1957), whose whole work is dedicated to a standardized representation of rhetorical education in the ancient world; even Henri I. Marrou, *A History of Education in Antiquity* (trans. George Lamb; New York: New American Library, 1956), and Werner Jaeger, *Paideia: The Ideals of Greek Culture* (3 vols.; trans. Gilbert Highet; New York: Oxford University Press, 1943–45), are guilty of the same homogenizing tendencies.

It may be necessary, if only for the sake of argument, to ask for some sense of subtlety: First, it must be kept in mind that since the Roman Imperium was very late in establishing public schools, education was widely available, but was not necessarily standardized nor widely employed. Second, using treatises written by those whose interests lay in offering the highest educational advancement for students as the standard for determining the education of the general population on the one hand, and the background of the authors of the *Kleinliteratur* (folk literature) of the New Testament on the other, may be problematical. Third, while it is true that *progymnasmata* may have been introduced at the level of grammatical education, we just aren't certain how much exposure to rhetoric the student at this level was given. Thus, while it is apparent that the New Testament authors use the elaboration exercise and other rhetorical structures to develop their narrative, there may be other influences at work, and the differences between the 'standard' rhetoric and 'early Christian' rhetoric may also be one of educational (not to mention cultural, i.e. Hellenistic Jewish) experience.

36. Mack, *Rhetoric and the New Testament*, pp. 30-31 (31). His educational elitism and Hellenophilic tendencies come through quite clearly at times: 'Only by

'To be engulfed in the culture of Hellenism meant to have ears trained for the rhetoric of speech. Rhetoric provided the rules for making critical judgments in the course of all forms of social intercourse.'[37]

It should not come as a surprise, therefore, that when 'we' turn to the argumentation of early Christianity, as represented by the traditions of the New Testament, that 'we' find these same structures and strategies. It should also not come as a surprise that Mack can conclude from this that there was a cognitive awareness of these strategies within traditions and communities from which they came. Therefore, any deviation from these standard structures are calculated, and thereby become the means for discussing the unique[!] features of early Christian discourse. And since Mack's rhetorical theory emphasizes the connection between discourse and context, rhetorical criticism can discover the underlying social issues present as the various communities faced issues of social formation and spoke to them.[38]

It is in particular with regard to the exercises found in the *progymnasmata* that he turns his attention. And this next step, while touched upon and worked through in *Rhetoric and the New Testament*, is more thoroughly explored and expanded upon in **Patterns of Persuasion in the Gospels**, a book which he co-authored with Dr Vernon Robbins. Here he sets out a description of the use and role of the handbooks at the turn of the century, and the state of rhetorical theory which they reflect. These handbooks were used by educators whose students had completed their secondary education, and were ready for an introduction into the advanced stages of rhetorical composition.[39] They provided a structured curriculum with exercises and graded lessons for

gaining some grasp of the theory and practice of rhetoric in a culture *dominated* [?!] by literary education is it possible to understand the rhetorical effectiveness for *Greco-Roman* ears of compositions like the gospels that were crafted in keeping with its rules' (emphases mine). See Mack, 'Elaboration of the Chreia in the Hellenistic School', in B. Mack and V. Robbins, *Patterns of Persuasion in the Gospels* (Sonoma, CA: Polebridge Press, 1989), pp. 31-67 (32). It is perhaps irreverent of me to point out that in fact very few people could afford a literary education at the time, and that there were many other 'ears' than just Greco-Romans who would have been listening to the traditions behind the Gospels and even the Gospels themselves.

37. Mack, *Rhetoric and the New Testament*, p. 31.

38. Mack, *Rhetoric and the New Testament*, p. 94.

39. Mack, 'Elaboration of the Chreia in the Hellenistic School', in Mack and Robbins, *Patterns of Persuasion in the Gospels*, p. 31.

teachers whose students were already familiar with literary studies. In general, these lessons began with a discussion of literary forms (fable, historical episode, anecdote) which were not, strictly speaking, rhetorical in nature, but which did draw upon the experiences of the student provided by previous instruction on writing, reading, grammar.[40] They then introduced new forms and argumentative structures (commonplaces, praise and blame, comparison, speech-in-character, description), eventually leading to highly advanced exercises of presenting and defending a thesis, and introducing new legislation.[41] It was a carefully orchestrated pedagogy from simple to more complex compositional forms, from mimetic to analytical to compositional exercises. Throughout it all the student would be drilled in every important aspect of [Greco-Roman!] rhetorical theory and technique: analysis of issues, construction of persuasive presentation, practice in composition in all major speech types, and even the more fundamental experience in style, delivery and diction.[42] 'Rhetorical purpose governed every exercise, even the more simple ones such as learning to paraphrase and amplify a stock anecdote: students were to learn the means by which speech was effective or persuasive.'[43]

---

40. Mack, 'Elaboration of the Chreia in the Hellenistic School', in Mack and Robbins, *Patterns of Persuasion in the Gospels*, p. 34. Mack also indicates the implications of the integration of literary with rhetorical studies at this stage of the history of rhetorical theory and practice. These include an awareness of the argumentative effectiveness of narrative material, an impact upon contemporary literature which saw composition guided by rhetorical as well as literary concerns, and a consolidation of the structures of argumentation with exercises known as 'elaboration'. In other words, rhetoric expanded to include narrative as well as discursive forms. Therefore, we should not be surprised to find specifically rhetorical structures in the Gospel narratives, structures not strictly limited to Jesus' speeches, but fundamentally controlling sayings collections and 'pronouncement stories'. We may even find in the material a hermeneutical application of 'elaboration' within the Gospels which sought to interpret not just Jewish tradition, but sayings and actions of Jesus. Cf. pp. 63-65. The impact upon the fundamental presuppositions of form criticism this discovery implies will be considered later.

41. Mack, 'Elaboration of the Chreia in the Hellenistic School', in Mack and Robbins, *Patterns of Persuasion in the Gospels*, p. 34.

42. Mack, 'Elaboration of the Chreia in the Hellenistic School', in Mack and Robbins, *Patterns of Persuasion in the Gospels*, p. 35.

43. Mack, 'Elaboration of the Chreia in the Hellenistic School', in Mack and Robbins, *Patterns of Persuasion in the Gospels*, p. 35.

One of the most important exercises for the understanding of the composition of the New Testament Gospels found in the handbooks is the *chreia* and its 'elaboration'. A *chreia* is 'a brief statement or action with pointedness attributed to a definite person or something like a person'.[44] Both maxims and anecdotal rejoinders counted as *chreiai*, and it was their particularly incisive quality that teachers of rhetoric appreciated. They saw in them challenges to conventional logic and argumentative reasoning, as distillations of the essential rhetorical situation in which a speaker displays rhetorical skill and ability to manipulate his way out of a challenging circumstance. 'The chreia could be seen, in other words, as a mini-speech situation complete with speaker, speech, and audience, and evaluated as to its use of rhetorical forms of argumentation.'[45] Thus, some exercises focused upon its internal dynamics, and tested the student's ability to expand the circumstances and response so as to display more clearly its rhetorical power.[46] On the

44. Translated in Robbins, 'Chreia & Pronouncement Story in Synoptic Studies', in Mack and Robbins, *Patterns of Persuasion in the Gospels*, p. 11. *Chreiai* differ from '(1) brief accounts of important circumstances and events in the life of the person, (2) brief accounts of a person's typical behavior, characteristics, virtues, nicknames, and so forth, (3) lists of precepts or wise advice attributed to the person, as well as (4) lists of what Diogenes [Laertius] called a person's views or doctrines that cover a wide variety of philosophical and ethical matters'. Cf. Mack, 'Elaboration of the Chreia in the Hellenistic School', in Mack and Robbins, *Patterns of Persuasion in the Gospels*, p. 46, summarizing Diogenes Laertius.

45. Mack, 'Elaboration of the Chreia in the Hellenistic School', in Mack and Robbins, *Patterns of Persuasion in the Gospels*, p. 36.

46. Mack, 'Elaboration of the Chreia in the Hellenistic School', in Mack and Robbins, *Patterns of Persuasion in the Gospels*, pp. 36-37 lists the various exercises developed by Theon (210.3-6): **recitation** emphasizes clarity of style and diction, and includes the ability to paraphrase; **inflection** is a series of exercises in which the main verb is conjugated by changing the number of the persons referred to in the *chreia*, and the proper nouns are declined by changing the phrases introducing the *chreia*. Both of these, while not immediately relevant to rhetorical development, nevertheless prepared the student for flexibility regarding the use and introduction of a *chreia* within an argument. But it is especially with respect to the exercises of **expansion** and **abbreviation** that the student came to learn the skills of argumentative composition. In the former case, the student was asked to elaborate a brief *chreia* by adding details of circumstance or of important background information regarding the people involved, by developing a greater dialogue structure leading up to the final statement or action. In the latter case, the student would be

other hand, its maxim-like quality allowed it to be expanded externally, and exercises were developed which tested the student's ability to embed the *chreia* appropriately within a greater argumentative structure.[47]

Mack describes the *chreia* tradition in terms of a complex development from an originally incisive argumentative form perhaps first practiced by the Cynics, to a more domesticated tradition in which *chreiai* were selected for use in rhetorical exercises based upon their social appropriateness (Theon, Hermogenes). *Chreiai* themselves, beginning as pithy statements or actions by Cynics [only?] which critique a particular aspect of a given social system, were soon chosen by traditional ethical standards of whether the individual was of good character, or whether the statements were useful.[48] The pedagogy of rhetoric developed around the concept of *mimēsis* and the idea that by listening,

called upon to reduce the *chreia* to its most important argumentative core, to provide the minimal, but complete circumstances in which the force of the statement or action might be made clear.

47. Mack, 'Elaboration of the Chreia in the Hellenistic School', in Mack and Robbins, *Patterns of Persuasion in the Gospels*, pp. 37-39 continues the list of exercises, these now focusing upon external expansion within an argumentative structure. Theon now suggests the *chreia* be considered from the point of view of commentary and critique in which the student should argue whether it is true, honorable, expedient, or whether it has been spoken by some other person of distinction. The first three of these categories correspond to the argumentative issues defining the three traditional genres (true = judicial; honorable = epideictic; expedient = deliberative) and constitute a portion of what were termed 'final proofs', others including what is right, lawful, pleasant, easy and necessary. These are argumentative appeals to cultural conventions, be they legal codes, social conventions or philosophical ideals. They indicate a trend in rhetorical theory that suggest that the most persuasive appeals were those to traditional and conservative norms. As indicated, this strategy was built into the very structure and goal of persuasive discourse, whether the context be legal, ceremonial or governmental. Furthermore, the fourth category, that of witness or citation, an appeal which could be used in any argumentative context, perpetuates this conservative trend.

Finally, Theon suggests the *chreia* be analyzed by means of **refutation** and **confirmation**. He only gives a list of strategies for refutation, which includes arguments from the quality of diction (obscure, loquacious, elliptical), arguments from the quality of logic (impossible, implausible, false) and arguments from the quality of ethics (unsuitable, useless, shameful). Confirmation would set out to test the *chreia* from the point of view of the 'opposites' of these.

memorizing, repeating and following the 'sound' advice of others, good moral character would be built into the student. Even rhetorical argumentative strategy, as developed during the Second Sophistic, and testified to in the elaboration exercises of Hermogenes,[49] shows a theory of persuasion that depended upon appeals to the conservative ethical, legal and philosophical values. Rationales, analogies, examples, witnesses, exhortative appeals, all of which depended upon socially sanctioned texts, analysis, interpretations and morals, were now woven into the very fabric of argumentative structure and strategy. Rhetoric, by the time of the New Testament, had begun its transition to domestication for the use of maintaining the status quo.[50]

48. This did not necessarily exclude the *chreiai* of Diogenes or the Cynic School, according to Bonner, *Education in Ancient Rome*, p. 257, citing G. von Wartensleben, *Begriff der griechischen Chreia und Beiträge zur Geschichte ihrer Form* (Heidelberg, 1901).

49. One should keep in mind that the works of Hermogenes come from the second century CE and were at first most influential among Greek, not Roman, rhetorical theorists. His impact upon the West does not come until Priscian's translation around 500 CE, and it is only during the Renaissance when he became as popular in Europe as he was in the East. See Kennedy, *Classical Rhetoric*, pp. 103, 164. In other words, while he may be reflecting the status of rhetorical theory up to the point of writing, and therefore may represent the kind of discourse structures available to early Christian apologetics, one may want to explore more cautiously the 'normative' status of his work at the time and place of the New Testament writings. This is perhaps, however, more interesting a question than significant a counter-argument to Mack's theses.

50. Cf. Mack, *The Lost Gospel: The Book of Q and Christian Origins* (San Francisco: HarperCollins, 1993), pp. 197-200, for a similar, though abbreviated treatment of the issue.

Such a simplification of rhetoric into general trends is not exactly accurate. As early as the fifth and fourth centuries BCE, Plato and Isocrates were criticizing rhetoricians ('sophists') for their relativism, particularly regarding their ability to argue both sides of an issue. Isocrates especially called for rhetors to be of good moral character, using noble topics and examples to prove their point. One should further consider the point that in Aristotle's *Rhetorica ad Alexandrum* 1421b it is suggested that with the issues to be decided through deliberative oratory, the final topics to which one might appeal included whether the decision would be just, lawful, expedient, honorable, easy or necessary. In general, then, we have here an example from about the fourth century BCE of a rhetorical practice appealing to very conservative social values.

What does it mean, therefore, that Mack wishes to portray a systematic development from social critique to conservative support of values in rhetorical theory in

The early Christian communities seem to be aware of these rhetorical strategies (*chreiai*, 'topics', citations) and structures (specifically the elaboration). However, compared to the normative rhetorical systems as understood by Mack, they added certain unique features in their attempt to justify their experimental social formations. Several examples can be given.

For instance, with respect to the 'final categories' Mack notes an awareness on the part of the early Christians regarding their use in traditional argumentation. Nevertheless, a 'transformation' of the values typically appealed to is found [how these are 'transformations' from a norm, and not an appeal to the norms of a different audience is left unclear]: Paul's 'law of christ' is a substitute symbol for Greek *nomos* used in appeals to what is 'legal'. Social designations were changed through the new self descriptions of 'kingdom of god' and *ekklēsia,* with resulting changes in the concepts of what is 'good' or 'right'. There is even some indication that early Christians added a new value to the 'final categories', that of 'blessed'.[51]

Another example of the 'transformation' of rhetorical strategies in early Christianity is the use of citation and non-technical proofs. Narrative traditions abound with references to 'witnesses' (human, divine, demonic and angelic), 'miracles', scriptural citations and prophetic fulfillment, divine covenants.[52] For the most part, these were highly argumentative and newly invented proofs, often either created or uniquely interpreted to supply authority and legitimation for the new social formations and experimentations taking place.

this period? There has certainly developed during this time a political trend away from the experimentation with democracy, and one does sense in the early Roman Empire a growing interest in declamation because the circumstance of real debate and oratorical influence have been severely curtailed. Nevertheless, one suspects here a presentation which seeks to describe the general rhetorical development of theory from social experimentation to social consolidation in order to emphasize a similar development in the Gospel traditions of Jesus: Mack's portrait of Jesus as Cynic-critic becomes the normative portrait of rhetorical integrity which is altered through later rhetorical techniques of conservatism. The result is a portrait of a struggle as the community seeks to maintain its originating experimentation through a discourse which can no longer speak to or for it. One wonders how much of this is wishful thinking for 'pristine origins' and how much is actual rhetorical discourse phenomenon and restriction.

51. Mack, *Rhetoric and the New Testament*, pp. 38-39.
52. Mack, *Rhetoric and the New Testament*, pp. 39-40.

Furthermore, the early Christian communities, when confronted with the need to provide technical proofs based upon accepted and expected topics, found it necessary to reconceive the traditional means of argumentation. Historical examples, for instance, seem to be limited strictly to Jesus, whose attributes and authority became mythical in proportion, the exemplar against which all others were judged. Early Christian discourse seems to avoid altogether the typical references to Greek figures, and any reference to Jewish heroes (particularly, David) were used in contrast to traditional interpretation.[53] Analogies, or parables, while usually 'invented' from typical examples of social or natural phenomenon, were given in Christian argumentation a new twist where 'we' see a tendency toward the odd, the curious, the disruptive, the unusual.[54] Rather than using analogies as an argumentative means of securing adherence to a proposition through appeals to 'universal truth', early Christians used them to justify their own new social experiments as somehow unique.

In addition, early Christian discourse is highly polemical, and replete with appeals to external authorities for legitimation of the propositions under discussion. Argumentative strategies, especially those exhibited within the *chreiai* traditions, are primarily concerned with developing contrasts between the followers of Jesus and the dominant social milieu represented by the stock Pharisee character. Debates are frequently depicted, but the terms of the debate, and the resulting authoritative pronouncement by Jesus, show no attempt at integrating dominant social norms, personages, witnesses or values. Instead, discussion is cut off without any attempt at persuasion, and the pronouncements are legitimated strictly by appeal to the assumed authority of Jesus himself.[55]

From these characteristics, it is obvious that early Christian social discourse did not concern itself with developing and justifying the convictions upon which was founded the social formation. Rather, the discourse simply assumed them, and sought to demonstrate how Christian social groups' conventions, which might seem questionable from

53. Mack, *Rhetoric and the New Testament*, p. 95; cf. also Mack and Robbins, 'Conclusion', in Mack and Robbins, *Patterns of Persuasion in the Gospels*, pp. 204-205.

54. Mack, *Rhetoric and the New Testament*, p. 40-41, 95; cf. also Mack and Robbins, 'Conclusion', in Mack and Robbins, *Patterns of Persuasion in the Gospels*, p. 205.

55. Mack, *Rhetoric and the New Testament*, pp. 96-97.

one set of convictions, could be justified in terms of a new set of convictions.[56] In order for such a discourse to function as argumentation at all, the values to which it appealed had to be shared already with the audience it addressed.[57] It simply could not have been persuasive to an audience of supposed objectors, as no attempt is made to appeal to their values. It would not have been fashioned as persuasive appeal to its own Christian context, as the audience is apparently already convinced. 'Perhaps we are to understand it as the quest of a new movement for its own appropriate topics... [T]he traditional values and canons of both its Jewish past and its Hellenistic environment are no longer adequate. By searching through its own emerging stock of convictions, memories, and narrative lore, the new movement must craft its own proofs for its own new system of values.'[58] What 'we' see in early Christian discourse, to put it more simply, is an experimentation with the development of the communities' own *paideia*.

It would not seem that elaboration, since it depended upon shared values and sought to offer support to 'approved' *chreiai*, would be an appropriate means of developing early Christian argumentation, topics and structures. Nevertheless, it was to the elaboration pattern that the communities turned in developing its *paideia*, albeit in a 'transformed' state. Beginning with *chreiai* attributed to Jesus, which exhibit the same tendency toward social critique as found in Cynic *chreiai*, the Christian communities used the elaboration pattern to justify social experiments in conflict. New examples, analogies and contrary arguments needed to be created. The patterns as developed in Hermogenes are 'altered', so that the rationale for the *chreia* and its interpretation are given only at the end, thus putting Jesus in the position of becoming his own authority,[59] whose pronouncement is now seen as a rebuttal within a context of debate. The elaboration becomes a means, thereby, for the

56. Mack, 'The Anointing of Jesus: Elaboration within a Chreia', in Mack and Robbins, *Patterns of Persuasion in the Gospels*, p. 104.

57. Mack, 'The Anointing of Jesus: Elaboration within a Chreia', in Mack and Robbins, *Patterns of Persuasion in the Gospels*, pp. 104-105.

58. Mack, 'The Anointing of Jesus: Elaboration within a Chreia', in Mack and Robbins, *Patterns of Persuasion in the Gospels*, p. 105.

59. Mack, 'The Anointing of Jesus: Elaboration within a Chreia', in Mack and Robbins, *Patterns of Persuasion in the Gospels*, p. 105; cf. also Mack and Robbins, 'Conclusion', in Mack and Robbins, *Patterns of Persuasion in the Gospels*, pp. 205-206.

early Christian communities to reflect upon the differences between their own value systems and those of the dominant culture, without any attempt to appeal to commonality. Not only is authoritative self-referential citation enough to legitimate a concept, but the fundamental concepts of definition ('kingdom of god', 'kingdom of heaven', both used in final proofs throughout this discourse) are themselves only given content by means of contrast to outside systems.[60]

How can 'we' explain the development from Cynic *chreiai* to domesticating elaboration? Mack suggests that 'we' may be able to reconstruct from the rhetoric of the discourse stages in social development. The aphoristic quality to many of the *chreiai* would indicate a stage at which some differences between the early Jesus movements and the dominant Jewish culture were recognized,[61] but without a set program in place to which these movements might refer. At this stage tensions need not have been extreme, separation not the intended discursive goal. Social experimentation may have been the guiding paradigm, with the critique aimed at the incongruencies of traditional forms of authority found in the dominant cultural milieu.[62] The *chreia* core indicates an insightful critique-from-within, a position of debate-with-engagement. At some important social juncture, however, a terrible and painful separation must have occurred.[63] As a result, *chreiai* are elaborated as means of justifying social experimentation now in opposition to the dominant culture. Boundary markers, self-definitions, leadership roles, rituals and rites for entry, defenses of values and practices abound in the discourse at this stage. Justification is needed, and a movement whose impetus was to question traditional forms of authority must now wrestle with the consolidation of authority and the question of whose teaching will now guide it. The new *paideia* turned back to the figure of Jesus as the locus of authority and legitimation in the developing circumstances. The Jesus of the *chreiai* exhibits a different sense of authority than the Jesus portrayed in the elaborations.[64] More and more

60. Mack, 'The Anointing of Jesus: Elaboration within a Chreia', in Mack and Robbins, *Patterns of Persuasion in the Gospels*, p. 159.

61. Mack and Robbins, 'Conclusion', in Mack and Robbins, *Patterns of Persuasion in the Gospels*, p. 207.

62. Mack, *Rhetoric and the New Testament*, p. 98.

63. Mack and Robbins, 'Conclusion', in Mack and Robbins, *Patterns of Persuasion in the Gospels*, p. 207.

64. Mack and Robbins, 'Conclusion', in Mack and Robbins, *Patterns of Per-*

authority devolves onto this singular figure, upon whose position as founding teacher is used to justify every argumentative appeal in these traditions. The subversion of Hellenistic rhetoric generates a portrait of an individual whose every pronouncement is unquestionable, whose every statement was final.[65] The pattern of debate portrayed in this tradition is an inauthentic exchange, because in order for the argumentation to be successful, it needed to appeal to the authoritative position of Jesus, which is precisely the issue the opponents of the movement would have rejected.[66] Once this pattern was taken up into the Gospel versions of the origins of the movement, it became the legitimated paradigm for Christian discourse by consolidating all argumentative situations and strategies into a unified mythological portrait of Jesus as teacher and christ.[67]

In other words, *the 'same' development in the rhetorical theory toward domestication of argumentative practices for purposes of supporting and legitimating the social status quo of imperial Hellenic and Roman Empires is also found in the traditions of early Christianity.* What was once a movement of social experimentation set within an argumentative context of the internal critique of traditional orders of authority now becomes by the time of the writing of the Gospels a movement whose rhetoric not only adapted the models of the dominant culture, but then used them to justify and legitimate its own (alternative) authoritative structures. The result is a discourse that bristles with divisiveness, a rhetoric whose argumentative strategies depend upon exclusively internal appeals to inductive authoritative pronouncements.

How much more can 'we' discover concerning the historical and social developments that led to this point, and to the resulting impact it has made upon Christian theology and western culture? How many different lines of argumentation, and the various group histories they represent, can 'we' discover from a careful reading of the Gospels? When 'we' pull apart the mono-mythic portrayal of the origins of Christianity in the life of Jesus, what will 'we' find as the essential ingredients of a developing social enterprise? What contributions to the

suasion in the Gospels, p. 208.

65. Mack and Robbins, 'Conclusion', in Mack and Robbins, *Patterns of Persuasion in the Gospels*, p. 208.

66. Mack, *Rhetoric and the New Testament*, p. 100.

67. Mack, *Rhetoric and the New Testament*, pp. 99-100.

portrait of the history of this enterprise can 'we' discern in the Gospel authors, particularly Mark? If you recall, these were the questions with which Mack began his quest, which he defined explicitly not as a quest for the historical Jesus, but for the reconstruction of early Christian social development and the myth of unique origins which it helped to generate. And now, with the full background of the rhetorical theory and criticism which he has been using in his attempt to fulfill this quest, we can turn to the results as offered in his formidable presentation of Christian origins, *A Myth of Innocence: Mark and Christian Origins*.[68]

In this extensive and intriguing work we find brought together into a unified presentation all of the previous discussions concerning the re-configuration of the historical-critical endeavor of New Testament scholarship, the survey and analysis of previous scholarly efforts as the justification for his new critical goal, and the methodological application of the sociology of literature to help him. Simply put, his goal is to assess the impact of the Gospel of Mark upon the traditions brought together in this Gospel.[69] His method is a *traditionsgeschichtliche* reconstruction of the social origins and textual histories of these traditions, which provide the background relief against which he can then determine the unique changes wrought by the Gospel of Mark. It is based upon a sociology of literature which is described in terms very similar to those used to define 'rhetorical criticism' in the works we have so far discussed.[70] The result is a portrait of Mark as a mosaic of varying traditions originating within a myriad of contexts, a portrait which now unifies them into an apocalyptic 'myth of origins' stemming from a community undergoing rejection and seeking justification for its own social formation. This myth of origins has not only determined the direction of the twentieth-century quest for the historical Jesus,[71] but

---

68. Philadelphia: Fortress Press, 1988.

69. Mack, *A Myth of Innocence*, p. 12.

70. Mack, *A Myth of Innocence*, pp. 17-22, esp. p. 20: 'If the requirement of the study is to reconstruct social and literary histories that created the climate for Mark's own composition, the trick must be to find a way to locate particular texts at specific junctures of social formation in order to be able to assess their mutual interrelations.' Cf. Mack, *Rhetoric and the New Testament*, p. 93: '[Rhetorics'] promise is that a rhetorical perspective on language and literature may make it possible to treat New Testament texts both as literary compositions and documents of early Christian social history at one and the same time'.

71. Mack, *A Myth of Innocence*, pp. 1-9.

its apocalyptic orientation and polemical rhetoric is the driving influence behind much of the history of western civilization, especially the American myth of innocence.[72]

He begins his survey of the narrative traditions by first presenting a description of the dominant cultural and social settings within which, and as reaction to which, they were generated.[73] Interestingly enough, against this background, he sets the stage by extrapolating from the earliest aphoristic layers of the Q tradition[74] a general portrait of Jesus as a Cynic-like teacher of anti-conventional wisdom within a context of a thoroughly Hellenistic Galilean culture.[75] His reconstruction of Galilee runs contrary to traditional ones[76] which tend to emphasize an apocalyptic, revolutionary fervor among the inhabitants, a unified concept of messianic expectation and the future restoration of Israel within the general religious culture, and the dominance of Pharisaism throughout the local population. But what is most striking is Mack's willingness to begin his reconstruction of tradition history with his own version of Jesus![77] Apparently his argument has shifted from 'we cannot go back as far as Jesus' to 'we cannot ascribe to Jesus an originary impulse which gives rise to all the various movements stemming from him'. He has located in Jesus a social critique, but one without a definite program; a religious piety, but one lacking interest in any specific Jewish institution; a following which experienced some sense of social transformation, but without any specific boundaries or self-definition.[78] This is a very humble beginning for the myriad of social formations that explode onto the scene upon his death, but the lack of a particular teaching or program would help to explain the diversity of interests which were then fostered by these groups and justified by attribution to

72. Mack, *A Myth of Innocence*, pp. 368-76.

73. Mack, *A Myth of Innocence*, pp. 27-52.

74. Which, building upon Kloppenborg's thesis, he distributes among three layers and five stages in social experimentation. Cf. Mack, *The Lost Gospel*, pp. 105-88.

75. Mack, *A Myth of Innocence*, pp. 53-77.

76. Cf. also Mack, *The Lost Gospel*, pp. 51-68.

77. In Mack, *The Lost Gospel*, he has shifted his emphasis away from implications concerning Jesus himself and moved more appropriately [with respect to consistency within his own model] to implications concerning the earliest material we have from the Q community, who are then given credit for ascribing to Jesus this Cynic-sage persona. Cf. p. 203.

78. Mack, *A Myth of Innocence*, pp. 63-64; 73-77.

Jesus. Jesus may have done *something*, but it wasn't very extensive, or very structured, thus explaining the myriad of traditions ascribed to him ['one should not underestimate the attraction of a Cynic-like sagery capable of enticing individuals into forming a discursive association'].[79]

What that something could have been, postulates Mack, can be found in the earliest traditions in the central importance of gathering for meals. Such a social custom was widespread throughout the Hellenistic period, extremely important for trade, business and association.[80] Jesus' own involvement in such a practice would provide occasions for the type of discourse Mack ascribes to him: a discourse composed of parables, aphorisms, discussions on the type of lifestyle he advocated and pursued, all taking place in a casual environment of close association of people from diverse social backgrounds and stations. Such social practice could easily be continued by the movements he left behind after his death, movements which now begin to recognize the unique quality of the associations, which begin to reflect upon definitions and boundaries of the groups, upon questions of ritual and leadership. Each group would solve these situations in its own way, and yet be able to share in common gatherings. Each group would also interact differently with the dominant cultural setting in which it developed, and would generate a rhetoric of experimentation and justification by reference to its founding figure, Jesus.

Thus, the complex social histories of the various groups arising from Jesus can be explained by reference to the social custom of sharing a common meal. It seems 'we' have found the golden apple of historical criticism after all!

Against this reconstructed socio-historical setting he is then able to describe the development of traditions through several different social junctures of self-definition, conflict and experimentation, always leading up to the specific contributions to their reinterpretation within Mark's Gospel. The meaning of the textual tradition, understood as the rhetorical intention, changes according to the social setting implied by its performance. Parables, for example, when placed within a broad Jewish context in the mouth of the Cynic-Jewish Jesus, could be understood as a subversion of Jewish values but with the goal of reflection upon the irregularities of the dominant culture.[81] When set

79. Mack, *The Lost Gospel*, p. 203.
80. Mack, *A Myth of Innocence*, pp. 80-81.
81. Mack, *A Myth of Innocence*, p. 149.

within the later context of the developing Jesus movements undergoing their own social experimentation (which generated their own parabolic discourse), the subversive element became interpreted as disruptive, as inaugurating a new time and social space now in practice and distinct from the dominant culture.[82] Mark has promoted this trend by adding an apocalyptic interpretation to this disruption. For him the parable tradition is now a reinterpretation of Greek educational tradition (*paideia*),[83] one that no longer emphasizes the *accessibility* of instruction and enculturation. Instead, for Mark the parables act as mysterious allegories of the eschatological kingdom understandable only to members of his own community. Rather than a means of clarification and example, they act as a means of exclusion and the elimination of the chance to communicate with those outside the community.[84]

Pronouncement stories, as 'we' have seen, were originally Cynic-like *chreiai* of social criticism,[85] then domesticated by later Jesus movements into polemic against the synagogue.[86] Mark enhanced the picture of the authoritative nature of Jesus found in the later tradition by coupling the characterization of Jesus as teacher with that of Jesus as son of god/son of man. He further defines his teaching in terms of apocalyptic pronouncement, which is met with controversy and ultimately rejection. Here, too, then, the instruction of Jesus is not meant to edify, clarify and educate, but to divide those who accept it from those who reject it.[87]

The pre-Markan and pre-Johannine miracle collection[88] was a reinterpretation of the Exodus and wilderness miracles, whereby Jesus reconstitutes the new congregation of Israel whose composition runs counter to traditional Jewish concepts.[89] Jesus turns to those people whose social status within the dominant Jewish culture would be marginal, and by means of his own power brings them together into a new society not in opposition to, but as an alternative to traditional views of

82. Mack, *A Myth of Innocence*, p. 150.
83. Mack, *A Myth of Innocence*, pp. 157-60.
84. Mack, *A Myth of Innocence*, pp. 165-71.
85. Mack, *A Myth of Innocence*, pp. 179-86.
86. Mack, *A Myth of Innocence*, pp. 195-99.
87. Mack, A *Myth of Innocence*, pp. 205-207.
88. Mack, *A Myth of Innocence*, pp. 215-22.
89. Mack, *A Myth of Innocence*, p. 223.

Israel.[90] In Mark, miracles serve to legitimate the apocalyptic instruction of Jesus set within contexts of conflict with religious and governing authorities.[91] As proof of his station and authority, the miracle stories reinforce the injustice of the later rejection of Jesus by these leaders, thereby legitimating their prophesied destruction. Here again 'we' see the rhetoric of polemic and rejection.

The portrait of Jesus as son of god whose ministry represents the advent of the kingdom of god now displayed through the power of his miraculous acts, sets up the atoning significance of the passion narrative, a traditional concern of the Hellenistic christ cult movements. Mack's most controversial thesis suggests that the passion narrative is the sole composition of Mark, a theory that runs completely contrary to Protestant scholarly consensus which attempts to ground Christian faith in this historical event. In the passion story Mark brings together the larger narrative elements of prediction/fulfillment, conflict/vindication, which are then woven into a framework introducing the christ cult movement's traditions concerning his last meal and his atoning death/resurrection.[92] The guiding narrative principle is the wisdom story of the persecution and vindication of the Righteous One as martyr.[93] The result is a whole new myth of origins in which the diverse portraits from the Jesus movements converge to create an apocalyptic story of the divinely ordained son of god who enters into a world hostile to his teaching, a world which refuses to recognize his authority as manifest in miracles and proclamation, and which therefore culpably rejects him and kills him. Nevertheless, his innocence has been vindicated through both his resurrection and the eschatological signs of the destruction of the Temple and Jerusalem. Mark thereby provides a testimony which attempts to explain the failure of his movement to make headway within Judaism, a failure and rejection portrayed in the life of its founder, to be vindicated only by the destruction of the outside hostile world.[94]

Mark wrote such a Gospel to speak to the concerns and experiences of his community who were undergoing the hardships of expulsion from the synagogue, and had lived through the turbulent times of the

---

90. Mack, *A Myth of Innocence*, pp. 223-24.
91. Mack, *A Myth of Innocence*, pp. 230-42.
92. Mack, *A Myth of Innocence*, p. 276.
93. Mack, *A Myth of Innocence*, pp. 265-70.
94. See his summary in Mack, *A Myth of Innocence*, pp. 353-55.

First Jewish Rebellion.[95] This group had attempted a reform within Judaism that went against traditional ritual laws of purity and allowed for an association of individuals which included the socially marginal.[96] They justified this reform on the basis of their own social experimentation and on memories of Jesus. This wasn't enough. Their reform was rejected, they were expelled from synagogues, and withdrew from the hostile world they had encountered in persecution and through times of great social upheaval. They were in need of justifying their existence outside of the institutions of Judaism and the recent historical turmoil they experienced and witnessed. Thus the impulse was created for a revision of Israel's epic history, one in which the founder of their sect would have to be portrayed as more authoritative than the leaders of the dominant religious institutions, one that would culminate in Jesus and the Jesus movements who would then be the only legitimate heirs of the epic promises.[97]

Mark sought to turn the failure of the community into a sign for its legitimacy by providing a foundational myth which would serve to unite the myriad Jesus and christ cult traditions into a single conceptual structure.[98] He had very definite ideas concerning the future of these movements, and edited together those social practices and traditions he thought important to the identity of the community into an apocalyptic framework which gave them legitimacy and hope for future vindication.[99] Jesus' authoritative teachings provided the argumentative justification for the community's formation, his life the paradigmatic example of faith in the face of rejection, his apocalyptic vindication the indication that he and his followers were the true heirs of Judaism's epic promises.[100] Mark did not write his Gospel out of concern for historical accuracy, but out of a context of turmoil which needed to be addressed for the sake of the future of the community.

His impact upon Christianity extended far beyond his immediate context, however, as his story became the narrative structure upon which every other canonical tradition was built. His myth of origins became

95. Mack, *A Myth of Innocence*, p. 315.
96. Mack, *A Myth of Innocence*, p. 318, 'the enclave of the unclean as the true inheritors of the promises to Israel'.
97. Mack, *A Myth of Innocence*, p. 318.
98. Mack, *A Myth of Innocence*, p. 319.
99. Mack, *A Myth of Innocence*, p. 319.
100. Mack, *A Myth of Innocence*, pp. 355-56.

the foundation of future recitals, one that was elaborated but never fundamentally altered.[101] Transformed over the years through the symbolic ritual re-enactment of pilgrimage, liturgy and eucharist, the core of the narrative story, the historical foundational myth in which all Christians participate through these acts, remains intact.[102] Even the post-Enlightenment attempt to reconstruct anthropological, linguistic, astronomical histories, etc., and biblical studies' quest for the historical Jesus, continue to perpetuate Mark's notion of origins.[103]

But his impact is not limited to religious and even academented fields, nor to the concept of an original event. In western civilization, and especially in America, 'we' see played out in 'our' own history concepts of destiny and origin very similar to that in Mark: a social experiment in a new world full of the exuberance and innocence of a new beginning, of a disruption of history (read: beginning of Mark's Gospel), is set in motion with a mandate of bringing freedom to the world (read: Jesus' messianic mission). But recently 'we' are losing 'our' sense of certainty, 'our' mandate has come under fire, and 'our' actions in the national and international arena are met with increasing criticism (read: Jewish persecution of Jesus). An ever-increasing sense of unjustified persecution has taken hold, and 'we' have begun to draw the lines, close the doors, turn away from a hostile world that rejects 'us' (read: Mark's community). But 'we' are convinced of 'our' innocence, and interpret criticism as the rejection from a world that cannot and will not understand or accept 'our' divinely sanctioned mandate (read: christ as martyr). Their fate, sealed by their rejection, will be utter apocalyptic destruction, and we, as Christians and Americans, will find vindication through their persecution (read: returning son of man). The Markan apocalyptic myth of origins has become the legitimating religious paradigm of the scapegoat-pogrom practiced throughout the history of (particularly) American civilization.[104]

We have come full circle. All that Mack set out to find in 'Gilgamesh and the Wizard of Oz' he has fulfilled with this portrait of early Christian social history. All that is needed [esp. in light of the criticisms he eventually encountered] is perhaps a little extension of the picture, perhaps a change in tone regarding the importance such a history has for

---

101. Mack, *A Myth of Innocence*, pp. 356-57.
102. Mack, *A Myth of Innocence*, pp. 361-68.
103. Mack, *A Myth of Innocence*, p. 368.
104. Mack, *A Myth of Innocence*, pp. 368-76.

modern [American] Christians, and the effort he envisioned a decade ago will be just about complete. This is precisely what he accomplishes in the final work we shall consider here, ***The Lost Gospel***. What Mack uncovers in light of his model of rhetoric-as-intimately-tied-to-social-context is a carefully developed pattern of social exploration and consolidation in the Q community, a pattern which will become lost in the ensuing history of Christian composition, consolidation and canonization [and one to which, as we shall see, he will advocate a return as a model for modern Christian *mimēsis*].

Mack builds upon Kloppenberg's thesis of [now up to three] layers of accretion in the Q material by identifying five stages in the social development of the community. The Q^1 material represents two stages.[105] The earliest is comprised of an aphoristic discourse replete with maxims, imperatives and admonitions, all of which attribute to Jesus a playful critique of social conventions, a critique which took place in public and that challenged the members of this collective to 'behave with integrity despite the social consequences'.[106] Beliefs were not a major concern, social critique was not systematic, and while there was a definite sense that a movement was being formed, it had not yet taken on characteristics of one that focused upon broad social reform.[107] If there is a parallel to contemporaneous movements and/or lifestyles, it would be that of the Cynics.

Eventually this aphoristic core was collected into blocks of material. Codification resulted in certain imperatives being elaborated into community rules 'by formulating argumentations to support their importance and reveal their appropriateness'.[108] The discourse now expands to include references to [a non-apocalyptic view of] the rule of god,[109] an express appeal to nature as the manifestation of divine Wisdom, and an attempt to embed the movement within Israel's epic history. The picture of Jesus being developed is that of a founder-teacher giving instructions [doctrines, *doxai, dogmata*] 'for the manner of life that should characterize his school'.[110] There is evidence of expansion and growth; of a network of groups who traveled and hence relied upon

105. Cf. Mack, *The Lost Gospel*, pp. 105-30.
106. Mack, *The Lost Gospel*, p. 203.
107. Mack, *The Lost Gospel*, pp. 120-21.
108. Mack, *The Lost Gospel*, p. 203.
109. Mack, *The Lost Gospel*, pp. 123-27.
110. Mack, *The Lost Gospel*, pp. 203-204.

hospitality of sympathetic families;[111] of a sense of a mission to people to embrace the 'rule of god' as an appropriate alternative response to the broader social systems. There is a growing formation and identity being fashioned, as questions concerning 'what it meant to live in accordance with the rule of god would have to be worked out in relation to persons and problems within the group'. 'We' witness the beginnings of the growing pangs of a group that moved from Cynic-like critique of the social world to a group developing to the point where questions of identity needed to be considered.

It was these growing pangs that eventually gave way to the rhetoric of judgment and anger witnessed in the materials comprising Q^2. Sometime prior to this redactional layer social conflict within the close circles of acquaintances took place, as members of the Jesus movement experienced rejection and condemnation. The polemical nature of the resulting discourse would not have arisen out of 'weariness with reproach or a discouragement born of dashed expectations'.[112] Rather, it must have stemmed from the questions being pondered during the second, 'identity-formative' stage: loyalty to the movement must have been of central concern; disruption of social bonds, particularly the family, seems to be a major issue;[113] the world is now castigated for its lack of sympathy and understanding. Questions of just who were the authentic bearers of Jewish tradition must have arisen, as conflicts between the Jesus movement and fellow Jews grew to a burning intensity. Gradually,[114] Jesus' role in the community as founding teacher is shored up by attributing to him a remarkable level of authority: now 'Jesus would refer to himself as his own authority, set for his teachings as community code, and accept as a matter of course his own importance as the one who intended from the first to set the standard for what the movement must become'.[115] It is to him that the language of judgment and prophetic pronouncement eventually was ascribed.

The material in Q^2 also reflects the next, fourth stage when the movement solidifies, has boundaries and begins to ponder its social role and purpose. The whole sweep of Jewish epic history came under review and was plundered for the sake of a new vision of the direction in

111. Mack, *The Lost Gospel*, pp. 128-30.
112. Mack, *The Lost Gospel*, p. 204.
113. Mack, *The Lost Gospel*, pp. 140-42.
114. Cf. Mack, *The Lost Gospel*, pp. 137-40.
115. Mack, *The Lost Gospel*, p. 137.

which that history was meant to culminate. Here the Q people found their place under the sun, as various stories [Jonah, Queen of the South, Noah, Lot and the city of Sodom] were used both as 'a warning to their detractors and as a subtle suggestion that the epic of Israel championed lone figures and marginal peoples'.[116] In order to secure this place, they made reference to two significant mythological figures in Israel's epic of history—that of Wisdom [who had been present 'at the foundations of the world'][117] and the apocalyptic son of man [who would usher in a future, just order of creation].[118] Both these figures, as well as the notion of a line of prophets, the mechanism of prediction and fulfillment, and the projection of a final judgment,[119] all converged upon the figure of Jesus who came to be pictured 'as knowing everything from the beginning to the end of time, including how he himself fit into God's grand scheme'.[120] The Q people at this stage have begun to formulate a myth of origins for their unique role in God's plan: 'The whole sweep of history was now in review, but of course the instruction Jesus had to offer from that grand perspective was not for the public ear. And so the voice of Wisdom's child took on a tinge of revelation discourse, private knowledge for in-house use as the community came to terms with its subcultural assignment.'[121]

When 'we' finally come to the last stages of redaction in Q^3, a total transformation of the social situation appears to have taken place, perhaps precipitated by events related to the Roman–Jewish war.[122] Mack describes three or four shifts in attitude that can be discerned from the evidence in this layer, shifts that come to show a remarkable accommodation to their Jewish origins and identity: while the mythology of Jesus makes its final move from Jesus as child of Wisdom and apocalyptic son of man to Jesus as the son of god,[123] and while the Q

116 Mack, *The Lost Gospel*, p. 146.

117. Cf., for a discussion on the figure of Wisdom, Mack, *The Lost Gospel*, pp. 149-52.

118. Mack, *The Lost Gospel*, pp. 159-61.

119. Mack, *The Lost Gospel*, p. 161.

120. Mack, *The Lost Gospel*, p. 163.

121. Mack, *The Lost Gospel*, p. 204.

122. Mack, *The Lost Gospel*, p. 171.

123. Mack, *The Lost Gospel*, pp. 173-74.

community took advantage of the destruction of the Temple in Jerusalem to think of themselves as the heir's of Israel's Wisdom,[124] it is also clear that the Jewish Scriptures were confirmed as authoritative to the community.[125] 'We' also see a kind of retreat 'from the vigor with which these people had engaged their social environment to a kind of resignation, an acceptance of the fact that the rule of God was a matter of personal and ethical integrity'.[126] It appears that while the community survived the war, the cost of its survival entailed some significant new reflections regarding its relationship to the world around them.

Here is the end of the history Mack can discern from the rhetorical strategies found in Q, since from this point on, Q disappears into the narrative Gospel tradition. What, then, does Q's history represent for Mack? What is the impact of his careful thesis, and upon what areas of interest (of acadamnia, *ekklēsia*)? First of all come the important challenges to current and traditional concepts of the development of early Christian history, theology and self-understanding. I shall quote liberally from his own assessment:

> ...Q's story puts the Jesus movements in the center of the picture as the dominant form of early group formations in the wake of Jesus, and it forces the modern historian to have another look at the congregations of the Christ. The congregations of the Christ will now have to be accounted for as a particular development within the Jesus movements, not as the earliest form of Christian persuasion and standard against which the Jesus movements have appeared as diluted accommodations to banal mentalities.
>
> The history of the Q movement demonstrates that several mythologies of Jesus as a divine agent were possible without any recourse to martyrological notions. The mythology of Jesus as an envoy of wisdom, or even as the manifest incarnation of wisdom's child was not generated by any experience or notion of Jesus' resurrection from the dead. It was, as we have seen, generated in the course of myth-making in the genre of the teachings of a teacher.
>
> The discovery of Q also cautions us about the traditional view that Christianity emerged as a reformation of the religion of Judaism. Even the appeal to the epic of Israel was an ad hoc strategy that was not integral to the primary motivations of the Jesus movement. Other ideological resources were as much at play, including popular forms of Hellenistic philosophy and the mythology of wisdom. The attraction of the

124. Mack, *The Lost Gospel*, pp. 174-75.
125. Mack, *The Lost Gospel*, p. 176.
126. Mack, *The Lost Gospel*, pp. 204-205.

new community was not rooted in a plan to reform a religious tradition that had missed its calling, or in a clarion call to start a new world religion based on a recent revelation, but in the enhancement of human values experienced in the process of social formation itself.[127]

Q challenges the whole New Testament and biblical historical-critical account of the origins of early Christianity by 'offering another, more plausible account of the first forty years...a more believable group of people...[and] documentation for the Jesus movement that the narrative gospels cannot provide for the congregational fiction they project'.[128] And since the Gospels are the 'cornerstone' of Christianity's mythic world, to find evidence that undermines its veracity is bound to send significant tremors throughout the whole edifice of Christian faith and practice.

Furthermore, the implications of these challenges cannot easily be dismissed, since, as Mack points out, there is no recourse to canonical standards that can [and have traditionally been used by Christian exegetes and historians to] exclude the Q material from consideration. Indeed, 'Q is foundational to the very composition of the narrative Gospels. Take Q away and they fall into fragments without narrative or instructional significance.'[129]

That is not to say that the narrative Gospels did not make their own significant contribution to early Christian myth-making processes. Indeed, the reason Q was left behind was that it was simply inadequate for the tasks confronting the nascent church, the tasks of consolidation and institutionalization. The narrative Gospels provided 'a chain of tradition that not only linked Jesus with the epic traditions of Israel but also with the disciples as the apostles of the church. The purpose of the gospels as instruction literature was less important than their authorization of the disciples as those who knew Jesus personally and whose own teachings and writings were therefore trustworthy records of what Jesus had said the church should be.'[130] And if the disciples were guarantors of this tradition, those whom they appointed must also be recognized as authorities within the developing church structures.

This latter move also bolstered the very early tradition of letter writing, which by the second century [1 and 2 Peter, the Pastorals] helped

127. Mack, *The Lost Gospel*, p. 213.
128. Mack, *The Lost Gospel*, p. 238.
129. Mack, *The Lost Gospel*, p. 241.
130. Mack, *The Lost Gospel*, p. 230.

to consolidate the authoritative role of bishop as appointed by the apostles to carry on the mission of oversight and instruction of future believers. 'This myth of a chain of tradition from Jesus through the apostles and on to the bishops is similar to the Greek notion of the succession of teachers in the tradition of a philosophic school. It therefore developed quite naturally among Christians and granted legitimacy and authority to the office of the bishop and to his instructions to the churches.'[131] The result, however, was a diminishment of the importance of the teachings attributed to Jesus.

> Jesus was still the guarantor for the truth of the church's instruction, but the sharp edge given to his own sayings as the sole source for Christian instruction was dulled. It was no longer necessary to attribute every instruction to the founder-teacher. Instruction *about* Jesus was now just as important as instruction *from* Jesus, and the instructions from Jesus needed a great deal of interpretation in order to clarify their import for Christian faith, piety, and virtue.[132]

Thus, Q became superseded: its instructions were no longer sufficient, it did not name any apostles, and its focus upon the singular authority of Jesus for instruction had become unimportant. It becomes absorbed into a new mythic structure which soon comes to dominate the interpretive tradition of Christian origins, even to the point of dominating the historical (as 'opposed' to the theological) reconstruction of events by biblical exegesis in this century. By bringing this 'lost gospel' to the fore, by exploring its traditions on their own terms, what Mack has done is take 'us' back to the very beginnings, the foundations of the earliest Christian material. He has stripped away the myth of 'unique' origins and found a complex and very human enterprise of people 'responding to their times in understandable ways, investing intellectual energy in their evolving social experiments, and developing mythologies just as any society-in-the-making does'.[133]

Mack has fulfilled the huge task of demythologization first instituted by the form critics under Bultmann, and has produced the most consistent picture of early Christianity to come out of this century: consistent, insofar as every theological presupposition made by previous critics has been exposed as part of the mythic process of Christianity

131. Mack, *The Lost Gospel*, pp. 232-33.
132. Mack, *The Lost Gospel*, p. 233.
133. Mack, *The Lost Gospel*, p. 213.

itself; consistent, insofar as the *multiplicity* of social origins and perspectives has been maintained, but also strictly and coherently accounted for; consistent, insofar as the program with which he started out has produced the kind of results he was anticipating, but is now backed up with an important new/old [read: authoritative] methodology—rhetoric. Beginning with a reconstruction of a monolithic and universally practiced/known ancient rhetorical tradition of argumentation and composition, Mack can trace the argumentative trajectories of early Christianity as stages in the social developments in the history of the various groups of Jesus followers and Hellenist christ-cult members. Each stage, as the rhetorical history shows, is a further remove from, a domestication of, an earliest 'core' of teachings which reflect no cohesive social program, but an *attitude* critical of early Hellenistic Palestinian society. And as criticism became domestication became apocalyptic rejection, 'we' become further and further removed from 'our' roots, that is, 'we' witness not just the benign social experimentations and adaptations of a group confronting adversity, but the malignant turn of vituperation and rejection, of the shutting down and cutting off of communicative channels. As a rhetorical social historian, Mack helps 'us' to identify and locate within New Testament traditions the sources/ models of rhetorical practices which today shape some of the most devastating and terrifying perspectives [and political policies] of American messianism and fundamentalist propaganda. He also helps 'us' to see how, in the beginning, at the most 'authentic' foundations of Christian instruction, it was not always so. Rhetoric, as a tool for the biblical historian, helps 'us' not only to see how the things said way back then have given shape to the things 'we' say and do today, but also to find 'in the beginning' an alternative and legitimating source for a critique of these very same traditions.

Hermeneutical Center—Historical-Critical Reconstruction
The impact Mack''s model of early Christian historical and social development makes upon New Testament studies, if persuasive, would be notable, if not revolutionary. In particular, his schema of multiple social formations in search of justification and defense, and its presence within the canonical textual tradition, is an important alternative to the standard 'Jesus-*kerygma*-Gospel' trajectory of traditional biblical scholarship. In taking the lateness of the various argumentative performances he discerns seriously, and in exposing the quest for the historical Jesus

as grounded in the mythical concept of origins first developed by Mark, he has given the influence of early Christian experimentation its long-neglected due.

However, the questions which I think would be appropriate at this point to address through a rhetoric of power would not include whether this reconstruction is accurate or persuasive. [In some respects, and within certain critical circles, it may very well be both.] Instead, it may prove more fruitful to take two other approaches in pondering the significance of his work. First, how has this 'revisionist history' been carried out, and what implications could his method have for biblical-critical studies in the future? Second, why has this task been carried out at all? With respect to the former question, the presentation of ancient rhetorical theory and its modern developments which help to fashion and justify a new criticism, may be of profound [if limited] impact.

For example, the insights of rhetorical theory (both ancient and modern) completely undermine the form- and redaction-critical assumptions regarding that nature of ancient compositional traditions and expectations. Pronouncement stories, now seen as *chreiai*, are embedded *within* contexts of performance [not acontextually distilled to a minimalist 'core'], as ancient rhetorical principles of composition demanded a recognition of the connection between setting and saying/action and an adaptation of the saying according to the 'needs' of the speech context and social circumstances.[134] Furthermore, the presence of *elaboration* in the Gospels suggests a whole new emphasis upon the *argumentative* purposes of the sayings traditions, also calling into question the form- and redaction-critical assumptions regarding 'collections', 'additions', 'insertions', 'layers', etc., as later, almost accidental connections/accretions/distortions.[135] Finally, an awareness of ancient rhetorical precepts makes 'us' aware of the *domestication* (i.e. the impact of conservative culture upon rhetorical structures, particularly elaboration and thesis) of the sayings tradition, and provides a means for exploring the perspectives of the early Christian movements regarding the means by which they justified their relationship to the culture at

134. Mack, 'Elaboration of the Chreia in the Hellenistic School', in Mack and Robbins, *Patterns of Persuasion in the Gospels*, p. 66, and Mack and Robbins, 'Conclusion', in Mack and Robbins, *Patterns of Persuasion in the Gospels*, p. 201.

135. Mack, 'The Anointing of Jesus: Elaboration within a Chreia', in Mack and Robbins, *Patterns of Persuasion in the Gospels*, p. 105.

large.[136] Rhetoric, as a method of exploring antiquarian customs (and expectations) of composition and communicative exchange, strikes at the heart of all previous concepts regarding tradition-history: what was once a single trajectory from authoritative 'pronouncement and instruction' of Jesus, through a development of oral and thematic collections and accretions at the service of *kerygma* proclamation, to the final culmination in the Gospel story of the life of Jesus, must now be completely reassessed in light of new insights brought by awareness of ancient rhetorical practices.

Furthermore, and building upon this, Mack's rhetorical foundation to his model of social development and historiography allows for an incredible sensitivity to the *changing* circumstances and the *multiplicity* of argumentative exchanges and experimentation confronting early Christian social movements. As different assumptions are made, as shifting shapes of oratorical *ethos* and rhetorical *pathos* are experimented with, Mack discerns subtle but significant alterations in the implications such strategies hold for the contexts within which they took place. Adaptation to audiences, the selection of certain argumentative forms, the alteration and/or rejection of other traditional means of persuasion, belie attempts of early Christian groups to adapt to developing circumstances. With the New Rhetoric's emphasis upon the social aspects of argumentative communication (indeed, *all* communication), and with ancient rhetoric's dominance of Greco-Roman preceptive traditions as a norm against which to judge early Christian rhetorical practice, Mack has recognized an important means of identifying the *variety* of social experimentations at work in the traditions behind the Gospels' narratives. Here, again, he has broken the hegemony of the single trajectory of development in Christian history.

Still, there are some strange inconsistencies concerning the claims made by him regarding rhetoric's impact upon methodological issues in exegesis [which we shall explore immediately], as well as some troubling concepts regarding the philosophy of rhetoric informing his own critical application of it upon the biblical texts [which will be elaborated particularly in our discussion of his hermeneutics of 'text' and 'context']. First is, for someone who recognizes and chastises the limitations of form and redaction criticism, it appears that rhetoric is used simply to rescue them both, or at least to salvage important aspects of

---

136. Mack and Robbins, 'Conclusion', in Mack and Robbins, *Patterns of Persuasion in the Gospels*, p. 201.

the historical project which they began: Mack actively undermines the assumptions regarding the approach to compositional techniques and communicative traditions of the ancient world assumed particularly by form criticism [whose tentacles reached out and affected source, redaction, social scientific, cultural-anthropological and cultural-comparative, parables, indeed *any* criticism based upon diachronic analysis of the text]. However, Mack's conception and application of rhetoric and the social sciences, though advanced as more promising and 'accurate' methodological tools for critical analysis of these ancient texts, produce results that fit into the same program of *Traditionsgeschichte*. Mack's quest is no different from any of the other previous quests before him, because, like theirs, his is a quest for origins: on the one hand, Mack downplays the potential for discovering authentic pronouncements, teachings and social formations stemming from the life of Jesus himself. Instead, all portraits and attributed sayings of Jesus are now understood as examples of rhetorical *mimēsis* and *prosōpopoieia* (speech-in-character), typical rhetorical exercises in the ancient world.[137] Nevertheless, Mack applies rhetorical-critical tools upon the textual traditions and sources in an effort to advance conclusions concerning the 'earliest' collection of sayings and evidence of social construction. Indeed, these conclusions go so far as to offer a portrait of Jesus that is constructed out of an aphoristic core.[138] Granted, it is not an impressive portrait: Jesus is seen now as a figure without a movement or social teaching, whose characteristic traits seem to be limited to a general critical posture with respect to the dominant cultural milieu. If this portrait is acceptable, then Mack's theory that an originary foundational event should not be located in the life of Jesus seems to be feasible: Jesus could not have supplied the direction and self-understanding of his movement, because he did not have one. Nevertheless, here is a significant conclusion regarding this solitary

137. Mack and Robbins, 'Conclusion', in Mack and Robbins, *Patterns of Persuasion in the Gospels*, p. 202.
138. Cf. discussions and conclusions in Mack, *A Myth of Innocence*, p. 60 (Q), p. 61 (parables), p. 62 (pronouncement stories), pp. 63-64 (Jesus' social critique), pp. 67-69 and pp. 73-74 (parallels between Jesus and Cynics). These conclusions are made in spite of the very cautious remarks regarding the particularly idiosyncratic nature of a tradition which remembers 'speeches-in-character' in Mack and Robbins, 'Conclusion', in Mack and Robbins, *Patterns of Persuasion in the Gospels*, p. 202.

figure, a conclusion that may be contrary to all previous attempts made concerning him, but one which Mack advances as an authoritative and genuine portrait of Jesus.

On the other hand, Mack peels back the layers of social development and rhetorical adaptation [read: accretion?] to locate *other* possible origins for the myths that became Christianity. At one point he suggests that one source might be the gathering for meals, a conclusion that simply shifts the originary event of Christianity away from the historical figure of Jesus himself to that of a shared social custom. ['We' look for a golden apple, and find a golden orange.][139] Later, however, he seems less willing to identify any one common practice (shared among the groups of Jesus movements and christ cults) as the possible context in and from which the vastly different images of Jesus would have been fashioned. Nevertheless, while he perhaps finally rejects his own analogous attempt to discern a unitary myth of origin [whether identified with an individual or with a vague social custom or posture], this does not keep him from perpetuating an approach to the biblical materials analogous to all previous critical efforts to hunt for these origins: Mack cannot help using a series of [literary] 'events' (i.e. rhetorical performances reflected in the narrative traditions) to trace generative 'causes' (i.e. assumed social phenomena at work behind, hence giving shape to these literary events) through a detailed sequence of developments in the chronology of the early Christian experiments, starting with the earliest discernible attempts at social formation and explaining every step along the way to canonization and beyond [I shall return to this point shortly]. Indeed, throughout this project, Mack *builds upon* the results of source-critical work, discerns and explicates 'layers' of traditions in minute fashion [form and redaction-criticism as analogs, if not foundations], and outlines chronological developments in careful detail [Pentateuchal and Gospel *Traditionsgeschichte* as analogs]. Rhetoric has been adopted as a better, perhaps more relevant and methodologically more 'accurate' means of recognizing compositional technique and traditions, but it has been done so simply to supplement the same project: he may have fixed the broken pieces, he may even have replaced the mechanism, but it is still the same clock.

Second, in spite of himself Mack's historiography cannot seem to break away from efforts at identifying 'the unique'. Oddly, this impact

139. Mack, *A Myth of Innocence*, pp. 63-64, 73-77, cited above.

extends to rhetorical theory [both modern and ancient] itself which he applies through a method that could be called a 'study of contrasts': he begins with a portrait of rhetoric in the ancient world, one which emphasizes the 'normative' and 'universal' nature of rhetorical education throughout the Roman Empire. This allows him to pursue Christian rhetoric as a variation, a deviation. His method pits one against the other. For example, Mack argues that the overwhelmingly authoritative portrait of Jesus in contexts of debate shuts out the potential for persuasion, since it assumes no common ground between participants. He arrives at this conclusion by comparing Christian elaboration with the pattern developed by Hermogenes and notes that there are no appeals to traditional cultural values and acceptable cultural figures; in other words, Christians are not playing the rhetorical game 'correctly'. From this he deduces a *paideia* function to these stories: they are not made to be persuasive externally, they are made to justify and authenticate new social experimentation by reference to an internally acceptable figure (Jesus). That is one possible explanation. But, eliminate the *contrast* to Hermogenes, and it is possible to create a scenario wherein these elaborations were seen as an *entirely* effective means of external persuasion, generating an overwhelmingly powerful *ethos* of the character of Jesus, one that just might have been attractive to some important (even if *indirectly* mentioned) groups who may or may not have existed outside the community generating these arguments [and responding to others!]. If this is the case, then the social-conflict 'context' need not exist as central to our understanding of these performances at all: Jesus' authority was not seen as eliminating discourse, but was entirely effective to perpetuate discourse and debate.

The result of establishing a single 'norm' and then contrasting Christian discourse with it is a strangely acontextual portrait, a pursuit of the 'unique' without embedding the results in the rich cultural diversity that constituted the Roman Empire. It seems to me a more advantageous approach would be a descriptive and *comparative* [versus a *contrastive*] approach. For one thing, just because the most significant rhetorical systems we have from that [or any other] time [and place] are Greco-Roman does not eliminate the awareness of other persuasive strategies and systems in other Mediterranean cultures.[140] The emphasis

140. Even within Greco-Roman preceptive tradition, Thomas Conley, *Rhetoric in the European Tradition* (White Plains, NY: Longman, 1990), finds *four* distinctive rhetorical ideals: Platonic 'rhetoric as pursuit of philosophical Truth', Aris-

Mack puts on the overwhelmingly universal and normative nature of this tradition eliminates the chance to describe other 'rhetorical' patterns that may be at work in early Christian discourse which, after all, also confronted native populations of several cultures throughout that region of the world [and often confronted its own variations and controversies].[141] If we were to turn our attention to argumentative phenomena 'as they were', this would break open the potential for expanding the whole discourse context to include not just the education of Hellenist city dwellers, but rural folk tellers, the speech and strategies of Palestinian and Diaspora Jews, colonized cultures and people throughout the Mediterranean, etc. Greco-Roman educational 'norms' would be but one in a myriad of traditions, albeit one to which the [varying-in-degree] educated authors of the Gospels were most likely

totelian 'rhetorical and dialectical pursuit of persuasion', Gorgianic 'rhetoric as manipulation of audience to secure the aims of the speaker', and Isocratean-Ciceronian 'rhetoric as setting forth the best possible arguments in effort of acting in spite of incomplete knowledge of Truth'. Note also, for example, the numerous references to vying and varying philosophies of rhetoric found throughout the literature: Aristotle, *Ars Rhetorica*, argues implicitly and explicitly with (but also adapts aspects of) Plato and Gorgias; Quintilian, *Institutio Oratoria*, also quite often surveys the handbooks and other treatises on rhetoric before settling on his own definition and presentation; Cicero, *De Oratore*, discusses several different perspectives concerning rhetorical theory and education.

141. Kennedy, *Classical Rhetoric*, pp. 4-6 makes a similar distinction between 'descriptive' and 'prescriptive' rhetorical theories, first by distinguishing instead between 'primary' rhetoric, whose emphasis was upon invention and persuasive public speech, and 'secondary' rhetoric, whose emphasis is the collection and analysis of rhetorical techniques of eloquence (e.g. collections of tropes and figures of speech and thought). Later, on p. 8, he considers the difference between conceptualized rhetoric which is induced (by observation of traditional and conventional practice) and one which is deduced (from principles, whether based upon psychological or philosophical conceptions of effective communication). What I am suggesting is that by emphasizing primarily rhetoric whose techniques are developed through induction when addressing the ancient texts and rhetorical traditions, we open up the possibility of discovering different communicative norms.

This is especially important when considering the fact that Jewish education tradition did not seem to have conceptualized its discourse. Yet, Jewish conventions of both historical epic traditions and symbolic universe were an integral part of early Christian religious instruction and propaganda. It is likely that Christian *paideia* which may have differed significantly from Greco-Roman models of discourse simply intuitively combined or applied Jewish or other discourse traditions.

exposed [but not the *only* one]. The study-in-comparison [not to discern just contrasts, but also similarities] would be much more rich, much more extensive, and will be able to test just how 'unique' early Christian rhetoric might have been.

Third, Mack has taken a strange tact with respect to the nature of rhetorical theory [his 'philosophy of rhetoric'] by emphasizing an instrumental (perhaps even causative) approach to rhetoric's *technē* and preceptive tradition which results in a thesis that approaches identifiable differences in rhetorical performance as indicating shifts in social development. That is, if a rhetor follows the rules of discourse as established and understood throughout her/his culture, then 'we' can anticipate the genre, purpose, intention and effectiveness of a performance given the context. A rhetor is presented with a particular circumstance and will apply the rules appropriately. From this, it is theoretically possible to analyze the discourse and ascertain the circumstances. [Is this an 'affirming the consequent' fallacy: if A ('context'), then B ('response'). B ('response'), therefore A ('context')?] It is upon this implied basis of the nature of communication that historical reconstructions of social settings can be attempted: if 'we' can gather together enough similar rhetorical strategies, 'we' can assume a shared 'context' to which it is directed. Variations of rhetorical strategies in the tradition record variations in stages of social development.

To some degree, and to be fair, Mack is often very good at recognizing the flexibility available to an orator or author. He does, in fact, emphasize throughout his discussion that no practice ever looked like the theory, that genres were often combined, steps rearranged or eliminated, etc.[142] Indeed, once he turns to various Gospel examples, he uses his reconstructed rhetorical theory as a very flexible heuristic device which helps him to describe features of early Christian discourse. With respect to the function of analogy, parable and example, as well as the particularly authoritative and polemical role Jesus plays in the pronouncement material, he has certainly given 'us' some important insights. Even in discovering the presence of *chreiai* and elaboration in the Gospel tradition and noting the argumentative dimension that narrative now takes on is a major contribution. But all this flexibility becomes the means for arrestation in socio-historical reconstruction:

142. Esp. Mack, 'Elaboration of the Chreia in the Hellenistic School', in Mack and Robbins, *Patterns of Persuasion in the Gospels*, pp. 52-53, 64, 198; Mack, *Rhetoric and the New Testament*, pp. 35, 49.

the freedom of the rhetor to shift according to argumentative situations becomes lost in a nearly behaviorist theory of rhetoric, as every difference in utterance is now evidence of a shift in social dynamics.

Part of the problem begins with the reduction of rhetorical theory and criticism to tools for historiography. Indeed, for Mack the definition of rhetorical criticism *is* a historiography taking the particular form of 'an approach to texts with an eye to social histories'.[143] It is not just that the (new) rhetorical criticism emphasizes argumentation over aesthetic description, reconstructs discourse according to persuasive strategy and discusses potential effectiveness, considers the role of authority of speaker and discourse, and maps out the varying stages of argumentative strategies. It is that all of this is to be done with the eventual goal of reconstructing and describing social setting.[144] The 'second coming' of rhetoric is not seen as a descriptive and critical means of analyzing 'effective' communication, with emphasis upon invention, arrangement and performance. It is instead the heralded savior of the floundering historical-critical method, bringing with it a new world order to the chaos of biblical inquiry which had hitherto seen its efforts at social and historical reconstruction exiled by modern literary methods and theories of communication. There is something quite apocalyptic about all this.

Two issues are at stake here. First, should historiography be part of the definition and intended goal of rhetorical criticism? While Mack is keenly aware of the focus and concern of rhetoric upon persuasion, his own argumentative description of rhetorical theory and criticism suggests a change in the program. His definition of rhetorical theory, as theory of argumentation 'immersing speech event in social situation', downplays the rhetorical aspect of invention, and overemphasizes the methodological focus as description of social-setting.

Second, what does a rhetorical theory of communication bring to the question of the relationship between 'text' and 'context'? Mack has built a theory of communication which presumes that 'context' causes content. He is careful to indicate that it is also a part of his interest to discern the impact of a 'text'/performance upon a social setting.[145] He

143. Mack, *Rhetoric and the New Testament*, p. 17. Emphasis mine.
144. Mack, *Rhetoric and the New Testament*, pp. 19-24.
145. Cf. Mack, *Rhetoric and the New Testament*, p. 13, where he suggests that among the issues developing in the late 1970s and 1980s in New Testament studies are questions concerning 'the role of literature within a culture and the effective difference a piece of writing might make within a given social history'.

even implies an interest in the possibility that different social contexts may engender different responses to the same performance.[146] Nevertheless, his assumed construction of this communicative situation does not allow for the *creation* of a rhetorical exigence through the rhetorical act itself. Not all argumentative situations are historical situations: they can become so through definition and address, emphasis and argumentation dedicated to the activity of making a historical event an event of rhetorical significance. He is assuming a social and historical core behind every utterance, and wishes to get at that core by reference to the discourse it has generated.

The issues here are concerned with (a) the communicative role of the 'text' and 'context' in Mack's rhetorical theory and (b) where he locates 'authority' in his exegetical interpretation. What we want to explore is a careful reading of the interaction between 'text' and 'context' implicit in his method, and the pursuant understanding of communication that justifies his attempt to generate social description from rhetorical performance. From this we can ascertain those systems and assumptions used to legitimate his exegetical reading of the text, and use this discovery as a heuristic device to assess the conclusions of the remaining scholars with which this work is concerned.

There are several distinct notions concerning the function of 'text' and 'context' in his exegesis. First, texts are used intertextually as a means of providing a literary 'context' contemporary with the particular tradition upon which he is focusing. This context is very extensive, including the works of Greek and Roman rhetoricians as a means of discerning rhetorical patterns; the works of Greco-Roman literature, including biographies, memorabilia, sayings collections, histories and epistles as a means of comparing forms, genres, structures and cultural concepts; Hebrew Scriptures and Hellenist Jewish literature as a means of grounding significant socio-religious ideals, concepts and terms. 'Text' here identifies important influences and traditions provided by the dominant cultural 'contexts' within which the various Jesus and christ cult movements and Gospel authors were writing. Argumentative

---

146. 'Eventually, rhetorical criticism may be called upon to rank the various authorities to which early Christians appealed and evaluate them in terms of their persuasive force from various social perspectives' (Mack, *Rhetoric and the New Testament*, pp. 23-24). This could be extended to include analysis of a particular claim to authority found in a tradition and the varying responses to that claim from different social perspectives.

strategy is determined by analyzing the presence of contrasts with, reinterpretations of, and/or implicit or explicit references to these other traditions, most particularly the Greco-Roman rhetorical *preceptive* tradition. 'Textuality' is a socially embedded construct in need of other contemporary socio-literary traditions in order to ascertain intended communicative purpose and effect.

The New Testament texts that he addresses are slightly different in origin, composition and function. Narratives, speeches and sayings, even epistles are analyzed. In *A Myth of Innocence*, narrative materials and literary forms (parable, pronouncement and miracle collections) are analyzed in tradition historical stages, with a great deal of weight given to the reconstructed Q material (showing two [and in *The Lost Gospel*, three] distinct layers of interpretation), the rhetorical dynamic and social setting at each stage compared to previous and future alterations. In *Patterns of Persuasion in the Gospels*, elaboration structures are analyzed from within the received Gospel tradition, rhetorical strategies determined by the presence and function of various argumentative figures in the elaboration, conclusions being offered regarding the implications upon social history. In *Rhetoric and the New Testament*, he argues for the presence of various rhetorical structures at several stages of social history: Jesus movement traditions (Q, pre-Markan pronouncement stories), Pauline epistles, the epistle to the Hebrews, and the Gospels–Acts. The rhetorical structure and persuasive impact of each of these is assessed by reference to the social setting ('context') from which it arises and to which it addresses itself. 'Text' here means both reconstructed and written material set within both an immediate and greater (canonical) textual and (social) contextual setting.

According to Mack, therefore, a 'text' is a historically embedded communicative act which he addresses from the perspective of argumentative impact. The methodological limitation of this assessment arrests the performative influence at the point of concurrent 'context'. Discourse is developed in, informed by, and interacts with literary, cultural and social traditions at the time of its expression. 'Text' and 'context' influence and effect one another, and Mack is particularly sensitive to this issue when he shows how changing social settings bring about new rhetorical interpretations of earlier traditions. However, while he is explicitly aware of the theoretical impact of argumentation to influence changes upon the historical setting, it is only addressed in terms of changes to the discourse, not in terms of actual persuasion.

Effectiveness can only be reconstructed by reference to a specific 'context' to which argumentative insights and strategy of a specific performance would be a most fitting response and upon which it would have the greatest influence. And this 'context' would have to be historically simultaneous with the utterance. Ultimately, Mack is a historian and is only interested in assessing the persuasive power, dynamic and impact of discourse as performed to its intended original audience(s).

It is important to note, however, that this assessment is not based upon a notion of singular performance to a 'virginal' audience whose potential responses are reconstructed based upon 'very narrowly prescribed circumstances and in a very specific social context'.[147] He rejects these notions outright. There is a great deal of profound insight garnered from a concept of constant and varying experimentations and reinterpretations of traditions and values, all of which can be discerned through the many rhetorical strategic trajectories. Constant influence and exchange in the discourse is noted, many performances and audiences discerned and explored. But where he gets into trouble is when he defines rhetorical criticism as a study of human discourse that

> takes the historical moment of a human exchange seriously in order to assess the quality of an encounter and the merits of an argumentation. It takes the social circumstances seriously in order to view the exchange from the perspective of each participant. Rhetorical criticism of the New Testament asks the modern reader to join the biblical critic in the work of judging the effectiveness of a human performance at a particular moment in early Christian history. [148]

The questions to ask are, 'Why judge that *particular* moment in history? Why ask the modern reader to "join the biblical critic" for this thoroughly *antiquarian* effort?' Because it is *this* moment, this *early* history that is assumed to be authoritative for Christian praxis. And there is one profound result to this hermeneutical assumption: it places the biblical critic as authoritative judge concerning the 'authenticity' of any practical application (interpretation) of the Tradition. Mack wants to arrest rhetorical-critical interpretation and impact of the biblical material *in the past*, where its original 'intention' and 'effect' can become the critical basis upon which to judge any further elaboration, alteration, inculcation. Indeed, this is precisely what he does when he

147. Mack, *A Myth of Innocence*, pp. 148-49.
148. Mack, *Rhetoric and the New Testament*, pp. 102-103.

explores every social development in terms of new rhetorical interpretations upon earlier discourses. At the heart of his hermeneutic is an assumption that the further back 'we' go, the more authoritative 'our' understanding of what Christianity was/is 'really' about.

At first, the implications of this hermeneutic were explored in some of the most vociferous condemnations of Christian argumentative traditions, particularly with respect to the polemical, inflammatory and divisive qualities of early Christian rhetoric which became canonized [and emphasized] first in Mark, then in the subsequent Gospels. The New Testament Gospel traditions, inheriting all these argumentative trajectories and attributing them to Jesus within a new myth of origins, become the examples *par excellence* of Christian discourse, which thereby sanctioned their vituperative rhetoric as paradigmatic examples to follow.[149] The question Mack posed is one of authority: in light of the polemical and divisive nature of early Christian rhetoric, should the New Testament be the model for modern Christian discourse?

Mack's explicit intention was to undermine the connection between biblical scholarship and hermeneutics, and ultimately the authority of the New Testament for the modern Christian community. Rhetorical criticism as a historical-critical enterprise becomes a means of discerning the early argumentative exchanges taking place during the formative, turbulent years of the struggling Jesus and christ cult movements. As an exegetical enterprise, these early struggles and the discourse they brought about become the authoritative contexts for determining the understanding and use of New Testament traditions. Later applications of these texts are affected by the original dynamics which produced them. By emphasizing the historically embedded nature of communication, rhetoric poses serious questions of social consequence for biblical hermeneutics, which is now confronted with argumentative strategies and postures which may tend to undermine traditional philosophical and ethical definitions of Christian faith.[150] The authority of the New Testament is thereby undermined, becoming a collection of discourse examples from which to pick and choose, now with a greater sensitivity to the multitude of interactive traditions in a struggle for self-definition.[151]

149. Mack, *Rhetoric and the New Testament*, p. 99.
150. Mack, *Rhetoric and the New Testament*, p. 102.
151. Mack, *Rhetoric and the New Testament*, p. 102.

This is Protestantism pushed to a new level: Reformation cries of 'back to the Bible' and the ensuing loss of intervening community/ church tradition as a standard for Christian faith and practice has forced Protestant scholars to turn to the historical enterprise in order to discern a core and foundational event/theology. This is the heart of the exegetical endeavor: by establishing an interpretation of the biblical text upon a historical norm there is an objective standard with which to judge current Christian faith and practice. Biblical studies and hermeneutics have had to go hand in hand, otherwise: (1) Protestant churches have no standard against which to judge their interpretation of the Bible (church tradition is explicitly excluded, but is nevertheless effectively present); and (2) biblical studies as an institution would be unimportant, a movement of scholarly inquiry pursuing esoteric methods in an effort to reconstruct ancient history.

Mack sought to eliminate this connection, bringing down the traditional authoritative systems and structures of Christianity. Accepting the authoritative role history plays in the methodological enterprise, he rendered the biblical text questionable at best, useless at worst for biblical hermeneutics. Mack pursued Protestant biblical scholarship in order to reconstruct its connection completely with traditional Christian faith: authority lies in history, but history shows 'us' a development away from 'authentic' Christian praxis. On the one hand, Mack asserts in *A Myth of Innocence* that one either has to accept this perception and its results (as many fundamentalist and millenarian movements do), or completely reassess the authority of the Bible. 'The hermeneutical value of a rhetorical criticism of the New Testament may therefore lie not in supplying models of discourse for twentieth-century Christians but in its challenge to the very notion of biblical hermeneutics as an essential grounding and guide for Christian faith and practice.'[152]

Later, however, this condemnation has given way to a brand new emphasis shown in his work on Q. Here we find a change of heart, a whole new rhetorical strategy vis-à-vis his contemporary audience in which he argues that the treasures he has discovered in the reconstruction of the Q social experiment lie not only at the core of Christian praxis [hence are *the* authentic Christian Tradition], but are also therefore *valuable* for Christian *mimēsis*.

---

152. Mack, *Rhetoric and the New Testament*, p. 102.

Q represents a movement that understood the significance of Jesus in terms of his instruction, not in terms of a christ-savior or messiah with a program for reforming Second-Temple Judaism. It represents a group who attached no importance to reports or traditions concerning Jesus' death and resurrection, who did not emphasize 'salvation' through personal, spiritual transformation.[153] Q runs entirely contrary to the whole christ-cult tradition that came to dominate historical depictions of the events in the life of Jesus and the church. The earliest traditions of the Jesus movements neither knew nor imagined everything we have come to believe about him: 'the baptism of Jesus; his conflict with the Jewish authorities and their plot to kill him; Jesus' instruction to the disciples; Jesus' transfiguration, march to Jerusalem, last supper, trial, and crucifixion as king of the Jews; and finally, his resurrection from the dead and the stories of the empty tomb'.[154] What Q reflects, and allows 'us' to reflect upon, is the very *human* process of mythmaking at work in the Gospels and christ-cult traditions, a mythmaking with no basis in historical fact.

The new project for Mack, in light of these discoveries, is education and enlightenment of the public, acadamnia, the church, the media, indeed the whole of western and American culture and tradition. 'Christian myth and western culture go together…Christian myth and American culture also go together.'[155] But it is both the persistent inability of Christians and Americans [in particular] to see how these myths work, and the virtual impossibility for them to recognizes these myths *as myths*, which keeps 'us' from tackling the huge social issues confronting 'us'.

> What we do not know or talk about is the mythic equation, how [factors of gender, ethnicity, social position, economic status, national loyalty, cultural tradition, religion, ideology and lifestyle] are rooted in mythologies, how myths surface to inform new patterns of motivation and association, how they impinge upon the creation of new mythologies, and how a mythology works in return to inform and support a particular social configuration. We do not know how to talk about the mentalities that underlie a culture's system of meanings, values, and attitudes.[156]

153. Mack, *The Lost Gospel*, pp. 245-46.
154. Mack, *The Lost Gospel*, p. 247.
155. Mack, *The Lost Gospel*, p. 251.
156. Mack, *The Lost Gospel*, p. 253.

But perhaps 'we' should learn how, and perhaps the time is ripe for such an exploration. And, low and behold, here comes Q as an important contribution to this process.

By debunking the 'historicity' of the narrative Gospel account, Q helps 'us' to place Christian mythology

> among the many mythologies and ideologies of the religions and cultures of the world. The Christian myth can be studied as any other myth is studied. It can be evaluated for its proposal of ways to solve social problems, construct sane societies, and symbolize human values. The gospel can be discussed as an enculturating mythology, and the question of its influence in American culture can be pursued without the constant interruption of questions and claims about historical truth of unique events.[157]

Q, according to Mack, helps 'us' to decenter the hegemony and chauvinism of the Christian myth in [and over] our country, in [and over] our culture, in [and over] our world.

Q also gives Christians of all persuasions the chance to reflect upon their relationship to the world. Two problems have arisen in the face of the growth of myriad voices within our culture, among varying cultures, and between nations, all of whom are struggling to find ways to work together. The first is the form of Christian mission 'with its implicit claim to know what is best for other people', as people are beginning to ask whether persuasion that takes the form of a mandate to 'convert' the world to this one religion is an appropriate task.[158] The second is the Christian myth's propensity to perpetrate and perpetuate abuses of power, as a culture's *messianic* self-conception justifies its continual interference into other people's matters by making reference to the model of a mythic superhero who appears out of nowhere to right the world's wrongs and bring salvation. Q could help in the process of solving these problems, not by providing ready-made answers, but by shifting the focus away from the myths in the New Testament and on to the *people* who produced them.[159] Q helps 'us' to catch a glimpse of an intellectual rigor, of the struggling attempts of a people to adapt a social vision to the problems confronting them. The resulting rules governing the group were seen as 'effective not because of some external authority, but by virtue of the agreements a community reaches in choosing to

157. Mack, *The Lost Gospel*, p. 254.
158. Mack, *The Lost Gospel*, p. 255.
159. Mack, *The Lost Gospel*, p. 256.

be guided by them'. There is nothing 'eternal' and 'essentialist' about such rules. Rather, it has *always* been the case that throughout history Christians have taken 'what they had in hand and coined new myths for new circumstances in the interest of compelling social visions'. Q's challenge of Christians 'is therefore an invitation to join the human race, to see ourselves with our myths on our hands and mythmaking as our task'.[160]

There are some interesting implications to ponder here. The first that strikes home is that the biblical historian's work is not irrelevant to the world at all: Mack has found a 'golden apple', one that promises to offer a 'wisdom' to both 'our' culture and 'our' Christian community, a wisdom long distorted, even hidden. Interesting how he argues for its relevance: Q's pedigree is unshakeable, coming out of the sanctioned canon of Christian literature. Furthermore, its claim to be the *earliest* tradition 'we' have of the Jesus movements authenticates its message [relationship to Jesus appears to be the primary approach for legitimization: a new 'apostolic' succession]. Tradition, if not what we thought Tradition entailed, asserts its hegemony in the apologetic and deliberative rhetoric of Mack's work.

Interesting how the 'solution' to 'our' 'problems' always seems to be in the past. 'Interesting', because access to the past, to its 'meaning' and 'intention' is available only through the historiographic enterprise, an enterprise given further support by reference to a hermeneutic which arrests interpretive authority to 'what it must have meant back then'. 'Interesting', because the critical tools are therefore only in the hands of those who have been initiated into the mysteries of their application. 'Interesting', because when the Bible's only authentic and authoritative message to the present and future is that which it said and meant in the past, the only authentic and authoritative messenger is the biblical critic. In Mack's work, whether that message is one of hatred, bigotry and rejection, hence one that should be discarded for fear of precipitating apocalyptic doom; or whether it is a message of hope for the future hidden far away in the recesses of time: at the heart, at the center of history stands the biblical scholar as the one who can provide all the answers. Is there a messiah complex here after all?

160. All quotes in this paragraph from Mack, *The Lost Gospel*, p. 257.

b. *Vernon Robbins*

When we turn to Robbins, the methodological similarities to Mack are apparent: rhetorical analysis of the Gospel materials helps provide sociological data upon which to reconstruct the values and norms of the intended audience. Specifically, Robbins is interested in analyzing the relationship between this audience and the culture-at-large in order to discern a cultural-literary tradition. His emphasis, however, focuses more directly upon the presence of ancient rhetorical forms and strategies, the impact of intertextuality as an index of cultural-literary forms and expectation. In other words, whereas Mack has emphasized the *social* in 'socio-rhetorical' exegesis, Robbins emphasizes the *rhetorical*. Nevertheless, the question posed to the Gospel texts is whether their literary rhetorical strategy can be used to pursue the same pluralistic goals of the modern liberal critical agenda. Ultimately, the heart of interpretive authority continues to lie in historical reconstruction, and the pursuit continues to be for an objective historical norm with which to interpret rhetorical effectiveness not just in ancient contexts, but for today. And, once again, at the center stands the expert exegete.

When we survey Robbins, we shall avoid a strictly chronological account of the development of his hermeneutical model, and focus instead upon clusters of articles and essays which seem to represent similar rhetorical strategies and philosophies. We shall begin with his monograph, *Jesus the Teacher*, wherein he introduces the so-called 'socio-rhetorical model'. We shall then turn to several articles published in *Semeia* and *Forum* which detail his method and its application, where he develops a rhetorical model thoroughly grounded in ancient Greco-Roman education and rhetoric. Finally, we shall return to *Jesus the Teacher*, this time focusing upon the introduction to the new paperback edition wherein he elucidates the hermeneutical and ideological presuppositions of his method, and compare these with an article entitled 'Rhetoric and Biblical Criticism' he co-authored with John H. Patton in 1980. We shall note that, like Mack, where he began determines where he ends up.

Survey of Methodology and Results

Robbins's first major exploration into the field of socio-rhetorical criticism, a term which he in fact introduces, is found in his [turgid] monograph, **Jesus the Teacher**. In the foreword to the paperback edition[161] he provides a theoretical overview and explication of his method, its assumptions and goals. He defines 'socio-rhetorical' inferences as the observation that 'a well-known social environment in the culture could play a key role in the rhetoric of a literary narrative'.[162] By a careful analysis of the rhetoric of a given saying, story or narrative, the social structures and systems of belief and practices out of which they arose and to which they respond can be reconstructed. The procedure is a four-step process through which the scholar becomes in essence a cultural anthropologist, an individual who uses the New Testament 'to perform fieldwork that yield[s] data with which [s/he] would accept the tasks of interpretation, generalization, deduction, and introspection', confronting 'the reality that New Testament texts are foreign to our literature, society, economics, politics, and culture'.[163]

The first step focuses intently upon the biblical text itself, a form of 'intrinsic criticism' which seeks to determine the 'rhetorical-literary features internal to the text'.[164] The second step is a study of the historical intertextuality of the text, a comparison of the literary features of the Bible to Jewish and Greco-Roman conventional literary forms and traditions. The third step is to reconstruct the social environment of the biblical text by reference to the implicit and explicit social values and systems determined by means of the previous two steps.[165] [We shall return to the fourth step in the next section.] Through this procedure, 'we' come to see not only the traditions prevalent in the historical and social circumstances and literary environment of the biblical texts, the tacit assumptions which provide the context of meaning for the rhetorical-narrative performance, but any unique contributions and subtle alterations of them by the biblical author.

---

161. Vernon K. Robbins, *Jesus the Teacher: A Socio-Rhetorical Interpretation of Mark* (Philadelphia: Fortress Press, 1984; paperback edition, with a new introduction, 1992).

162. Robbins, *Jesus the Teacher*, 'Introduction to the Paperback Edition', p. xix.

163. Robbins, 'Introduction to the Paperback Edition', p. xxi.

164. Robbins, 'Introduction to the Paperback Edition', p. xxiii.

165. Robbins, 'Introduction to the Paperback Edition', pp. xx, xxiii. These steps will later be combined in Robbins's exploration of ancient rhetorical forms prevalent in Mediterranean education, esp. focusing upon the prominence of the *chreia*-elaboration exercises found in the handbooks and the *progymnasmata*, as well as analyzing the aphorisms of Jesus by means of Aristotelian rhetorical theory.

When turning to the Gospel of Mark, Robbins's early work in 'intrinsic analysis' takes its cue from Kenneth Burke's concept of form: 'A work has form in so far as one part of it leads a reader to anticipate another part, to be gratified by the sequence.'[166] A careful analysis of Mark reveals four kinds of form present in the rhetoric of the Gospel, each contributing to the movement and unity of the presentation of the ministry of Jesus: (1) minor forms, traditionally studied by form critics, include controversy stories, miracles, parables, sayings, even metaphors, antithesis and parallelism. These forms 'represent folklore from sectors of early Christianity that participated in the Jesus movement' which perpetuate the identity of the movement over against established sectors of Jewish society. While their presence in Mark claims to provide a vision that is new and rebellious, they actually serve the traditional and conservative function of perpetuating the established norms of the group.[167] (2) Progressive forms are either 'logical', which serve to build up narrative systems of expectation/fulfillment much as though the narrative presents a coherent argument and helps the reader to anticipate events, or 'qualitative', which are unexpected developments and characteristics that come to be 'acceptable' to the [sympathetic] reader only after events have occurred.[168] (3) Repetitive forms lend structure to the narrative by giving repeated emphasis to a narrative principle through variation, that is by repeating the same thing in different ways.[169] (4) Conventional forms are those literary traditions which in their application serve to raise expectations prior to the act of reading. These can include the minor forms [tropes, figures], but Robbins chooses to concentrate upon general rhetorical forms and overarching literary traditions which provide the background to reading Mark's Gospel in its intertextual context.[170] With these tools, Robbins develops his thesis that Mark represents a variation upon 'the portrayal of a cycle of relationships between teacher and disciple from the moment of call to discipleship until the time of the death of the teacher [which] is a conventional form in Mediterranean literature'.[171]

---

166. Kenneth Burke, *Counter-Statement* (Berkeley: University of California Press, 1968), p. 124, as quoted in Robbins, *Jesus the Teacher*, p. 7.

167. Robbins, *Jesus the Teacher*, pp. 7-8.

168. Robbins, *Jesus the Teacher*, pp. 9-10.

169. Robbins, *Jesus the Teacher*, p. 10.

170. Robbins, *Jesus the Teacher*, p. 10.

171. Robbins, *Jesus the Teacher*, p. 11.

Robbins begins his outline of the structure of Mark by reference to repetitive forms, in particular the presence of what he terms 'three-step progressions'. Reviewing the presence of repetitions-of-three in series and scenes throughout the Gospel,[172] he notes that with respect to the most well-known example of the triple prediction of the passion (8.31; 9.31; 10.33-34), each prediction takes place within a similar narrative framework: the first step of narrative progression sees Jesus as the center of action, leading his disciples from one location to another (8.27-30; 9.30-32; 10.32-34). The second step sees Jesus interacting with others (8.31-33; 9.33-34; 10.35-40), which leads to the third step wherein Jesus summons his disciples and instructs them in discipleship (8.34–9.1; 9.35-50; 10.41-45).

Using this as a heuristic model, Robbins searches the Gospel for similar three-step progressions, finding several (1.14-20; 3.7-19; 6.1-13; 8.27–9.1; 10.46–11.11; and 13.1-37). 'Each three-step progression inaugurates a section of material that explores new attributes in the identity of Jesus and new dimensions in the responsibilities of discipleship.'[173] The result is the following outline in which the character of Jesus as teacher and the character of disciples as followers are developed: Jesus is introduced as 'son of god', and the disciples respond simply by leaving everything upon their summons and following him. Jesus' ability to heal is then identified with the title 'son of god', while he prepares a select group of twelve to carry on his ministry of healing. Jesus as a rejected prophet sends out the twelve with instruction concerning their actions when they are rejected. Jesus then discusses his identity as the suffering, dying and rising son of man, and summons the disciples to a way of life defined in terms of acceptance of loss of life as a means of gaining life. As authoritative son of David, Jesus elicits the disciples' preparation for his entry into Jerusalem and the Temple. After predicting the destruction of the Temple and defining his role as future son of man and the dying messiah-king, Peter, Andrew, James and John are given the responsibility of carrying on Jesus' program (gospel) at a time when he is absent from them and when they will face circumstances of difficulty similar to those Jesus will soon face. Robbins has not only discovered a carefully integrated narrative structure with which to provide an outline of events and developments within the Gospel, but has also displayed a progression of the relationship between Jesus

---

172. Robbins, *Jesus the Teacher*, pp. 19-22.
173. Robbins, *Jesus the Teacher*, pp. 25-47 (46).

and the disciples that shows a unified narrative program of Jesus' thought and actions.

This program is then compared to conventional literature in the Mediterranean environment at the time of the writing of Mark's Gospel. Robbins turns first to prophetic literature of the Hebrew Bible to discern a pattern wherein: '1. the word of the Lord comes to the prophet; 2. the prophet announces the word of the Lord; 3. events occur according to the words of the Lord that the prophet announces'.[174] In contrast, Mark alters this pattern fundamentally at the very first step: 'There are no repetitive forms in Mark insisting that the word of the Lord comes to Jesus. Instead, the action and speech of Jesus himself gains center stage.'[175] The social dimension of this alteration shifts from that of a prophet whose authority derives from the lord, to that of a prophet-teacher who transmits a system of thought and belief he himself embodies. The rhetorical significance of this alteration arises with a shift from the integrity of the prophet being secured by the intervention of the lord in history, to that wherein the action and speech of a prophet-teacher finds integrity through his own lifestyle consistent with his instruction.[176] It is a shift from prophet to a disciple-gathering teacher, a socio-rhetorical phenomenon which finds parallels in many other literary examples of contemporary Greek literature, particularly the *apomnemoneumata*, the only extant example of which 'we' see for Mark's time in Xenophon's *Memorabilia*. The socio-rhetorical pattern underlying Xenophon's portrait of Socrates contains three essential elements: '(1) the teacher himself does what he teaches others to do; (2) the teacher interacts with others through speech to teach the system of thought and action he embodies; and (3) through his teaching and action the teacher transmits a religio-ethical system of thought and action to later generations through his disciple-companions'.[177]

The remainder of the book is devoted to a comparative analysis of the rhetorical form of the Gospel as it integrates the progressive and repetitive forms into the conventional forms of both biblical Hebrew prophetic tradition and the Greco-Roman tradition of disciple-gathering teachers. Robbins identifies three major divisions which shape the significant phases of the relationship between disciple and teacher: the first

174. Robbins, *Jesus the Teacher*, p. 58.
175. Robbins, *Jesus the Teacher*, p. 59.
176. Robbins, *Jesus the Teacher*, p. 59.
177. Robbins, *Jesus the Teacher*, p. 64.

is the gathering of disciples found in 1.1-13. Here is defined Jesus' fundamental role as teacher, whose 'call to a student-disciple represents the first moment in the relationship [between them]. This moment results in the resolve of the disciple to associate extensively with the teacher in order to learn through discussion and observation.'[178] And yet, the role of Jesus and the role of the disciples in the Gospel of Mark are composite, unique portraits when compared with the conventional literature of both Israelite and Hellenistic traditions and the Greco-Roman role of itinerant teachers. On the one hand, Jesus' call to individuals is reminiscent of Yahweh's call to both Abraham and Moses in the LXX. 'Jesus' commands, directions, and explanations take the place of Yahweh's commands, directions, and explanations...The attributes of Jesus' character, action, and speech unfold much like the attributes of Yahweh's character, action, and speech in biblical narrative, while the attributes of the disciples unfold much like the attributes of the prophets.'[179] On the other hand, this merger is not complete, since Jesus' autonomy is limited to his mortality. Indeed it is Yahweh who both empowers, sanctions Jesus' ministry and limits his autonomy by requiring him to accept his death. In Jewish tradition Yahweh alone is autonomous in wisdom and power. This is in fact a unique combination of both Jewish and Greco-Roman traditions found in Mark: 'a basic dimension of the "messianic" nature of Jesus' activity in Mark arises from the adaptation of the autonomous stature of the teacher in Greco-Roman tradition and the subsequent importation of this emphasis on autonomy into Jewish tradition where God has been the dominant autonomous figure'.[180] The Greco-Roman literary tradition of the figure of the itinerant philosopher teacher portrays an individual whose authoritative wisdom and power leads him to gather disciple-companions in order to transmit a system of thought and action to them. It is this autonomy that Mark displays in Jesus, one which continually gets Jesus into trouble as various Pharisees, scribes and priests condemn him for usurping Yahweh's unique position. Mark thereby revolutionizes Jewish tradition when Jesus' knowledge of the gospel of god allows him to take over Yahweh's role of teaching, calling and commissioning, and yet Mark remains fully within Jewish tradition when Jesus' mortality becomes his definitive limitation.

178. Robbins, *Jesus the Teacher*, p. 114.
179. Robbins, *Jesus the Teacher*, p. 119.
180. Robbins, *Jesus the Teacher*, p. 116.

The intermediate phase, found in Mk 3.7–12.44, is the period of instruction and learning. Here, too, Greco-Roman tradition with its emphasis upon comprehension has transformed Jewish tradition with its expectation of obedience and the threat of punishment if there is disobedience. The Gospel of Mark downplays the decisive tests and punishments of biblical literature, relegating any threat of judgment and punishment until the end.[181] The emphasis is instead upon education and the clarification of ambiguities, complexities and paradoxes of the religio-ethical system; the test of comprehension is applied by assessing the person's fulfillment of the new role demanded by the system *throughout* her/his adult life.[182] Indeed, the parallels between Mark's portrait of the developing relationship of Jesus to his disciples and those found in Xenophon's *Memorabilia*, Philostratus's *Apollonius of Tyana*, and the Socratic dialogues show a similar four-stage progression: (1) the initial instruction of the teacher's system to the disciple(s) [Mk 3.7–5.43//*Memorabilia* 4.3.1-18//*Apollonius* 1.21-40//*Theaetetus* 151E–160E], (2) demonstration to the disciple(s) of the superiority of the new system over that of the dominant traditional system, which may lead to incomprehension and confusion on the part of the disciple(s) [Mk 6.1–8.26//*Memorabilia* 4.4.1-25//*Apollonius* 2//*Theaetetus* 160E–186E//*Meno* 70A–79E], (3) intense educational exploration of the central dimensions of the system between teacher and disciple(s) in an effort to overcome incomprehension [Mk 8.27–10.45//*Memorabilia* 4.5.1-12//*Apollonius* 3//*Theaetetus* 187A–210D//*Meno* 79E–89C], and (4) the public presentation of the system by both teacher and disciple(s), setting the stage for confrontation between the teacher and authority figures representing the dominant traditional system which accelerates the teacher's ultimate demise [Mk 10.46–12.44//*Memorabilia* 4.6.1-15//*Apollonius* 4–6//*Meno* 89D–100C].[183] These parallels show that the 'system of thought and action in the Gospel of Mark is more like the religio-ethical system of [these Greco-Roman socio-rhetorical traditions] than the covenant system that informs the stories of Abraham, Moses, Elijah, and Elisha'.[184]

---

181. Robbins, *Jesus the Teacher*, p. 166.
182. Robbins, *Jesus the Teacher*, p. 167.
183. Robbins, *Jesus the Teacher*, pp. 126-55, for a survey and comparison of the Greco-Roman and Jewish socio-rhetorical traditions.
184. Robbins, *Jesus the Teacher*, p. 167.

After the four stages of the teaching/learning phase of the relationship between disciple and teacher, the final phase begins. Herein 'we' find in both Mark and *Memorabilia* parallel progressions: (a) preparation for separation from the teacher [Mk 13.1–37//*Memorabilia* 4.7.1-10] and (b) the teacher's acceptance of death [Mk 14.1–15.47//*Memorabilia* 4.8.1-11].[185] Nevertheless, even here 'we' see a unique mingling of both Jewish and Greco-Roman traditions: the genre of farewell speeches found in biblical and extra-canonical Jewish literature[186] is transformed in Mark 13 through the convention of the temple dialogue found throughout Greco-Roman literature.[187] The biblical and Jewish tradition of the suffering righteous one is informed by the Greco-Roman tradition of the king dying as a benefit for his people[188] to help Mark provide for 'the possibility for living with the offense of the crucifixion of the Messiah'.[189] By means of this unique combination of cultural traditions, Mark has provided a story that transforms Jesus from a disciple-gathering teacher into a Jewish messiah who dies as an ultimate example of dedication to both his own religio-ethical system and to his followers, thus becoming a true king through whom the kingdom of god is near at hand.

With this careful exercise in intrinsic analysis and comparative literary studies, Robbins offers a significant introduction to what will become a formidable trend in American biblical scholarship [i.e. rhetorical criticism]. He has contributed to the concept of narrative rhetorical structures through his analysis of repetitive, conventional and progressive forms found throughout the Gospel: repetitive forms serve the important rhetorical function of argumentative amplification, the reinforcement of character traits, and the pattern of narrative expectation and fulfillment; conventional forms serve the important rhetorical function of implicit appeal to shared values, presumptions, 'facts' and 'truths' through social and literary intertextual references; progressive forms give the narrative an argumentative structure, even a sense of logical progression through assertion, demonstration and implicit conclusion as new narrative stages are reached.[190] Robbins has also

185. Robbins, *Jesus the Teacher*, pp. 172-73.
186. Robbins, *Jesus the Teacher,* pp. 173-78.
187. Robbins, *Jesus the Teacher*, pp. 178-79.
188. Robbins, *Jesus the Teacher*, pp. 187-91.
189. Robbins, *Jesus the Teacher*, p. 191.
190. Robbins, *Jesus the Teacher*, pp. 197-209.

provided a very careful and detailed argument documenting the impact of Greco-Roman social and literary traditions upon the composition of the Gospel of Mark, breaking open for discussion the question of the contribution made by concurrent Mediterranean culture to all aspects of the traditioning process surrounding the sayings attributed to Jesus, as well as to the stories concerning his life. He, and others following him, will seize upon the relationship between inner-textual forms and inter-textual argumentative customs as means by which to discern the social influences at work in giving shape to the traditions concerning the teachings and life of Jesus.

In particular, Robbins begins to focus exclusively upon specific rhetorical handbooks and treatises extant at the time of the writing of the Gospels (dropping the modern rhetorical insights of Burke) in order to discern the impact they may have had upon developing Jesus traditions, specifically with respect to the aphorisms and collections of sayings attributed to Jesus. He considers the state of rhetorical education and its effect on composition by referring to the exercises found in Theon's *Progymnasmata*, especially the instruction concerning *chreia* and its elaboration. He then combines this with Aristotle's interest in enthymemes and the classification of argumentation into three broad genres (epideictic, forensic, deliberative). The result is an attempt at social reconstruction by means of analysis of implied syllogistic premises which provide both the shared values presumed in and the intended rhetorical effect of a given performance. The effect of such an approach to the Gospel traditions is not only to give emphasis to the *Hellenistic* milieu informing and impacting upon the Jesus material [in contrast to the traditional comparison with Jewish theology and tradi-tion], but also to reconsider the whole form-critical and *traditions-geschichtliche* enterprise through insights garnered from ancient rhetori-cal practice.

An early article, '**Pronouncement Stories and Jesus' Blessing of the Children: A Rhetorical Approach**',[191] provides a typical sample: traditional approaches to Jesus' aphorisms in the Gospels [i.e. form-criticism] consider the actions and settings of Jesus to be secondary accretions to the more original saying. However, turning to Theon's *Progymnasmata* 'we' see that the history of *chreia* traditions shows that actions are often as important as sayings, and in some instances

191. Vernon K. Robbins, *Semeia* 29 (1983), pp. 43-74.

actions are *prior* in the tradition to which sayings become attached as a means of explanation or clarification. Thus, with the presence of speaker, speech/demonstration and audience shown to be integral to a *chreia*, 'we' have before 'us' a rhetorical situation in which *ethos* (character), *logos* (thought) and *pathos* (response) play an important role in interpretation.[192] With this insight, his rhetorical analysis of sayings in which children play a prominent role in the saying and action of Jesus in response to a particular question or situation shows 'a specific image of Jesus' character (ethos) by means of pointed speech and action (logos) designed to evoke a positive response (pathos) toward a particular system of thought and action perpetuated by early Christians'.[193]

So, for example, 'we' find in the sayings tradition of the synoptics a *chreia* in which children are said to belong to the kingdom. Matthew's version in 19.13-15 shows a mixed *chreia*, wherein Jesus responds to his disciples' hindrance of the children by means of a statement ('Let the children come to me, and do not hinder them, for to such belongs the kingdom of heaven') and an action (laying his hands on the children). Jesus' action reinforces by example his speech (*logos*), thus creating an *ethos* which is both morally favorable and consistent, and providing positive response (*pathos*) by including the little children in the kingdom.[194] Mark's (10.13-16) is also a mixed *chreia,* whose unique feature is the presence of a maxim ('Truly I say to you, whoever does not receive the kingdom of god like a child shall never enter it') which both contributes to Jesus' *ethos* and 'links this specific story with the argumentation about children, kingdom and discipleship that the author is developing in Mark 9.30–10.31'.[195] More importantly, the presence of this maxim arises out of a process, as evidenced in Greco-Roman literature,[196] in which a specific saying can develop into a general saying, and was therefore unlikely to be 'an originally independent dominical saying' inserted later.[197] Finally, Luke's version (18.15-17) is a straightforward sayings *chreia* which includes the maxim, but emphasizes the speech of Jesus by removing the action of laying on

192. Robbins, 'Jesus' Blessing of the Children', pp. 44-45.
193. Robbins, 'Jesus' Blessing of the Children', p. 48.
194. Robbins, 'Jesus' Blessing of the Children', pp. 53-55.
195. Robbins, 'Jesus' Blessing of the Children', p. 60.
196. Cf. Robbins, 'Jesus' Blessing of the Children', pp. 56-59.
197. Robbins, 'Jesus' Blessing of the Children', p. 58, quoting Rudolf Bultmann, *History of the Synoptic Tradition* (trans. J. Marsh; New York, 1963), p. 47.

hands.[198] This phenomenon helps the unit to contribute to the narrative argumentative Gospel context in which is built a sequence of three stories ending with maxims (18.14, 16-17, 29-30) which describe the means by which a person may enter the kingdom.[199]

The *chreia* concerning who is the greatest in the kingdom was originally an action *chreia* which underwent a 'natural tendency to add some kind of statement after a demonstrative action as the story was told in an extended literary setting'.[200] In this case, the mixed *chreia* 'we' studied above, which depicts Jesus 'receiving' the children as examples of 'one who is greatest', provided an *ethos* of Jesus which became springboard for the saying 'whoever receives one such child in my name receives me'. Luke (9.46-48) once again enhances the mixed *chreia* with addition of a maxim ('for he who is the least among you is the one who is great'), thus securing Jesus' *ethos* through the rationale (*logos*) the maxim provides.[201] Matthew (18.1-5) provides two additional maxims in support of final statement on 'receiving', the first statement being an adaptation of the saying found in the *chreia* tradition 'we' explored above ('Truly, I say to you, unless you turn and become like children, you will never enter the kingdom of heaven', cf. Lk. 18.17; Mk 10.15), while the second is an adaptation of a free-floating maxim concerning humility and entry into the kingdom.[202] Finally, Mark (9.33-37) is a three-part story, wherein the question concerning the greatest is answered first by inserting a maxim of reversal/sacrifice ('If anyone would be first, he must be last of all and servant of all') which serves to tie the story to the greater narrative rhetorical Gospel context (8.31–10.45), next by an the action of placing a child in their midst, and finally by the 'receiving' saying.[203]

Finally, Robbins notes in the *Gospel of Thomas* and in John the tendency of maxims and settings, when once formed out of a sayings-*chreia* trajectory, 'to be used in literary units that…developed by generalizing both the settings and the sayings that existed in previous

198. Robbins, 'Jesus' Blessing of the Children', p. 61.
199. Robbins, 'Jesus' Blessing of the Children', pp. 61-62.
200. Robbins, 'Jesus' Blessing of the Children', p. 63.
201. Robbins, 'Jesus' Blessing of the Children', pp. 65-66.
202. Robbins, 'Jesus' Blessing of the Children', pp. 66-68.
203. Robbins, 'Jesus' Blessing of the Children', pp. 68-69.

chreia traditions'.[204] Examples are found in *Gospel of Thomas* 22 and Jn 3.1-21, the former springboarding from an observation of Jesus' concerning children to series of statements,[205] the latter simply presuming a generalized *ethos* about Jesus, the kingdom and children in developing 'a dialogue that extends into a discourse on believing heavenly things'.[206]

The results of these analyses are clear: saying and setting are integral to the interpretation of the *chreia*. In some cases the action on the part of Jesus may have been the original core upon which the saying was built for the sake of clarification. Maxims were not free-floating logia, but arose as a consequence of the Gospel author's rhetorical strategy. The Gospel authors' elaborations of the *chreiai* are well within what 'we' would expect given Greco-Roman educational tradition, being constructed to serve their rhetorical needs. Thus, Robbins suggests five revisions for the investigation of traditions about Jesus in the Gospels: (1) the interrelation between rhetoric within the story and rhetoric of the Gospel context should be explored; (2) the scholar should be open to the possibility that the action of Jesus may be at the heart of the tradition, which would have spawned varying attempts at clarification; (3) maxims often naturally arose through a rhetorical process that sought general application to a specific saying, and should be distinguished from popular maxims; (4) components integral to the original form of a *chreia* tradition need to be distinguished from those arising through influence of another *chreia* tradition; (5) dialogues can be composed for the sole purpose of presenting various maxims, which is a different process from that of *chreiai* to which maxims have been added or from out of which maxims have arisen.[207]

These insights provide an important means by which to begin to construct an alternative methodological system that discerns changes in discourse traditions reflective of new or differing social circumstances, eventually leading to the potential of developing a criterion of authenticity to be applied to sayings attributed to Jesus. He offers an example of the usefulness of these insights in his follow-up article, entitled

---

204. Robbins, 'Jesus' Blessing of the Children', p. 69.
205. Robbins, 'Jesus' Blessing of the Children', pp. 70-72, with parallels to Xenophon's *Memorabilia*.
206. Robbins, 'Jesus' Blessing of the Children', pp. 72-73 (73).
207. Robbins, 'Jesus' Blessing of the Children', pp. 73-74.

'**Pragmatic Relations as a Criterion for Authentic Sayings**',[208] an analysis of the beatitudes in their Matthean and Lukan form.[209] The resulting 'network of communication' is compared to other sayings in the Jesus tradition to determine any common 'postured meaning effect' whose tenacity might provide a criterion for authenticity.

He explicates the results of his studies on *chreia* elaboration into a methodological principle and gives it a name, 'criterion of pragmatic relations'. 'The purpose is to formulate a systematic approach for analyzing the relations of implications and explications in single or grouped sayings...[by using] the *extant fields of discourse in the texts* as an aid for understanding the development of fields of discourse in the tradition.' The extent fields are 'viewed as sectors of the network of communication which functioned in, around and through the situations, actions, and speech of Jesus and his followers', presuming that the later developments in the tradition emerged through bridging earlier ones.[210]

A close rhetorical reading of Matthew's beatitudes (5.3-12) reveals a series of enthymemes which produces an 'accumulative' or 'qualitative' sequence of states of being. Each beatitude introduces a quality that sets up another quality, which in turn is accepted as appropriate in relation to the other preceding qualities: from 'poor in spirit', to 'those who mourn', 'the meek', 'those who hunger and thirst for righteousness', 'the merciful', 'the pure in heart', 'the peacemakers', 'those who are persecuted for righteousness' sake', and, finally, 'you when men

---

208. Vernon K. Robbins, *Forum* 1.3 (1985), pp. 35-63.

209. Robbins, 'Pragmatic Relations', pp. 38-46, 50-51, explores the Q-source performance of the tradition, but does so in order to show that the scholarly reconstruction shows no relation to any performance we have. Scholars have (1) imported the syllogistic structure of the Matthean beatitude form into the Lukan tradition (which shows no easily reconstructed 'logical' reasoning), (2) imported the deductive reasoning governing the Lukan tradition into the Matthean tradition (which is accumulative and inductive), and (3) eliminated the spiritual field of discourse presumed by Matthew ('poor in *spirit*', 'hunger and thirst *for righteousness*') and the intersubjective form of Luke ('Blessed are the poor, for *yours* is the kingdom of God').

Cf. the discussion of contrasting performances given below. They assume that a more universal and propositional form lies at the heart of tradition, reconstructing more logically clear statements that make sense in reconstructed settings which the tradition does not itself exhibit.

210. Robbins, 'Pragmatic Relations', pp. 37-38. Emphasis mine.

revile, persecute, and utter all manner of evil against you'.[211] The central Matthean beatitude that lies at the heart of this 'spiritual field' seems to be the enthymeme in Mt. 5.10: 'Blessed are those who are persecuted for righteousness' sake, for theirs is the kingdom of heaven'. If stated in a syllogistic form, it would look like:

Unstated Premise:	Blessed are those to whom the kingdom of heaven belongs.
Stated Premise:	The kingdom of heaven belongs to those who are are persecuted for righteousness' sake.
Conclusion:	Therefore, blessed are those who are persecuted for righteousness' sake.

The attribute of 'righteousness' lies at the heart of the syllogism, logically relating the kingdom of heaven to those who are blessed. Every other beatitude[212] explores an 'attribute of character' associated with righteousness: being 'poor in spirit', 'mourning', being 'meek', 'hungering and thirsting for righteousness', being 'merciful', being 'pure in heart', and being 'peacemakers'.[213] The accumulation of enthymemes appears to describe various states of spiritual being, states which are attributable to the righteousness of the kingdom of heaven.

In contrast, the Lukan beatitudes in 6.20-22 show a logical progression from a physical state of poverty to a biological state of hunger and an emotional state of weeping.[214] Furthermore, they also display a personal rather than a universal vision. This is made quite clear when 'we' compare the syllogisms underlying the parallel enthymemes in Mt. 5.2 and Lk. 6.20:

Unstated:	*Blessed are those to whom the kingdom of heaven belongs.*	**Stated:**	Yours is the kingdom of god.
Stated:	The kingdom of heaven belongs to the poor in spirit.	**Unstated:**	*You are poor.*
Conclusion:	Therefore, blessed are the poor in spirit.	**Conclusion:**	Therefore, blessed are the poor.

There is a postured meaning effect in the first three beatitudes of Luke which reveals a unique, personal vision, similar to that found in

---

211. Robbins, 'Pragmatic Relations', p. 49.

212. With the exception of Mt. 5.11-12, which 'operates out of the logic of analogy with the prophets'. Cf. Robbins, 'Pragmatic Relations', p. 50.

213. Robbins, 'Pragmatic Relations', p. 50.

214. Robbins, 'Pragmatic Relations', p. 51.

other aphorisms attributed to Jesus.[215] Rather than arguing from a general state of blessing of any to whom the kingdom belongs and deducing therefrom the particular attributes of this state, Luke reasons from the particular social and physical state (of poverty, hunger and weeping) to the general state of blessing.

Robbins suggests that if such a pragmatic relation (not the specific 'postured meaning effect', but the modality of personal vision and argumentation from particular to general) were to lie at the foundation of the tradition, it would explain the later developments found in Matthew: as 'we' have seen in his work on the pronouncement stories above, it is typical that a saying reflecting a personal vision related to a specific situation attracts attempts at broader applicability. In this case, Matthew does so by working out the implicit logic at work in the enthymeme, transforming it from an intersubjective second-person relationship to a third-person 'proverbial' and universal logical form (from 'you are poor and therefore blessed' to 'blessed is anyone to whom the kingdom belongs, and among those are the poor in spirit'). This can then itself be expanded by application to a general spiritual field (from economic 'poverty' which is broad, but still socially specific, to 'spiritual poverty' which even the powerful and rich can attain).[216]

Turning from this analysis of the deductive use of premises in the beatitudes, Robbins considers the inductive use of examples to support propositions, such as found in Mt. 5.38-42. Here 'we' have a proposition ('Do not resist one who is evil') given argumentative support through several examples, the first three of which describe responses to evil acts arising from the ascribed status of social and political subjectivity ('But if anyone strikes you on the right cheek, turn to him the other also', 'if anyone would sue you and take your coat, let him have your cloak as well', and 'if any one forces you to go one mile, go with him two miles'). This presumes a similar social situation (poverty, weakness) as that described in the first three Lukan beatitudes. Furthermore, each of the examples are intersubjective, second-person addresses, as in the Lukan beatitudes. 'We' also see that the specific examples reason toward a general proposition, also as found in the Lukan beatitudes.[217] Hence, an integrated field of discourse emerges:

215. Robbins, 'Pragmatic Relations', p. 52.
216. Robbins, 'Pragmatic Relations', pp. 53-56.
217. Robbins, 'Pragmatic Relations', pp. 58-59.

Blessed are the poor, for yours is the kingdom of god.

Blessed are those who hunger now, for you shall be satisfied.

Blessed are those who weep now, for you shall laugh.

If anyone strikes you on the right cheek, turn to him the other also;

and if anyone would sue you and take your coat, let him have your cloak as well;

and if anyone forces you to go one mile, go with him two miles.

In this integrated setting, the first three deductive propositions and the last three inductive examples create an inferential bridge that works toward the implicit proposition, 'Blessed are you who are abused and oppressed'. [How suspiciously revolutionary!] This, in turn, is remarkably similar to the beatitudes found in Mt. 5.11 ('Blessed are you when people revile you and persecute you and utter all kinds of evil against you falsely on my account') and in Lk. 6.22 ('Blessed are you when people hate you, and when they exclude you, revile you, and defame you on account of the son of man').[218] 'We' can thus begin to trace the origins of a unique [Aha!] and personal vision found in intersubjective sayings related to specific settings that speak of ascribed social standing and its experiences. Here 'we' are beginning to see how a careful rhetorical reading (informed by contemporaneous pedagogical handbooks of rhetorical instruction) of *extant* traditions can help us *better* to uncover the network of values and beliefs at work in the sayings of and stories about Jesus, eventually helping us to construct social histories [and perhaps even a criterion by which to determine an authentic core of sayings from Jesus!].

It is this social turn that he more fully explores in the articles leading up to the publication of ***Patterns of Persuasion***[219] [we shall not be considering this book itself, however]. In doing so, he enlists the help of Aristotelian genre classifications of argumentative discourse and the implications they make concerning the role of audience and setting upon speech: forensic (which emphasizes a rhetoric of accusation and defense, thereby asking an audience to judge guilt or innocence), deliberative (which emphasizes a rhetoric of expediency, thereby asking an

218. Robbins, 'Pragmatic Relations', pp. 59-60.

219. In which, interestingly enough, Robbins consistently refuses to draw out any inferences of social setting and situation when analyzing the *chreia* tradition of the Gospels. He instead limits his focus to analyses of the rhetoric within *chreiai* and their relationship to the rhetorical context of the Gospel tradition wherein the given *chreia* was performed/elaborated.

audience to accept advice concerning future conduct), and epideictic (which emphasizes a rhetoric of praise or blame, thereby seeking to strengthen an audience's adherence to beliefs and values it already holds, but which have come under question).[220] Yet, as we have already seen in our exploration of Mack, Robbins emphasizes the significant alteration of Aristotelian rhetorical theory as a result of the breakdown of the traditional social forums in which these three genres were confined and defined: as a result of the Roman Imperium, which saw the loss of the independence of the city-states, the sayings attributed to Jesus were composed during a period where civil ceremony, law courts and civic assemblies were no longer the dominant social settings. Thus, 'we' see a number of the sayings of Jesus arise from settings that are not limited to the three conventional arenas of rhetoric. This is significant, since the social environment helped to control the rhetorical utterance through social convention:

> For example, a speaker's use of deliberative or epideictic rhetoric in a courtroom will rarely remove the dominance of the judicial social structure—a jury and judge will proceed with a pronouncement of guilt or innocence. By contrast, when someone launches an accusation in a grainfield or the town square, a speaker may use deliberative or epideictic rhetoric so skillfully that the judicial setting is transformed into an exhibition of praise or blame or a deliberation about future action.[221]

In other words, the social setting itself no longer controls the kind of rhetoric that will dominate the story. It is the interaction between rhetorical strategies of the speaker and the dynamics of the situation that will determine the intended (and possibly transformative) rhetorical effect and the 'kind of situation it turns out to be'.[222]

Take, for example, Mt. 5.21-48, which James Williams, in his essay on *paraenesis* in the Semeia volume dedicated to this issue, suggests provides examples of sacrifice within a rhetorical strategy of excess. Williams suggests with regard to Mt. 5.38-42:

> To take this style of rhetoric literally would be just as foolish as trying to obey the teaching on adultery by engaging in self-mutilation (5.27-30). If someone hit me am I to say 'Now hit me again'? If I were to lose

---

220. Robbins, 'Pronouncement Stories from a Rhetorical Perspective', *Forum* 4.2 (1988), pp. 3-32 (20).
221. Robbins, 'Pronouncement Stories from a Rhetorical Perspective', p. 21.
222. Robbins, 'Pronouncement Stories from a Rhetorical Perspective', p. 21.

$1,000 in a lawsuit, should I offer the winning party another one thousand on Christian principles?[223]

According to Robbins, this is a misreading of the situation: 'the antitheses have changed judicial (forensic) rhetoric into deliberative rhetoric. In other words, commandments that could be perceived as laws triable in a law court are transformed into guidelines that function as advice for maintaining honor in a political arena where citizens assemble to make decisions about group action.'[224] They are not so much laws offered in the context of *Gesellschaft* (culture) [of particularly Jewish society whose legal foundation is the Torah and its interpretation] but in the context of Christian *Gemeinschaft* (community). The Sermon on the Mount transforms commands into advice in order to secure and maintain honor among those who identify themselves as Christians: 'Where will judgment occur for the one who looks at a woman lustfully? Not in a law court where a verdict on adultery could be sought. Rather, people in the community will disapprove of or publicly denounce the man who looks at a woman lustfully.'[225] The concern with divorce is the same: it is not the legal matter that is at issue, but the issue of shame or honor one holds within a community which can indict an individual among his or her associates for the breakup of marital bonds.[226] Even the antithesis about killing, which speaks explicitly of judicial consequences (5.21-26) of liability to judgment, council and *Gehenna*, is referring to inner-community structures and the standing of the individual within the community.[227] Given the change in the rhetorical situation, 'we' can then begin to explore the social setting of these antitheses and ask whether the rhetoric is in fact 'excessive' at all, or rather appropriate to the implicit sacrificial demands of honor within certain social circumstances.[228]

Consider also 1 Tim. 2.11-15, which Robbins suggests moves from deliberative toward judicial rhetoric, an aspect that Jerome Quinn, in the same volume, completely ignores. The assertion 'Let a womon

223. James Williams, 'Paraenesis, Excess and Ethics', *Semeia* 50 (1990), pp. 163-87.
224. Vernon K. Robbins, 'A Socio-Rhetorical Response: Contexts of Interaction and Forms of Exhortation', *Semeia* 50 (1990), pp. 261-71 (264).
225. Robbins, 'A Socio-Rhetorical Response', p. 264.
226. Robbins, 'A Socio-Rhetorical Response', p. 264.
227. Robbins, 'A Socio-Rhetorical Response', p. 265.
228. Robbins, 'A Socio-Rhetorical Response', pp. 266-67.

learn in silence with full submission' is supported with rationalizations that help to articulate and defend it: 'I *permit* no womon to teach or to have authority over a man; she is to keep silence. For Adam was formed first, then Eve; and Adam was not deceived, but the womon was deceived and became a transgressor.' The result is a shift from concern with honor and shame within *Gemeinschaft* to declaration of what is and is not considered an infraction of what is permitted, somewhat akin to legal characteristics of *Gesellschaft*.[229] This judicially charged rhetoric results in a powerfully authoritative pronouncement which secures the behavior of womyn who will face consequences in an environment where people are told what is permitted and is not permitted.[230]

Here, Robbins finally makes the step from innertextual rhetoric and intertextual comparison to the social implications of such an analysis. Up to this point, the 'social' in 'socio-rhetorical criticism' has been limited to the hermeneutical implications concerning the relationship between a saying and its narrative setting. The most that has been derived from such an implication is that rhetoric emphasizes the pragmatic dimension of a communicative act: the meaning of a saying is determined by a 'context' in which it functions. 'The saying has meaning through the relation of items to one another in the saying and the relation of those related items to other things, often present in sayings, actions, or other expressed or unexpressed phenomena in the world.'[231] So far Robbins has explored these phenomena strictly in terms of narrative context, whether 'narrative' is limited strictly to the brief description of the setting in which a saying is uttered (or an act performed), or expanded to include the literary and argumentative context of the Gospel in which the story takes place, or even beyond these confines to include cultural and literary traditions of the time in which the story was remembered and eventually written down. The 'social' in all of this is the argument that (1) saying and setting are inseparable (the 'social' context mentioned in the *chreia*), (2) Jesus traditions exhibit the impact of classical rhetorical education (the 'social' context implicit in the fact that Jesus sayings are *chreiai*), and (3) Gospel authors are rhetors (the 'social' context implicit in the fact that rhetorical education and cultural literary traditions helped to shape the form of the Gospels).

229. Robbins, 'A Socio-Rhetorical Response', p. 270.
230. Robbins, 'A Socio-Rhetorical Response', p. 270.
231. Robbins, 'Pragmatic Relations', p. 38.

His expansion is now such that the 'social' dimension to argumentation is the implicit relationship of audience and speaker made through argumentative strategy. Meaning of rhetorical text is determined by the rhetorical genre in which the text operates: if a text is 'forensic', this implies a relationship between 'speaker' and 'audience' (whether understood as characters within the text, or as implied author and implied reader of the text) which would bring a much different interpretative meaning than if the text were 'deliberative' or 'epideictic'. This meaning would also, in turn, shed light upon the historical contextual circumstances out of which the text arose.[232]

Thus, rhetorical criticism operates within the biblical exegetical hermeneutic which asserts the priority of reconstructing the historical 'context' of not just intertextual contemporaneous argumentative and literary traditions, but also the social 'contexts' that are reflected in the values and argumentative 'intention' of the traditions. The question to be put to Robbins at this point is, 'Why?' Here I believe we enter into

232. Thus, Robbins opts for a 'deliberative' rather than, say, Williams's 'judicial' reading of the Sermon on the Mount, fully aware of the interpretive impact this would have upon the analysis of the argumentative dynamics and intentions, and upon the resultant understanding of the social context out of which the argument [supposedly] developed. It is not clear, however, how Robbins derives his 'deliberative' understanding of this text other than sheer interpretive assumption: it can just as cogently be argued that the Matthean Jesus' ethos is so pronounced, any declaration on his part is rhetorically presumed to be authoritative, hence binding upon the community. Is this 'advice' or 'law'? Is there any limitation to Jesus' pronouncements in Matthew such that they appear to be restricted simply to the social dynamics of a community, or rather is not his rhetoric proclaimed to be valid anywhere, for all time (cf. Mt. 5.17-20; 28.20)? If presumed limited to a particular community, what makes his authority such that it is different from the author of 1 Timothy? Do they not both assert standards of behavior and then back them up with argumentation which articulates and defends them? Finally, is it the case that 'deliberative' only concerns itself with expediency and advice? Does it not also concern itself with legal practice, and also take place in a setting wherein decisions concerning 'what is and is not permitted' are binding? It is certainly the case that the determination of rhetorical genre is one important means of classification providing the interpretive filter through which a text may be understood. It is not clear how the genre is to be determined by the analyst: whether from reconstructed authorial intention, innertextual analysis, intertextual comparison, or at the time [throughout history] of its reception. [Genre is an inventional strategy, not an analytical tool; indeed, it seems to be used 'inventionally' when appealed to as means of analysis and interpretation.]

the heart of the matter, for given the *inventional* aspects of the Aristotelian genre classifications as Robbins applies them (i.e. they are no longer reflective of social settings, but are argumentative strategies that place the audience in certain roles and reflect an argumentative 'intention' on the part of the tradition), there is nothing to keep him from asserting that the social 'context' thereby discerned can be met with *at any time the text is taken up.* In other words, the restriction of social 'context' to ancient historical context of composition is not at all *necessary* given his emphasis upon *inventionality.* So, 'why' continue to make historical reconstruction a priority and goal? His answer lies in his *ethical* position [*how* it is an 'ethic' will be shown in the next section] of adhering to the belief in the biblical text's *foreign-ness,* a belief informing all his work since *Jesus the Teacher.* I suggest that it is *here* we can begin to uncover the disciplinary power systems constraining his rhetorical-critical efforts.

For, on the one hand, Robbins is correct to assert the 'foreign-ness' of the Gospels, given their antiquity and the social and cultural milieu of their production. On the other hand, he falls into the trap of every interpreter by assuming that it is this 'foreign-ness' that should become the object of interpretation and the foundation of further reception of the text. This is seen throughout his work: his exploration into 'intertextuality' is limited to comparisons with traditions and texts extant at the time of the writing of the Gospel material. 'Innertextual' dynamics are more freely explored by application of both modern and ancient rhetorical filters, but are either again compared only with 'intertexts' of the time, or are used for the sake of the historiographical project of discerning 'authentic' sayings of Jesus [both of which are pursued for the sake of identifying the 'uniqueness' of the Christian message]. Even when the 'social' aspect of 'socio-rhetorical criticism' begins to gain prominence in his critical work, the hermeneutical assumptions of historiography [capriciously] assert their hegemony. Genre studies of texts are used to reconstruct historical 'contexts' of performance and to assert a hermeneutically central authoritative 'intention': a Gospel author has chosen to depict Jesus in a particular way due to the impact of certain social and historical circumstances, thus making these circumstances available to the critic *through* the rhetoric of the text. All of rhetoric's inventional power is [unnecessarily] reduced and used as a tool of historiography, as 'texts' and their 'meanings' are explored for the sake of reconstructing[!] their historical 'contexts' of composition.

My point is that the pursuit of historiography is not 'wrong' per se, but it is a particularly *interested* pursuit in biblical studies, one dedicated to the cause of perpetuating the institutional interests of the field. And it is Robbins's adherence to the [value] concept of the 'foreignness' of the Bible which assures disciplinary identification and control of interpretation. [We shall explore this more thoroughly in the next section.] As such, biblical rhetorical critics, as expert [historical] interpreters of the Bible, are claiming a position of tremendous power.

But, lest I appear to be exaggerating, it is in fact to the *specific* and explicit end of maintaining disciplinary identity that Robbins openly pursues his socio-rhetorical critical method, as he states in an apologetic article entitled '**Rhetoric and Biblical Criticism**'[233] he wrote with John Patton [*prior* to the publication of *Jesus the Teacher*]. Here (t)he(y) try [desperately] to set biblical studies back into the heart of liberal arts acadamnia by offering a rather thorough survey of early rhetorical-critical efforts of previous decades by biblical scholars. They make it explicit that this survey is meant

> to (1) disclose ways in which biblical criticism addresses fundamental rhetorical issues, (2) describe the importance of particular contributions to the understanding of rhetorical forms, and (3) trace the implications of biblical criticism for interpreting the nature and structure of meaning [in order] to suggest that biblical critics are *active participants* in the current quest for methodological refinement, philosophical formulation, and mediation between practice and theory in the investigation of language, speech, text, and meaning.[234]

According to them, the contribution biblical critics could claim to make is 'an awareness of rhetorical and aesthetic nuance of meaning within forms and structures [in the particular] dimension of literature by which language escapes itself to produce meaning beyond the banal, the unambiguous, and the conventional...'[235] Biblical rhetorical analysis reveals the significance of form that 'unites consciousness, history, and ultimacy in demonstrable patterns of meaning'[236] so that one can fulfill

---

233. Vernon K. Robbins and John H. Patton, 'Rhetoric and Biblical Criticism', *Quarterly Journal of Speech* 66.4 (1980), pp. 327-37.

234. Robbins and Patton, 'Rhetoric and Biblical Criticism', p. 329. Emphases mine.

235. Robbins and Patton, 'Rhetoric and Biblical Criticism', p. 335.

236. Robbins and Patton, 'Rhetoric and Biblical Criticism', p. 336.

the *obligation* to 'seek those ultimate world-pictures and stories which best[!?] answer to the total experience of mankind'.[237]

On the one hand, this is an impassioned plea for building bridges between disciplines, for 'making present' the common ground shared between biblical scholars and other rhetorical critics. It is an attempt at offering justification to other humanistic efforts for the distinctive characteristics that rhetorical criticism of the Bible could contribute to liberal arts education. On the other hand, let us note the specific nature of the contribution as seen by Robbins and Patton: it is not just that other disciplines have something to learn from rhetorical criticism of the Bible ('the patterns of consciousness and culture'; the social patterns 'which govern and constrain the use of forms'; the disclosure of the 'life-world of rhetors and audiences within which meaning is constituted' and the 'historical conditions or exigences that generate and sustain particular practices of dialogue, narration, epistle, and poem'),[238] which could be said about the contributions of any discipline in an interdisciplinary endeavor. It is that particularly *biblical* rhetorical analysis *gets to the foundations of existence, to the shared universals, to the ultimate and transcendent extremes of language and thought.* [Is there a latent ideology of fascism in the idea of finding 'total' experience and 'ultimate' world-pictures/stories? Why the implicit plea for unification under a monomyth?] What better way to *apologize* for this particular disciplinary endeavor and *deliberate* upon its potential role in the humanities?

I am not suggesting that the historiographic project of biblical studies in general, nor even Robbins's own work specifically, explicitly conceives itself in any such sinister fashion. What I am suggesting is that 'we' find here several notions of power converging through his rhetorical-critical methodology: the rhetoric of 'historiography', which asserts hermeneutic hegemony of reconstructed original 'meaning effect', hence shoring up the ramparts of disciplinary boundaries, meets with

237. Robbins and Patton, 'Rhetoric and Biblical Criticism', p. 335, quoting Amos Wilder, *Theopoetic: Theology and the Religious Imagination* (Philadelphia: Fortress Press, 1976), p. 80. Note the obligation inherent in Wilder's quotation, 'We *must* seek...', and its acceptance by Robbins and Patton in their assessment, 'the relevance of Wilder's conceptions for rhetorical scholars *may best be reflected in his recommendation...*'

238. Robbins and Patton, 'Rhetoric and Biblical Criticism', p. 329.

the rhetoric of 'ultimacy', which asserts the importance of *biblical* contributions to other humanistic endeavors. This potent combination results in a *missionary* project for biblical studies, one that can best [only?] be carried on through the practices of the historian-as-exegete. There is at work here an ideology dedicated to maintaining the centrality of his role as humanist interpreter of the biblical text.

Hermeneutical Center—Historical-Critical Reconstruction

Interestingly, Robbins touches upon the issue of 'ideology' as the last of his four steps comprising 'socio-rhetorical criticism'. Here we see the potential for a self-reflecting [*museful*] turn within his method to consider the 'interests', assumptions, world-views, *pouvoir/savoir* systems at work not only in the biblical texts and traditions, but also in biblical interpretation, even biblical studies as academented institution. Unfortunately, this potential is realized [if at all] only *within* the institutional discourse domain of biblical exegesis, rather than reflecting upon/against it.

At first, he turns his attention to the 'ideology' of interpretive approaches, by which he means the critical presuppositions that inform a personal *Weltanschauung*. This *Weltanschauung* considers 'the body and the culture of the body to be as important as the mind and the culture of the mind'.[239] It informs an effort that attempts to unite in a theory of communication the social and historical factors contributing the meaning of an utterance in its 'context'.[240] The issue is set within the context of biblical exegesis, which attempts (a) to read the text and (b) to open the world of the text. The questions are, (a) *how* should one read a biblical text, and (b) *which world* of a biblical text is one trying to open?[241] Rejecting the 'New Critical' isolation of the text in which the 'world of the text' is read in a 'house of language',[242] he wants to explore the social functions of language in an 'interdisciplinary method grounded in a multidisciplinary approach that uses both trans-disci-

---

239. Robbins, 'Introduction to the Paperback Edition', p. xxii.

240. Cf. Robbins, 'Introduction to the Paperback Edition', p. xxiv, where he speaks of the effort to 'establish an environment that brings together the narratorial and social dimensions of language in texts', by which he clearly means historical reconstruction.

241. Robbins, 'Introduction to the Paperback Edition', p. xxiii.

242. Robbins, 'Introduction to the Paperback Edition', p. xxiv.

plinary and disciplinary practices in its interpretive strategies'.[243] He means he wants a method that combines a social semiotic[244] approach to culture and language with a thematic approach to literary and cultural traditions[245] and which is open to the contribution of several socio-literary interpretive strategies. Such a method emphasizes the 'texture' of a text, the cognitive, emotive, social and material meaning potential of the network of signification and communication in texts.[246]

Once again, Robbins indicates a potential here for a method that emphasizes the role of textual reception and the impact of hermeneutical ideology in the interpretation of a biblical text. He is very explicit about this:

> On the one hand, this means that texts have no meanings in and of themselves. Texts contain signs to which reader-interpreters attribute meanings. On the other hand, this means that texts receive meanings as people living in social environments attribute meanings to them. In other words, every meaning perceived to be in a text is attributed to signs in that text by a reader-interpreter. The meanings in the text are dependent on the kinds of knowledge the reader-interpreter brings to the text.[247]

The problem is, while Robbins is so emphatic about the *social* construct of meaning, even to the point of admitting to the impossibility of securing a single and controllable meaning to a 'text', he nevertheless allows the historical 'context' to assert its hegemony in interpretation, due to his commitment to the belief in the biblical text's *foreign-ness*. In other words, his concern with the 'social meanings and social conversation in which the language in the text is engaged'[248] as an ideological 'texture' is considered *solely within and by means of the historical-critical enterprise of exegesis*, since it is only by this means that the text's foreign-ness is both maintained and deciphered.

This is unfortunate, since there is a *recognized* potential here for interpreting textual and social 'engagement' in terms of 'reception-

---

243. Robbins, 'Introduction to the Paperback Edition', p. xxiv.

244. He understand 'semiotics' to be a *multidisciplinary* method that studies 'everything in a culture as a form of communication' in order to seek 'similarities and differences that both interrelate and differentiate phenomena' (Robbins, 'Introduction to the Paperback Edition', p. xxv).

245. Robbins, 'Introduction to the Paperback Edition', p. xxv.

246. Robbins, 'Introduction to the Paperback Edition', p. xxvii.

247. Robbins, 'Introduction to the Paperback Edition', p. xxix.

248. Robbins, 'Introduction to the Paperback Edition', p. xxix.

through-time-and-context'. Disappointingly, this potential is eliminated by the commitment to the historical-critical paradigm: every example he gives of the application of socio-rhetorical method as he has defined it, examples running from John Elliott's *A Home for the Homeless*[249] to Ched Myers's *Binding the Strong Man*,[250] Mack's *A Myth of Innocence*, Bernard Brandon Scott's *Hear Then the Parable*[251] and Clarice Martin's 'A Chamberlain's Journey',[252] are all limited to hermeneutical interpretation of 'texts' and the generation of authoritative meaning in reconstructed socio-historical 'contexts'. At no point does he ask about the ideology behind the exegetical method itself and its presuppositions concerning the nature of 'text' and 'context' in the generation of 'meaning'. He has yet to ask about the role of the 'social' (i.e. academentia-as-ideological-institution) in the pursuit of biblical interpretation *itself.*

What he does, instead, is argue that the awareness of the 'foreignness' of the text which his method generates, that is, the authoritative role historical 'context' plays in the exegetical interpretation of 'text', keeps[!?] the interpreter from imposing his own ideology upon the text. 'The reading equips the narratorial voices with as much social, cultural, and ideological information about ancient Mediterranean culture [as is available to the scholar]' thus opening up the 'foreign world of the text in a manner that richly informs our faith and lives as we live in the midst of foreign cultures at the turn of the century...'[253] But not only is 'our faith' strengthened through socio-rhetorical criticism, but socio-rhetorical criticism also provides the means by which 'Western Christianity [can] be a leader in the work of reconciliation and equitable distribution of food, wealth, and respect on the planet earth during the twenty-first century'.[254] This is quite a powerful contribution: socio-rhetorical criticism and its sensitivity to the 'texture' of the 'text' becomes the heralded savior of Christianity [note the ideology of 'purity' implicit in the emphasis upon 'foreign-ness' of the 'text', and with it the implicit 'sanctification' of the Bible through this interpretive means] making 'us' more sensitive to the plurality of cultural voices and differences in the world, hence 'strengthening' 'our' faith. But this isn't

---

249. Philadelphia: Fortress Press, 1981.
250. Maryknoll, NY: Orbis Books, 1988.
251. Minneapolis: Fortress Press, 1989.
252. *Semeia* 47 (1989), pp. 105-35.
253. Robbins, 'Introduction to the Paperback Edition', p. xxxviii.
254. Robbins, 'Introduction to the Paperback Edition', p. xxxviii.

all: through this strengthening [sensitizing] of 'our' faith 'we' can become *leaders* in the effort to solve the world's problems! [This is no longer an academented analog of 'missionizing' as we saw above and with Mack; this is also now an explicitly religious missionizing guided by a liberal agenda.]

Sadly, the emphasis upon the historical and social 'foreign-ness' of the biblical text as the 'context' of interpretation, undermines his own agenda. His method of 'democratization' of interpretation brings History and Tradition (Bible) right back to the center of authority, the access to which is only through elite, academented means. That his interpretive method excludes these same foreign cultures by its own elite access to knowledge, that it takes away the authority of others outside the realm of biblical scholarship to interpret texts according to the social, cultural and ideological systems in which they receive the biblical text, that neither history nor the Bible necessarily provide the answers for the world's ills, never crosses his mind. Instead, he presumes a liberal agenda of an elite 'who know better' and are in a 'better position' to help the world solve its problems.

Once again, and not for the last time, rhetoric comes to the aid of biblical studies, justifying the relevance of the discipline by reference to a deeply embedded ideology of the 'messianic' call of the west.[255]

255. Unfortunately, the promise of the socio-rhetorical [totalizing] methodological superstructure to bring together the multidisciplinary tasks of interpretation still can't seem to escape these same difficulties of engaging in reconstruction of historical 'meaning effects' for the sake of 'equipping the interpreter for exploring the convictions, beliefs, values, actions and attitudes in other religions at the present time'. [Vernon K. Robbins, *What Is Socio-Rhetorical Criticism?* (Guides to Biblical Scholarship, New Testament Series; ed. Dan O. Via, Jr; Minneapolis: Fortress Press, forthcoming), prepublication draft, p. 232.] While Robbins recognizes the *symphonic, symbiotic* and *museful* nature of his paradigm, and while he draws from a number of examples of works which embrace modern methods and critical insights, at no point does he discuss the reasons for the centrality of a hermeneutic of original 'meaning' in his paradigm. Nor does he envision the potential for socio-rhetorical criticism to engage in innertextual, intertextual, socio-cultural textual, ideological textual interpretations of the Bible outside of its first-century 'contexts'. [The question to raise at this point is whether the paradigm itself isn't so thoroughly directed to historical reconstruction of originary 'meaning effect' that it *precludes* any other historicist readings, i.e. reading *through* time.]

c. *Antoinette Wire*

As we turn now to Antoinette Wire's seminal work, ***The Corinthian Women Prophets: A Reconstruction through Paul's Rhetoric***,[256] we will see that her argumentative effect is similar to those so far explored: a socio-historical reconstruction through argumentative strategies that were taken up in response to the rhetorical situation of the first-century [in this case, Corinthian] Christian community. She, with all the others, uses rhetorical criticism to shore up the institutional boundaries of biblical studies as a historicist discipline.

As an alternative to an approach that compares Pauline argumentative dynamics with Jewish and Greco-Roman rhetorical traditions, an analysis in which Paul's argumentation would be developed through the self-conscious application of contemporary rhetorical methods within his socio-historical milieu, Wire eliminates attention to authorial intention, turning instead to the means of persuasion applied in his correspondence.[257] Whether or not he was aware and made use of a specific rhetorical tradition is not relevant here. Instead, Wire wants to analyze the persuasive dynamics within the letter itself, how they function to persuade, rather than identifying specific forms (outlines, topics, tropes, colors, etc.). This frees her from the hegemony of research into ancient rhetorical models, turning instead to the movement instituted by Perelman and Olbrechts-Tyteca known as the 'New Rhetoric'. Like Mack, she defends this move by arguing that this modern model maintains important theoretical and practical divisions and analysis found in ancient Greco-Roman rhetoric. The contribution the New Rhetoric makes, however, lies in its emphasis upon the persuasive dimension of all discourse, focusing upon 'how words function to persuade'.[258]

Survey of Scholarship

The theoretical difficulty facing historical reconstruction of a social situation through the rhetoric in a text (even one as discursive as Paul's letter, which addresses an explicit cluster of circumstances within the life history of a particular community) is the tension created in the model between rhetoric as descriptive of persuasive argumentation and rhetoric as prescriptive. While modern rhetorical theory is founded

256. Minneapolis: Fortress Press, 1990.
257. Wire, *Corinthian Women Prophets*, p. 2.
258. Wire, *Corinthian Women Prophets*, p. 2.

upon observations of 'how people who have any freedom use it to persuade each other' (i.e. rhetoric as descriptive), it also requires the rhetor to secure assent by analyzing the addressed audience effectively, by shaping her/his argument according to their expectations and values (i.e. rhetoric as prescription). 'Because everything spoken must be shaped for them, the measure of the audience as the speaker knows it can be read in the arguments that are chosen.'[259]

This emphasis upon the theoretical role of an audience in argumentation allows Wire to reconstruct the socio-historical circumstance of a particular sector of the audience (Corinthian womyn prophets) through Paul's rhetoric. His letter comes at a later stage of an ongoing dialogue between Paul and the Corinthian community, and thus the argumentative situation of 1 Corinthians reflects 'the influence of earlier stages of the discussion on the argumentative possibilities'.[260] Paul must read effectively this circumscribed situation and gauge his audience as accurately as possible, 'to use their language, to work from where they are in order to move them toward where [he wants] them to be'.[261] Prescriptive demands on effective persuasion in a rhetorical situation helps Wire to reconstruct the rhetorical situation from which the letter arises,

259. Wire, *Corinthian Women Prophets*, p. 3. This is, in fact, the definition offered by Perelman and Olbrechts-Tyteca in their work, *The New Rhetoric: A Treatise on Argumentation* (Notre Dame, IN: University of Notre Dame Press, 1969), pp. 96, 491, for the concept of argumentative situation, which is quite different than the concept of the rhetorical situation proposed by Lloyd Bitzer, 'The Rhetorical Situation', *Philosophy & Rhetoric* 1.1 (1968), pp. 1-14. The difference is important to note since Perelman and Olbrechts-Tyteca emphasize primarily the discursive dimension of the rhetorical act, while Bitzer's pragmatic approach allows for a socio-historical approach. That is, the rhetorical situation lies outside of the discourse and interacts with it and is acted upon by it once the discourse is delivered. The argumentative situation is generated both before the discourse and through it; this latter dimension is esp. important in analyzing the rhetorical strategy, as it emphasizes the impact upon the rhetorical situation *through the discourse itself*: the argumentative situation changes and develops within the discourse. If Wire had not confused these two concepts, she would have seen that the relationship between Paul and the community could not be reduced to theological dogma and social position. She would have noticed that through the discourse several stages of theological ideas were being developed, that several social interrelations were being experienced and were shifting throughout the argument.

260. Wire, *Corinthian Women Prophets*, p. 3, quoting Perelman and Olbrechts-Tyteca, *The New Rhetoric*, p. 491.

261. Wire, *Corinthian Women Prophets*, p. 3.

to which it responds, and upon which it hopes to have an influence. This rhetorical situation is proposed with the purpose of providing a coherent, unifying description of the circumstances of the Corinthian community. Ultimately, it becomes the springboard from which she hopes to provide the theological and sociological position not only of the Corinthian church, but specifically of the Corinthian womyn prophets. Consistently, the portrait provides not simply a complement to the discussion, the other side of the implied dialogue, but a *contrast* to Paul's own theology and world-view.

Her method employs the rhetorical model proposed by Perelman and Olbrechts-Tyteca in their work *The New Rhetoric*. It is a close reading of the argumentative dynamics of Paul's letter to the Corinthians, one that uses a two-step approach. The first step is an analysis of what is called the 'techniques of argumentation' employed by Paul throughout the letter. These she terms the 'textual rhetoric', and she collects the various examples under Perelman/Olbrechts-Tyteca's fourfold divisions:

Dissociative arguments. According to Wire, these are arguments in which 'assumed structures of reality are broken apart to provoke new understanding, as when reality is dissociated from appearance, the concrete from the abstract, or the divine from the human'.[262] Paul's use of this technique of argumentation is extensive, and she groups them around several themes.

The first theme (argumentation dissociating principle from practice) will serve as an example for the rest. By dissociating principle from practice Paul hopes effectively to qualify important claims to authority made by the Corinthian community. Such examples include 1 Cor. 6.12a and 6.12b ('All things are authorized me, but not all things are

---

262. Wire, *Corinthian Women Prophets*, p. 7. Unfortunately, this definition is not exactly what Perelman and Olbrechts-Tyteca had in mind. Dissociative argumentation, more specifically, takes place when an individual is confronted with incompatibilities and attempts to reconcile them. All dissociative argumentation is analogous to the single philosophical pair 'appearance/reality' and takes the form 'X and Y might appear to be contradictory, but a more careful exploration reveals a deeper reality from which both X and Y originate, and hence they are in fact complementary'. Cf. Chaim Perelman, *The Realm of Rhetoric* (Notre Dame, IN: University of Notre Dame Press, 1982), pp. 126-37, and Perelman and Olbrechts-Tyteca, *The New Rhetoric*, pp. 411-59.

useful. All things are authorized me, but I will not fall under the authority of anything'), 10.23a and 10.23b ('All things are authorized, but not all things are useful. All things are authorized, but not all things are constructive'). Assuming that the principle admitted by Paul in the first half of these statements is one which at least the Corinthian community shares with Paul, at most asserts independently of Paul, by agreeing with these principles he is able to reflect his audience's position well enough to then qualify their application of them. In fact, as Wire suggests, his qualification of the principle of freedom is so severe as to reverse it in practice: sexual practices, eating in temples, marriage, celibacy and acting on one's knowledge are all limited or censored through Paul's argumentation, argumentation founded upon what Wire identifies as dissociative strategies.[263]

Other themes include:

- Arguments dissociating thought from reality (3.18 'If any among you in this age think they are wise, let them become fools that they may become wise'), in which boasts from members of the community are deflated as mere thought, not based in reality at all;[264]

- Private sphere from public sphere (14.34-35 'Let the womyn be silent in the churches...And if they want to learn, let them inquire of their husbands at home, for it is shameful for a womon to speak in church'), in which Paul argues that the church is to be understood as public space, and hence all behavioral norms are to be judged as such. Home is seen as the place in which 'people's energy... their lively interest in such things as food, sex, unveiled prayer, money, inquiry and ecstasy' are to take place, sanctioning church space as undefiled and undisruptive;[265]

- Self-benefit from community benefit (14.3-4 'Those who prophesy speak to people to build up and encourage and strengthen. Those who speak in tongues build themselves up, but those who prophesy build up the church'), an argumentative strategy in which Paul affirms their spiritual

---

263. Wire, *Corinthian Women Prophets*, pp. 13-14.
264. Wire, *Corinthian Women Prophets*, pp. 14-15.
265. Wire, *Corinthian Women Prophets*, pp. 15-17.

power and gifts, but subordinates their application to the good of the community;[266]

- Shame from honor (1.27 'god chose the world's foolish things to shame those who are wise'), in which Paul emphasizes the activity of god to choose those socially marginal in order to shame those socially powerful. He does not, however, suggest that such a volition implies a reversal of social station;[267]

- Human from divine/flesh from spirit (15.50 'But I say this, brethren: Flesh and Blood cannot inherit the kingdom of god, nor can the perishable inherit the imperishable'), which seeks to condemn certain behavior as indicative of human or fleshly, thus antithetical to the spiritual status claimed by some in the community in order to justify this behavior.[268]

Quasi-logical argument. These appeal to the logic of common sense, 'wholes are made up of parts, contradictions exclude each other, things the same or similar are to be treated as such'.[269] Paul relies primarily upon arguments from definition and arguments from justice, although a uniquely religious rhetorical category left unexplored by Perelman and Olbrechts-Tyteca is Paul's use of arguments of divine retribution.

- Arguments from definition (11.3 'But I want you to know that of every man the head is christ, and the head of womon is man, and the head of christ is god') depend not upon empirical reality, but upon a stated universal or logical quality from which important strategic implications can be based. They do not depend upon evidence, but simply assert, and usually so when there are competing definitions.[270] It is a rhetorically powerful tool, since it simply assumes acceptance of the definition, from whence all implications must also be accepted. Paul uses this strategy

266. Wire, *Corinthian Women Prophets*, pp. 17-19.
267. Wire, *Corinthian Women Prophets*, pp. 19-21.
268. Wire, *Corinthian Women Prophets*, pp. 21-23.
269. Wire, *Corinthian Women Prophets*, p. 7.
270. Wire, *Corinthian Women Prophets*, pp 23-24.

to address the question of wisdom (1.18) in his argumentative attempt to undermine alternative claims to authority by uniting the community under a single Gospel. He also uses it to address the role of womyn in the church (11.3), and even appeals to a definition of the nature of god (14.33), in both cases seeking to control what he sees to be disruptive behavior by womyn in the worship service. Finally, his definition of love (ch. 13) also serves the greater argumentative purpose of deflating alternative claims to authority which he sees as disruptive and dividing the community through particular worship practices.

- Arguments from justice (7.3 'Let the man give what he owes to his wife, likewise also the wife to the husband') demand that it is logical that identical cases be treated identically, and equivalent treatment be given to equivalent cases. Paul invokes this strategy especially when addressing issues of marriage.[271] But he also uses it to assert his right to church support (9.5-6), and to justify the implication of certain social practices with respect to womyn prophets (11.4-5a, 11-12).

- Arguments from divine reciprocity of human acts are of two different kinds. The first, according to Wire, is the divine passive 'used to state that God reciprocates and surpasses all human knowledge of God' (13.12b 'Now I know in part, but then I shall know even as I have been known').[272] The second kind shows retribution, the pronouncement of a sentence of death for polluting god (11.29-30 'For those who eat and drink without discerning the body seal their own sentence with eating and drinking. This is the reason many among you are weak and sick and several die'). The quasi-logical nature of this strategy lies in the notion of consequences from acts, guaranteed by intervention from the cosmic dimension. This is an important contribution to rhetorical theory, only minimally anal-

---

271. Wire, *Corinthian Women Prophets*, p. 25.
272. Wire, *Corinthian Women Prophets*, p. 26.

ogous to the application of legal principle in circumstances of violation of laws.[273]

Arguments based upon the structure of reality. Wire identifies their presence and function and says that 'These arguments appeal to relations of cause and effect and relations people have to their acts, the latter including arguments from authority, custom, and other more symbolic kinds of co-existence'.[274] According to Perelman, such arguments draw from a *recognized* liaison between elements of reality in order to pass 'from what is accepted to what we wish to have accepted'.[275] Thus, if elements are understood to have a causal tie between them, then argumentation 'can be directed toward the search for causes, the determination of effects, and the evaluation of a fact by its consequences'.[276] A person can be judged according to her/his actions, attitudes, works, or on the basis of her/his relationship to a group or status-perception. Recognized symbolic relationships can be appealed to or exploited for effect (e.g. flag burning, communion). In every case, an argument based upon an appeal to the structure of reality attempts to legitimate and support a rhetorical or argumentative position by appeal to acceptable standards and interpretations of reality. Ultimately, it is an appeal to tradition.

- Arguments from what is written concentrate around issues of church practice in Paul's effort to constrain Corinthian behavior in worship, moral and financial matters. These are almost exclusively appeals to Jewish written traditions, whether explicitly quoted (10.7), summarized (10.5-6) or generalized (14.34). 'The accent is on warning. Paul primarily uses the Scripture as a rein on the Corinthians, including the women.'[277]

- Arguments from god's calling appeal to the incumbent position and/or behavior one is expected to adopt while a

273. Wire, *Corinthian Women Prophets*, pp. 26-27. It is the notion of the curse, the reliance not upon the organizations of state power and enforcement, but upon a world-view that extends beyond immediate human intervention. It is 'justice' elevated to a universal and personified power.

274. Wire, *Corinthian Women Prophets*, p. 7.

275. Perelman, *The Realm of Rhetoric*, p. 81.

276. Perelman, *The Realm of Rhetoric*, pp. 81-82.

277. Wire, *Corinthian Women Prophets*, p. 29.

member of a group living within a particular tradition. Paul makes use of this strategy, particularly concentrating on the volitional status of the Corinthians in the introductory section of the letter, where it is most important for him to recall and re-establish a common ground with his audience. Through an appeal to their relationship to him and others in the participation in the 'partnership' of christ (1.9), Paul not only confirms his own relationship to them, but sets up a broad base of authority by reference to their calling 'to be saints together with *all those in every place* who call on the name of our lord Jesus christ' (1.2). The use of this appeal, however, is not just in reminding them of their calling, but in argumentatively defining the consequences, which Paul clearly understands to be an impact upon the hopes and desire and values of the believing community, but not upon the social status. Whether they appear in the discussion of wisdom (1.22-29) or in marriage and household questions (7.15-24), Paul uses appeals to god's calling ultimately to argue that the social standing of the believer within the community is not affected by her/his volitional status.[278]

• Related to his appeal to volition through which he emphasizes the communal nature of the status of the believer in the faithing community is his argumentative appeals to universal church practice. In every case (4.17; 7.17; 11.16; 14.32-36) Paul uses this strategy authoritatively and definitively to claim validity for his particular interpretation of the social consequences of membership in the community. Marriage and prophecy in particular bring about such appeals, where Paul must ultimately make use of an argument from justice: if others elsewhere behave in such a way, then you must conform to their behavior, since you are all under the same calling.[279]

• Finally, to secure several argumentative points, Paul appeals to traditions that trace their authority back to the lord. These concentrate, once again, in those sections of

278. Wire, *Corinthian Women Prophets*, pp. 30-31.
279. Wire, *Corinthian Women Prophets*, pp. 31-33.

the letter concerning marriage practice (7.10-11) and prophecy (14.37-38), but in one instance Paul also makes use of a command of the lord in a digression concerning his apostolic behavior and relation to the community (9.14).[280]

Arguments establishing the structure of reality. These are arguments appealing to *mimēsis* and analogy, making use of examples, illustrations, metaphors, models in order to provide paradigms of behavior. In contrast to arguments that appeal to the structure of reality, '[arguments establishing reality] do not deduce from common sense or from assumptions about how reality is structured but work to establish this structure. Here the argument moves from the particular to the general: examples seek to prove a rule; illustration is satisfied to highlight a rule; models or anti-models stand for more than themselves; analogy and metaphor speak through particular images.'[281]

Wire discerns in Paul two primary classifications, both of which are necessitated out of the lack of traditional models for early Christian communities to follow, thereby forcing Paul to develop his own *paideia.*

- The use of Paul or christ as model to follow, in every case, presents a model of voluntary sacrifice (10.32–11.1; 14.18-20, etc.), betraying Paul's own experience of the gospel as one which has brought him from a relatively high social status to a relatively meager one. He becomes for the community an example of the new structure of reality into which the community has been called, a calling that he shares with them. Through him generalizations can be drawn, and ultimately the community comes to imitate christ. Paul's argumentation rests not upon the significance of christ's resurrection and the status a believer shares in participating through this resurrection, but upon christ's voluntary sacrifice upon the cross and the social implications drawn therefrom.[282]

- Analogy of christ's subordination to god (3.21-23; 11.3; 15.23-28). 'Three times in this letter Paul takes up a pair

280. Wire, *Corinthian Women Prophets*, pp. 33-35.
281. Wire, *Corinthian Women Prophets*, p. 7. Cf. also Perelman, *The Realm of Rhetoric*, pp. 106-25.
282. Wire, *Corinthian Women Prophets*, pp. 35-36.

of terms in human experience and subordinates one term to the other as lower to higher, the higher term to Christ, and Christ to God. In each context the point being debated is not the relations of Christ and God, but the order of the original two terms. This indicates that Christ is being subordinated to God as an argument to confirm a distinctive ordering of the other two terms…The analogy here does not appeal to a better-known human relation but to a divine relationship, constructing human reality less by a suggestive parallel case than by an authoritative divine case.'[283] In order for this argument to be effective, the members of the audience must accept christ as the key link between themselves and god. The question is whether they understand this link in the subordinate terms Paul uses.

Throughout the careful exploration of each of these techniques of argumentation, Wire draws conclusions concerning the composition and theological self-understanding not only of the groups Paul is implicitly or explicitly addressing, but of the impact such arguments may have upon the Corinthian womyn. Often this is achieved through interpolation: in 1 Cor. 6.12, 13; 7.1b-2; 8.1b, 7a; and 10.23, Paul dissociates the principle of the authority of the believer from its practice. Regardless of whether the principle is a Corinthian slogan or a position he himself presented to the Corinthian community earlier, his argument's effectiveness depends upon him so well reflecting his hearers' views in agreeing with them in principle 'that they will be open to his qualification in practice'.[284] 'We' may thus surmise that the Corinthian community, and hence by extension the Corinthian womyn prophets, conceives itself as having authority to do all things (6.12), having all knowledge (8.1), eating what it likes (6.13), and living in freedom from sex-role obligations (7.1).[285] Wire often discerns a stance in opposition to Paul's argumentation by means of the strategies applied by Paul. Arguments from definition are assumed to imply contesting definitions, and Wire concludes that 'there

283. Wire, *Corinthian Women Prophets*, p. 37.
284. Wire, *Corinthian Women Prophets*, p. 13.
285. Wire, *Corinthian Women Prophets*, p. 14. Cf. also p. 27, where she similarly interpolates, 'In these arguments from retribution, the primary group addressed is not the Corinthian women, but they are included because Paul attacks the community at large'.

is no direct evidence showing that the Corinthian women or men used definitions that Paul is reworking or that they reworked his definitions, although some of this is almost unavoidable in verbal confrontations'.[286] Given this, it is possible for her to suggest that Paul's particular definition of the cross as *god's* foolishness and weakness builds upon the common ground of early Christian crucifixion traditions, but stands in contrast to Corinthians's understanding of the cross as 'the obvious weakness and foolishness of *human* life, the life *out of which* God raises Christ and those who are in Christ [emphasis mine]'.[287]

A similar conclusion is drawn from Paul's use of arguments attempting to establish the structure of reality: Paul's appeals to the analogy of christ's subordination to God to provide an authoritative basis for justifying his own arguments for social structures of subordination. In one instance, he undermines Corinthian appeals to specific religious leaders as figures representing distinctive theologies by setting the leaders under the community, which is itself set under christ (3.21-23). He thereby rhetorically eliminates the means by which differing groups can appeal to traditions that particularly undermine Paul's own instructions, since all belong to christ. In contrast, Wire suggests that 'the Corinthians do not understand their relation to Christ through baptism as one of being owned—at least not in a way that conflicts with their allegiance to persons who baptized them'.[288] Similarly, Paul argues at the end of 1 Corinthians that they 'remain subject to death until death is at last made subject to Christ at his triumph, and then ultimately Christ will be made subject to God'.[289] In contrast, Wire suggests that the Corinthians do not see themselves as subordinated under death, but that through christ death has given way to life. Arguments attempting to structure reality imply an alternative, even opposite, view of reality. Terms must be shared by both speaker and audience for such arguments to be effective (in these examples, both Paul and the Corinthians are arguing over the practical implications of the significance of christ and his relationship to god), but by the fact that Paul argues for one structure of reality, Wire implies an alternative must be present.[290]

286. Wire, *Corinthian Women Prophets*, p. 24.
287. Wire, *Corinthian Women Prophets*, p. 24.
288. Wire, *Corinthian Women Prophets*, p. 37.
289. Wire, *Corinthian Women Prophets*, p. 38.
290. While such may be the case, it must be determined by more contextual factors than the selection of locus alone. It is theoretically possible that arguments

For Wire, dissociative arguments are perhaps the most direct means of securing the theological position of the Corinthian audience through Paul's rhetoric. Arguments dissociating thought from reality, private from public, self- from community-benefit, human from divine, show that Paul is wrestling with concepts and principles shared between himself and his audience, but with which he disagrees with the social and practical application on the part of the Corinthians. Throughout Paul's arguments he brings specific behavior under question, from which 'we' discover that womyn are separating from their husbands/ fiancés, are praying and prophesying in the church, that people are eating food to idols in public places, that the community exercises spiritual gifts, among many other things. His technique of dissociation, however, reveals that he and they do not agree as to the value of the practices: Paul deflates the Corinthian's boasts of wisdom and knowledge as unfounded.[291] He attempts to regulate certain public behavior back into the private sphere of the home.[292] He attempts to establish a distinction between behavior which he understands as boastful and arrogant from behavior which through self-control helps to incorporate concern for the community's weaker and poorer members.[293] He argues for an interpretation of spiritual-divine behavior that differs from current practices within the community.[294] In every case, Paul is arguing for more restrictive, socially acceptable and conservative behavior as the implication of their life in christ. Thus, according to Wire, the Corinthians 'must' embrace an alternative theological interpretation of their baptismal experience: the fullness of the expression of wisdom and spiritual power through worship services of prophecy and tongues which are shared gifts without order or limitation, through public witnessing of the universal power of god-in-christ by eating food to idols, by social advancement of traditionally disadvantaged groups, by advancement of the power of the Spirit within the community through personal displays of spiritual authority, by not differentiating between home and communal space during services (hence not limiting certain behavior to a more 'appropriately' private space), by the multitude of

establishing structures of reality may be drawing from implicitly accepted values which are then made explicit in order to create greater adherence to them.

291. Wire, *Corinthian Women Prophets*, pp. 14-15.
292. Wire, *Corinthian Women Prophets*, pp. 16-17.
293. Wire, *Corinthian Women Prophets*, pp. 18-19.
294. Wire, *Corinthian Women Prophets*, pp. 20-23.

authority and leadership roles prevalent in the worship service and community. Piecing this together, Wire discerns through Paul's argument not only the explicit codes both he and the community share, not only the explicit social patterns he cannot accept within the community, but behind them both the fundamental underlying theological division: Paul's is a god of order; the Corinthian's is a god of freedom. In dissociative argumentation, Wire finds that Paul and Corinthians agree on the terms (christ, baptism, god, resurrection, wisdom, Spirit, community of faith, etc.), but not on the practical implications.

Wire can also find very specific and explicit references to Corinthian practices, upon which she can build her social and theological portrait of the community. These coalesce around arguments based upon the structure of reality, where, for example, appeals to universal church practice also serve as a contrast to Corinthian practice.[295] 1 Corinthians 1.26-27 also reflects specific and direct evidence of the social standing of some of the members of the Corinthian community. When Paul argues for the reversal of people's desire which results from god's calling, however, he argues against the reversal of their social standing, emphasizing instead god's attempt at making the wise of this world look foolish by calling the foolish of this world. The Corinthians, however, must have thought otherwise, or else Paul would not have needed to press this point.[296]

These tentative results are next elaborated through her analysis of what she terms the 'structural rhetoric' of the letter. In the following chapters, she integrates the analysis of techniques of argumentation into a presentation of the broader argumentative dynamics and strategies Paul uses to persuade his Corinthian audiences. Breaking up the letter into six major units, she hopes to highlight its argumentative dynamics in the developing discourse, which provide her with insights into the rhetorical situation: 1 Corinthians 1–4, in which Paul reconstitutes his

---

295. Wire, *Corinthian Women Prophets*, pp. 32-33.

296. Wire, *Corinthian Women Prophets*, p. 31. In the same way, dissociative arguments may reflect implicit practices of Paul's audience. E.g. the argumentative strategy in 2.12-15 which considers distinction between human and divine, between flesh and spirit, assumes that the Corinthians understand the distinction; Paul feels no need to elaborate or defend this dissociation. He does, however, attack certain Corinthian behavior as fleshly, which indicates a conflict between him and them over the concept of what constitutes life in the spirit. Thus, Wire can hope to build upon these rhetorical clues in her reconstruction of theology and practice at Corinth.

wisdom *ethos* in order to assert his authority over the community; 1 Corinthians 5–7, in which Paul addresses what he believes is flagrantly immoral sexual behavior of individuals, and judiciously urges certain groups of now-consecrated womyn to adopt the more socially conservative institution of marriage as the means by which to curtail such behavior; 1 Corinthians 8–11, in which Paul ties immorality to the issues of idolatry and the threat of pollution brought about by members of the community in their zeal to witness to the wisdom and authority granted through christ; 1 Cor. 11.2-6, in which Paul considers the potential for idolatry in the authority displayed by womyn prophets and seeks to curtail it by adopting socially conservative dress; 1 Corinthians 12–14, in which Paul further curtails prophetic freedom by distinguishing and prioritizing among spiritual gifts, and carefully structuring and limiting forms of communal worship; and 1 Corinthians 15–16, in which he reflects upon his own resurrection theology and its social implications, arguing for the centrality of his gospel in the community which he seeks to guarantee by reference to his own network of social contacts. I shall summarize the argumentative strategy of each of these sections, being careful to integrate them into a coherent rhetorical direction is united under a central theological aim: to persuade the Corinthian community to adopt Paul's more socially conservative wisdom gospel and to restrict certain of its fundamental practices which reflect social transformation.

The central issue is the definition and resulting social implications of the role of wisdom in Corinthian theology.[297] There is 'a wisdom, freedom, and fluency in the church—perhaps particularly among its prophesying women—that threatens Paul's gospel and leadership'.[298] The most immediate problem facing Paul, addressed in **1 Corinthians 1–4**, is his ethos and authoritative standing vis-à-vis the Corinthian community. In order to respond to the social and behavioral implications of the Corinthians' wisdom theology, he must first secure his claim to wisdom, hence his relationship to the community.

Paul's eventual rhetorical position of authority is derived from two distinct strategies. First, he must reconstruct his power base by arguing for position of leadership in the community. Acknowledging the abundance of 'verbal, mental and spiritual wealth'[299] Paul can nevertheless

297. Wire, *Corinthian Women Prophets*, p. 48.
298. Wire, *Corinthian Women Prophets*, p. 15.
299. Wire, *Corinthian Women Prophets*, p. 40.

shame their recent divisions over leaders and theology as absurd and a sign of spiritual immaturity. Dissociating himself from the contentions, he establishes a hierarchy under which the whole congregation is united by belonging to christ, who in turn belongs to god. This secures his role as an outside mediator, from which position he can then subsume all rival leaders (i.e. Apollos) under a hierarchy in which Paul asserts his role as more fundamental to the community. Paul's ministry and instruction is to champion 'God's gift, God's written work, God's judgment, God's possession of them, in each case presented as the limit to human claims'.[300] Under such teaching it is Paul's life of shame, homelessness, sacrifice and abuse which becomes the only authentic expression of life in the gospel. This stands, however, in sharp contrast to the Corinthians' claims to authority and power. Asserting that limitation and sacrifice is the true example of power and wisdom, as experienced in his own ministry, Paul now feels on rhetorically high moral ground, in a position to stake a claim for authority over the community. He has managed through these first four chapters to argue from a position of comparatively weak *ethos* to one that claims ultimate strength over the community.

His second strategy is to justify this claim by redefining the nature and implication of wisdom as distinct from that understood and practiced at Corinth. In a distinct 'wisdom digression' (1.18–2.16) he refutes the charge of 'not speaking wisdom in Corinth' in three ways: (1) he argues that christ as god's power and wisdom is identified as the continuing event of the word of the cross, which is 'foolishness to the lost, but to those being saved it is god's power'. This definition then allows Paul (2) to dissociate christ's wisdom from worldly wisdom, emphasizing the implication that such an understanding of wisdom legitimates sacrifice and weakness in the face of worldly power. He can thereby (3) shame the Corinthians as having misunderstood worldly wisdom for christ's wisdom, proved by the contentions. As such, they are therefore not mature enough for Paul to have spoken wisdom, of which he himself becomes the model in contrast to Corinthian practice. Through such a digression, Paul is now in a superior position from which to support his authoritative claim over the community.

Paul takes immediate advantage of his rhetorically superior *ethos* by putting the Corinthian community on the defensive: in **1 Corinthians**

---

300. Wire, *Corinthian Women Prophets*, p. 44.

5–7 Paul condemns what he sees as sexual excess and social disarray, pointing to examples such as the community's acceptance of what he believes to be an unnatural marriage arrangement, inner-community lawsuits, and the flagrancy of men attending prostitutes. This becomes a rhetorically important accusation, an argumentative context of social and spiritual chaos within the community which he can use to justify his attempt to restructure the Corinthian community. He argues that under current circumstances of spiritual immaturity, there is a pervasive, realistic and ominous threat of extreme immorality and spiritual bankruptcy within the community. In an effort to address this situation, he turns his focus upon the Corinthian womyn, who are a prominent and powerful sector of the community. It is particularly their behavior and their social situation that he seeks to modify, urging them to adopt his own alternative social agenda as a solution to the current situation. The rhetoric at first is cautious, 'judicious', as he offers advice concerning the womyn who have voluntarily withdrawn from sexual relationship with men (whether as wives separated from husbands, as widows or as virgins). While recognizing the advantages of singular devotion, he nevertheless dissociates principle from practice in an effort to justify marriage as the institution best suited to curtail sexual and behavioral excess and immorality so rhetorically prevalent in the community. Responding to very strong claims to authority and knowledge by the womyn, Paul adopts a rhetoric of reciprocity and mutual responsibility upon both sexes, appearing to offer womyn equality within the marital relationship. Paul's advice, based upon his concern with social and moral excess, is to emphasize spiritual authority as an expression of self-control and self-abnegation in order to avoid evil. In every case, a position of freedom and authority for the womyn in principle is limited to the practice of self-sacrifice for the sake of the community. The result is instruction for womyn which leads them back to the traditionally private and socially limiting sexual/marriage roles.

In **1 Corinthians 8–11**, Paul can now employ his model of limitation and sacrifice to countermand what he sees as excessive behavior regarding the question of eating food to idols. Paul offers another rhetorical example of immoral practice, eating food sacrificed to idols, which threatens to pollute the community as a result of excessive demands for freedom. This provides Paul with the opportunity to argue again for the sacrifice of principle for a practice that builds up the common good. The issues are fundamental: does participation in christ overcome barriers of pollution and transcend religious divisions, or is social and religious identity with christ fundamental and exclusive? The theological contrasts implicit here once again play up the nature and question of authority granted the believer through wisdom: 'is authority that rises from participation in Christ to be restricted so as not to offend, or is it to be exercised openly as a witness of the one God to all people?'[301] Paul once again opts for a more conservative, 'constructive' interpretation of this authority: 'watch that your very authority not become a stumbling block to the weak' (8.9) and 'all things are authorized, but not all things are constructive' (10.23). In 9.1-27, he offers himself as a model of such behavior: by all rights, he is in a position to exercise his authority to demand support from the church, as well as to exercise his freedom from the law. Neither of these he does, but rather adjusts his behavior for the sake of the common good, for the sake of expediency in the building up of the community. The issue isn't simply the question of adapting to the needs of the weakest member of the community, but rather issues of strength and authority that threaten to unseat god. This is made clear when he offers the Israelites as anti-model in 10.1-13. Here Paul argues that they, like the Corinthians, could boast of spiritual authority, but were punished because they misused it. The Corinthians, too, are in need of curtailing their exercise of authority, lest it lead them astray. By partaking of food sacrificed to idols, as well as the cup and the loaf which makes them participants of christ, they are threatening to pollute the very body of christ which would provoke divine retribution: consider the recent sicknesses and deaths in the congregation. Idolatry and controversy surrounding the lord's meal unite under the issue of pollution: it is not only that the Corinthians should seek the building up of the community by reference to needs of the spiritually weakest members, but that participation in the meal requires an exclusivity concerned with the protection of the community and christ himself from pollution which threatens to bring divine retribution. Exercise of spiritual authority leads to immorality and threat of destruction.

In **1 Cor. 11.2–6** he inserts into the middle of this discussion the issue of head coverings for women prophets. At first, he praises their adherence to tradition, but immediately offers a correction to their practice by defining a hierarchical structure of subordination: christ is sub-

---

301. Wire, *Corinthian Women Prophets*, p. 98.

ordinate to god, man is subordinate to christ, and womon is subordinate to man. The remaining complex of arguments attempts to elaborate and justify this modification, aiming to secure adherence to a more socially acceptable practice of wearing a head covering. The question is, how do the issues of female prophecy and the lord's supper fit into the context of idolatry? The answer, according to Wire, is the continuation of the concept of idolatry being defined as the unlimited exercise of authority: Paul defines the threat to god's glory by locating it in womon as the glory of the male, who in turn is the image and glory of god according to an interpretation of Genesis.[302] As long as the womon exercises her full authority, she threatens idolatry by usurping her position and competing with god. Paul's concept of such competition between the human and divine world requires womyn to wear garments which (may) represent their social inferiority.[303]

The affective, perhaps even intended *telos* of Paul's argument is reached in the regulation of spiritual behavior in Corinthian worship found in **1 Corinthians 12–14**, achieving its apex with the final authoritative demand for womyn's silence during the service. Paul seeks to differentiate between the various gifts of the Spirit in an attempt to regulate and delegate their expression.[304] He urges the Corinthians to be zealous for the 'greater gifts', which he has hierarchically defined in such a way to exalt apostleship and prophecy, for the sake of the common good. Paul wishes to dissociate prophecy from speaking in tongues, emphasizing the rational content of prophecy and its suitability to witness and foster belief in those outside the community. He castigates *glōssolalia* as private divine speech which acts as a 'sign of stumbling' to test and prove unbelief, and hence does not serve to build up community. Paul also emphasizes the need for regulation of such speech-acts within the worship service, limiting the number and order of prophetic proclamation, controlling ecstatic prayer by requiring its interpretation. He does this in an effort to shift the purpose of worship away from the Corinthian's theology of communal speaking and unlimited expression of wisdom, instead moving toward the needs of listen-

302. Wire, *Corinthian Women Prophets*, p. 133.
303. Wire, *Corinthian Women Prophets*, p. 130; cf. her Appendix 8 for various interpretations regarding this issue.
304. Wire, *Corinthian Women Prophets*, pp. 135-38.

ing, understanding and reflection, once again for the sake of community upbuilding.[305]

This persistent emphasis upon sacrificing individual experience of wisdom for the sake of the community, of regulating communal worship under individual leadership, of limiting the social consequences of a life of freedom in the Spirit to the needs of the weakest members of the community (not to mention, for the sake of the threat of generating controversy among those outside of the congregation), all lead Paul to what he views as the central source of the problems he encounters in the community: the role of womyn in the leadership and worship of the Corinthian congregation. With this particular group seeking to explore the newly experienced freedom and social mobility through a theology of life in the Spirit, Paul is persistent in his effort throughout the letter to restrict and control their behavior for the sake of the common good. His rhetorical aim eventually leads to his final solution: 'let the womyn be silent in the churches'. Rather than inspired speech, Paul limits the womyn to inspirational silence, authoritatively hammering home by every rhetorical means (appeal to prophecy, appeal to law, shame, social castigation) his attempt to overthrow their centrally powerful position in the community and replace theirs with his own more conservative agenda: 'let everything be done decently and in order'.[306] The social consequences, not to mention theological, 'we' have seen developing throughout: he assumes greater and greater authority, pushing the womyn further and further outside of the power structures of the congregation as he manages not only to restrict their behavior, but to implicate them for the supposedly rampant immorality under which the congregation is suffering.[307]

The theological center upon which this letter revolves is finally and climactically explored in the **1 Corinthians 15–16**. Having addressed the practical affairs of the congregation, and having rhetorically 'succeeded' in identifying and subjugating his opposition, he can now turn to the fundamental theological controversy giving rise to the issues and behaviors of the community Paul rejects. The issue focuses upon the question of the nature of the resurrection: does it represent an event that

305. Wire, *Corinthian Women Prophets*, pp. 146-49.

306. Wire, *Corinthian Women Prophets*, pp. 152-58.

307. See esp. Wire, *Corinthian Women Prophets*, pp. 153-54, concerning the rhetorical strategies used to implicate the Corinthian womyn prophets, and pp. 155-56, concerning the centrality of their position in the congregation.

takes place within present reality, a transformation in the life of the believer? Or is it reserved for a future time, a transformation that will only touch upon the life of the believer at the end of the age? Paul emphasizes the limitation of the access of the believer to the experience of the resurrection: using a familiar tradition of christ's dying and rising he legitimates his claim to be the final member by creating a select, formally transmitted list of witnesses to christ's resurrection,[308] thereby undermining any claim on the part of the members of the congregation to have experienced the living, resurrected christ. Paul denies any access to the transformative experience of resurrection among the living, reserving the transformation of the body into spiritual existence until the end time at which point a carefully organized and orchestrated series of events will eventually lead to all things being subjected to christ, and then finally christ himself being subjected to god.[309] This is a very thoughtful theological argument which serves as justification for every rhetorical strategy Paul has employed in his letter. Through it he has managed to stake a claim to authority over the community, being both the final witness to the resurrection and hence the origin of tradition to the Corinthians. Paul has also introduced a cosmological history which emphasizes not only order and position, but which provides a model of subjugation in christ's role in that history. Finally, he has so thoroughly dissociated the present physical age from the spiritual age to come, that he restricts any socially transformative experience of believer to another time and place. The result is a theological justification of his socially conservative program which has aimed at restricting the behavior and social position of members in the community, particularly the Corinthian womyn prophets: everyone has her place, and there is a place for everyone. Finally, Paul seeks to secure the implementation of this agenda by appeals to a network of individuals working for him (Timothy, Stephanus, Fortunatus, Achaicus), by reference to his own connections with those whom the Corinthians respect (Apollos, Prisca, Aquila), and ultimately by reference to his own plans to come to the community and his instructions to them concerning the collection (echoing his threats in 4.14-21, reinforced by the curse in 16.22).

---

308. Wire, *Corinthian Women Prophets*, p. 163.
309. Wire, *Corinthian Women Prophets*, pp. 163-69.

Hermeneutical Authority—The Historical-Critical Paradigm

Throughout this clear and coherent description of Paul's argument, Wire has been careful to balance each rhetorical position with both explicit and implicit indications of the Corinthian congregation's position. Every argumentative strategy found in Paul's rhetoric offers Wire the chance to reconstruct an alternative perspective which would explain the social practices apparently encouraged within the community that he is addressing. She generates this reconstruction through an interpolation of the results of her rhetorical analysis, an interpolation based upon certain assumptions regarding motivational and situational factors: (1) every aspect of the letter to the Corinthians is motivational and intentional speech reflecting Paul's perspective; (2) the letter is addressed to his audience, hence attempting to reflect their values in his effort to persuade them. Thus, his audience impacts Paul's rhetoric; (3) the intensity of argumentation on Paul's part reflects a proportional intensity of opposition to him in Corinth; and (4) womyn prophets play a role in the audience (whether directly or indirectly) and are impacted by Paul's rhetoric (whether directly or indirectly).[310] Thus, every means of interpolation begins with the rhetorical evidence, but then seeks to reconstruct the situation from the perspective of the Corinthian congregation by asking: what would the theological and social issues be which would give rise to Paul's argument? How can 'we' factor out Paul's perspective in order to give a reasonable and defensible alternative that gives rise to his concerns? What are the social factors giving rise to the conflicts between Paul and the Corinthians? What differing theological positions are discernible in Paul's rhetoric, and that would help to provide a coherency to his argumentation? Wire, by means of such questions, seeks to discern the rhetorical situation giving rise to the correspondence.

Wire offers a reconstruction of the rhetorical situation that centers upon contrasting interpretations of the wisdom theology prevalent at Corinth, and the social implications that lead Paul to argue against apparently prevalent behavior and practices. Paul and the Corinthians share a common theological foundation, that of christ crucified and resurrected. Paul's rhetoric, however, betrays the fact that neither he nor they agree upon the implications of this theology, upon the interpretation of the terms and concepts they share. Wire's contention is that

---

310. Wire, *Corinthian Women Prophets*, pp. 8-9.

the Corinthians see in wisdom the means whereby they overcome their previous socially disadvantaged position by expressing equality and power in the spirit. In contrast, Paul's own wisdom theology demands sacrifice, which results in the abrogation of the claim of social advantage and power. Both Paul and the Corinthians hold in common the example of christ as god's wisdom, but whereas Paul defines wisdom by the example of the cross, the Corinthians define it in terms of the resurrection and the power implicit in a theology that emphasizes the transformation of the believer, a transformation having socially advantageous consequences.

Based upon this reconstruction of the rhetorical situation, Wire offers a model of the social mobility and status of the Corinthian womyn prophets. The model offers a socio-historical context that would provide the experiential basis for both the Corinthian wisdom theology with which Paul is interacting and the specific social questions addressed to and by him. In this model she suggests that 'the social status of the Corinthian womyn prophets at the time that they are called seems to be mixed on one indicator (free/slave) and low in every other indicator: wisdom, power, rank, ethnic support, and gender'.[311] A close reading of the letter, however, evidences a change of status: wisdom instruction at the time of baptism, the cultivation of prophecy and tongues in the worship service, and the evidence of womyn abstaining from sexual relations and redefining their socio-sexual roles, all lead her to conclude that 'it appears that the Corinthian woman prophet has experienced a surge of status in wisdom, power, and honor…'[312]

On the other hand, Paul's own perceived loss of status through his conversion to Christianity, his exhortation to mimic such loss, and his theology of voluntary sacrifice[313] must be seen within the context of his social position not only as a free Jewish male, but as a member of a (presumably wealthy) Hellenistic Jewish family granted Roman citizenship. His immediate loss of status within the Jewish community (and the resulting persecutions he endures) is aggravated by the larger context in which his Jewish legal and moral tradition emphasizes voluntary sacrifice of social status within the Roman Empire for the sake of Jewish identity. This, in turn, should be set against the broad context of social mobility and fluidity among various classes of the first century as

311. Wire, *Corinthian Women Prophets*, p. 93.
312. Wire, *Corinthian Women Prophets*, p. 65.
313. Wire, *Corinthian Women Prophets*, p. 69.

a result of technological advancements, as well as economic and colonial stability. As a result, there is evidence of 'disarray' among members of the advantaged classes who decry the usurpation of their power and position by the 'rising hordes'. An acute sense of downward mobility motivates Paul's argumentative position vis-à-vis the upward mobility of the Corinthian womyn prophets.

Therefore, where Paul has experienced a loss of social position as a result of his conversion, certain members of the Corinthian congregation have experienced a significant advancement. Paul is fighting what he perceives to be a decay of social structures by fighting to retain what Mary Douglas has called a 'high grid/strong group' position by securing discipline, fighting pollution and defining group boundaries. In contrast, the Corinthians are upwardly mobile, moving toward a 'low grid/weak group' structure by downplaying concerns about ritual purity, and by traversing group boundaries by sharing at several tables. The Corinthians have found new social power which they want to exercise here and now; Paul has seen himself as losing his social position, and wishes to use himself as a model of sacrifice in an effort to keep the Corinthians from usurping more and creating controversy.[314]

Rhetoric has provided Wire with a means by which to factor into analysis the situational and motivational[315] aspects of Paul's discourse. Through Paul's rhetoric, therefore, Wire reconstructs the contrasting theological position of the Corinthians which is the basis for their own experience of christ as the wisdom of god: they reject the emphasis upon the future resurrection of the dead, stressing instead the experience of the living resurrection in the life of the believer through participation in the dying and rising of christ in baptism.[316] The active participation of the believer in christ, the free access to the living god made present in the worship of the community, 'liberates people from an old humanity bound in the structures of sin, stratified as male or female, slave or free'.[317] God is not identified with order and structure, but with disruption 'that overwhelms the structures that ossify life'.[318] The life of the new humanity that puts on god's image 'is not split between privilege and deprivation or reward and punishment but is a

---

314. Wire, *Corinthian Women Prophets*, pp. 188-95.
315. Wire, *Corinthian Women Prophets*, pp. 8-9.
316. Wire, *Corinthian Women Prophets*, pp. 167-68.
317. Wire, *Corinthian Women Prophets*, p. 176.
318. Wire, *Corinthian Women Prophets*, p. 176.

single identity in Christ where people mediate God to each other in prophecy and each other to God in prayer'.[319] God is not a god of the dead, but of the living, and the power experienced through him manifests itself here and now, accessible to everyone.

This is a very persuasive reconstruction, based upon a careful analysis of the discourse of the letter, striving to provide a coherent picture of the situation that would bring about this letter. The contrasts are defensible, grounded further in social analysis and serve to provide a context within which both parties would argue. Wire's emphasis is consistently upon the argumentative dynamics of the letter, rightfully analyzing every topic pursued, argument offered, discussion undertaken, advice given, with the aim in view that Paul was seeking to affect a change in his relationship to the audience, to alter their behavior and gain their adherence to particular values. She is careful, however, not to reduce the complex argumentative dynamics to a single genre category. Her emphasis upon modern rhetorical methods keeps her from focusing upon argumentative forms, classification of figures at the expense of the dynamism of the rhetoric. She consistently asks 'us' to consider strategy, motivation in 'our' effort to understand and reconstruct the situation from both Paul's and the Corinthian's perspective.

On the other hand, the reconstruction assumes a posture of thorough controversy, downplaying Pauline biblical authority so much that ultimately Paul's argumentative position is not given the benefit of the doubt, while the Corinthians are painted in a very positive light. I don't find this [personally] problematic per se: Paul can be painted purple, dressed in drag and sacrificed to volcanoes, as far as that goes. The question is: can we approach the same evidence she uncovers in a slightly different fashion, one which needn't assume the worst of Paul? And the answer is, 'Of course'.

The motivational aspects of Paul's argumentation, the assumption that he is developing a strategy out of his perspective, a perspective that interprets the rhetorical situation and gives shape to its presentation, are important to recognize and adjust for when attempting to factor out of his rhetoric a reasonable presentation of his interlocutors. The results of his argumentation, with respect particularly to the womyn prophets in the congregation who may certainly be a prominent and powerful sector, do indeed emphasize a concern for social acceptability and

---

319. Wire, *Corinthian Women Prophets*, p. 176.

respectability, and in some cases even a return to the social status quo. Such appears to be the case with respect to his advice for the married and for slaves (esp. 7.17-24) and his silence of the womyn during worship (14.34-36). Acceptability also appears to be the case in his advice concerning the prevalence of tongues (esp. 14.23-25) and concerning food to idols (esp. 10.31-33), as well as head coverings for female prophets (11.2-6). But it is an example of assuming the worst of Paul when suggesting these motives stem from a personal loss of social prestige, that they are an attempt to wrestle away from the socially disadvantaged any gain in power and authority they have taken at his (and his followers') expense. Why can we not assume higher motives?

It appears that together with his concern for social acceptability and respectability, Paul is genuinely interested in building up the community, both through outreach and through practices that take into account the need to address those who are spiritually weak. Paul's use of dissociative argumentation is consistently applied to those who assume a posture of strength, his references to tradition and universal practice seek to undermine prevalent concepts of authority in the community, his quasi-logical argumentation seeks to redefine the nature and expression of spiritual knowledge and authority, and his use of himself and christ as models to follow reinforce these definitions. In other words, he is having to address a very powerful sector in the community, and uses every argumentational strategy in his arsenal in an effort to both alter their behavior and to reconsider the theological foundations they may be using to justify their practices. It is true that throughout his letter these strategies emphasize subordination, that he is attempting through them to secure his own position within and over the community. But even if we accept a level of self interest here, could it also not be the case that the circumstances call for just such an intervention, in order to curb the potential (if not real) abuses of the exercise of authority of this powerful group? As 'founder' of the community, Paul is in just the sort of position of responsibility that would motivate his strategy.

On the other hand, it is nowhere apparent that his appeals to community benefit and his use of the spiritually weak to curb the authority of the strong in the community are appeals for his sake or for the sake of his followers. They instead appear to be genuine concern for those in the community who are at the time of the writing the most (spiritually and/or socially) disadvantaged (8.10-13; 10.24-29; 11.22). It is certainly the case that often the answer to these concerns comes at the expense of womyn in the community: the advice regarding marriage uses the womyn as a means of controlling male immorality; social respectability requires they wear suitable garb which (may) represent their inferior status; eating and food preparation may have repercussions regarding their role as hostesses and their participation in the communal meal; the contradictory statements in 11.2-6 and 14.34-36 make the silence of womyn during worship the target of his argument even at the expense of consistency; the implicit relationship Wire builds between womyn prophets and the theology of wisdom and freedom would also suggest that Paul's restraints would affect their social freedom and authority directly and indirectly. But, if we look more closely, for example, at the question of sexual relations as considered in ch. 7, I would suggest we find here not a consistent program of marriage and a return to traditional family and social values, but a series of arguments and a collection of advice that are much more of a mishmash than anything else. True, the argument begins with a programmatic statement: 'but because of cases of sexual immorality, each man should have his own wife and each womon her own husband' (v. 2). This is further supported by another: 'let each of you remain in the condition in which you were called' (v. 20; cf. v. 17). But this ideal is also quickly nuanced: 'I wish that all were as I myself am' (v. 7). This tension is exhibited throughout: Paul emphasizes the *lack* of social disruption as a result of their calling in advice to the married, those married to unbelievers, and to slaves, but he also considers the marriage state as quite inferior to that which allows full freedom to 'be anxious about the affairs of the lord' (v. 34) and in a very confusing argument tells slaves that their ultimate devotion is also to the lord (v. 22). Is there a coherence here? I would suggest only in that Paul is attempting to reconcile these opposites ('as I am' versus 'as you were called') in the best way possible: 'but each has a particular gift from god, one having one kind and another a different kind' (v. 7). The only other alternative is to assume the absolute worst of Paul, that he does not intend his advice to the virgins and widows to be 'real' advice at all, it is only a ruse to qualm any suspicions on their part while he effectively usurps their authority by handing the decision to marry to the men. This may be 'true', but it is only an interpretive assumption, demanding a coherence in strategy and argumentation, not to mention a deviousness, which may not be there.

Or consider ch. 12: are the distinctions among gifts of the Spirit in fact dissociative arguments, creating distinctions for the sake of controlling and limiting expression in worship, or are they arguments from justice in which each gift is given its due, and all of them are considered from the point of view of building up the community? If the former, then Wire is right to suggest that Paul is inhibiting spiritual expression, fighting against a group whose theological self-understanding centers upon the full and free expression of wisdom, prayer and prophecy without distinction. But if the latter, then Paul is arguing for greater access of the myriad of gifts of the Spirit, and it is Paul who is attempting to provide a way in which wisdom, prayer and prophecy are each given their due place in worship, against those whose power has allowed them to usurp one form of expression over another.

The simple question to ask is: why cannot we assume Paul is correct when he perceives the need to intervene for the sake of the community's weaker members, and for the sake of respectability of the community with regards to the greater society? Must we assume hyperbole in every example Paul gives of strife and the abuse of authority in the community? What if a now-important segment of the congregation, even in their zeal for experiencing a newly won freedom and authority, *has* gone 'too far'? The strange thing is, when considering the portrait offered by Wire of this new movement, it seems to have done just that: demands for social reconstruction within society and among members, refusal to concern themselves with appearances to outsiders and with possible misunderstanding by 'weak' insiders, charismatic display as the focus and legitimation of authority, unstructured and often ecstatic worship at the expense of some members of the congregation, apparent sloganeering, dismissal of a theology of the resurrection of the dead, all make it sound just like the kind of chaos Paul is describing and attempting to control.

Of course there is the issue: 'too far' according to *whom?* It was certainly not 'too far' for those who were practicing such things. It is apparently not 'too far' for Wire, who seems to be very sympathetic to the chorus of once-silenced voices whose demands for freedom she seeks to amplify again. It *was* evidently 'too far' for Paul, whose rhetoric has been effective enough throughout the history of the church and scholarship to have defined and rejected the position of these members of the Corinthian congregation. But ultimately, Wire is not interested in accepting and rescuing Paul's perspective, since Paul has many followers in biblical circles who can do that for him. What she wants to do is rescue those whose theology stands in contrast and perhaps even in contest with Paul, to bring out the 'voices in the distance'. She assumes that these voices are the ones we need to hear. But how can we be sure that theirs is really nothing more than her own, amplified through the institutional rhetoric of historicist inquiry?

But this is an inherently unfair argument: *all* reconstruction is rhetorically motivated, working within the frameworks and starting points of institutionally inscribed argumentation. The question we are here to ask is not whether one interpretation is 'better' than another [that depends on a lot of factors, primarily those that constitute (are held by) the 'audience' of critical analysis], but whether our rhetoric of power can discern the limitations and presumptions (the institutional and disciplinary assumptions) accepted by her and affecting her application of rhetorical criticism.

Wire is keen to point out that Paul's discourse provides a perception, a perspective on the social and historical situation confronting him at Corinth. Rhetorical theory emphasizes the persuasive dimension of discourse, claiming for its domain those aspects of daily life wherein truth is never certain, conclusions are never compulsory, differing values interact and demand various intensities of allegiance. Even under circumstances wherein the stakes are high, such as religion which demands the total transformation of the life of the believer, which speaks of eternal propositions of truth and life, a rhetorical [particularly a Third Sophistic] approach to religious discourse breaks open the dynamics of persuasion in the application of principles to daily life. As such, authoritative and dogmatic claims to theological certainty are aberrations, not taking seriously the struggle to gain adherence, to which Paul's letter itself witnesses:

> [R]hetoric is not concerned with demonstrating absolute truth, scientific or dogmatic, but with argument concerning what is probable, aiming to increase adherence to these presented for approval. In so far as biblical authority is taken in the popular sense as the absolute authority of the biblical writer's point of view, there is no experience of Paul's letter as rhetoric. Respect for biblical authority presupposes that Paul is right and excludes the possibility of weighing his arguments in the balance.[320]

The implications are as profound as those so far discussed by all previous authors we have met, for if the biblical texts are not approached with dogmatic/canonical propositions of divinely ordained authority,

320. Wire, *Corinthian Women Prophets*, pp. 9-10. Cf. the excellent discussion on pp. 10-11.

then the texts are free to exercise persuasion, perhaps even as they were originally 'intended' to do.[321] Rhetoric usurps dogmatics as the *telos* of biblical interpretation: the issue is no longer to develop a 'better' understanding of the biblical text in order to live out more fully the implications and practices of one's faith and beliefs according to the 'word of god'. Rather, it is to ask whether or not biblical texts are *persuasive*, or, more profoundly, *which* of them [or other texts/perspectives] are persuasive to the believer [within her/his faithing community(?)]. Approaching biblical texts as persuasive texts may break open theological discussions which would no longer be dominated by issues of authority (i.e. *who* is interpreting, *what* can be interpreted, etc.), but would provide a forum in which arguments, warrants, justifications are tested, accepted, rejected, etc. (i.e. *how* interpretation is being done). This approach allows for the participation of traditionally 'silenced voices within and around'[322] the biblical textual and interpretational tradition, giving them a chance to participate in the ensuing debate. 'Texts' become a fluid and dynamic force, their 'persuasive' dimension is dependent upon circumstances of audience [time/space] and is not eternally secure, their authority can be embraced, denied, partially adopted.

Thus does Wire undermine the authority of biblical tradition and canon, demanding from the texts a reasonability/persuasivity which is no longer dependent upon its authority within the community. In this way, too, is biblical studies as an exegetical effort potentially transformed: away from an interest in strict historiography-for-the-sake-of-authoritative-meaning and toward an approach that lifts up argumentation, rhetorical strategy and dynamics for critical appraisal [a criticism presumably performed within the 'context' of the modern interpreter]. There is a potential for embracing a full spectrum of 'intentionalities' and 'motivations' in biblical exegesis and interpretation, not just those of the 'author', nor those in the 'text', but of all those voices that surround the 'text', both at the time of its inception, and throughout time in its varying and various 'performances' [including the performances rendered by the interpreter him/herself, even the critical analyst]. Here

321. Wire, *Corinthian Women Prophets*, p. 11.

322. Wire, *Corinthian Women Prophets*, p. 11. One example of such an expansion on a canonical level is the current interest and acceptance of traditionally apocryphal literature as important evidence in the reconstruction of early Christian origins by some groups of predominantly American scholars.

is where the Bible as *power* can be explored and experienced in its fullest form(s) and expression(s).

It is unfortunate, therefore, that Wire does not explore the implications of this potential, but instead restricts rhetoric to a tool for historiography by embedding its critical practice within a larger project of reconstructing social histories. While Wire is aware of the experimental nature of rhetoric, that is, the interest and function of rhetorical methods to attempt to achieve adherence, through discourse, to certain values which inform and affect action,[323] it remains for her the 'by-product' of her method, whose specific goal is the reconstruction of the role of the Corinthian womyn within the rhetorical situation.[324]

> The rhetorical method, *which reconstructs the audiences conduct and view in its understanding of a writer's argument*, deals with women's view where they had a significant role in an audience.[325]

Once again, rhetorical strategies in the 'text' are used as a means for discerning implicitly shared values and explicitly motivated strategies through which the discourse 'context' can be reconstructed. And this discourse 'context' is one that is *restricted* to the historical and social situation at the time of writing. While the biblical canonical 'texts' themselves are no longer given *theological* authority, their ancient historical 'contexts' of generation and performance are still given the central critical role of the goal of biblical interpretation [i.e. they are given *critical* authority]. 'Texts' continue to be understood by reference to their historical 'contexts', their rhetoric used as a tool for reconstructing authorial 'intention' in response to a specific rhetorical and argumentative situation, their consequences critiqued from within the confines of their generative/originating 'exigence' which becomes the prototype for modern critical appraisal. While it is important for rhetoric to ponder the implications and effects of power generated through/in/with 'texts' in specific 'contexts' *during* history, Wire never questions why this particular performance should be the critical center of attention. She simply assumes that 'reconstructing the audience's conduct and view in its understanding of a writer's argument…where [womyn] had a significant role in the audience' is a reconstruction of the *first* audi-

323. Wire, *Corinthian Women Prophets*, p. 6: 'The by-product will be a clear picture of the author's act of writing in the rhetorical situation…'
324. Wire, *Corinthian Women Prophets*, p. 6.
325. Wire, *Corinthian Women Prophets*, p. 6.

ence. To this end, she remains immersed in the disciplinary rhetoric, the institutional power structure of biblical studies as historiography which hermeneutically restricts access to those who are equipped to perform the elite task of historical reconstruction. The Bible may lose authority, but the interpretive structures [hence, the interpreter] do[es] not.

But there is, unfortunately, more: it is her use of rhetorical analysis to reduce argumentative dynamics and multiple rhetorical strategies to theological doctrines. This is an inherently *acontextual* move in spite of her effort to use these doctrines as a means of contextualizing discourse in social systems. It reduces 'text' as activity to 'contexts' of propositions, which are then in turn set within an alternative 'context' of social description. But while propositions [ideologies?] and social settings are important factors to consider in rhetorical analysis, it is their arrestation in *ancient* history that becomes hermeneutically central for modern critical appraisal. This is the notion that history can 'speak' to us, that recovered histories of oppressed or marginalized groups can become useful means of discerning a heritage. The reduction of rhetorical strategies to theological systems and propositions, coupled with the recovery of heritage, allows her the rhetorical move of *relevance*, the ability to transcend the immediate boundaries of time to a point where 'we' can decide between Paul's christ-crucified and the Corinthians' christ-resurrected, noting the potential of each position's effects by using the historical context as an example of consequences: social conservatism versus social freedom. The problem is, such rhetoric-turned-theology is, of course, the other side of the biblical studies coin: the search for a historical foundation to theological truth, the pursuit of 'authentic' Tradition.

It is important to note that her own tradition runs counter to the sanctioned, distortive, destructive and boringly ass-umed patriarchal tradition that governs not only theological, but historical-critical interpretive traditions [assumptions, models and results] of the Bible. Nevertheless, it is still an appeal to Tradition, to legitimation of theological concepts by immersing them in the past, at the original moment of conception/construction. Why do I find this bothersome? Because 'theology', when mixed with historiography, has important institutional consequences, all of which simply serve to shore up the role of the biblical historical exegete in the life of acadamnia and the church. The end results may be different, but the game remains the same: as with every other scholar we have and will consider here, her rhetorical model uses the 'text' as a window into the social and historical circumstances of the original audience, and does so with the explicit purpose [and reductive result] of discerning alternative [but nevertheless *within the canon*] theo-logical/-social/-political doctrines now located 'in the beginning'. Historiography combines with theology to locate radically new interpretations in an old Tradition. And who remains the one best suited to help 'give voice' to these lost, but perhaps 'authentic' alternative doctrines? The biblical exegete-as-historian.

d. *Elisabeth Schüssler Fiorenza*

Like Mack, Robbins and Wire, the value of rhetoric to the historical-critical enterprise for Schüssler Fiorenza lies in its ability to address both ancient and modern concerns of the scholar. As an ancient theory of communication, it is 'one of the oldest forms of literary [*sic*] criticism that explores the particular historical uses of language in specific social political situations'.[326] Its pervasive influence in the cultural setting of the early Christian communities is evidenced by the appearance of rhetorical forms and structures in the New Testament texts themselves. It can thereby become a means of understanding the discourse strategies and, hence, sociopolitical postures embedded in the performance at the time.

As a modern theory of argumentation, insights from discourse theory, reader-response criticism and a recognition of the political dimensions of interpretation and historiography can combine with it to provide a new integrative paradigm in biblical interpretation. This paradigm would bring together the critical models and interests of literary studies, hermeneutics and social world description,[327] but also more than this: rhetoric as ideology critique of interpretive practices begins to impact Schüssler Fiorenza's efforts to expose the 'motivational', the 'intentional' dynamics of *all* discourse. Rhetoric, for the first time among the scholars we have been addressing, is explicitly employed in order to discern levels of power not only within the historical context of the biblical performance(s) [from oral tradition through Gospel composition

---

326. Elisabeth Schüssler Fiorenza, 'Rhetorical Situation and Historical Reconstruction in I Corinthians', *New Testament Studies* 33 (1987), pp. 386-403 (386).
327. Schüssler Fiorenza, 'Rhetorical Situation', p. 386.

and beyond to canonization], but [finally!] within the contexts of interpretation themselves, including *in particular* the institutional and disciplinary rhetoric of biblical exegesis as historiography. As such, it
becomes an important critical tool for describing the values, interests,
argumentative strategies and aims of not only biblical authors, but biblical scholarship and hermeneutical interpretation as well.[328]

Survey of Scholarship
Elisabeth Schüssler Fiorenza's quest is the reconstitution of Christian
faith and practice within an alternative community committed to exploring new models of biblical theology, interpretation, liturgical and ritual
practice, and institutional reform. This religious community of self-
identified womyn and womyn-identified men takes as its central programmatic goal the eventual liberation of both womyn and men of all
races, classes and cultures from the oppressive and exploitative structures, systems and ideology of patriarchy, including those at work within religious institutions and theological traditions. Schüssler Fiorenza
wonders *whether* biblical texts and interpretive traditions should be
thought of as authoritative and *to what end* they should be employed.
To answer these questions, she develops a highly complex model of
feminist theology, incorporating a wide variety of hermeneutical systems, all of which are rooted in the experiences and *praxis* of womyn-
church [as public, democratic space].[329]

The Bible remains important for her not only because she and her
community have come out of and continue to identify with their Judeo-
Christian religious heritage, but also because the text and its interpretive tradition have made and continue to make a profound impact
upon the social context in which they practice their commitment to liberation. For Schüssler Fiorenza, the Bible and its function in contem-

328. Elisabeth Schüssler Fiorenza, 'The Ethics of Biblical Interpretation: De-
Centering Biblical Scholarship', *Journal of Biblical Literature* 107.1 (1988), pp. 3-
17 (4).

329. For the following survey, initially developed within a typology of three
categories ('Toward a Feminist Critical Hermeneutic', 'Toward a Feminist Critical
Method', and 'Toward a Feminist Model of Historical Construction') cf. also Elisabeth Schüssler Fiorenza, *In Memory of Her: A Feminist Theological Reconstruction of Christian Origins* (New York: Crossroad, 1984), pp. 1-95. I have decided to
adopt the typology developed in her later essays, to which I refer throughout this
survey, for reasons of greater specificity and clarity.

porary society and throughout history are fundamental areas in which a feminist ideological critique of both society and scholarship must take place: as a tool for the perpetuation and legitimation of patriarchal structures (particularly family structures),[330] the Bible has been one of the most profound forces of political and economic oppression, used frequently as an authoritative means by which womyn's attempts at social, political, legal and economic reforms have been undermined. On the other hand, it has also been a source of inspiration for groups and movements in the struggle for justice, equality and liberation. Its powerful influence over western philosophical and legal thought, religious tradition, moral and ethical development, social (particularly familial) systems cannot be overlooked, rejected or ignored if successful implementation of feminist revolutionary reconstruction is to be achieved. If knowledge is the key to power, then biblical interpretive methods must be developed within a feminist hermeneutic of *praxis* which can wrestle away the Bible from those who wish to use it as a tool for oppression and exploitation.

Schüssler Fiorenza remains committed to historical-critical exegesis as a means by which womyn-church can claim the Bible as part of their own heritage and tradition. In order to do so, however, biblical historical criticism must be shaped by a new paradigm of historical inquiry and reconstruction that rejects the objectivist-realist presumptions of androcentric historical scholarship. Such scholarship perpetuates an 'impartial, value-neutral, objective-descriptive, scientific-antiquarian' method that 'understands its androcentric sources as "data" and its own androcentric language and narrative as totally divorced from contemporary concerns'.[331] Under the influence of such a paradigm, biblical

330. For an explanation and elaboration of her concept of 'patriarchy' and its implications for 'womyn-church', cf. Elisabeth Schüssler Fiorenza, 'The Will to Choose or to Reject: Continuing our Critical Work', in Letty M. Russell, *Feminist Interpretation of the Bible* (Philadelphia: Westminster Press, 1985), pp. 125-36 (127-29); cf. also Elisabeth Schüssler Fiorenza, 'Women-Church: The Hermeneutical Center of Feminist Biblical Interpretation', in Schüssler Fiorenza, *Bread Not Stone: The Challenge of Feminist Biblical Interpretation* (Boston: Beacon Press, 1984), pp. 1-22 (5-8).

331. Elisabeth Schüssler Fiorenza, 'Remembering the Past in Creating the Future: Historical-Critical Scholarship and Feminist Biblical Interpretation', in Adela Collins, *Feminist Perspectives on Biblical Scholarship* (Chico, CA: Scholars Press, 1985), pp. 44-55 (47). This same article is also found in Schüssler Fiorenza, *Bread Not Stone*, pp. 93-115.

historical reconstruction does not, indeed *cannot* conceive of womyn as central to and participants in the developing movements of early Christianity. Rather, it considers the 'woman-question' topically, regarding both womyn and the textual evidence that speaks of them as exceptional and distinctive from the broader historical picture and scholarly effort. Rejecting this paradigm, Schüssler Fiorenza embraces in its stead a constructivist epistemology that understands all historical investigation and resulting reconstruction as 'interested': 'facts' ('data', 'sources') do not emerge as mirrors of past events, but are made *present* to the scholar through investigative models, are selected and ordered into a coherent narrative account that seeks to ascribe historical significance to them, and are presented with a rhetorical aim which seeks to influence the attitude of the intended audience regarding the results. History is never simply a history *of,* but always a history *for.*[332]

Her own model of historical-critical reconstruction approaches the biblical text as an androcentric document that reflects the patriarchal perspectives of their authors and the traditions they drew upon. It is informed by a '**hermeneutics of suspicion**' which sees the Bible as a *prescriptive* portrait of the history of the early churches, especially with regard to the relationship of men to womyn (and other socially marginal groups). This hermeneutic helps the feminist historian to detect the patriarchal ideological distortions informing both the portrait and intentionality of the biblical texts, to become sensitive to inconsistencies and incoherences in the portrait of womyn painted by these androcentric texts, and from them to reconstruct the social and institutional systems of the early churches in such a way as to 'locate women's historic role not just at the margin of social-ecclesial relations but also in the center of them'.[333] Schüssler Fiorenza's approach is not 'topical': she does not limit her efforts to those texts and traditions that speak explicitly and exceptionally of womyn, since such a method would continue to perpetuate their marginal status. Instead, she takes on *all* texts and asks about the implications and effects such traditions, teachings, structures and practices might have had upon womyn (children, slaves and other socially marginal groups). Where there are silences in the texts regarding womyn, Schüssler Fiorenza fills these out by exploring new cognitive models that attempt to provide a consistency to the 'clues' which *do* make mention of them. In this way, biblical history is

332. Schüssler Fiorenza, 'Remembering the Past', pp. 48-55.
333. Schüssler Fiorenza, 'Remembering the Past', p. 44.

also womyn's history: her effort at historical reconstruction considers the role of womyn in the early churches, their participation in the developing thought and structures of these communities, the experiences they shared, the struggles they endured, the losses they suffered. A 'constructivist' historical criticism no longer views the Bible as a history *of* the ministry of Jesus and early Christians, but sees both biblical text and its interpretation as a historical rhetoric *for* certain groups and communities, in her case, *for* the community of womyn-church.

Historical-critical inquiry takes place within a feminist theology of liberation whose hermeneutical criterion of authority is centered not around the biblical text, but upon womyn's experience in the struggle for freedom from the structures of patriarchal oppression. Both Christian feminist apologists and postbiblical feminists 'not only overlook the experiences of women in biblical religion, but also assume that the Bible has authority independently of the community to which it belongs'.[334] Schüssler Fiorenza rejects the 'mythical-archetypal' paradigm of biblical interpretation prevalent in contemporary hermeneutical approaches to the text,[335] a paradigm that takes 'the historically limited experiences and texts and posits them as universals, which then become authoritative and normative for all times and cultures'.[336] This paradigm is at work not only within the doctrinal approach to the biblical text as verbally inspired revelation,[337] but can also be found working within the historical-factual approach that posits as theologically authoritative that which is historically reliable,[338] as well as within any neo-orthodox 'canon-within-the-canon' approach that attempts to identify a single theological tradition in the text as the standard by which to judge other biblical traditions.[339] Schüssler Fiorenza rejects as the point of departure for feminist critical interpretation of the Bible the normative authority of the biblical archetype, and instead begins with

334. Schüssler Fiorenza, 'Women-Church', pp. 1-22.

335. Schüssler Fiorenza, 'Women-Church', pp. 10-15; cf. a more detailed discussion in, '"For the Sake of our Salvation": Biblical Interpretation and the Community of Faith', in Schüssler Fiorenza, *Bread Not Stone*, pp. 23-42.

336. Schüssler Fiorenza, 'Women-Church', p. 10.

337. Cf. Schüssler Fiorenza, 'Women-Church', pp. 10-11, and '"For the Sake of our Salvation"', pp. 25-28.

338. Cf. Schüssler Fiorenza, 'Women-Church', p. 11, and '"For the Sake of our Salvation"', pp. 28-32.

339. Schüssler Fiorenza, 'Women-Church', pp. 12-13, and Schüssler Fiorenza, *In Memory of Her*, pp. 14-21.

womyn's contemporary experiences of their struggle against racism, sexism and poverty as oppressive systems of patriarchy and with a systematic exploration of these systems in feminist theory.[340] The Bible becomes not mythic archetype, but historical prototype, a prototype historical criticism has revealed to be a collection of texts and traditions that were *theological responses to historical-communal situations.*[341]

If this is so, and given that hermeneutical authority is located within the experience of womyn-church to choose or reject biblical texts and traditions, then a feminist biblical interpretation must also be based upon a '**hermeneutics of critical evaluation**'. Such a hermeneutic would be founded upon a systematic exploration of womyn's historical experiences of oppression and liberation, and would therefrom derive criteria that would help the interpreter to 'sort through particular biblical texts and test out in a process of critical analysis and evaluation how much their content and function perpetrates and legitimates patriarchal structures, not only in their original historical contexts but also in our contemporary situation'.[342] Rather than assuming a correlation between the biblical text and the feminist principles that are fundamental to womyn-church, a critical approach must bring to bear the full force of a feminist critique, since historically the text and its interpretive tradition have been powerful tools of womyn's oppression. At the same time, a 'hermeneutics of critical evaluation' would also bring to light the feminist liberating content and function of certain texts which the community could then employ as both paradigm and resource in its ongoing development and engagement in liberatory *praxis*.

Schüssler Fiorenza would next incorporate the results of feminist critical analysis of the biblical text into a '**hermeneutics of proclamation**' which would 'assess the Bible's theological significance and power for the contemporary community of faith'[343] and would insist upon undermining the presumed authority of patriarchal scriptural texts and their role in the liturgy of the community.[344] 'Feminist theology must first of all denounce all texts and traditions that

340. Schüssler Fiorenza, 'Women-Church', p. 14.

341. Schüssler Fiorenza, 'Women-Church', p. 11, and '"For the Sake of our Salvation"', pp. 33-36.

342. Schüssler Fiorenza, 'Continuing our Critical Work', pp. 131.

343. Schüssler Fiorenza, 'Women-Church', p. 18.

344. Schüssler Fiorenza, 'Continuing our Critical Work', p. 132.

perpetrate and legitimate oppressive patriarchal structures and ideologies' and do so with hermeneutical priority over their proclamation in Christian worship, their inclusion in the lectionary, and their instruction in catechesis. A careful historical-critical assessment must be complemented by a political-critical feminist evaluation which would 'assess the interaction of patriarchal biblical texts with contemporary culture'[345] and would reject any text found to further sexist, racist or colonial militarist aims.[346] On the other hand, 'those texts that are identified as transcending their patriarchal contexts and as articulating a liberating vision of human freedom and wholeness should receive their proper place in the liturgy and teaching of the churches'.[347]

At the same time, a hermeneutics of proclamation must be balanced by a critical '**hermeneutics of remembrance**' which 'recovers *all* biblical texts and traditions through feminist historical reconstruction'.[348] Since feminism is not defined on the basis of essential sexual differences but upon 'the common historical experience of women as collaborating or struggling participants in patriarchal culture and biblical history',[349] then feminist meaning is grounded in the recounting of that experience, even in and through androcentric texts and traditions. Rather than relinquishing patriarchal biblical tradition and abandoning the memory of earlier womyn in this history, such a hermeneutics reclaims their suffering, struggles and victories through the subversive power of the re-membered past. A 'hermeneutics of remembrance' develops theoretical models of historical reconstruction that cut through the androcentric biblical texts and endeavors to place womyn not on the periphery but at the center of biblical community and history. These models 'allow a glimpse of the early Christian movements as the discipleship of equals, the reality of women's commitment and leadership in these movements'[350] and the gradual and difficult process of patriarchalization that takes place through the prescriptive injunctions found

345. Schüssler Fiorenza, 'Women-Church', p. 18.

346. Schüssler Fiorenza, 'Women-Church', p. 18; 'Continuing our Critical Work', pp. 132-33.

347. Schüssler Fiorenza, 'Women-Church', pp. 18-19.

348. Schüssler Fiorenza, 'Continuing our Critical Work', p. 133.

349. Schüssler Fiorenza, 'Women-Church', p. 19; cf. also, 'Discipleship and Patriarchy: Toward a Feminist Evaluative Hermeneutics', in Schüssler Fiorenza, *Bread Not Stone*, pp. 84-92 (86, 88).

350. Schüssler Fiorenza, 'Women-Church', p. 20.

in the later stages of the tradition. They help 'us' to see that 'patriarchal structures are not inherent to Christian community, although they have become historically dominant'.[351] A 'hermeneutics of remembrance' can thereby reclaim biblical history as the history of womyn, and can keep alive the memory of the 'struggle, life and leadership of biblical women who spoke and acted in the power of the Spirit'.[352]

Finally, interpretation through remembrance and proclamation must be supplemented by a '**hermeneutics of creative ritualization**' which allows womyn and womyn-church to enter into the biblical story with the help of historical imagination, artistic recreation and liturgical celebration. The Bible as a formative prototype has inspired artistic creativity and literary embellishment throughout the centuries in the form of legend and apocryphal texts, liturgy and sacred hymns, feast days and liturgical cycles, 'lives' of the saints and writings of the church 'fathers'. Feminists reclaim this same imaginative freedom and popular creativity in order to rewrite biblical stories, reformulate patriarchal prayers and biblical injunctions from the perspective of the discipleship of equals, to elaborate upon the feminist remnants that have survived in the biblical texts and other traditions, and create feminist rituals for celebrating early Christian foremothers and their struggles.[353] 'Only by reclaiming our religious imagination and our ritual powers of naming can women-church dream new dreams and see new visions.'[354]

It appears that throughout this discussion one can identify the central interpretive principle characteristic of the feminist-critical model that Schüssler Fiorenza is herein proposing as being the principle of critical evaluation based upon the lived experience of womyn suffering and struggling under patriarchy. Her call for liberation, while embracing other liberation theologies' assertion that 'all theology knowingly or not is by definition always engaged for or against the oppressed',[355] nevertheless distinguishes itself from these by its assertion that neither the 'god of the oppressed' nor the educational hermeneutic advanced by

351. Schüssler Fiorenza, 'Continuing our Critical Work', p. 134.

352. Schüssler Fiorenza, 'Women-Church', p. 20.

353. Schüssler Fiorenza, 'Continuing our Critical Work', p. 135; cf. 'Women-Church', p. 21.

354. Schüssler Fiorenza, 'Continuing our Critical Work', p. 135.

355. Schüssler Fiorenza, 'Scripture in the Liberation Struggle', in Schüssler Fiorenza, *Discipleship of Equals: A Critical Feminist Ekklesialogy of Liberation* (New York: Crossroad, 1993), p. 45.

liberation theologies can speak to womyn unless and until a critical evaluative principle of the use of the Bible and the identification of the 'oppressed' as *womyn* first take place: while god may have been a 'god of/for the oppressed', it was rarely, if ever the case that god was a 'god of/for womyn'. Indeed, '[s]ince the Bible was and is used against women's demand for equality and liberation from societal, cultural and ecclesial sexism, [feminist liberation theology] must conceive of this task first in critical terms before it can attempt to formulate a hermeneutics of liberation'.[356] Schüssler Fiorenza therefore defines the task of feminist liberation theology not in terms of rescuing the Bible from its androcentric nature and misogynist tendencies, but as the task of critically comprehending 'how the Bible functions in the oppression of women or the poor, and thus [preventing] its misuse for further oppression'.[357] Feminist liberation theology incorporates a critical evaluative hermeneutic as a new interpretive paradigm that has as its aim emancipatory *praxis* seeking to 'transform the patriarchal household code ethics and its institutional structures if women and the Christian church are to have a feminist Christian future'.[358]

The particular circumstance we need to explore is the developing role that rhetoric begins to play within this hermeneutic system. Early efforts show an interest in rhetoric as a critical tool for socio-historical reconstruction of biblical textual traditions, justified as a means by which to control or limit interpretive potentialities. Such is the case, for example, in her work on Revelation, '**Visionary Rhetoric and Socio-Political Situation**'.[359] Here she argues that the letter is a mythico-poetic work of visionary rhetoric, thereby rejecting both essentialist theological and abstractionist philosophical approaches to its evocative symbolic language.[360] As 'poetic-rhetorical' construction of an alternative symbolic universe, an adequate interpretation of Revelation 'must first explore the poetic-evocative character of its language and symbols' and then 'assess its rhetorical dynamics in a "proportional" reading of

---

356. Schüssler Fiorenza, 'Scripture in the Liberation Struggle', p. 53; cf. also 'Toward a Critical-Theological Self-Understanding of Biblical Scholarship', in *Bread Not Stone*, pp. 136-41.

357. Schüssler Fiorenza, 'Scripture in the Liberation Struggle', p. 57.

358. Schüssler Fiorenza, 'Discipleship and Patriarchy', p. 92.

359. In *The Book of Revelation: Justice and Judgment* (Philadelphia: Fortress Press, 1985), pp. 181-203.

360. Schüssler Fiorenza, 'Visionary Rhetoric', pp. 183-86.

its symbols to elucidate their particular interrelations and the author's persuasive goals' in order to show how and why 'the construction of the symbolic universe of Revelation is a "fitting" response to its historical-rhetorical situation'.[361] Not just 'any' meaning is possible, but the interpretation of this text 'must make "sense" with regard to the overall structure of the book as well as with respect to its "function" within a particular historical situation'.[362] And it is both this structure and this function that rhetoric helps bring to light.

Turning specifically to Rev. 14.1-5, Schüssler Fiorenza argues that the strategic position and textual relations of the symbols and images of this text have a specific, persuasive function within the overall compositional movement of Rev. 10.1–15.5. The vision of the 144,000 with the divine name on their foreheads is an antithetical vision to those of the dragon and the two beasts, and continues the motif of the measuring of the Temple, the two witnesses and the womon with the child.[363] Indeed, this episode shows a multitude of connections to both visions and auditions present throughout the entire book, all of which serve the persuasive function of 'motivating [the] audience to make their decision for salvation and for the word of God in the face of the destructive power represented by the beasts and Babylon as the symbols of Rome'.[364] The choice facing the audience is 'either to worship the anti-divine powers embodied by Rome and to become "followers" of the Beast (cf. 13.2-4), or to worship God and to become "companions" of the Lamb on Mount Zion. This decision jeopardizes either their lives and fortunes here and now or their future lives and share in the New Jerusalem, Mount Zion.'[365] The persuasive direction of these passages is not only to get the audience to choose *against* the worship of the Beast, but to stake their very lives *for* the worship of god.

When the question comes to reconstruction, therefore, Schüssler Fiorenza attempts to generate a portrait of the socio-historical circumstances in which and to which such rhetoric is generated as a 'fitting' response: the rhetorical situation[366] draws forth a particular rhetorical

---

361. Schüssler Fiorenza, 'Visionary Rhetoric', p. 183.
362. Schüssler Fiorenza, 'Visionary Rhetoric', p. 187.
363. Schüssler Fiorenza, 'Visionary Rhetoric', p. 188.
364. Schüssler Fiorenza, 'Visionary Rhetoric', p. 189.
365. Schüssler Fiorenza, 'Visionary Rhetoric', p. 191.
366. Bitzer, 'The Rhetorical Situation', pp. 1-14. This is her most serious flaw. With the publication of this article came an intense debate concerning Bitzer's

response and not vice versa. It is characterized both by a controlling exigency, 'which specifies the mode of discourse to be chosen and the change to be effected', and urgency. Furthermore, it is constituted by the constraints 'which affect the audience's decision or action and those which are limitations imposed on the author'.[367] All these characteristics provide the guidelines for determining a response that is 'fit'. Assuming that the author of Revelation has successfully accounted for the particular rhetorical situation which s/he confronts, Schüssler Fiorenza can thereby reconstruct the historical circumstances to which the letter was responding.

Specifically, these circumstances included harassment, persecution and hostility, particularly under the Flavians ('especially Domitian'), which challenged a Christian's faith in the face of the promotion and enforcement of the imperial cult. 'The political situation was aggravated and the necessity to make a decision [between Christianity and the imperial cult] became more pressing because Jewish Christians like John could less and less claim Jewish political privileges for themselves.'[368] Furthermore, 'not only among Jews but also among Christians there was a tendency to adapt and acquiesce to the political powers'.[369] In the face of these challenges, 'John advocates an uncompromising theological stance toward the imperial religion because, for him and his followers, the dehumanizing powers of Rome and its vassals have become so destructive and oppressive that a compromise with them would mean an affirmation of 'those who destroy the earth' (11.18)'.[370] The author of the letter was attempting to construct a

concept of the 'rhetorical situation'. The issues can perhaps best be summarized as to whether his account of the relationship between rhetorical situation and historical fact is normative or descriptive: If it is descriptive, then some very serious objections can be raised, namely that historical exigencies don't create rhetorical response, but rather the other way around: Through rhetoric an event, whether real or unreal, can be made important enough to address persuasively.

For further discussion of these and other related issues in response to Bitzer's article, see Richard E. Vatz, 'The Myth of the Rhetorical Situation', *Philosophy & Rhetoric* 6.3 (1973), pp. 154-61; Alan Brinton, 'Situation in the Theory of Rhetoric', *Philosophy & Rhetoric* 14.4 (1981), pp. 234-48, and references in n. 2 on p. 247 in this same article.

367. Schüssler Fiorenza, 'Visionary Rhetoric', p. 192.
368. Schüssler Fiorenza, 'Visionary Rhetoric', p. 194.
369. Schüssler Fiorenza, 'Visionary Rhetoric', p. 195.
370. Schüssler Fiorenza, 'Visionary Rhetoric', p. 196.

symbolic universe 'that is mythological insofar as it represents a conception of reality that points to the ongoing determination of the world by sacred forces', thus endowing the suffering and terror encountered by both the individual Christian and the community as a whole under Flavian rule with a sense of 'purpose' and 'meaning' by reference to a 'cosmic order of justice and power'.[371] According to Schüssler Fiorenza, then, the letter was responding to the particular circumstances of the 'rhetorical situation' of persecution in a 'fitting' manner by taking the audience through the transformative 'dramatic-cathartic' journey from alienation through purification to redemption in an effort to 'move' the audience 'to control their fear and to sustain their vision'[372] in the face of the difficulties they confronted under the Roman Imperium.

But in an important move which strives to assess the impact of the vision and dramatic-symbolic action of this letter upon the *contemporary* audience, Schüssler Fiorenza points out the hermeneutical potential of the 'rhetorical situation': the 'fittedness' of the rhetorical response by the author of Revelation can be met with time and again, wherever the 'rhetorical situation' of 'a social-political-religious "tension" generated by oppression and persecution persists or re-occurs'.[373] Therefore, if the letter is best understood as an appeal for 'the realization of God's justice and power', it can only be understood by those 'who hunger and thirst for justice'.[374] However, where a totally different 'rhetorical situation' exists, the letter is no longer 'fit', and indeed the prevalence of misogynist images of womyn throughout the text would 'perpetuate prejudice and injustice if it is not "translated" into a contemporary "rhetorical situation" to which it can be a "fitting" rhetorical response'.[375] With this single statement it becomes clear that rhetorical 'fit' is not conceived *exclusively* as dependent upon the historical circumstances of origination, but is also informed by a hermeneutic principle founded upon an avowed ethical principal of liberation which controls the rhetorical intentionality/effect of the text. Rhetorical-critical analysis conceives argumentation as being context-dependent (thus making accessible its 'controlling' historical exigencies and

---

371. Schüssler Fiorenza, 'Visionary Rhetoric', p. 197.
372. Schüssler Fiorenza, 'Visionary Rhetoric', p. 198.
373. Schüssler Fiorenza, 'Visionary Rhetoric', p. 199.
374. Schüssler Fiorenza, 'Visionary Rhetoric', p. 198.
375. Schüssler Fiorenza, 'Visionary Rhetoric', p. 199.

constraints), but also accessible to future 'rhetorical situational' analogs and 'fit' readings.

Other efforts continue to suggest this relationship between rhetoric as tool for historical-rhetorical reconstruction [exegesis] and hermeneutic assessment within contemporary standards and situations. However, in an important expansion of the critical gaze, rhetoric as a critical approach to discourse begins slowly to turn from application of a given model exclusively *within* the framework of biblical exegesis and hermeneutic application, toward an assessment of the discourse practices of exegesis themselves as 'persuasive' and 'motivational/motivated' (hence, 'rhetorical') efforts of the community of interpreters. This turn can be seen in her article, '**Rhetorical Situation and Historical Reconstruction in I Corinthians**', wherein she suggests that rhetorical criticism must distinguish between the historical argumentative setting, the implied or inscribed rhetorical setting, and the rhetorical situation of contemporary interpretation.[376] This results in a four-step model: (1) identification of rhetorical interests and models in contemporary interpretation; (2) identification of rhetorical arrangements, interests and perspectives of the 'author'; (3) reconstruction of the historical-rhetorical situation of the letter; and finally (4) an assessment of the rhetoric in terms of its function for early Christian self-understanding and community, one that seeks to 'develop a responsible ethical and evaluative theological criticism'.[377] She develops and then tests this proposed model on Paul's 'first' letter to the Corinthians.

This letter, it seems, is an extremely seductive text for socio-historical critics, since in it perhaps the most detailed descriptions can be found of group constitution, social customs, values, religious practices and traditions concerning a specific congregation in a well-known city. The apparent rise and interaction of factions within the community, advice regarding social customs and practices, discussions regarding interpretation of fundamental theological doctrines of Christian self-definition, the implicit struggle of Paul's position vis-à-vis the Corinthians and other missionaries, all give the historical critic the sense that here 'we' have unprecedented access to the day-to-day workings of a particular Hellenist Christian community. If rhetorical criticism, with

376. Schüssler Fiorenza, 'Rhetorical Situation', p. 388.
377. Schüssler Fiorenza, 'Rhetorical Situation', pp. 388-89.

its emphasis upon persuasion, can bring out the political posturing of Paul's discourse, valuable new insight can be brought to the interactive dimension of the social situation of a Pauline community, perhaps with implications concerning Paul's own mission.

The first step necessary to bring these goals about is to distinguish between the authorial argumentative intention within the letter from the actual historical situation when the modern interpreter approaches the text.[378] Reader-response criticism first introduced the concept of the 'implied author' who is a construct which the real reader creates gradually in the process of reading the work,[379] a process carefully guided by the real author through the production of embedded textual strategies.[380] The importance of this notion for traditional interpretation of this particular letter becomes apparent in the critical literature. So much of the information important to understanding 1 Corinthians is left presupposed or unexplained. Biblical scholars supply implicit information regarding the social structures and value systems by reference to Jewish symbol systems, pagan religion and mystery cults, philosophical schools, Hellenistic Judaism and Gnosticism, and/or social data from socio-anthropological models. Unfortunately, they do so within the

---

378. Schüssler Fiorenza, 'Rhetorical Situation', p. 388.

379. Schüssler Fiorenza, 'Rhetorical Situation', p. 389. Here she refers to Wayne Booth's original definition as offered in *The Rhetoric of Fiction* (Chicago: University of Chicago Press, 2nd edn, 1983).

380. Schüssler Fiorenza, 'Rhetorical Situation and Historical Reconstruction', p. 389. She is very specific about the power of the reconstruction of the implied author lying in the hands of the real author, or at least in the dynamics of the text. She refers here to the definition offered by Edward V. McKnight, *The Bible and the Reader: An Introduction to Literary Criticism* (Philadelphia: Fortress Press, 1985), p. 102. One understands why she wishes to emphasize the textual or authorial control over this construct, given the traditional biblical critical penchant for accepting Paul's word regarding the situation he confronts. Nevertheless, there are significant alternatives, most notably Stanley Fish's emphasis upon the institutional interpretive strategies when constructing the implied author's intention, which would better suit her purposes. Cf., e.g., Stanley Fish, 'Interpreting the *Variorum*', in Jane P. Tompkins (ed.), *Reader-Response Criticism: From Formalism to Post-Structuralism* (Baltimore: The Johns Hopkins University Press, 1980), pp. 70-100; and see also more recently *idem*, *Is There a Text in This Class?* (Cambridge, MA: Harvard University Press, 1982); *idem*, *Doing What Comes Naturally: Change, Rhetoric and the Practice of Theory in Literary and Legal Studies* (London: Duke University Press, 1989).

rhetorical posture and constructs of Paul's argumentation. This becomes especially apparent when they describe the situation in the Corinthian community as one of conflict between Paul and Corinthian 'opponents' who are 'foolish, immature, arrogant, divisive, individualistic, unrealistic illusionists, libertine enthusiasts, or boasting spiritualists who misunderstood the preaching of Paul in terms of "realized eschatology"'.[381] The authority of the implied author construct, secured through Paul's apostolic and canonical position in biblical tradition, continues to impact upon the interpretation of the letter in a way that keeps scholars from questioning the argumentative and rhetorical intention and perspective. What if Paul's apostleship and his letters had been condemned as somehow heretical? Would we then accept his portrayal of the Corinthian situation? These questions belie an underlying rhetorical approach to biblical interpretive models, questioning the interests and systems of power behind investigative and interpretive assumptions regarding Pauline authority.

The goal of the second step is to outline the inherent argumentative strategies in the descriptions of and addressed to these circumstances. By laying out the rhetorical strategies embedded in the letter, 'we' get a good idea of the kind of audience *as perceived by Paul* and the ways in which he sets out to influence them.[382] In ancient rhetorical tradition, the description of the function of the audience in argumentative strategy is typically defined in terms of rhetorical 'genre'. Schüssler Fiorenza turns to Aristotelian classifications and describes the *Sitz im Leben* of each: forensic in the courtroom, wherein the audience judges past actions; deliberative in the forum, wherein the audience judges future action; and epideictic in the marketplace or amphitheater, where the audience judges 'the oratory of the speaker in order to award praise or blame'.[383] After analyzing previous attempts by others to define the letter as either epideictic or forensic,[384] she argues for a deliberative classification: 1 Cor. 1.10 appeals to unity of the congregation in order that they may, in the future, take action in their best interest on issues

---

381. Schüssler Fiorenza, 'Rhetorical Situation', pp. 389-90.
382. Schüssler Fiorenza, 'Rhetorical Situation', p. 389, 391.
383. Schüssler Fiorenza, 'Rhetorical Situation', p. 391.
384. Schüssler Fiorenza, 'Rhetorical Situation', pp. 390-93. See my own assessment of these arguments, including her own, in 'Re-discovering and Re-inventing Rhetoric', *Scriptura* 50 (1994), pp. 1-22.

under discussion (marriage and sexuality, meat sacrificed to idols, worship, resurrection, collection for the saints). When Paul exhorts the Corinthians to subject themselves and give recognition to people such as Stephanas (16.15-18), it is apparent that the inscribed audience being asked to make such decisions is composed of those 'who have either social status or missionary status or both'.[385]

Now that the implicit audience and its argumentative role in the rhetorical strategy of the letter have been discerned, the next step is once again to reconstruct a plausible historical situation to which the letter would be a 'fitting' response.[386] Schüssler Fiorenza suggests that the rhetorical situation of the 'first' letter to the Corinthians can best be understood as dealing with the issue (*stasis*) of jurisdiction, that is, the question of the authority of the speaker to address and settle the issue. The Corinthian community was in the midst of discussion and debates concerning social customs and values arising from their 'new self-understanding expressed in the pre-Pauline baptismal formula in Gal. 3.28' which were in direct conflict with the dominant 'patriarchal status division between Greeks and Jews, slave and free, men and women, rich and poor, wise and uneducated'.[387] In particular, the implications of 'no longer male and female' raised important questions concerning marriage, family, sexual practices and participation in worship for womyn. The community decided to write to different missionaries for their advice, since these missionaries and their differing theological emphases gave rise to these questions in the first place.[388] As the deliberative strategy of the letter indicates, the community is understood to be in a position to evaluate and determine its future course of action. Paul, however, gets wind from Chloe's people that some in the community do not accept his authority, as he appears to be least qualified in terms of 'pneumatic competence: he preaches on the elementary level and, as for actual pastoral experience, he hasn't shown up for a long time and does not live a lifestyle appropriate to an apostle'.[389] He therefore must seek to strengthen his position in order to secure their acceptance of his instruction over others. He does this by redefining the discussion in terms of party divisions threatening to undermine the unity

385. Schüssler Fiorenza, 'Rhetorical Situation', p. 393.
386. Schüssler Fiorenza, 'Rhetorical Situation', pp. 387-88.
387. Schüssler Fiorenza, 'Rhetorical Situation', p. 397.
388. Schüssler Fiorenza, 'Rhetorical Situation', p. 398.
389. Schüssler Fiorenza, 'Rhetorical Situation', p. 398.

of the congregation,[390] thus putting alternative instruction on the defensive. He then introduces a hierarchical structure of patriarchal subordination (God, Christ, Paul, Apollos, Timothy, Stephanas) 'not only into the social relationships of the *ekklēsia,* but into its symbolic universe as well by arrogating the authority of God, the "father", for himself'.[391] This now secures his position over the community as sole father and founder, thereby undermining 'the persuasive-consensual authority based on pneumatic competence accessible to all'.[392] He then uses this hierarchical model to appeal to those who, like himself and Stephanas, were of higher social and educational status, and apparently did not include womyn.[393]

From this reconstruction it appears that Paul's interpretation and experience of his new life in christ differs from that of some of the members of the Corinthian community. For them, the baptismal understanding of 'life in christ' meant living in the new creation here and now, free from restrictive social structures of subordination. But for Paul, his new life has been one of suffering, hardships and trials which will be recompensed in the future.[394] The question the biblical scholar must now pose in the final step is what were the practical implications for such a position upon the historical situation and the Corinthian community? It appears that Paul is the [an?] *origin* of Christian patriarchalism in the early missionary movement,[395] a reconception of social relationships that will have powerful consequences upon the socially

390. Schüssler Fiorenza, 'Rhetorical Situation', p. 396.
391. Schüssler Fiorenza, 'Rhetorical Situation', p. 397.
392. Schüssler Fiorenza, 'Rhetorical Situation', p. 397.
393. Schüssler Fiorenza, 'Rhetorical Situation', p. 399.
394. Schüssler Fiorenza, 'Rhetorical Situation', p. 400.
395. Schüssler Fiorenza, 'Rhetorical Situation', p. 397. One has seen this conclusion before, discussed in her book *In Memory of Her*, esp. Chapter 6. One begins to get the suspicion that biblical historical critics, who had an intuitive understanding of the social structures and development of early Christianity, have found in rhetorical criticism a model which simply helps them assert these reconstructions by reference to 'newly discovered' argumentative strategies. This in and of itself may be a good reason to call for the halt in the use of rhetoric as a tool for historiography. Another good reason is recognizing that argumentative strategies take on new meanings as different contexts are confronted, even if the textual performance (in the case of the Bible) remains the same. Using rhetorical strategies as a means of generating historical contexts becomes, therefore, extremely problematic, hence allowing the critic a great deal of freedom in reconstructing the setting.

marginal as Christianity develops. In this light, 'we' must ask ourselves whether Paul's experience of becoming a follower of christ and its incumbent demand for the relinquishment of authority and status should be normative for us. Whose perspective do 'we' find more acceptable, the Corinthians' or Paul's?

Throughout this discussion, Schüssler Fiorenza has been at pains to discern the difference between Pauline rhetorical perspectives and the socio-historical circumstances of performance. She has thereby clearly decentered the authority of Paul, as his argumentation becomes an experiment in persuasion which must be assessed according to the rhetorical situation. Particularly in the first and fourth steps of her model, she shifts the power of portrayal of the historical setting away from the biblical canonical tradition and into the hands of the scholar, who must now assess not only previous scholarly inquiry, models and conclusions, but even the assertions of biblical rhetoric itself. Rhetoric continues to act as a critical tool of historical inquiry into the situation of origination wherein its argumentative/persuasive intentionality is to be judged. However, similar to Mack and Wire, New Testament texts have thereby lost their authoritative dimension and instead become examples of a developing argumentative strategy.

The goal of the rhetorical critic is to determine the rhetorical intent and assess its effect within the socio-historical context of performance. However, modern interpreters have tended to view the rhetorical historical situation of the New Testament from the perspective of the (implied) author of a particular text. Even when Mack or Robbins emphasizes the argumentative dimension and effectiveness of a performance tradition, they do so from the point of view of the rhetorical intention: what does this *chreia*, this elaboration pattern, this gospel seek to argue, and how does it compare with normative or conventional standards? In contrast, a decentered rhetorical criticism sees the performance as one among many actual and potential perspectives upon a particular setting or situation. Such a view of biblical critical discourse emphasizes the political ethical dimension of biblical scholarship and its own rhetorical strategies. The public character of biblical interpretation, made explicit by means of the rhetorical emphasis upon argumentation, requires the recognition of certain incumbent responsibilities regarding literary readings and historical reconstructions. It also requires the recognition of 'our' own scholarly interests and the institutional forms that give sanction to particular investigative traditions and communities.

In the context of the androcentric history of biblical studies and religion, models of inquiry were developed that stressed an apolitical detachment, an objectivist positivism in the pursuit of historical reconstruction. This scientist ethos of value-free inquiry was 'shaped by the struggle of biblical scholarship to free itself from dogmatic and ecclesiastical controls...[and] corresponded to the professionalization of academic life and the rise of the university'.[396] Biblical studies sought to prove itself as an objective discipline analogous to the natural sciences by rejecting any accountability to, reflection upon or responsibility for sociopolitical factors it in fact influences.[397] However, there is a marked difference in the type of audience and the impact upon it that these disciplines address. Science, through technological advancement, has generated a public awareness of the benefits it has provided for human welfare. On the other hand, biblical scholarship has simply assumed its importance for the public at large, and has turned instead to fostering power relationships with organized religion 'whose dominant leadership has been more concerned with the defense of the status quo than with any human betterment accruing form new religious insights'.[398] Objectivist inquiry is, in fact, ideological.

Schüssler Fiorenza views rhetoric as the means of exposing the argumentative and political assumptions of objectivist inquiry. By recasting discourse in terms of the interaction of perspectives and values, rhetoric generates an awareness of the dimension of power in communication. Rhetoric exposes the political character of the claim of value-neutral investigation that seeks to deny the impact of its socio-historical location upon the hermeneutical and theoretical character of its mode of inquiry. Calling for the decentering of the dominant scientist ethos by recentering it in a critical 'praxis for liberation',[399] Schüssler Fiorenza hopes to emphasize an awareness of the tentative and value-laden nature of biblical interpretation and the plurality of meaning and effect as an inherent potential in any text. She proposes a double ethical stan-

396. Schüssler Fiorenza, 'The Ethics of Biblical Interpretation', p. 11.
397. Schüssler Fiorenza, 'The Ethics of Biblical Interpretation', pp. 9-10.
398. Schüssler Fiorenza, 'The Ethics of Biblical Interpretation', p. 13, quoting Leroy Waterman, 'Biblical Studies in a New Setting', *Journal of Biblical Literature* 66 (1947), pp. 1-14 (5).
399. Schüssler Fiorenza, 'The Ethics of Biblical Interpretation', p. 9.

dard which addresses the recognition of the 'ethical consequences and political functions of biblical texts in their historical as well as in their contemporary sociopolitical context'.[400]

First, she proposes an 'ethics of historical reading', which seeks to evaluate and critically assess the values and authority claims of the biblical text by concentrating upon the limited 'original meanings' of a text within its historical contexts. 'Such a historical reading seeks to give the text its due by asserting its original meanings over and against later dogmatic usurpations. It makes the assimilation of the text to our own experience and interests more difficult and thereby keeps alive the "irritation" of the original text by challenging our own assumptions, world view, and practices.'[401] The point here is not to enforce and support the claims to authority that the biblical text makes, but to relativize them by contextualizing them. Such is the intention behind the fourth step of her model, and is part of what we noted above as her 'hermeneutics of remembrance'.

But Schüssler Fiorenza doesn't stop there. She is not interested in abandoning the text. Instead, she wishes to maintain a link with tradition, but one that is governed by what she calls an 'ethics of accountability' extending to the consequences of the biblical text and its meanings. Biblical studies must take responsibility not only for reconstruction of original meanings within historical contexts, but also for the ethical and social consequences of their espoused values in both the ancient *and* modern world.[402] The Bible has been used throughout history as the authoritative source for justification of oppression, violence, warfare, bigotry, slavery, misogyny and colonialization. The question the biblical scholar must pose is whether such uses are indeed inherent within the text.[403] The normative status of the biblical text requires the scholar to make explicit the important implications of such traditions, where they exist, upon the community. The biblical scholar must turn and face the very real social consequences of maintaining a distance, in both method and audience, from the world outside of institutional academentia and religion. This separation becomes surrender in the

---

400. Schüssler Fiorenza, 'The Ethics of Biblical Interpretation', p. 15.
401. Schüssler Fiorenza, 'The Ethics of Biblical Interpretation', p. 14.
402. Schüssler Fiorenza, 'The Ethics of Biblical Interpretation', p. 15.
403. Schüssler Fiorenza, 'The Ethics of Biblical Interpretation', p. 15.

face of a populist fundamentalist movement which stresses antidemocratic authoritarianism and fosters personal prejudice.[404] A rhetorical biblical model of investigation can counteract this tendency, if made available to the public, by offering a decentered perspective regarding the authority of biblical argumentation. She refuses to deconstruct the authority of the text to the point of total irrelevance for the needs of a culturally pluralist twentieth-century world. She does, however, wish to introduce into interpretive discourse dynamics an authoritative liberationist agenda that becomes the standard against which biblical interpretation must be judged, an agenda rooted firmly within the experiences of womyn-church.

Schüssler Fiorenza expands the horizons of rhetorical criticism to include biblical scholarly inquiry itself, addressing the political and conventional systems inherent in the discipline. The question of the location of 'authority' in biblical interpretation now considers the role of the interpreter in the perpetuation of scholarly models of inquiry, the sociopolitical contexts of their application, and the implications of their conclusions.[405] This reconceptualization of biblical scholarship in rhetorical terms provides a framework wherein historical, archaeological, social, political, literary and theological approaches are integrated with an ethical political awareness of the interpretative process itself. This rhetorical hermeneutic approaches the biblical text not as scientific evidence of historical reality, but as discourse directed by perspectives constructing symbolic worlds.[406] These alternative symbolic universes cannot be approached by methods developed within academemented contexts of supposed 'value-neutral' inquiry and scientific objectivism that seeks to reduce New Testament discourse to historical data free from dogmatic and theological claims.[407] Instead, both the biblical texts and their competing interpretations must be viewed as 'explicit articulation[s] of...rhetorical strategies, interested perspectives, ethical criteria, theoretical frameworks, religious presuppositions, and sociopolitical locations for critical public discussion'.[408] A rhetorical approach to biblical studies and biblical texts emphasizes the authorial aims and

---

404. Schüssler Fiorenza, 'The Ethics of Biblical Interpretation', p. 16.
405. Schüssler Fiorenza, 'The Ethics of Biblical Interpretation', pp. 13-17.
406. Schüssler Fiorenza, 'The Ethics of Biblical Interpretation', pp. 13-14.
407. Schüssler Fiorenza, 'The Ethics of Biblical Interpretation', p. 11.
408. Schüssler Fiorenza, 'The Ethics of Biblical Interpretation', p. 14.

strategies, as well as audience perceptions and constructions, as political and religious discourse practices.[409]

It is the elaboration of the implications of this rhetorical approach which she addresses explicitly in her recent monograph, *But She Said*.[410] Here her hermeneutical model of feminist liberationist interpretation becomes supplemented and suffused throughout with insights culled from an explicitly and specifically *rhetorical* approach to biblical interpretation. Indeed, in what is perhaps the most programmatic declaration of the rhetorical directions she will pursue in the book,[411] Schüssler Fiorenza at times appears to contrast [albeit, for the sake of completion, supplementation, perhaps even redefinition] rhetoric with hermeneutics,[412] resulting in a 'critical feminist rhetorical model of interpretation' which not only informs the hermeneutic model she developed in *Bread Not Stone*,[413] but also sees itself as utilizing and integrating a wide variety of feminist biblical interpretive approaches[414] 'in order to recast biblical studies in *rhetorical* terms'.[415] Biblical interpretive practice (including its hermeneutical foundations), redefined as specifically *rhetorical* practice, is now directed toward the critical goal of displaying

> how biblical texts and their contemporary interpretations [including their hermeneutical theoretical assumptions, whether implicitly or explicitly engaged] are both political and religious. Authorial aims, point of view, narrative strategies, persuasive means, and authorial closure, as well as the audience's [and interpreter's] perceptions [including methods and

409. Schüssler Fiorenza, 'The Ethics of Biblical Interpretation', p. 4.

410. Elisabeth Schüssler Fiorenza, *But She Said: Feminist Practices of Biblical Interpretation* (Boston: Beacon Press, 1992).

411. Cf. Schüssler Fiorenza, *But She Said*, pp. 40-48.

412. Cf., e.g., Schüssler Fiorenza, *But She Said*, p. 41: 'Whereas hermeneutical theory seeks to explore and to appreciate the meaning of texts, rhetorical interpretation and its theoethical interrogation of texts and symbolic worlds pays attention to the kinds of effects biblical discourses produce and how they produce them.' Cf. also p. 46: 'Whereas hermeneutics seeks to explore and to appreciate the meaning of texts, rhetorical interpretation pays attention both to the kind of sociosymbolic worlds and moral universes biblical discourses produce, and to the way these discourses produce them.'

413. Cf. Schüssler Fiorenza, *But She Said*, pp. 57-76.

414. Schüssler Fiorenza, *But She Said*, pp. 21-39.

415. Schüssler Fiorenza, *But She Said*, p. 40. Emphasis mine.

paradigmata, traditions, the external forms and 'entextualization' of discursive power], are rhetorical practices which have determined not only the Bible's production but also its subsequent interpretations [critical tools, analytical boundaries, etc.].[416]

This shift from a hermeneutical paradigm [of 'meaning'] to a rhetorical one [of pragmatic intentions and effects] has broad consequences for biblical interpretation, not only with respect to the posture one takes regarding the Bible's rhetoric and authority, nor only to the political and ethical functions of interpretation within both Christianity and western cultures, but also with respect to the academented systems and discursive practices themselves that sanction interpretive methods and govern both the means and ends of critical inquiry.

While Schüssler Fiorenza goes on to explore the particular hermeneutic-rhetorical space of feminist critical theory in general [a 'democratic' *ekklēsia*],[417] and varying strategies of feminist biblical interpretation in particular,[418] it is to the academented institutional structures (which are among the 'framing conditions'[419] of interpretation-as-praxis) to which I wish to turn as an example of the kind of inquiry which suggest a kinship to that I envision taking shape through a rhetoric of power. For here, indeed, we see for the first time among our scholars the tentative break *through* the disciplinary walls and boundaries that have constrained and defined rhetorical criticism in biblical exegesis. It is not my argument to suggest that *only* through rhetoric could such a critique take place (since similar critiques are found throughout her works, incited by her feminist-liberationist hermeneutic, and have been offered by others as well), but that we begin to see in her works rhetoric as a critical strategy and approach that pushes [if not quite overcomes] the boundaries of its otherwise strictly constrained application within exegetical disciplinary practices. Rhetoric is no longer limited to a tool for historical-critical reconstruction [although it continues to be that in her work], but turns its analytical gaze outside the *biblical* texts to include in its field of critical vision *interpretive* 'texts' and 'contexts'. In her hands, rhetoric becomes a tool for exposing implicit and explicit discourses and systems of power in its many manifestations within biblical studies.

---

416. Schüssler Fiorenza, *But She Said*, p. 46.
417. Cf. Schüssler Fiorenza, *But She Said*, pp. 102-32.
418. Cf., e.g., Schüssler Fiorenza, *But She Said*, pp. 195-217.
419. Schüssler Fiorenza, *But She Said*, p. 10.

The contribution unique among those we have been exploring in this tome to which I wish to turn explicitly is the analysis of institutional settings that reinforce traditional (i.e. objectivist, positivist, androcentric) biblical interpretive practices. Her analysis focuses particularly upon the systems of socialization that students confront when educated into the discourse practices of biblical academented and theological interpretation. These systems are driven by a double agenda [socialization into 'scientific' theological thinking and into professional training] which 'entails a change of discursive frameworks from a discourse of acceptance of the Bible as a cultural icon, or from a discourse of obedience to it as the word of G-d, to a critical academic discourse that assumes the authority of inquiry and scholarship in challenging the cultural and doctrinal authority of the Bible'.[420] Historically, the origins of the shift from religious to scholarly authority can be traced back to the transformation of the curriculum of higher education based upon the model of German scientific research in the late nineteenth century. This shift resulted not only in a fundamental revision of the structure the university, 'side-lining' the Bible and religion in college education, but also constituted and ensured the hegemony of 'objective method, scientific value-neutrality, and disinterested research' as a paradigm of all critical and analytical pursuits in any and every field of inquiry, including biblical studies and theological 'sciences'.[421] And, of course, we have been exploring the implicit systems of power at work within such a paradigm: the elevation of an essentially limited (if not actively distortive) perspective ['whitemale'] to that of universal and authoritative standard for inquiry and conclusion regarding 'truth', 'understanding', 'meaning' and 'reality'.[422] Such a paradigm actively denies its 'hermeneutic-theoretical character and "androcentric" optic. It also masks [its] sociohistorical location, as well as [its] sociopolitical... interests.'[423]

Pedagogical approaches, procedures of validation and styles of reasoning,[424] all serve to reinforce the 'disinterested', objectivist herme-

420. Schüssler Fiorenza, *But She Said*, pp. 172-73.

421. Schüssler Fiorenza, *But She Said*, pp. 173-74.

422. Cf. her citation of Elisabeth Minnich, *Transforming Knowledge* (Philadelphia: Temple University Press, 1990) in Schüssler Fiorenza, *But She Said*, pp. 188-89.

423. Schüssler Fiorenza, *But She Said*, p. 174.

424. Cf. Schüssler Fiorenza, *But She Said*, pp. 186-94.

neutic as authoritative status quo, thereby systematically silencing questions of interest to liberationist interpreters. By excluding students from participating in the active production of knowledge, all pedagogical systems ('banking', expert-apprentice, consumer and therapeutic models of education) serve only to perpetuate their passivity as consumers of information within a patriarchal-capitalist paradigm.[425] Systems of validation serve to reinforce the hegemony of the dominant discourse tradition of 'whitemale' scholarship by exclusively requiring proven ability in its methods and knowledge of its results in order to receive professional credentials.[426] Sanctioned rhetorical traditions and settings in which interpretive practices function enforce the quest for empirical statements and reject value judgments as non-/ir-rational positions to be excluded from the pursuit of knowledge. Even the seminar discussions and academented conferences prefer 'the mode of ascertaining truth [through] adversarial debate and the honing of arguments that can withstand the most acerbic assault…[similar] to forensic interrogation, to methods of arrest and discipline, to an understanding of logic and dialectic as police arts'.[427] These systems of power collude to 'internalize the entire constellation of beliefs, values, techniques, shared worldviews, and systems of knowledge as maps or guidelines for thinking and speaking in a "scholarly" way'[428] which in biblical and ecclesial contexts have been historically controlled by European males in positions of dominance seeking to exclude the voices (values, beliefs, assumptions, perspectives) of 'others' (womyn, colonial cultures, economically disadvantaged classes, etc.).

It is in particular the institutional discursive position of womyn as 'Other' that problematizes their entry into academented and ecclesiastical institutions of education. This position constitutes the basis of the socialization of womyn experience upon entry into acadamnia

---

425. Schüssler Fiorenza, *But She Said*, pp. 186-87.

426. Schüssler Fiorenza, *But She Said*, p. 189: 'Students being tested on their knowledge of biblical interpretation, for instance, will be certified if they know the "whitemale" Euro-American tradition of biblical interpretation. Their knowledge of African-American or feminist biblical interpretation does not count. Conversely, students who have no knowledge of either African-American, Hispanic, or feminist biblical interpretation will be certified as competent.'

427. Schüssler Fiorenza, *But She Said*, p. 191.

428. Schüssler Fiorenza, *But She Said*, p. 181.

under which they learn to mimic the dominant biblical-theological paradigm whose discourse practices renders their experiences, insights and
issues silent and irrelevant. On the other hand, this site of 'exclusion'
also provides the location from which such institutional systems can be
viewed, scrutinized, rejected and/or reformed. Schüssler Fiorenza envi-
sions the need to 'construct a different feminist discursive space for a
pedagogical practice of liberation...Feminists who engage in theological education in order to transform the patriarchal discourses of
church and academy can do so only if we become qualified residents
and remain foreign speakers at one and the same time.'[429] This position
of 'resident alien'[430] must remain the fundamental interpretive center,
since

> [i]f the dominant interpretive community acts somewhat like a police
> force, defending against unacceptable interpretations, then it becomes
> important to reflect on the social institutional location of a critical fem-
> inist interpretation for liberation in departments of religion and schools
> of theology. For whenever liberation discourses are displaced from their
> social location in emancipatory movements and become integrated into
> the institutional practices of church or academy, they become subject to
> the disciplinary pressures and requirements of these interpretive com-
> munities.

It is precisely these 'disciplinary pressures and requirements' that
Schüssler Fiorenza seeks to understand through a rhetorical approach to
biblical interpretation in an effort to carve out an alternative, liberating
space from which to change both 'institutional structures [and] the pedagogical practices of theological education'.[431]

As we have been exploring, a rhetorical approach to biblical studies
and education engages with interpretive paradigmata on several fronts:
on the one hand, it seeks out and exposes the implicit systems of power
that perpetrate and perpetuate traditional forms of dominance, rejecting
the claim to 'value-free' scholarship as the universalist foundation of
rationality and investigation. In this respect, it also therefore seeks to
create an awareness of the 'interestedness' of all scholarship, thereby
demanding ethical and political responsibility for interpretation. On the
other hand, it further seeks to reconstruct educational models whereby
'the discourses of biblical education [are] laid open for critical scrutiny

429. Schüssler Fiorenza, *But She Said*, p. 170; cf. also pp. 182-86.
430. Cf. Schüssler Fiorenza, *But She Said*, pp. 184-86.
431. Schüssler Fiorenza, *But She Said*, p. 172.

in such a way that all students can participate in their own professional education as speaking subjects'.[432] To this end, pedagogical practices must be directed toward not only critical awareness of the socio-historical location of traditional interpretive approaches and their methodological and hermeneutical assumptions, but also must begin with a critical exploration of the students' own 'experience, commitments, and questions, as well as...their theological presuppositions and frameworks'.[433] It must also explore and 'appreciate biblical interpretations which have been developed in sociocultural locations different from those of white elite church- or university-men', including those which have been developed 'in oppressed communities such as the Black Church or in emancipatory struggles'.[434] In this way, students begin to become aware of the interests of interpretations, interpreters and biblical texts; begin to consider the sociopolitical implications; begin to develop ways of asking critical questions and articulating their own interpretation 'rather than simply accepting and repeating the exegetical results of the masters in the field'.[435] A rhetorical approach to biblical interpretation does not limit its vision to issues of exegesis alone, but begins to make profound, fundamental changes to the entire structure of biblical and theological education and its underlying systems of power.

With Schüssler Fiorenza, therefore, we see the first example of the field of inquiry of biblical interpretation broadened through an explicitly *rhetorical* approach. Beginning as another methodological tool for historical-critical interpretation of the biblical text, rhetoric quickly takes on critical dimensions that demand from biblical scholars the recognition of systems of power at work in their discipline and practices. Rhetoric begins to transcend the strict disciplinary boundaries of the field in order to transform the field itself. It has become a *rhetoric of power*.

Hermeneutical Authority—The Historical-Critical Paradigm
In our own critical turn, that is, our own analysis of power of Schüssler Fiorenza's work, it is important to ponder the disciplinary edifices that remain intact in her interpretive paradigm. That is, in spite of important renovations, expansions and rededications of the structures of biblical

432. Schüssler Fiorenza, *But She Said*, p. 178.
433. Schüssler Fiorenza, *But She Said*, p. 179.
434. Schüssler Fiorenza, *But She Said*, p. 178.
435. Schüssler Fiorenza, *But She Said*, p. 179.

interpretation brought about by her approach, it is fascinating to consider what disciplinary framework and foundations remain largely present [even if suspiciously questioned, tested and then reconfigured] in the resulting program.

We have seen her rejection of antiquarian positivism of historical criticism whose scientific objectivism 'masks the extent to which the concept of objective social science and history is itself a theoretical construct'.[436] On the other hand, Schüssler Fiorenza also rejects what she identifies as positivist textualism: while feminist literary studies rightly eschews the 'referential fallacy' engaged when one assumes the fictive world and characters of the text as representational of the 'real' world and 'real' people, Schüssler Fiorenza nevertheless rejoins with the accusation that the implicit New Criticism of literary analysis 'cannot but remain ensconced in the rhetorical world projected by the androcentric text'[437] since it cannot reconstruct 'a historical world *different* from the androcentric world construction of the text'.[438] With this, Schüssler Fiorenza shows a commitment to the historical-critical discipline, although she re-envisions its ethical *telos*.

Just what the nature and implications of the impact of this *telos* upon the discipline entails, becomes clear in her rejection of postmodernism in its specific incarnation within the 'New Historicism'. According to Schüssler Fiorenza, postmodernism's devastating critique of abstract and universal Truth, and concurrently its immersion of 'validity' within historically contingent and constructed processes of knowing and doing, undermine any attempts to theorize agency for change.[439] If there is no unproblematic position of privilege, then postmodernism in its most consistent form must embrace an all-pervasive relativity. Schüssler Fiorenza rejects this conclusion, suggesting instead that womyn's own

---

436. Schüssler Fiorenza, *But She Said*, pp. 82-84 (84). This seems a bit unfair, in light of her own assertion that historical reconstructions are themselves discursive constructs: Must a claim for ontology be the only valid foundation for 'textual' interpretation? Just how strong an ontological claim does Schüssler Fiorenza make for her own ['textual'] histories? Furthermore, what precludes feminist literary studies from deconstructive analysis of the text's world? Is the text's androcentric narrative world indeed so monolithic as to withstand such deconstruction? Where then are the fissures which Schüssler Fiorenza herself uses to gain entry into her own discursive construct.['historical (re)construction']?

437. Schüssler Fiorenza, *But She Said*, p. 85.

438. Schüssler Fiorenza, *But She Said*, p. 86.

439. Schüssler Fiorenza, *But She Said*, pp. 87-88.

experiences of alienation have not necessarily lead to a 'relativist pluralism', but have rather compelled them 'to articulate a *different* knowledge and vision of the world, one that can inspire and sustain a liberating praxis'.[440] The key interpretive center for feminist historical reconstruction once again becomes the lived, historical, pragmatic experiences of struggle of the contemporary community in their commitment to envision and realize *praxis* for liberation of socially marginalized [on the basis of gender, but also on the basis of race and economics] womyn. Feminist rhetorical-historical reconstruction, while 'it recognizes the provisionality and multiplicity of knowledge as particular, situated, and "embodied", it does not abandon the claim to relative objectivity and historical validity'. Instead, it assesses this claim according to whether and how much reconstruction can make present 'the historical losers and their arguments—that is, how much they can make visible the symbolic world-constructions of those who have been made "invisible" in androcentric texts'.[441]

In other words, historical reconstruction has a new goal, shifted from traditional concerns with constructing [with an ontological claim to certainty] the events and personages (and their socio-cultural circumstances) of the past. It is, instead, a *critical* goal dedicated to emancipatory praxis of the *ekklēsia gynaikōn* and political assessment 'in terms of [its] implications and consequences for the struggle to transform patriarchal relations of oppression'.[442] Biblical 'texts' and their authority, historical reconstructions as 'texts' and their authority, are all subsumed under the 'context' of the *rhetorical* space within which early Christian origins are to be (re)constructed from a feminist perspective. Indeed, '[s]uch a feminist theological perspective, positioned in the rhetorical space of the *ekklēsia gynaikōn*, provides the critical norm and criterion by which all biblical traditions and writings must be assembled into a historical model'.[443] A feminist version of objectivity, while acknowledging 'the provisionality and multiplicity of local knowledge' as embodied ideological practice, embraces a hermeneutics of suspicion that 'recognizes the androcentric ideological construction of reality in language, texts, and other religious-cultural representations' and reads them 'against the grain'. Its purpose is to 'disclose

---

440. Schüssler Fiorenza, *But She Said*, p. 89. Emphasis hers.
441. Schüssler Fiorenza, *But She Said*, pp. 33-34.
442. Schüssler Fiorenza, *But She Said*, p. 197.
443. Schüssler Fiorenza, *But She Said*, p. 141.

and unravel "the politics of Otherness" inscribed in and constructed by the androcentric text because feminists experience and theorize about a historical reality in which "the [excluded] others" are present and active [in their reconstructions]'.[444] Feminist theory, and its efforts at historical reconstruction, rejects postmodernism's proclivity to inaction because it understands itself as *committed* to a sociopolitical movement for change.

Yet, while her model does not maintain the *ethical* priority of the biblical text and androcentric historical [-interpretive] tradition, it does assert their *methodological* authority. This is clear, insofar as exegesis, even when rhetorically reconfigured, continues to be practiced as historical reconstruction [of revisionist biblical history and/or authorial rhetorical 'intention']. She cannot re-envision exegesis as anything else, since she is committed to a historicist quest for the recovery of womyn's agency in social, political and particularly ecclesiastical history. The Bible becomes a resource for this agenda, and the wide range of traditional interpretive methods remain the primary tools for its enactment, even if its political and ethical setting and purpose have been redirected. This not only secures a central position for the biblical 'text', but ensures a central and significant role for the very institutions and methods of scholarship whose power she wants[?] to diffuse.

The difficulty is, feminist historiography and interpretation of the Bible dedicated to the (re)construction of a new socio-historical reality [or at least a *different* one], walks a fine line between rejecting 'objective certainty' and asserting ontological 'reality'. Schüssler Fiorenza assures 'us' that such imaginative reconstruction is not a fictive fantasy, but rather a historical imagination that has been partially instantiated 'in the historical struggles of "the subordinated others" who have refused to be defined by the patriarchal politics of inequality, subordination and dehumanization'.[445] The ontological basis, however, seems to be confused by this and other statements: does rhetorical historical reconstruction claim ontological status for its results with respect to the past, the present or the future? The answer is clouded by the all-subsuming 'context' of the ethical imperatives of the contemporary community for whom such reconstruction is performed.

If its claim is that the results are indeed ontologically grounded in the past, then it is difficult to assess the standard by which to judge its

444. Schüssler Fiorenza, *But She Said*, p. 90.
445. Schüssler Fiorenza, *But She Said*, p. 92.

results with respect to historical 'accuracy'. According to Schüssler Fiorenza, feminist historical reconstruction does not offer its alternative constructs of 'reality' as 'given facts' 'but as plausible "subtext" to the androcentric text'.[446] Its explicit criterion of success is met not through claims to objectivism, but 'on the *explanatory power* of the heuristic models and arguments generated to comprehend history as the reality not only of Western elite men but also of the subordinated and dehumanized others'.[447] It achieves its goal 'when it can make those whom the androcentric text marginalizes or excludes centrally present as historical actors'. It rejects the notion of 'the true meaning of the text itself' in favor of the criterion of contemporary political assessment of the consequences of the interpretive act.[448] One sees here the potential collapse of ontology into epistemology, at least insofar as critical interpretive efforts are concerned. What we may also see is an attempt to have her cake and eat it, too: if there is no 'objective' reality, but only interested reality, how can 'we' stake any ontological claim to 'our' reconstructive efforts when all 'we' are asserting is 'our' epistemological stance? But if 'all we have' is 'our' epistemological position, isn't any historical reconstruction at some level [being the result of rhetorical and discursive practices] always *fictive*?[449]

But if this is the case, if in arguing for an 'ethical' standard of consequences regarding both biblical texts and interpretive traditions, a standard that ultimately usurps the authority of the 'text' over the community, we can make no ontological claim to 'reality' [or at least a claim which can be assessed as somehow 'real' and 'accurate': the Holocaust *did* happen, but the only way to argue for such a position is through the introduction of ontological claims of some sort upon which to reject statements to the contrary], then why bother with the system of exegetical-as-historiography practice at all? In other words, if the 'context' of modern/current struggle for liberation is so authoritative that it becomes the standard by which to judge historical-critical reconstruction, why bother with any claims to any rhetorical construct of 'reality'

446. Schüssler Fiorenza, *But She Said*, p. 96.
447. Schüssler Fiorenza, *But She Said*, p. 101.
448. Schüssler Fiorenza, *But She Said*, p. 197.
449. I'm not attempting to insert an 'objectivist' and transhistorical Archimedian point as the basis for my critique. I am trying to show the collapse of ontology into epistemology.

regarding its results? Why bother with history at all, why not just make the whole thing up?

There may be a very good reason to keep wanting to turn to history as a fundamental arena of Schüssler Fiorenza's hermeneutical-rhetorical praxis: the quest for agency, which is a quest for action, responsibility and legitimation. And yet, if the 'context' of the modern community is that of the praxis of liberation *here* and *now* in the struggle for all possible *futures* of freedom [a 'context' that authorizes the interpretation and use of the biblical 'text'], why must 'agency' be defined by history? Because of the assumed legitimating role of Tradition. And if the Tradition of the fathers of early [through modern] Christianity isn't acceptable, find a useable past, construct a new/old Tradition to which one can point in its stead. At the heart of her hermeneutic lies the centrality of historical Tradition; every aspect of the program turns around it: hermeneutics of suspicion questioning history's rhetorical construction; hermeneutics of remembrance commemorating its fallen victims/heroines; hermeneutics of proclamation displaying its affirming examples as models for inspiration and emulation; hermeneutics of imagination giving its silenced voices the chance to speak. From history 'we' find examples to mimic and anti-models to avoid. From history 'we' find 'our' location, learn 'our' lessons, meet 'our' heroines, castigate 'our' oppressors, identify the systems and structures of power in its broad developments and movements. From history 'we' begin the quest for a new present and a better future. It is a search for, and creation of, a Tradition in which a liberating praxis can be situated. Even if that Tradition can make no claim to ontological existence.

The point I wish to make is not so much that the pursuit of Tradition through historical reconstruction is not somehow a persuasive and effective rhetorical strategy [given her community]. Nor is my point that we should ground such a pursuit in prestructuralist claim to 'objectivity'. The point I wish to make is the interesting pragmatic result of the continued fascination with historical reconstruction and recovery of liberationist Tradition: that, even in spite of her democratizing action and her authoritative shift of discursive power to the living community of believers at work in the struggle for liberation, the result is the continuation and assurance of the status and position of the historical interpreter to the task of liberation, and with it, the broader structures of disciplinary power, of methods and critical focus remain intact [even if the façade may have been changed, the edifice reno-vated]. That is, even historical reconstruction for liberation, based upon the rejection of objectivist scientist inquiry, is still historical recon-struction, the search for origins, the recreation of a Tradition with roots to the past. It is still a disciplinary structure of interpretation that over-writes the sources and reconstructs both text and ontology through discursive practices of 'entextualization' and intellectual activity. It still leaves standing the fundamental assumption that if only 'we' interpret more honestly, (re)construct 'texts', speak or imagine or write History, somehow something is going to change, whether through 'our' dis-course, or alongside it. What I am interested in is the continued pres-ence of power of precisely those systems which Schüssler Fiorenza wants to wrestle under her control. And while I am not totally con-vinced she has failed to do so, I am also not convinced she has suc-ceeded or can succeed.

non-Chapter 4e

MUSINGS ON 'THE (NEW) RHETORICAL CRITICISM(S)
AND
NEW TESTAMENT EXEGESIS'

From one point of view, the [acadamnian] aspires to the condition of the music-hall comedian. Being incapable of altering his[/her] wares to suit a prevailing taste, if there be any, [s/]he naturally desires a state of society in which they may become popular.

The Use of Poetry and the Use of Criticism
T.S. Eliot

An analysis of the function of the (new) rhetorical criticism(s) has exposed the fundamental presuppositions of this approach as practiced by these important scholars. For each of them, I would argue, the understanding of the rhetorical *effect* of a discourse is directed by a hermeneutic that continues to locate textual 'meaning' in the original act/context/event of composition and performance. The dialogic interaction between rhetor and audience is restricted in their rhetorical-critical analysis of the text to the generative circumstances out of which the work arose and to which it was immediately addressed. The methodological focus is therefore directed toward the effort of reconstructing the historical 'context' to which the 'author' addresses her/his 'text' whose meaning can only be understood as a 'fitting' response to this 'context'. The 'meaning' of a 'text' resides, then, in this complex of ancient events and circumstances that gave rise to the rhetorical a(rtifa)ct(s) culminating in the production of the biblical textual traditions. It is this reconstructed meaning-as-historical-meaning that is the hermeneutical center [the authoritative touchstone] for further textual interpretation and application. The resulting locus of power for biblical interpretation, therefore, resides in the hands of the exegete-as-historian, and this is a power not to be taken lightly [after all, we are talking about struggles for determining authoritative interpretive control over the Bible!], and is enforced through restricted initiation into methodological norms [what else is education?].

The question which is of great interest [if not of vital importance] to a rhetoric of power is, 'Where does this particular formulation of rhetorical analysis stem from, and what are the forces at work that ensure its continued [persistent] dominance over the interpretive field?' Uncovering ideologies of power at work in the discourse of the (new) rhetorical-critical exegesis of the New Testament is an important step, but also points the way to a series of important questions concerning the [(genea-)logical, not necessarily chronological] 'origins' of these systems of power. For the quest for biblical 'meaning' in general, and the particular form that has taken shape in the discourse of these rhetorical scholars, belies a very important set of circumstances (social, historical, theoretical, methodological, pedagogic) to which the efforts of these scholars address their work (and which, in turn, are shaping their work). There is a tension exhibited in each of their pursuits, a tension that wrestles with concerns of relevance of their scholarly efforts to contemporary social and religious issues, while at the same time attempting to maintain a unique disciplinary identity and control over the discourse. There is also a tension between pursuing the full implications and ramifications of a rhetorical approach to interpretation and the habits of inquiry firmly entrenched in their methods, the latter of which so thoroughly permeate their analyses that none of them ultimately questions the legitimacy of historical-critical reconstruction or sees the interpretive closure and ideological distortions of power it exerts upon their work. Perhaps we can introduce suggestive areas of further [future] (re)search into the 'origins' of this ideology and power by looking at the hegemony of the historical-critical paradigm at work in the discipline of biblical studies [a paradigm which has been considered *definitional* for the discipline].

Readings through a Rhetoric of Power

The Academented Context of Power and Biblical Studies
How we approach the quest for the origins of the limitations of the (new) rhetorical criticism(s) will, of course, determine *what* we find. There are several directions that a rhetoric of power, as informed in particular by Steven Mailloux's 'rhetorical hermeneutics', could take.

On the one hand, we can trace the influence of critical historicism upon biblical interpretation through a chronological reconstruction of the significant developments in the study of the Bible. Such a reconstruction could not possibly take into account all the factors contributing to the eventual dominance of exegetical readings informed by a hermeneutics of historical reconstruction. After all, such factors would include social and political upheavals, technological and economic developments, as well as philosophical 'revolutions' and fundamental transformations within systems of education. Nevertheless, we can offer here at least the broad outlines of chronological development as a preliminary 'background' for further reflections.

The most 'obvious' origin of a historical-critical approach to biblical interpretation can be traced back to the Reformation and Luther's call for Scripture as the only and final source of revelation (*scriptura scripturae interpres*), coupled with an interpretive hermeneutic (inherited, in part, from Scholasticism) which stressed the 'literal, ordinary, natural sense' of the text. What was unique among the Reformers was the authority they ascribed to the Bible: for them, the Bible *alone* became the authoritative *locus* from which church faith, doctrine and practices were to be judged and determined, thereby undermining the traditional understanding of the Bible as only one of several 'pillars of the faith'. As such, the Bible not only became the subject of intense investigative and interpretive activity, but this activity was to take place outside of the traditional spheres of theological and dogmatic tradition, often resulting in exegetical interpretations that ran contrary to patristic exegesis, council doctrines, etc. In effect, as one interpreter has put it, '[t]he reformers, in the interest of reform, were actually driving a wedge between the Bible and the Church'.[1]

This 'wedge' has haunted biblical interpretation ever since, for one of the most pressing issues confronting the Reformers was determining the means by which to authenticate and validate interpretation, if not by church dogma or theological tradition. The christ-centric interpretation of Luther, or Calvin's 'confirmation by the internal testimony of the holy spirit', both developed essentially privatized, 'subjective' means by which to confirm interpretive validity, opening the door to a wide

---

1.   Terence J. Keegan, *Interpreting the Bible: A Popular Introduction to Biblical Hermeneutics* (New York: Paulist Press, 1985), p. 19.

variety of groups who flourished in the seventeenth and early eighteenth centuries (Quakers, Anabaptists, Ranters, Seekers, etc.). In reaction to these 'radical sectarians', Lutherans, Calvinists and Anglicans would return, ironically enough, to dogma-centered standards, resulting in an orthodoxy as harrowing [and dangerous] as any Inquisition had been.

But another alternative began to assert itself in the wake of Renaissance humanism: the rise of classical philology and the study of Greco-Roman 'classics', and the division of theology and philosophy heralded by the works of Descartes, Hobbes and Spinoza. That is, many scholars of the Bible continued to argue for the validity of the application and results of critical methodologies for their efforts to reconstruct the biblical text, to search for sources behind the traditions of both the Pentateuch and Gospels, as well as to study the 'original' meaning of the texts in their historical (cultural and linguistic) 'contexts'. Their attempt to provide a rational foundation for the study of the Bible offered an important, though not yet comfortable, alternative for privatized interpretation on the one hand and conservative dogmatics on the other. But it also could not avoid, even in spite of apologetics offered to the contrary, further driving the 'wedge' between Bible and church.

The most prominent of such scholars during the sixteenth century was Erasmus of Rotterdam who set about the task of compiling the first ever critical edition of the Greek New Testament [published 1516]. Turning to the advances in classical philology in order to sort out the myriad of textual variants among the manuscripts available to him, he applied humanist principles of literary analysis in order to reconstruct what he believed was the 'original' text. The adequacy of his results (both with respect to the reconstructed text and his critical literary interpretation of them) was eventually questioned in the face of continued scrutiny (esp. by the Counter-Reformers). But in spite of this, and the threat of condemnation by orthodox opponents, there were others who continued to apply these methodological principles (and suffer for it). In the seventeenth century, for example, we see this work continued by R. Simon, whose *Histoire critique du Vieux Testament* (1678) and *Histoire critique du Nouveau Testament* (1689) were both condemned to be burned. Others whose interest in philology led them to produce critical editions of the Greek New Testament included J. Mill (1642–1707), J. Griesbach (1745–1812), C. Tischendorf (1815–74) and B. Westcott and F. Hort (1825–1901; 1828–92).

By the eighteenth century, the prominence of Enlightenment rationalism in philosophy and education set the stage for the critical-historical approach to the New Testament, first advocated by J. Semler (1725–88?) and especially W. Michaelis (1717–91). While they were perhaps the most vocal proponents for the application of a critical literary methodology to the biblical texts, efforts at reconstructing the life of Jesus based on rationalist/humanist methods can trace their inspiration back to the works of Reimarus (1694–1798). Here also we cannot overlook contributions made by G. Lessing (1729–81), J. Eichhorn (1752–1827), C. Lachmann (1793–1851) and H. Weisse (1801–66) in their attempts to reconstruct Gospel 'sources' and the early, 'authentic' teachings of Jesus. We should also note the contribution to hermeneutics and the important rationalist reconstruction of the life of Jesus presented by F. Schleiermacher in the late eighteenth century.

The most prominent historical critic of the New Testament of the early nineteenth century was undoubtedly F. Baur (1792–1860), whose reconstruction of early Christian history, inspired by B. Niebuhr's critical historiography (published 1810–12), was influenced by Hegelian dialectics. It was his thesis that the development of dogma could be traced through a process of thesis (early Jewish legalists)—antithesis (Paul as anti-legalist)—synthesis (Gospel and Epistles). He was also interested in the differences between Jesus as a Jewish preacher and the subsequent depictions of him in early Christian literature. Among his most important students were D. Strauss (1808–74), who constituted, even in spite of his own misgivings concerning its success, the nineteenth-century quest for the historical Jesus, a quest culminating in the work of A. Schweitzer (1875–1965) at the end of the nineteenth century, and picked up again in a 'New Quest' and even a 'Third Quest' in this century.

But it was particularly during the period between approximately 1830–1945 that the discipline of biblical studies could be said to have achieved its modern disciplinary identity, with an explosion of interpretive schools arising out the historical-critical paradigm (some of which we shall touch upon, below). This is a profound transformation [even usurpation] of disciplinary identity in the wake of centuries of theologically driven interpretation. Whereas historical-critical methodology since the Reformation had been employed either by critics of the church, or by a handful of assorted 'leaders' and scholars, by the nineteenth century critical historiography had become the adopted and sanctioned tool of biblical scholarship for disciplinary interpretive practice, the 'first' and fundamental means by which to 'study the Bible'. In spite of significant differences in [primarily theologically driven] reconstruction regarding the relationship of the New Testament to both the earthly ministry of Jesus and the missionary movements reflected in Paul's writing, regarding the conflict between Jewish and Gentile Christianity, regarding the relationship of Christianity to Hellenistic mystery religions, Gnosticism, Jewish Apocalyptism and rabbinic traditions, *biblical scholarship no longer doubted the relevance and importance of a historical approach to biblical interpretation.* This was true not only on the Continent, but in England and America, as well. Conflicts arose over issues of theological orthodoxy and/or spiritual emptiness of these disciplinary studies; over the theological implications and hence validity of approaching Jesus as a human (rather than divine) being; over the role of liberal humanism and German idealism informing these critical practices; over the hermeneutical gap between radical historical reconstruction and its relationship to the living community and modern believer, and so on. But, throughout these controversies, the thesis was presented and eventually achieved hegemony over biblical studies that its disciplinary self-definition and discourse practices were to be as a historical science dedicated to the study of primitive Christianity and its development.

This rather remarkable disciplinary transformation and consolidation was helped by a number of factors giving shape to acadamnia in general: the extraordinary successes achieved by the physical sciences and their objectivist methodologies, the growing importance of the German research university as a model for higher education and research, and thus the mimetic 'desire' within the humanities for developing their own critical 'objectivist' methods (as seen, e.g., in the empirical historical research model). The 'wedge' driven between church and Bible, between theology and exegesis, produced a 'gap' which was tenuously, arduously, but successfully filled by an 'objectivist', empirical historiography that provided the general rubric under which various lower and higher critical approaches could operate, giving them not only their disciplinary impetus and direction, but also the discursive means by which to produce analyses and defend/identify critical praxis.

On the other hand, we could supplement the above chronology with a fragmented genealogy of interpretive schools and their subsequent manifestation and impact upon the discipline as currently practiced, noting all the while their assumption of the historical-critical paradigm. Each time these schools rose to prominence, they occasioned bitter reaction both from other critical scholars [disciplinary infighting] but also especially from theologians who simply refused to accept the consequences of the critical achievements, since they so thoroughly undermined church teaching, tradition and dogma. Nevertheless, critical-literary, social-scientific, anthropological and historical tools became the norm for interpretation in an effort to reconstruct the history of early Christianity and 'original' meanings of biblical traditions.

Such was the case with the Tübingen school's Hegelian historical dialectics and its resultant portrait of Gentile versus Jewish Christianity. Their conclusions were eventually mediated and then rejected by A. Ritschl (1822–89), B. Weiss (1827–1918), A. Jülicher (1857–1938) and R. Lightfoot (1828–89).

Such was also the case with the rise of the *Religionsgeschichte* (religious history) school and its initial emphasis upon the relationship between early Christianity and contemporaneous intertestamental Judaism, thus the emphasis upon a 'thorough-going eschatology' of both Jesus and Paul. Soon, however, these conclusions gave way to growing disciplinary insight offered by research into Hellenistic mystery religions and Gnosticism and their impact upon New Testament traditions and authors. Still later, this swing toward Greco-Roman religious influences was counterbalanced by the work of Strack-Billerbeck (1922) and the discoveries at Qumran (1947), which returned to the question of the relationship between Jesus and the Palestinian Judaism of his time and its impact upon both his teaching and the developing Jesus movements.

Here we must also note the advent of a radical historicism introduced by W. Wrede (1859–1906) in his approach to both the Gospel and Pauline traditions, a skepticism whose ramifications sent shockwaves, both for and against, throughout the discipline in spite of the best efforts of J. Wellhausen (1844–1918), A. Harnack (1851–1930), M. Kähler (1835–1912) and P. Feine (1859–1933) to mediate and undermine this skepticism.

We might also speak of specific schools of methodology, such as the form-criticism of W. Kümmel (1905–), O. Dibelius (1883–1947) and R. Bultmann (1884–1976), in reaction to which G. Bornkamm (1901–77) and H. Conzelmann (1915–89) called for a redaction-critical approach to the Gospels in an effort to bring together the scattered fragments of tradition and to rescue the coherent narrative history as depicted by the Gospel authors from the near oblivion into which form criticism had sent it.

It was about this time that in biblical studies there came about a (re)turn to theology with the rise of the New Hermeneutics of R. Bultmann's followers, as well as the 'neo-orthodoxy' of K. Barth (1886–1968) and his followers. It is important to note that the time of this reaction to skeptical empirical historicism was the same period of crisis of culture met in Europe after the Great War. The German humanists in particular reacted to their erosion of power brought about by the academented turn toward empiricism and positivism by consolidating their relationship to the government through rhetorical appeal to Kantian anthropological humanism and the central role of education in *kulturelle Bildung* (cultural socialization). In biblical studies, this 'new emphasis upon theological interpretation' attempted to give direction to disciplinary practices, but could never completely displace the historical-critical paradigm.

It was not long before J. Robinson (1924–) chronicled important developments offered by new philosophies of history that would allow for a 'New Quest' to be given shape and justification. This return was aided tremendously by the incredible archaeological discoveries at Oxyrhynchus and Nag Hammadi.

More recently, a revival in the interest of Hellenistic romance literature and the handbooks of the Greco-Roman schools has helped scholars completely revise previous notions of 'first-century Palestinian Judaism' and 'Hellenistic' cultures, offering as thoroughly *complex* a picture of the cultures and religious practices of the times as the 'data' can sustain. The resultant 'Third Quest', helped by advances in sociohistorical methods, cultural anthropology and an awareness of the impact of politics and economics upon Mediterranean cultures under the Roman Imperium, has been willing to draw on a plurality of sources with a distinctive *lack* of *a priori* theological assumptions directing the work. The result has been an explosive and exciting fragmentation of the discipline, now informed by a myriad of methodological tools and close scrutiny of critical assumptions.[2]

---

2.   There has, of course, been recent growing interest in new literary theories and methods, such as narrative poetics and reader response, which have made an occasional foray into the discipline. It is my argument, however, that their significance has been limited. Only recently could the monolith of the historical-critical

Throughout it all, and even in spite of important methodological, theological and hermeneutical misgivings and criticisms, it has been the success of critical historiographical methodologies over the field that has dominated and defined biblical studies as a discipline in tension with its religious and theological roots/context.

My own application of a rhetoric of power, while interested in and benefited by both chronological and genealogical reconstruction of the discipline, will instead turn to the analysis of the 'origins' of the historian's power in biblical studies by assessing the discipline in terms of its discursive practices. It can thereby locate the *rhetorical* dynamics that give shape to and are given shape by specific academented systems of power. I want to ponder the disciplinary 'intentions' of the dominance of the historical-critical paradigm over biblical studies by judging the *effects* of the discursive practices as we have so far exposed them. I do so in order to ponder the power of biblical studies as an academented and critical pursuit of biblical interpretation, one that seeks to carve out for itself a territory of expertise and experts of interpretation, an effect not unique in academentia, nor in religion, but one which does have certain ramifications for the academented interpretation of the Bible with respect to religious systems.

We begin this brief excursion into unknown territory by asking a simple question: Within the context of biblical interpretation [i.e. within the structure of both academentia and *ekklēsia*], just what does the historical-critical paradigm *do* for biblical studies? And the answers, I believe, are quite evident.

First, it wrestles control for biblical interpretation away from those authorities whose legitimacy and power are founded in dogma and tradition. From the beginning, the call for a historical exegetical approach to the 'text' informed first by philology, and even earlier with Luther's call for an open canon, has met with vociferous condemnation by both Catholic and Protestant orthodoxies.[3] This has been the case

paradigm be showing signs of structural failure, particularly as a result of the rise of the postmodern critique of the positivist hermeneutics informing historical-critical analysis.

3. Cf., e.g., Nigel M. de S. Cameron, *Biblical Higher Criticism and the Defense of Infallibilism in 19th Century Britain* (Lewiston: Edwin Mellen Press, 1987). Cf. also Stephen Neill, *Interpretation of the New Testament 1861–1986* (Oxford: Oxford University Press, 1988), Chapter 1, 'Challenge to Orthodoxy',

throughout its history, from the book burnings of R. Simon's *Histoire critique du Vieux Testament* to the fate of the students of the *Religionsgeschichte* school who could not find faculty positions. Even today, members of the Jesus Seminar have lost their jobs and/or been threatened with dismissal for their continued participation in that project. Nevertheless, in spite of these threats of sanction, those who have pursued historical criticism have done so precisely in order to undermine orthodoxy's claim to authoritative instruction in and interpretation of the Bible.[4] It has offered itself as a rigorous, objective, scientific approach to biblical interpretation free from creedal formulations and theological ideologies predetermining the critical results, attempting to transform the field of theology and religion into an exclusively historical pursuit.[5]

Second, it provides biblical interpretation with a means of participating in the dramatic changes brought about in university education of the last 150 years or more, legitimating its continued presence as a discipline by appeal to its critical methodology. The origins of the transformation of university education, particularly the impact of positivist and objectivist inquiry in the humanities, is too complicated to trace out in detail at this point, but at least two important events must be singled out: the classical philology of C. Wolf (1750),[6] and the critical historicism of B. Niebuhr (published in 1810–12). However, we

pp. 1-34. For reception in American university education of these critical methods, cf. Jerry W. Brown, *The Rise of Biblical Criticism in America, 1800–1870: The New England Scholars* (Middletown, CT: Wesleyan University Press, 1969).

4. 'The "dogma of the New Testament" is actually one of the leading dogmas of the Catholic Church which, like so much else, the evangelical churches have taken over uncritically. When it has once been abandoned there is to be no talk of treating the New Testament books and the theology embedded in them as independent of time and space: in fact they are to be, and can only be, understood in light of their time and environment' (G. Krüger, *Das Dogma vom neuen Testament* [Programm Giessen, 1896], p. 5, quoted in Werner Kümmel, *The New Testament: The History of the Investigation of its Problems* [trans. S. McLean Gilmour and Howard C. Kee; Nashville: Abingdon Press, 1972], p. 303).

5. Bultmann stating baldly that 'there can be only one method for scientific New Testament research', namely 'the historical'. Paul de Legarde suggested that theology was 'exclusively a historical discipline'. Both quoted in Kümmel, *The New Testament*, p. 372 (Bultmann), p. 302 (Legarde).

6. Fritz K. Ringer, 'The German Academic Community', in Alexandra Oleson and John Voss (eds.), *The Organization of Knowledge in Modern America, 1860–1920* (Baltimore: The Johns Hopkins University Press, 1976), pp. 409-27 (412-13).

must not overlook the transformation of European education brought about by the agitation for a curriculum conducted in the vernacular languages (which also brought with it educational reforms leading to the eventual diminishing of the classical educational system), nor the transformation of philosophy by Descartes and Kant.

But the most important development in the history of European and American education came with the establishment of the German research university in the early nineteenth century. And when the institution of pure research met with the American trend towards vocational and professional areas of specialization in university education (furthered by the Morrill Act of 1862) and the Harvard elective system (1869), the result was explosive: there was an exponential increase in areas of specialization and departmentalization, a trend that signaled the downfall in Europe with the traditional four-faculty division of the university (Medicine, Theology, Law and Philosophy). This increase and proliferation of areas of specialization was felt in both Europe and America, particularly in the increased presence of departments dedicated to the empirical and social sciences.

Contributing to this growth was also the rise of industrialism, which brought certain economic forces to bear upon university education resulting in a proliferation of departments dedicated to empirical and social scientific pursuits. On America's part, endowments by merchants and industrialists, and government support for technical universities, had early on impacted upon American university education which developed a trend, now felt throughout the world, toward a proliferation of vocational and professional degrees.[7] Positivism and practical instruction have created a 'matrix of specialization' which has put tremendous pressure upon the liberal arts and humanities.[8]

---

7. For an excellent survey of these developments, cf. Fritz Malchup, *Knowledge: Its Creation, Distribution, and Economic Significance*. II. *The Branches of Learning* (Princeton, NJ: Princeton University Press, 1982), esp. pp. 130-71.

8. Cf. John Higham, 'The Matrix of Specialization', in Oleson and Voss (eds.), *The Organization of Knowledge in Modern America, 1860–1920*, pp. 3-18 (4-6). This growth has not been without its detractors: While in Europe, the critics of specialization have come from within the sciences themselves (emphasizing the loss of shared knowledge and the ensuing 'narrowness of mind'), in America its critics came [come] from outside the sciences and departments of applied studies ('liberal education' proponents from undergraduate humanities departments).

Theology could not escape these pressures: from its dominance over university education,[9] it is now one among a plethora of departments, itself being conducted under the paradigm of specialization which fosters distinctive discourse practices identifying a variety of approaches to the interpretation of the Bible [not to mention recent fragmentation of religious studies into its own departmental emphases: systematic theology, philosophy of religion, church history, religion and the arts, comparative religions, etc.]. Biblical studies, in adapting to the changes of educational philosophy brought about by the research university and the rise of specialized empirical research in Germany beginning around 1830, presented itself as a critical discipline by adopting the methods of critical, rigorous historical science. This culminated in a disciplinary boundary definition (tentative and always in tension with theology [Kümmel makes this tension clear, for instance]) by explicit appeal to a positivist historical paradigm. All of this is happening, particularly with references to impact made by the *Religionsgeschichte* school upon disciplinary practices,[10] at precisely the time when the German research university was reaching its dominance, and precisely at the time when historical positivism set the critical standard for research in the humanities. The Tübingen school, the *Religionsgeschichte* school, and Wrede's radical historicism set Christianity within the human cultural sphere available to objective research and hence departmental specialization (along with the rest of the humanistic and historical disciplines).[11] This ensured it a space in the new educational order being brought about by the research university.

9.   Cf. Malchup, *Knowledge*, pp. 121, 124-35.
10.   It is not this school's critical conclusions per se with which I am interested here, but the dominance in the discipline of an approach to theology and biblical interpretation which set its disciplinary sights upon the question of historical reconstruction by understanding Christianity as a phenomenon in history and impacted upon by religious and cultural traditions contemporary and older than its origins. This is a point also made by, e.g., Kurt Rudolph, 'Early Christianity as a Religious-Historical Phenomenon', in Birger A. Pearson (ed.), *The Future of Early Christianity* (Minneapolis: Fortress Press, 1991), pp. 9-19.
11.   It would be of immense value to take a closer look at parallels in argumentative strategy and the use of topoi which may exist between the general conflict raging on between 'positivist' and neo-Idealist movements in the humanistic and historical disciplines in German universities at this time, a conflict based on the issue of the role of education as *kulturelle Bildung* especially in the face of growing specialization, and those between historical critics and the theological opposition

In addition, specialization and vocational pressures at the university level brought about the establishment of academemed societies to advance the specific discourse practices of the biblical studies discipline. Thus, we see the establishment of the Society of Biblical Literature (1880), the Studiorum Novi Testamenti Societas (1947), the Catholic Biblical Association (1936), and the American Academy of Religion (1909). All of these societies serve not only to provide a forum for the exchange of research and information, but also to advance the careers of its members, to obtain grant money to further research, to lobby on behalf of members and on behalf of the discipline at the institutional and political level, to sponsor journals and establish disciplinary presses, and often act as liaison between independent and major press houses and scholars. All of these academemed societies, as well as others not listed, serve the purpose of strengthening and legitimating disciplinary identity and practices in the face of lost prestige and dominance.

Third, the historical-critical paradigm as the disciplinary boundary definition also serves to combat other populist hermeneutical approaches of the text, especially the hermeneutics of Protestant fundamentalism. The historical-critical paradigm usurps fundamentalist hermeneutics by questioning both the issue of inerrancy and the unitary, simple meaning of the text by both [appropriately] complicating the tradition and emphasizing the text's foreign-ness. This *foreign-ness* is configured not only [appropriately] in terms of its ancient provenance and linguistic expression, *but also* in terms of the myriad of methodological tools, the intensity of educational socialization in their application, as well as the historicist hermeneutics which asserts authority for the critically determined meaning of the 'text' according to the ancient context of its production and distribution. Hence, the Bible's meaning is determined not by the 'plain reading' of the 'text', a reading which may be informed by the contemporary historical, cultural and social context of the modern reader and/or faithing community, but by reference to the inaccessible [except to specialists] reconstruction of social and cultural factors at work in its production. The assumptions governing the exegetical endeavor are ones meant to reinforce a hierarchy of values and 'truths' about the role of the faithful in encountering the word of god.[12]

they encountered. Cf. Ringer, 'The German Academic Community', pp. 422-27. Cf. also Paul Bové, *Intellectuals in Power: A Genealogy of Critical Humanism* (New York: Columbia University Press, 1986).

    12.   Robert Funk, in his introductory essays to *The Five Gospels: The Search for*

Its rhetoric appeals to standards of interpretation that place the scholar-as-historical-specialist in the mediating role once held by the priest or pastor. Ironically, the *sola scriptura* of Protestantism which began the whole interpretive tradition culminating in the historical-critical interpretation of the 'text', but which also emphasized the Bible's interpretation *according to the Bible* (an angle analogous to that of modern fundamentalism), is now usurped for the Bible's interpretation according to the 'text' of the critical scholar.

But there are also certain ramifications [difficulties!] for biblical studies which come from having defined and carved out a disciplinary space according to the historical-critical paradigm. That is, certain systems of power ensue as a result of the codification of the discourse practices of the discipline according to a positivist historicist hermeneutics of biblical interpretation.

First to come to mind is the issue of 'canonicity'. This 'canonicity' includes, of course, the issue of source documents and their status within the discipline with respect to their importance to the pursuit of reconstructing the history of the Jesus movements and early missionary activity. 'Canonicity' also extends, therefore, to the question of the 'authenticity' and importance of those texts included in and excluded from the *biblical* canon (analogous to Luther's reconstitution of the canon, but determined not along theological lines or 'apostolic succession', but according to *scholarly* interests [once again the consolidation of power into the hands of the discipline]).[13] Further, 'canonicity' also includes the whole constellation of methodological tools and critical results sanctioned by the discipline through channels of academemed power and bureaucracy, for example, sanctioned by editorial boards of

the Authentic Words of Jesus (Sonoma, CA: Polebridge Press; New York, Macmillan, 1993), p. 35, describes this hierarchy unwittingly: 'Public attack on members of the Seminar is commonplace, coming especially from those who lack academic credentials.' Indeed, the rhetoric of the whole introduction is infused not only with the presumption of the certainty/correctness of positivism and objectivity, but also with arrogance exhibited at those non-academics who disagree with this Enlightenment hermeneutics [aka, fundamentalists]. Funk frequently draws upon the ethos of academentia in arguments against those outside acadamnia: Note the thorough listing of academic credentials of the members of the Seminar given in 'Roster of the Fellows of the Jesus Seminar', pp. 533-37, and the translation of the biblical texts given the title, 'The Scholars' Version'.

13. Cf. the recent call by the Jesus Seminar for a new canon.

journals and publishing houses, graduate faculty committees determining acceptability of thesis and dissertation proposals, peer review committees and tenure, issuance of grant money for research, etc. [nothing new in acadamnia, but certainly integral in maintaining standards of scholarship, with unavoidably *economic* consequences]. The particular *form* in which 'canonicity' is given expression in this discipline is the limitation of all things 'biblical studies' to the discourse practices of biblical interpretation according to the historical-critical paradigm that came to define the discipline. [And if not the reconstruction of early Christian history per se, nevertheless the paradigm of interpretation which places authoritative interpretation into the hands of the scholar: authorial (historically contextual) intention, original audience effect, even deconstructionist scholarly *elan...*]

Another [negative] consequence of this particular definition of biblical studies is the resultant tension between the [publicly, generally speaking] irrelevant academented pursuit of the Bible and dominant popular image of religion as fundamentalist, anti-educationalist fascism, a tension that puts biblical studies in the uneasy position of having no home at all. This is the perpetual tension of creedal affiliation and critical historiography. It is also a tension that arises only because the academented study of the Bible has been carried out as a positivist-historicist enterprise of interpretation, rather than, say, a field that also concerns itself with the 'meaning' and interpretation of the Bible and its impact upon western cultures (and beyond) throughout history ['biblical studies' as the study of the Bible's influence upon our world]. The result of this tension is the ever-shrinking domain of relevance of biblical studies: On the one hand, the historical-critical paradigm explicitly rejects denomination and creedal affiliation [or tries to], hence comes under suspicion and is always in jeopardy of losing economic support from denomination(s). Additionally, it requires a high degree of specialization and the socialization into a specific discourse, making it difficult for graduates of such programs to transfer [rhetorically] the results of critical scholarship to any other 'context' outside of academentia (e.g. particularly church/parish settings) [a difficulty reinforced by the fact that 'popular texts' are often derided by the discipline itself].

On the other hand, the diminishing role of the humanities in university education, not to mention the long-since general decline of prominence of 'theology' or 'divinity' at the university, makes biblical studies appear to be an 'elective' discipline. There are subtle, 'logically' contradictory, but 'rhetorically' effective factors at work here: dedicated *not* to the study of the role of religion in society, but to the pursuit of historical-critical reconstruction of a time 2000 years ago by focusing upon a specific area of the world and with appeal to a limited selection of texts, biblical studies, swimming in a sea of professional and scientific-business-technological departments, is seen as an oddity in an educational world [especially in America] dedicated to the pursuit of technological and economic advancement. This is exacerbated by the fact that the growing popular discourse concerning religion [again, esp. in America] has been dominated by conservative fundamentalism-turned-politics, thus contributing to the suspicion of the relevance of religion to the Enlightenment pursuit of knowledge free from reprisals from forces of dogmatism [even in spite of biblical studies' attempt to define itself precisely along these same Enlightenment principles].

Finally, the unbearable tension between positivist inquiry and theological relevance is often released in distortive critical results which hide doctrinal proclivities, yet at the same time try desperately to present the results of critical scholarship as relevant to the lives of believers. This tension has often surfaced in arguments concerning discussions of methodological presuppositions and conclusions, from the reactions against the Tübingen school's reconstruction of Christian origins in the Gentile- versus Jewish-Christian dialects, to the rejection of the *Religionsgeschichte* school's assertions regarding mystery cults, 'divine man' and Gnostic redeemer myths, to the explicit rejections of liberal Protestant theology by the thesis of a thoroughgoing Jewish eschatology of Jesus' teaching, and up through Mack's most recent rejection of the whole historical Jesus pursuit as founded upon a myth of unique origins. Creedal ideologies are perhaps unavoidable, directing analysis, if not in its explicit methodological application, nevertheless often in its justification regarding its concluding 'relevances' [for the life of the believer, for the community, etc.]. This distortive field arises from the conflict between theological conviction and rigorous critical-historicist inquiry, a conflict that is a consequence of a disciplinary definition limited to this historical task.

(New) Rhetorical Criticism(s) and the Historical-Critical Paradigm
Against this background we can begin to assess the impact the historical-critical paradigm has had upon the (new) rhetorical-critical

interpretation of the New Testament. That is, having seen the role that the historical-critical paradigm has played in defining the disciplinary boundaries and discursive practices of biblical studies, as well as exploring the 'reasons' for the dominance of this paradigm, it may now become easier to see why it is so 'instinctive' and 'natural' that the four scholars we have looked [and many more we only glanced] at simply adapt rhetoric to the historical-critical interpretation of the text.

My own interest, while elucidated by the development and genealogy of methods, lies in particular with the specifically *productive* aspects of disciplinary power which the (new) rhetorical criticism(s) engenders, but does so strictly within the confines of the historical-critical paradigm. That is, what is of interest to me is the specific, *new* characteristics of discursivity that the (new) rhetorical criticism(s) brings to the practice of biblical studies as a discipline of critical historiography.

For the (new) rhetorical criticism(s) has been adopted uncritically and unwittingly as a tool to be used within/under, and to further perpetrate/perpetuate, the hegemony of the historical-critical paradigm, thereby solidifying the hierarchy of scholar-exegete over lay-reader. The (new) rhetorical criticism(s) simply reinforces disciplinary boundaries by being used within/as an approach that continues to mystify the encounter of the 'text' as ancient, as 'other', hence in need of ['objective', disciplined] intercession by the scholar who thereby controls its interpretation. It does so, however, by means of its own specific discursive characteristics and disciplinary traditions/practices which make unique contributions to the strategies of defense and conservation of the hegemonic paradigm. How this is so needs to be explored carefully.

For example, the significant *inventional* and *prescriptive* concepts of 'rhetorical situation' and 'fittedness' are used in a deterministic fashion which hermeneutically locates the 'meaning' of a rhetorical a(rtifa)ct within the strict confines of its original performance. Under the hegemony of historical-critical exegesis, a rhetorical act becomes a 'fitting' response to a singular, particular situation and is therefore highly 'context'-ualized. Since this 'context' is assumedly defined as an ancient one, historical reconstruction becomes necessary to determine the rhetorical 'effect' and hence 'meaning' of the 'text'. Presuming the rhetorical act was 'fit', and presuming the rhetorical situation so constrained the rhetor in her/his response and is itself static/controllable/controlled, the exegete can work backward through the a(rtifa)ct to the situation. The resulting power dynamic is quite significant: the 'contextuality' of rhetoric's pragmatic and prescriptive tradition becomes the hermeneutic means whereby the significance of a rhetorical a(rtifa)ct, its 'intentionality' and 'meaning', is limited first and foremost [if not exclusively] to the original historical 'context'. A rhetorical approach to language and persuasive discourse has thereby become the means for constraining, controlling and limiting the biblical text's persuasive impact, for restricting its accessibility to an elite core of scholars who have discursively generated a disciplinary power-field in which they ensure themselves a position of authority over knowledge-control: interpretive dynamics and dissemination of rhetorical impact of the 'text' can only be met with through them [as historian-rhetoricians].

This runs counter to every explicit liberatory impulse and motivation expressed by these scholars, all of whom profess to embrace rhetoric as a means to engage in the struggle against the authoritative systems of dogmatic orthodoxy and biblical interpretive stricture: all of them celebrate rhetoric as a means of breaking open even further the question of canonical authority of the biblical text by demanding that it be approached not as eternal 'truth', but as religious *persuasion* informed by motivations influenced by, set within, and constitutive of struggles for community self-definition and questions of power [dogmatic and ecclesiastical]. Rhetoric is explicitly adopted as a means of bringing to light the multiplicity of perspectives, the plurality of voices giving shape to the tradition, even when those voices were [often violently (both physically and rhetorically)] censored and repressed, thereby lifting up as part of the tradition of biblical interpretation and community self-definition the *variety* of group, social and theological experimentations witnessed within the canon. Finally, all four find in rhetoric the means whereby they can trace to the very core of the biblical (New Testament) tradition their own liberal humanist agenda of liberation by finding evidence of movements and teachings that emphasized radical anti-authoritarian group structures and an ethics of egalitarian access to power (both spiritual and social) prior to orthodoxy's hierarchical consolidation.

Yet, in spite of these liberatory intentions [pretensions], by hermeneutically *arresting* the authoritative interpretive moment of the biblical text's rhetorical impact ('intentionality' and 'effect') at a specific [ancient] moment in time these scholars only fashion and consolidate for themselves a position of power within the confines of their discipline. Indeed, insofar as their interpretive methods require initiation into methodologies of both critical-historical research *and* rhetorical analysis, disciplinary *pouvoir/savoir* is further complicated and constituted. Since discipline restricts accessibility to the means of knowledge creation and dissemination, that is, to authoritative *loci* [both institutions and methodologies] of interpretation, power now firmly rests under the control of an elite core of liberal rhetorical historians. Thus, liberation is nothing other than an agenda of an elite and exclusivist class of interpreters effectively bent on consolidating and maintaining interpretive control of the biblical tradition by keeping the Bible's rhetorical 'meaning' and 'effect' inaccessible to all but a few who are methodologically equipped to reconstruct original (i.e. ancient) exigencies, 'intentions' and 'effects'. This is a 'palace rebellion', hardly meant at all to give populist movements for revolution or reform any authoritative position [ethos] in the pursuit of biblical interpretation.

This becomes clear when pondering the institutional 'effects' of subsuming rhetorical analysis under the disciplinary paradigm of historical exegesis, especially as these scholars have so fashioned their 'socio-rhetorical' methodological synthesis. Through their own interpretive models and practices, rhetoric becomes an important means by which the boundaries of biblical studies as a discipline are reinforced within the academy: rhetoric is used to perpetuate the historical-critical paradigm of reconstruction (of the original 'contexts' of production and performance) by overcoming important theoretical difficulties met with when literary-critical studies of the Bible began to feel the impact of a New Critical and reception-theoretical turn in the disciplinary discourse practices. By claiming, as Mack explicitly does, to 'bridge the gap' between historical-critical and literary-critical enterprises; by using it, as Robbins does, to build a comprehensive model for socio-historical research and literary-critical analysis; by building rhetoric, as Schüssler Fiorenza does, into a critical hermeneutics that maintains the ethical priority of historical-critical interpretation; by emphasizing the 'rhetorical setting' and 'exigency' in inventional theory, as Wire does: all these scholars refuse to let rhetoric out of the disciplinary cage; rhetoric is chained, through methodological strictures, to the machinery of historical reconstruction and its production. All the important self-reflection engendered by hermeneutics, literary theory and communication theory is dismissed as 'solved' by appeal to rhetoric's own theoretical traditions, effectively silencing the critique. Rhetoric, wielded in the hands of these scholars, helps maintain the hegemony of the historical-critical paradigm against both the questions brought to bear against its herme-neutic and theoretical presumptions and presuppositions and its neglect as the new literary methods began to attract attention.

To that end, rhetoric is also used to maintain disciplinary integrity by perpetuating a paradigm which makes biblical studies unique from other literary disciplines. As literary-critical methods began to encroach upon the disciplinary terrain, the definitional boundaries between liter-ary studies of texts-in-general and literary studies of the Bible began to fade. Scholars accustomed to understanding their role as experts in bib-lical history began to note the incursion of literary critics from other fields (e.g. Frank Kermode) effectively erase the investigative impetus that defined the field of biblical studies. If the Bible could be ap-proached as literature, even sacred literature, it becomes accessible to a myriad of methods, scholars and interpreters. But biblical studies is not the study of the Bible, per se; it is the study of biblical *history*. And rhetoric, as these scholars approach its application to the biblical text, simply serves the ends of writing biblical history.

Furthermore, rhetoric is also used to perpetuate the disciplinary boundaries of biblical studies by marking the Bible as *persuasive* dis-course, hence rescuing the historical 'meaning' of the text by offering it as a model (or anti-model) of rhetorical strategies to be employed (or critiqued and avoided) by the modern faithing community. In other words, rhetoric makes biblical studies *relevant* to ecclesiastical systems and structures, but nevertheless serves to identify the discipline as dis-tinct from theology: note how the emphasis on 'rhetorical practices', in spite of issues of utility for the modern community of faith, by being approached from the point of view of historical-critical reconstruction of 'meaning' and 'effect', also maintains disciplinary independence from ecclesiastical dogma and theology by grounding its results in terms of *persuasive discourse* and not theological tradition or cate-chetical instruction. Rhetoric is used to serve *disciplinary* ends (of *both* rhetoric and exegesis) and practices.

It is also interesting to note how rhetorical criticism serves as a point of prestige for biblical studies, insofar as 'rhetoric' is currently showing an incredible rise in prominence among the humanities [not in terms of departments (though also that), but in terms of its 'translativity' into several disciplines]. The 'rhetoric of inquiry' and 'critical rhetoric' movements of the past decade, not to mention the legitimacy of rhetoric to the area of philosophy [that might be saying a bit too much] resulting from the excursion of significant philosophers such as Perelman, Toulmin, Natanson, Johnson and Burke into the field of rhetoric: all give testimony to the impressive return of rhetoric to university education after 100 years of neglect and abuse. Biblical studies, by claiming to embrace rhetoric within its discipline, can participate in the 'rhetorical turn' of the humanities and sciences, thereby helping it to participate in a powerful new forefront of potential educational reform.

But this is an illusion, a hypocritical mask: while postmodern rhetorics are beginning to produce some of the most profound and (possibly) devastating de(con)structive critiques of disciplinary *pouvoir/savoir*, undermining the epistemological foundations of the liberal humanist educational system and its relationship to social, political and cultural centers of power, rhetoric within biblical studies simply serves to reinforce these very systems. Rhetoric, in the hands of the biblical historians, not only becomes a tool for the historical-critical enterprise [a result that is no surprise at all], but a very important theoretical means by which to *reconstitute* and *justify* the historical-critical disciplinary identity of biblical studies. This continued and persistent use of rhetoric towards such ends, I would suggest, constitutes one more example, this one resulting from its own distinctive disciplinary *pouvoir/savoir* of the conditions of biblical studies, of a 'rhetoric restrained', indeed *constrained*.

Tragically, one of the most obvious areas of de(con)structive critique available to these rhetorical critics of the Bible, an area that is one part of a constellation of systemic forces serving to maintain elite control over access to biblical interpretation, is never even pondered as a potential focus of rhetorical-critical assessment: the discipline of biblical interpretation itself. The reason for such an oversight [if 'oversight' could also imply the motivistic aspects of disciplinary survival that I am suggesting are at work] is quite obvious: biblical studies cannot be so critiqued, because to do so would mean that these critics would undermine their own basis of power. Such a critique would constitute a threat to their position, both economically [in immediate terms: the potential reconstitution of their departments in the wake of such a critique] and theoretically/hermeneutically [their loss of power otherwise secured by an interpretive paradigm which requires initiation into esoteric methods of historical-critical analysis]. Suffering from a liberal humanist belief, tenaciously ass-umed, in the function and role of the intellectual as intercessor between social forces/institutions of power and educational access to that power, these (new) rhetorical critics of the Bible secure their position as mediator by arguing for a rhetorical philosophy that arrests the critical moment at a point inaccessible to all but the modern historian.

In contrast, the question arises [and the attempts to answer this question are multitudinous and varied]: what would be the result if (new) rhetorical criticism(s) were given the chance to transform biblical studies according to a paradigm of power that focuses upon the ways in which the Bible is used (through argumentation, cultural values, specific discourse forms, by means of ideological infiltration of specific values and world-views) rhetorically? What if, instead of controlling interpretation by various theoretical means, rhetorical critics of the Bible simply took as their subject the stories, writings, moral rules, 'Law', faith(s), letters, interpretations, allusions, references to, depictions of, the values, judgments, presumptions, 'truths' and 'facts' in/of the Bible throughout history and culture, including both ancient, Medieval, modern, postmodern; including western and Eastern, northern and Southern, first world and First (third) World? I suggest such a shift would radically alter the disciplinary landscape, breaking open for immediate critical analysis the physical, ideological and theoretical manifestations of 'biblical' rhetoric and its relationship to systems of power/knowledge throughout histories and societies. And *this* would constitute a first, tentative and local step toward the necessary, radical transformation of academentia into something [perhaps] unavoidably related to, but also other than, its liberal humanist origins: a site where power, as both restrictive and creative, becomes an integral aspect of critical thought, analysis, discussion and action *for the sake of imagining new forms and strategies of power through an analytics that seeks out the fissures in the hegemonic systems of a society in order to break open new possibilities of freedom.*

In the next chapter, we shall ponder the implications, manifestations, ramifications and potential areas of exploration that just such a transformation might bring about with respect specifically to rhetorical theory, philosophy and critical praxis, especially of the Bible.

Chapter 5

MESSAGES IN A BOTTLE:
THE PROMISE(S) OF A RHETORIC OF POWER

Your reality, sir, is lies and balderdash, and I am delighted to say that I have no grasp of it whatsoever.

Baron Munchausen
Terry Gilliam

. . . But have I (that is, the ethos of the 'I') lost my 'serious' reader with this abrupt (and perhaps 'silly') turn-around statement? (I'm sure that I have lost my leftist 'colligs'!) Well, if I've lost him/her, then, so be it! (That's my purpose!) The concept of 'universal audience', or audiences themselves, is and are, as far as I'm concerned, highly overrated! They're best Lost! In respect to audiences, I would rather be 'celibate', but then again, from a distance, still engage audiences through 'a continuing, strange love letter'. We need to lose each other so that perhaps we might find each other, on different terms, again.

'Dear Jim, Susan, John, and "colligs" (drifting item. 1)'
Victor Vitanza

Scribbled Love Notes on Splintering Fragments of Thoughts

Drifting Fragment-Message 1
The issue at this point of this tome is not to present or defend a new totalizing model of rhetoric under which to subsume biblical studies, but just the opposite: to *fragment* and *disrupt* all previous and potential assumptions regarding what it would mean to develop and implement a 'rhetorical criticism' of the Bible. By which I mean: perhaps the very notion of what would constitute a 'rhetorical criticism' of the Bible needs to be reassessed.

What I am arguing is a delimitation of biblical interpretation by means of the translativity of rhetoric [i.e. the ability of rhetoric, as a study about discourse, to enter into discourse in order critically to disrupt the power paradigms at work in the discourse {'discourse' of course not limited to words or coherent processes at all, but to the incoherent actions, the 'slips', the forms and manifestations of social (economic, political, cultural, religious) ideologies as material (even if ephemeral) entities (including individuals)}] which could expand the notion of 'biblical studies' beyond a 'mere' interpretation of the 'text'.

That is, one important aspect of a rhetorical approach to biblical studies would be a concern with the rhetoric [said to be] *in* the text. Thus, a myriad of methods and their critical apparatuses could be employed to lift out certain dynamics of argumentation and persuasion at work in the multiple intentionalities reflected 'in' the 'text'. There is no getting around the 'fact' that the linguistic and communicative medium is such that it can be 'legitimately' [better: *has been* legitimated along certain lines] analyzed in terms of *deixis*, *modality* and other syntactic and semantic factors that are part of the linguistic code. It is also the case that argumentative strategies and the traditions of figures, tropes, colors could be 'identified' [excavated, 'invented'] and their play described [argued]. This could be done not only for the sake of understanding 'better' the rhetorical dynamics 'in' the 'text', but in a distinctly *vernacular* turn it could cause us to reconsider and reconstruct our own methodological principles and terms.

But immediately, a certain hesitation comes to mind. Why arrest the critical focus of rhetoric at the point of the *biblical* text? Why cannot a rhetorical approach to biblical studies also concern itself with the rhetoric 'in' other texts which themselves interpret the Bible, use the Bible argumentatively, appeal to the Bible in explicit or oblique forms (as traditions assumed to be biblical, e.g. theological and ethical texts). That is *precisely* the critical turn taken in this tome: A rhetorical approach to biblical studies can and *should* be expanded beyond the immediate purview of offering an interpretation of the Bible to include interpreting the *interpretations and interpreters of the Bible*. The eventual result would be a rhetorical approach that included as part of its analytical domain the cultural discourses in which the Bible constitutes an important aspect of argumentation.

This would further lead to a supplementary effort that ponders the implications of an approach to the rhetoric 'of' the Bible. By this is meant the study of the effects of the 'text' upon *broader* social and discourse 'contexts'. It would include analysis of the biblical traditions' power to support, even implicitly or deeply 'underground' [not a deep grammar, but the value-laden foundations upon which all argumentation takes place, the ideologies that are the 'implicit premises', but also perhaps the social traditions in which such argumentation functions], argumentation that depends upon the values, presumptions, judgments and 'truths' founded upon and with reference to biblical interpretive/theological (discourse) traditions. A rhetoric 'of' the text could include even specific forms of worship, for example, the 'rhetoric of sermons', the 'rhetoric of prayer', the 'rhetoric of mysticism', the 'rhetoric of systematic theology', etc. But it would note also both the persuasive power which the 'text' has had upon cultures throughout their histories, as well as the *powers* that presume an ideological foundation based upon the Bible. It could even be more subtle, such as, for example, traditions of thought processes [in the west] which presume all the trappings of monotheism (unified 'self', search for physical ['Big Bang'] and metaphysical 'origins' [phenomenology], etc.). And, again, such an exploration would not be directed solely at a critique of these discourses, but could return its critical gaze back upon rhetoric itself.

So conceived, 'biblical studies' would not be limited to the question of generating interpretations of the Bible; through a 'rhetoric revalued' it could be expanded to be the study of the Bible *in action*, throughout history and among cultures, and in its various guises. [Almost, but not quite it…]

Drifting Fragment-Message 2
The issue is not that we should embark upon the generation of a theory of *a*historical readings, as though such a thing were any longer deemed possible [reader response often seems to think so, however]. The issue is not that the rhetoric 'in' [even the rhetoric 'of'] the text is something that resides as a constant and immutable 'thing' or even 'dynamic' in the text which can be described apart from any historical context [this may be *precisely* the implication/problem of analyses of the rhetoric 'in' the text]. The point is to redefine the notion of history itself and the role it [the 'notion'] plays in the generation of rhetorical interpretations. That is, the authoritative 'meaning' of a 'text' is often generated in terms of the question of actual authorial 'intention'. This is one important tradition of justifying interpretations, that is, by appeal to what the author 'must have meant'. As such, history for interpreters of a text has been arrested at a single moment. We have frequently had cause to

explore the implicit and explicit ramifications of just such an approach, and we have time and again asked *why* arrest a text's meaning to such a moment.

The point is to break open the concept of history in such a way so as not to privilege a single moment in time. Or, better, to allow for interpretations that choose the moment in time in which to interpret and judge the text. If rhetoric is something that is an unavoidable exchange of energy among beings attempting to impact upon each other's behavior, and if this something occurs everyday, all the time, then a rhetorical approach of the Bible must be open to this exchange and *all* contexts and effects that take place *all* the time, *throughout* history. Authorial 'intentions' are met with in the context of language *exchange* which must also include the reader's/audience's/interpreter's 'intentions', hence rhetoric is enacted every time this exchange takes place. History becomes a concept no longer ephemeral or outside interpretation's domain, but is at work in *every* encounter between a 'text', its [new and changing] 'contexts', and its [mobile] 'audience'. It is no longer a distant moment in time that becomes the dominating court of appeal per se of our biblical-interpretive enterprise; instead, a rhetorical approach should be founded on a notion of both the *history* and *historicity* of the text and its various interpretations *through* time and in time. *This* is how the text's *materiality* can help us fracture and fragment disciplinary boundaries.

Indeed, therefore, rhetorical interpretations themselves would then be seen to take place *within* history, and not 'outside' or 'above' it. This is *rhetoric's* history and historicity, one which must be kept ever in view [particularly rhetoric's cultural and gender-role dimensions eclipsed in most studies concerning 'argumentation' and 'persuasion' which focus instead primarily upon the academented tradition]. Here we should also note rhetoric's mutability, that is, its changes and adaptations to new situations encountered throughout its history,[1] as well as its role in 'cultural contests and conflicts'[2] which gave/give further shape to its

1. Cf. Edwin Black, 'The Mutability of Rhetoric', in E. Black, *Rhetorical Questions: Studies of Public Discourse* (Chicago: University of Chicago Press, 1992), pp. 171-86.

2. Wilhelm Wuellner, 'Biblical Exegesis in the Light of the History and Historicity of Rhetoric and the Nature of the Rhetoric of Religion', in Stanley E. Porter and Thomas H. Olbricht (eds.), *Rhetoric and the New Testament: Essays from the 1992 Heidelberg Conference (Journal for the Study of the New Testament,*

traditions. Rhetoric and rhetorical-critical interpretations are developed within several different contexts which need to be addressed and understood: the context of the rhetorical 'canon' [both 'canon' of rhetorical literature, and 'canon' in which the interpreted work itself is set]; the social, cultural, ideological and institutional contexts in which both rhetoric and rhetorical-critical interpretation(s) are shaped; as well as the context of communicative technology by which the a(rtifa)ct is transmitted.[3] In *these* ways, rhetorical interpretations are unavoidably also historical readings. [Almost, but *still* not quite there...]

Drifting Fragment-Message 3
The consequences of a critical rhetorics might include a radical shift in power in the humanities and education, especially with respect to the kinds of *antihumanist* critiques of disciplinary systems of power which are currently being engaged. Here is, perhaps, the most important contribution of postmodern rhetorics: the chance to expose to view the underlying values, judgments, 'facts' and 'truths' of investigative disciplines and their discursive practices in an effort to tear down the boundaries, ponder the effects of power relations and systems of objectivity [subjugation] on the broader structures of social and political power.

One important aspect of this critique should include a radically new shift *away from* the humanist's interest in the individual consciousness, given specific form in rhetorical criticism when it focuses upon authorial intention (singular intentionality, but also even dual intentionalities: e.g. not just 'authors', but also audiences and/or various reader constructs). One interesting aspect of traditional rhetorical criticism is the insidious cult of personality reflected in analyses of rhetorical texts: the drive towards understanding, or simply appealing to, the coherent subject-consciousness which is the foundation of every rhetorical interpretation and pedagogy since at least Quintilian's *vir bonum*. Rather than focusing upon the individual's, and/or individual scholar's impact upon

Supplement Series, 90; Sheffield: Sheffield Academic Press, 1993), pp. 492-513 (498-501, 503-505).
      3.   These are the four aspects of 'materiality' which Wuellner identifies in 'Biblical Exegesis in the Light of the History and Historicity of Rhetoric', pp. 505-506. Cf. J. Hillis Miller, 'The Triumph of Theory, the Resistance to Reading, and the Question of the Material Base', *Publications of the Modern Language Association* 101.3 (1987), pp. 281-91.

history, rhetoric could be used anti-humanistically to break down and subvert the humanist belief in 'education' as means for 'cultural socialization' and its ties to western culture's economic and politically elite power base. A reconstitution of rhetoric away from humanist discourse traditions toward anti-humanist critique would understand 'persuasion' in terms of sanctioned acts of power/violence, 'canon' as approved discourse forms; and 'author' as controlling metaphor of interpretative limits. [This is getting closer, more interesting...]

Floating Flotsam and Jetsam

Ramus's education reform could be seen as related to the commodification, industrialization and standardization of merchandise due, in part, to the advent of typography and *its* commodification, industrialization and standardization of language/manuscript production. His educational reform reflected this when the merchant class embraced his efforts towards *quantification* of education.

It is also precisely with Ramus that a number of authors (e.g. Wuellner, Conley) have assigned the beginning of the end of rhetoric's power and influence in the education of the northern European cultures (where his reform was most directly felt). Interestingly, but not surprisingly, they attribute this 'death of rhetoric' to his division of rhetoric and dialectics, thus perpetuating disciplinary fixation upon issues of theory. What if the decline of rhetoric was not so much due to Ramus's impact upon rhetorical theory and praxis, but was simply 'inevitable'? What if rhetoric lost its impact because typography's world of uniformity, linearity and quantity was inimical to rhetoric's world of plurality, orality, tactility? What if rhetoric's steady decline could be shown to coincide with *print* culture's steady rise to power in the cultural psyche?

Now note: With the rise of telecommunication technology and the electronic age's tactility (esp. the reassertion of orality and nonlinearity) comes the resurrection of rhetoric. It coincides almost directly with the exponential growth in the variety and distribution of audio/visual communication technology and its embracing of tactility over and beyond print. Could the return to 'secondary orality', driven by technological changes in communication, be the *cause* of rhetoric's re-emergence?[4]

4. Cf. Marshall McLuhan, *The Guttenberg Galaxy: The Makings of Typographical Man* (Toronto: University of Toronto Press, 1962), pp. 192-202.

If so, then the future of rhetoric lies not in a return to early manuscript and late oral cultural traditions of rhetoric, but in embracing, learning, creating new analytical means by which persuasion is generated within this new world.[5] Here, too, is the historicity and materiality of rhetoric, which has implications not only for rhetoric, but biblical interpretation as well. [Yes, but...]

Drifting Fragment-Message 4
Given these discussions concerning the philosophical basis of the application of a 'rhetoric of power', its application is 'naturally' eclectic. The claim for eclecticism sends shivers down the spines of those who assume analytics' priority of rigorous, monologic inquiry. Yet, as a critical rhetoric engaged in the rhetoric of inquiry, a 'rhetoric of power' must be allowed to adapt to the discourse practices of the discipline it is critiquing, and thereby must be allowed the freedom to adopt, at will, a variety of approaches according to the circumstances of the critique [and the ability, skill, energy and time/space confines of the critic]. Eclecticism is necessary for survival, since the world is never reducible to systems, but thrives in chaos. Unless we are willing to adopt chaos as our partner/posture, rhetoric [if defined as its own, distinctive and mechanistic critical discipline] will be reduced once again to the study of tropes and figures, a trend already germinating in the reduction of rhetoric to questions of argumentation and persuasion as inherently *linguistic* and *rational* [conscious, intended] phenomena.

The cerebration of eclecticism is the demand that we take our rhetoric seriously, that we see argumentation and persuasion as operating in extra-[pre-? un-]linguistic forms, in irrational and nonrational ways. One needs to keep in mind the distortion of the modernist assumption,[6] that is, the belief that recourse to language 'alone' is recourse to power. This is precisely NOT the point, but rather, power is *also* reinforced through language [as also language is reinforced through power]. Awareness of

5.   Cf. Robert Fowler's discussion on the implications of 'secondary orality' and 'hypertextuality' upon biblical studies in 'How the Secondary Orality of the Electronic Age Can Awaken Us to the Primary Orality of Antiquity—or—What Hypertext Can Teach Us about the Bible', presented at the Annual Meeting of the Eastern Great Lakes Biblical Society, April 1994.

6.   As it is described by John Fekete, *The Critical Twilight: Explorations in the Ideology of Anglo-American Literary Theory from Eliot to McLuhan* (London: Routledge & Kegan Paul, 1977), esp. pp. v-xxv, 3-36.

materiality and historicity must also mean awareness of the limitations of language, interpretative praxis, even rhetoric.[7] This is why it was important that I have immersed my discourse analysis in this tome within specific institutional context(s) in history, to try to immerse my work within a material dimension. It is also clear that what I have done here is not enough, but merely acts as a signal for future critical activity that addresses a wider variety of systems of power more thoroughly. [Can concepts of 'materiality' and 'power' find a relationship through a reconstitution of an analytics of a rhetoric of power which is *more* than discursive in its focus? There must be another configuration...]

Love Notes from a Dead Friend

> The role of an intellectual is not to tell others what they have to do. By what right would [she/]he do so?...The work of an intellectual is not to shape others' political will; it is, through the analyses that [she/]he carries out in [her/]his own field, to question over and over again what is postulated as self-evident, to disturb people's mental habits, the way they do and think things, to dissipate what is familiar and accepted, to re-examine rules and institutions and on the basis of this re-problemat-ization (in which [she/]he carries out his specific task as an intellectual) to participate in the formation of a political will (in which [she/]he has [her/]his role to play as a citizen).[8]

> ...we would do well to ask ourselves 'what is the nature of our present?' ...I would like to say something about the function of any diagnosis concerning the nature of the present. It does not consist in simple charac-terization of what we are but, instead—by following lines of fragility in the present—in managing to grasp why and how that-which-is might no longer be that-which-is. In this sense, any description must always be made in accordance with these kinds of virtual fractures which open up the space of freedom understood as a space of concrete freedom, i.e., of possible transformation... It is fruitful in a certain way to describe that-which-is by making it appear as something that might not be, or that might not be as it is. Which is why this designation or description of the real never has a prescriptive value of the kind, 'because this is, that will

7.   James W. Hikins and Kenneth S. Zagacki, 'Rhetoric, Objectivism, and the Doctrine of Tolerance', in Ian Angus and Lenore Langsdorf (eds.), *The Critical Turn: Rhetoric and Philosophy in Postmodern Discourse* (Carbondale, IL: South-ern Illinois University, 1993), pp. 100-25.

8.   Michel Foucault, 'The Concern for Truth', in Lawrence D. Kritzman (ed.), *Politics, Philosophy and Culture* (London: Routledge, 1988), pp. 255-67 (265).

be'. It is also why, in my opinion, recourse to history…is meaningful to the extent that history serves to show how that-which-is has not always been; i.e., that the things which seem most evident to us are always formed in the confluence of encounters and chances, during the course of a precarious and fragile history.[9]

Drifting Fragment-Message 5

Rhetoric itself must be understood in relation to systems of power. From the perspective of a rhetoric of power, the purpose of rhetorical analysis becomes the exposure of this foundation at work in any 'discourse' for scrutiny, the systems of power it reflects and supports, and its limitations and inconsistencies. But rhetoric must in turn be viewed within its own systems of power. This is the necessary self-reflective [*museful*] turn that must take place, indeed must be part of *any* and *every* rhetorical reconfiguration of the discipline. The purpose of such a turn is not ideological confession, but the perpetuation of a process whereby rhetoric avoids the temptation of becoming another Grand Narrative, another Totalizing Discipline, lost in its own hypnotic gaze in the mirror. The self-reflective turn becomes the means by which rhetoric becomes its own Johnstonian 'wedge',[10] the means by which to crack the unicity of disciplinary 'normalcy' and coherence by exposing the unattended, the denied and repressed. Rhetoric must search for its own points of vulnerability, take aim and strike.

This is a uniquely Third Sophistic return to a reconfigured sense of the *dissoi logoi* (the ability to argue both sides of a point cogently), one that understands as inherent within every discourse lies its own repressed contradiction. A rhetoric of power must recognize its own moment of seduction by its own beautiful façade as the moment of abuse, now sublimated and repressed. It must not be mesmerized into a complacent belief in its own coherence.

> Instead of a communication (familial) triangle, which is a graphic/fascist *account* of how communication might/does take place across institutional/hegemonic codes, 'we' are more interested in Lacan's 'graph of desire' (Imaginary, Symbolic, the Real) which is a graphic representation of the constant misrepresentation of communication, of its impossibility in spite of institutional/hegemonic codes. Therein lies the stuff of

9.   Michel Foucault, 'Critical Theory/Intellectual History', in Kritzman (ed.), *Politics, Philosophy and Culture*, pp. 17-46 (36-37).

10.   Henry W. Johnstone, Jr, 'Reply', *Philosophy & Rhetoric* 20.2 (1987), pp. 129-38.

resistance and disruption! Lacan writes: 'The real [an 'Excluded' Third] is impossible'. This friction between the unsynthesized sections is 'our' celebration of noise. But besides Lacan's rethinking of the triangle, we are also interested in Serres's notion of entropic- or mis-communication in his ('our') triangle of *host, parasite*, and *interruption* (or 'Excluded Third'). What we really want to write about is to write about, as we always write about, two things—un/namely, *speaking at crossed purposes and interrupting*. (We love the word 'and'.)[11]

[Actually, we love the phrase '**yes, but**...']

Rhetoric cannot avoid its own disciplinary systems of power and stricture/structure. Power, like rhetoric, is unavoidable. A rhetorical approach which decenters disciplinary power [i.e. its translativity allows for rhetoric to intervene within disciplines in order to expose their argumentative assumptions, limitations and distortions, and thus...] puts rhetoricians themselves in a position of power. This is where the critical self-reflective gaze becomes instrumental in limiting abuses of such power, even if such abuses are unavoidable. This limitation is served by a reflective praxis 'that outlines for the subject the conditions of domination' in order to illuminate 'the possibilities of a new existence' *without* preconceived notions of what those possibilities might be, what the eventual *teloi* might look like. The Grand Inquisitor already knows what answers he will find, and the Authorizing Narrative Design controls both the questions and the answers. In contrast, a critical rhetorician must commit to the pursuit of *tolerance* and the pluralizing of discourse(s), that is, to the Sophistic pursuit of practice not for perfection's sake, but for future practices' sake; for the rough-and-tumble of engagement with the purpose not to secure 'truth' and 'right', but to contribute further to the development of understanding, exchange, learning and living.

Ultimately, rhetorical criticism cannot and should not help exegesis secure an authoritative meaning of the biblical text. Rhetoric, especially conceived as a rhetoric of power, is interested in the argumentative and persuasive effects of *all* approaches that seek to convince or persuade an audience to action, in analyzing the means whereby one interpretation seeks, and perhaps for a time achieves hegemony over others. As such, it does not engage the question of 'meaning' at all; it wants to ask what the *consequences* are of choosing one means by which to secure

11. Victor Vitanza, 'Selections from "Neo-Triplicity": A Post(modern)-script, or Excursus, or Re/Inter/View, May 1990', *Pre/Text* 11.3–4 (1990), pp. 269-70.

adherence to one interpretive 'meaning' as opposed to another, as well as to ask what the consequences *were* which contributed to its formulation and presentation.

A rhetorical approach to biblical studies, then, opens up for consideration [for the first time] the arenas of turmoil and struggle in which our interpretations contest with one another to be heard and adopted. And it does so while taking note not only of the myriad systems of power within the context of 'our' own struggle as biblical interpreters and rhetorical critics, but also considers the whole material history of which this struggle is but a minimal part. A rhetorical approach to biblical studies fragments and shatters previous disciplinary boundary-definitions/limitations by reconstituting the study of the Bible in the 'extended' terms of the Bible's continuing (ab)use(-ive impact) and argumentative engagement throughout time and space. It no longer limits its task to the production of 'authoritative' interpretive practices based on reconstructions of ancient history. Instead it turns its critical gaze to other ongoing interpretive engagements with the biblical text which have taken place throughout history and in history in order to assess their impact and strength. [Here we are getting *very* close...]

A Glass Shiv on the Beach
While the exploration of institutional disciplinary forces at work in (new) rhetorical criticism(s) of the Bible has been helpful in locating certain systems and constellations of power at work in constraining the interpretive field and praxis of rhetoric in/of the Bible, it is merely a preliminary step. Indeed, its analysis is not only incomplete, but perhaps even focused on what I would only suggest is an almost irrelevant issue: it is an exploration into the strategies of power employed to maintain a disciplinary interpretive paradigm. The impact of this hegemony, however, is limited strictly to those seeking to operate within this particular disciplinary system. While the 'effect' of this tome might be to attempt to formulate a critique leading to the reconstitution and reconfiguration of certain discursive practices, it is hardly the case that the current critique, as formulated, will have reverberations beyond the immediate group of scholars in this discipline. This is due primarily to its locality and intention: an argument for the adoption of a particular kind of theoretical and philosophical perspective informing the discipline's domain.

The next necessary step to take, the future direction of a rhetoric of power, must be to transform its strategy into an analytic of power which takes as its initial site the body of the individual and the constellation of the microforces of power which act upon it and constitute it as an 'object' of power. It would thus become an analytics that would consider not just discursive manifestation of power, but also non-discursive. What I wish to focus upon is the specific religious 'rhetorical-power' dimensions which may [or may not] be at work in the capillary level of network relations of power surrounding the individual: at work either in terms of having provided (historically) the analog or inspiration for certain practices (since transformed by their interaction with other systemic forces [e.g. monotheism; sacramental traditions; kinship systems; legal traditions; sacrificial systems]); or of explicit argumentative (both discursive and non-discursive [i.e., e.g., iconographic, architectural, symbolic]) strategies and their associated forms of power upon the social site of the body; or of ideological reverberations (values, presumptions, 'truths' and 'facts') at work on the cultural level (popular, intellectual, political and economic) in sustaining particular practices, both on the micro- and macro-levels of power, etc.

A rhetoric of power approach to biblical studies allows us to critique other interpreters and other interpretations in order that we might become active participants in and critics of the struggles in/of discipline and power. It is a commitment to avoid the practice of silencing the critics/critiques [in the search for 'the' 'right' interpretation] and to keep the conversation going, to fracture and fragment the relations of power at work in securing a unifying interpretation, to expose them to further critique, to test their assumptions, to keep us constantly questioning the nature and extent of the forces of power at work around us, to provide a space in the cracks of the wall of silence in order to allow further and multiple voices and interpretive and active possibilities to explore, express and enact new possibilities of freedom...

YES, BUT...

ASSORTED BIBLIOGRAPHIES

Main Sources

Andrews, James R., *The Practice of Rhetorical Criticism* (New York: Longmans, 2nd edn, 1990).

Angus, Ian, and Lenore Langsdorf (eds.), *The Critical Turn: Rhetoric and Philosophy in Postmodern Discourse* (Carbondale, IL: Southern Illinois University Press, 1993).

Arnett, Ronald C., 'Religious Rhetoric', *Journal of Communication and Religion* 12 (1989), pp. 1-28.

Arnett, Ronald C. (ed.), 'Interpretation of Various Religious Rhetorics', *Journal of Communication and Religion* 12 (1989), pp. 1-42.

Atkins, J.W.H., *Literary Criticism in Antiquity* (2 vols.; Glouchester, MA: Peter Smith, 2nd edn, 1961).

Bakhtin, Mikhail M., *The Dialogic Imagination: Four Essays* (ed. Michael Holquist; trans. Caryl Emerson and Michael Holquist; Austin, TX: University of Texas Press, 1981).

—*Speech Genres and Other Late Essays* (ed. V.M. McGee; trans. C. Emerson and M. Holquist; Austin, TX: University of Texas Press, 1986).

Baldwin, C.S., *Ancient Rhetoric and Poetic* (Glouchester, MA: Peter Smith, 1959).

Barilli, Renato, *Rhetoric* (trans. Guiliana Menozzi; Minneapolis: University of Minnesota Press, 1989).

Barrett, Harold, *The Sophists: Rhetoric, Democracy, and Plato's Idea of Sophistry* (Novato, CA: Chandler & Sharp, 1987).

Bator, Paul, 'The "Good Reasons Movement": A "Confounding" of Dialetic and Rhetoric?', *Philosophy & Rhetoric* 21.1 (1988), pp. 38-47.

Bauer, Dale M., and Susan Jarrett McKinstry (eds.), *Feminism, Bakhtin, and the Dialogic* (Albany, NY: State University of New York Press, 1991).

Beale, Walter H., *A Pragmatic Theory of Rhetoric* (Carbondale, IL: Southern Illinois University Press, 1987).

—'Rhetorical Performative Discourse: A New Theory of Epideictic', *Philosophy & Rhetoric* 11.4 (1978), pp. 221-45.

Benko, S., and J.J. O'Rouke, *The Catacombs and the Coliseum* (Valley Forge, PA: Judson, 1971).

Berthoff, Ann E., *Richards on Rhetoric: I.A. Richards Select Essays (1929–1974)* (New York: Oxford University Press, 1990).

Bessinger, Jess B., 'Oral to Written: Some Implications of the Anglo-Saxon Transition', *Explorations* 8 (1957), pp. 11-15.

Betz, Hans Dieter, *Galatians: A Commentary on Paul's Letter to the Churches in Galatia* (Philadelphia: Fortress Press, 1979).

—'The Literary Composition and Function of Paul's Letter to the Galatians', *New Testament Studies* 21 (1975), pp. 353-79.

Bitzer, Lloyd F., 'Functional Communication: A Situational Perspective', in E.E. White (ed.), *Rhetoric in Transition: Studies in the Nature and Uses of Rhetoric* (University Park, PA: Pennsylvania State University Press, 1980), pp. 21-38.

—'The Rhetorical Situation', *Philosophy & Rhetoric* 1.1 (1968), pp. 1-14.

Bitzer, Lloyd, and Edwin Black (eds.), *The Prospect of Rhetoric* (Englewood Cliffs, NJ: Prentice–Hall, 1971).

Black, C. Clifton, 'Rhetorical Criticism and Biblical Interpretation', *Expository Times* 100 (1989), pp. 252-58.

—'Rhetorical Criticism and the New Testament', *Proceedings* 8 (1988), pp. 77-92.

—Rhetorical Questions: The New Testament, Classical Rhetoric, and Current Interpretation', *Dialog* 29.1 (1990), pp. 62-70.

Black, Edwin, *Rhetorical Criticism: A Study in Method* (Madison, WI: University of Wisconsin Press, 2nd edn, 1978).

—*Rhetorical Questions: Studies of Public Discourse* (Chicago: University of Chicago Press, 1992).

Bolter, Jay David, *Writing Space: The Computer, Hypertext and the History of Writing* (Hillsdale, NJ: Lawrence Erlbaum, 1991).

Bonner, Stanley F., *Dionysius of Halicarnassus* (Cambridge: Cambridge University Press, 1939).

—*Education in Ancient Rome: From the Elder Cato to the Younger Pliny* (Berkeley: University of California Press, 1977).

—*Roman Declamation in the Late Republic and Early Empire* (Berkeley: University of California Press, 2nd edn, 1977).

Booth, A.D., 'Elementary and Secondary Education in the Roman Empire', *Florigelium* 1 (1979), pp. 1-14.

Booth, Wayne, *A Rhetoric of Irony* (Chicago: University of Chicago Press, 1974).

—*The Rhetoric of Fiction* (Chicago: University of Chicago Press, 2nd edn, 1983).

Bormann, Ernest, *Communication Theory* (New York: Holt, Rinehart & Winston, 1980).

—*The Force of Fantasy: Restoring the American Dream* (Carbondale, IL: Southern Illinois University Press, 1985).

—'Rhetorical Criticism and Significant Form: A Humanistic Approach', in K. Campbell and K. Jamieson (eds.), *Forms and Genre: Shaping Rhetorical Action* (Falls Church, VA: The Speech Communication Association, n.d.).

Botha, Jan, 'On the "Reinvention" of Rhetoric', *Scriptura* 31 (1989), pp. 14-31.

Bourdieu, Pierre, *Language and Symbolic Power* (ed. John B. Thompson; trans. Gino Raymond; Cambridge, MA: Harvard University Press, 1991).

Bové, Paul, *In the Wake of Theory* (Middletown, CN: University Press of New England, 1992).

—*Intellectuals in Power: A Genealogy of Critical Humanism* (New York: Columbia University Press, 1986).

—*Mastering Discourse: The Politics of Intellectual Culture* (Durham: Duke University Press, 1992).

Braet, Antoine, 'The Classical Doctrine of Status and the Rhetorical Theory of Argumentation', *Philosophy & Rhetoric* 20.2 (1987), pp. 79-93.

Brandt, William, *The Rhetoric of Argumentation* (Indianapolis: Bobbs–Merrill, 1970).

Brinton, Alan, 'Situation in the Theory of Rhetoric', *Philosophy & Rhetoric* 14.4 (1981), pp. 234-48.

Brock, B.L., R.L. Scott and J.W. Chesebro (eds.), *Methods of Rhetorical Criticism: A Twentieth Century Perspective* (Detroit: Wayne State University Press, 2nd rev. edn, 1980).

Brockriede, Wayne, 'Constructs, Experience, and Argument', *The Quarterly Journal of Speech* 71.2 (1985), pp. 151-63.

—'Rhetorical Criticism as Argument', *The Quarterly Journal of Speech* 60.2 (1974), pp. 165-74.

Brown, Jerry W., *The Rise of Biblical Criticism in America, 1800–1870: The New England Scholars* (Middletown, CT: Wesleyan University Press, 1969).

Brown, William R., 'The Holographic View of Argument', *Argumentation* 1 (1987), pp. 89-102.

Burke, Kenneth, *A Grammar of Motives* (Berkeley: University of California Press, 2nd edn, 1962).

—*A Rhetoric of Motives* (Berkeley: University of California Press, 1950).

—*Counter-Statement* (Berkeley: University of California Press, 1968).

—'Methodological Repression and/or Strategies of Containment', *Critical Inquiry* 5.2 (1978), pp. 401-16.

—'Motion, Action, and the Human Condition', in W.E. Tanner and J. Dean Bishop (eds.), *Rhetoric and Change* (Mesquite, TX: Ide House, 1982), pp. 78-94.

—*The Rhetoric of Religion: Studies in Logology* (Berkeley: University of California Press, 1961).

Cameron, Nigel M. de S., *Biblical Higher Criticism and the Defense of Infallibilism in 19th Century Britain* (Lewiston, NY: Edwin Mellen Press, 1987).

Clark, Donald Lemen, *Rhetoric in Greco-Roman Education* (Morningside Heights, NY: Columbia University Press, 1957).

Clarke, M.L., *Higher Education in the Ancient World* (London: Routledge & Kegan Paul, 1971).

—*Rhetoric at Rome: Historical Survey* (London: Cohen & West, 1953).

Conley, Thomas, *Rhetoric in the European Tradition* (White Plains, NY: Longman, 1990).

Connors, Robert J., Lisa S. Ede and Andrea A. Lunsford (eds.), *Essays on Classical Rhetoric and Modern Discourse* (Carbondale, IL: Southern Illinois University Press, 1984).

Consigny, Scott, 'Rhetoric and its Situations', *Philosophy & Rhetoric* 7.3 (1974), pp. 175-86.

Cooper, Charles, and Lee Odell (eds.), *Research on Composing* (Urbana, IL: National Council of Teachers of English, 1978).

Corbett, Edward P.J., *Classical Rhetoric for the Modern Student* (New York: Oxford University Press, 1965).

Costello, Edward, 'Modality and Textual Structuration', *PTL: A Journal for Descriptive Poetics and Theory of Literature* 4, pp. 299-314.

Courtes, Joseph, 'Rhetorique et semiotique: De quelques divergences et convergences', *Review of Science and Religion* 52 (1978), pp. 227-43.

Cox, J. Robert, and Charles A. Willard, *Advances in Argumentation Theory and Research* (Carbondale, IL: Southern Illinois University Press, 1982).

Cox, J. Robert, Malcom O. Sillars and Gregg B. Walker (eds.), *Argument and Social Practice: Proceedings of the Fourth SCA/AFA Conference on Argumentation* (Annandale, VA: Speech Communication Association, 1985).

Crusius, Timothy, 'A Case for Kenneth Burke's Dialectic and Rhetoric', *Philosophy & Rhetoric* 19.1 (1986), pp. 23-37.

Cunningham, David S., *Faithful Persuasion: In Aid of a Rhetoric of Christian Theology* (Notre Dame, IN: University of Notre Dame Press, 1991).

Cushman, D.P., and P.K. Tompkins, 'A Theory of Rhetoric for Contemporary Society', *Philosophy & Rhetoric* 13.1 (1980), pp. 43-67.

Czitrom, Daniel J., *Media and the American Mind: From Morse to McLuhan* (Chapel Hill: University of North Carolina Press, 1982).

Dearin, Roy, 'The Philosophical Basis of Chaim Perelman's Theory of Rhetoric', *Quarterly Journal of Speech* 55.3 (1969), pp. 213-24.

Dillon, George, *Rhetoric as Social Imagination: Exploration in the Interpersonal Function of Language* (Bloomington: Indiana University Press, 1986).

Dingwall, Robert, and Philip Lewis (eds.), *The Sociology of the Professions: Lawyers, Doctors, and Others* (New York, St Martin's Press, 1983).

Dreyfus, Hubert, and Paul Rabinow, *Michel Foucault: Beyond Structuralism and Hermeneutics* (Chicago: University of Chicago Press, 2nd edn, 1983).

Eagleton, Terry, *Criticism and Ideology* (London: Verso, 1978).

—*Literary Theory: An Introduction* (Minneapolis: University of Minnesota Press, 1983).

—*The Function of Criticism: From the Spectator to Post-Structuralism* (London: Verso, 1984).

—*The Ideology of the Aesthetic* (Cambridge, MA: Basil Blackwell, 1990).

—*The Significance of Theory* (Oxford: Basil Blackwell, 1990).

Eden, K., 'Hermeneutics and the Ancient Rhetorical Tradition', *Rhetorica* 5.1 (1987), pp. 59-86.

Ehninger, Douglas, *Influence, Belief, and Argument: An Introduction to Responsible Persuasion* (Glenview, IL: Scott, Foresman, 1974).

Eisenhut, W., *Einführung in die antike Rhetorik und ihre Geschichte* (Darmstadt: Wissenschaftliche Buchgesellschaft, 4th edn, 1990).

Eliot, T.S., *The Use of Poetry and the Use of Criticism* (repr.; Cambridge, MA: Harvard University Press, 1986).

Elsom, Helen, 'The New Testament and Greco-Roman Writing', in R. Alter and F. Kermode (eds.), *The Literary Guide to the Bible* (Cambridge, MA: Harvard University Press, 1987).

Enos, R.L., 'The Persuasive and Social Force of Logography in Ancient Greece', *Central States Speech Journal* 25.1 (1974), pp. 4-10.

—'When Rhetoric Was Outlawed in Rome: A Translation and Commentary of Suetonius' Treatise on Early Roman Rhetoricians', *Speech Monographs* 39 (1972), pp. 34-42.

Enzensberger, Hans M., *The Consciousness Industry: On Literature, Politics, and the Media* (New York: Seabury, 1974).

Eubanks, Ralph, 'An Axiological Analysis of Chaim Perelman's Theory of Practical Reasoning', in James Golden and Joseph Pilotta (eds.), *Practical Reasoning in Human Affairs: Studies in Honor of Chaim Perelman* (Dordrecht: D. Reidel Publishing Company, 1986), pp. 69-83.

Evans, G.R., *Old Arts and New Theology: The Beginnings of Theology as an Academic Discipline* (Oxford: Clarendon Press, 1980).

Eyre, J.J., 'Roman Education in the Late Republic and Early Empire', *Greece and Rome* NS 10 (1963), pp. 47-59.

Fahstock, Jeanne, and Marie Secor, *Readings in Argument* (New York: Random House, 1985).

Fekete, John, *The Critical Twilight: Explorations in the Ideology of Anglo-American Literary Theory from Eliot to McLuhan* (London: Routledge & Kegan Paul, 1977).

Felperin, Howard, *Beyond Deconstruction: The Uses and Abuses of Theory* (Oxford: Clarendon Press, 1985).

Fore, William F., *Mythmakers: Gospel, Culture, and the Media* (New York: Friendship Press, 1990).

Foss, Sonja K., Karen A. Foss and Robert Trapp (eds.), *Contemporary Perspectives on Rhetoric* (Prospect Heights, IL: Waveland, 2nd edn, 1991).

Foss, Sonja K. (ed.), *Rhetorical Criticism: Exploration and Practice* (Prospect Heights, IL: Waveland Press, 1989).

Foucault, Michel, *Archaeology of Knowledge and the Discourse on Language* (trans. A.M. Sheridan Smith; New York: Pantheon, 1972).

—'The Concern for Truth', in Lawrence D. Kritzman (ed.), *Politics, Philosophy and Culture* (London: Routledge, 1998), pp. 255-67.

—'Critical Theory/Intellectual History', in Kritzman (ed.), *Politics, Philosophy and Culture*, pp. 17-46.

Fowler, Robert M., 'How the Secondary Orality of the Electronic Age Can Awaken Us to the Primary Orality of Antiquity—or—What Hypertext Can Teach Us about the Bible', presented at the Annual Meeting of the Eastern Great Lakes Biblical Society, 1994.

—*Linguistic Criticism* (Oxford: Oxford University Press, 1986).

Freyne, Sean, *Galilee: From Alexander the Great to Hadrian* (Wilmington, DE: Michael Glazier; Notre Dame, IN: University of Notre Dame Press, 1980).

Führmann, M. (ed.), *Die antike Rhetorik* (Artemis Einführungen, 10; Munich: Artemis, 3rd edn, 1990).

Gadamer, Hans G., 'Rhetorik, Hermeneutik und Ideologiekritik: Metakritische Erörterungen zu Wahrheit und Methode', in K. Apel *et al.* (eds.), *Hermeneutik und Ideologiekritik* (Frankfurt-on-Main: Suhrkamp, 1971).

Gaustad, Edwin S., *A Religious History of America* (San Francisco: Harper & Row, 1990).

Genette, Gérard, 'La rhétorique restreinte', *Figures*, III (Paris: Editions du Seuil, 1983).

Gilliam, Terry, *The Adventures of Baron Munchausen* (RCA/Columbia Pictures, 1989).

Golden, J.L., Goodwin F. Berquist and William E. Coleman (eds.), *Essays on the Rhetoric of the Western World* (Dubuque, IA: Kendall/Hunt, 1990).

Golden, J.L., and J.J. Pilotta (eds.), *Practical Reasoning in Human Affairs: Studies in Honor of Chaim Perelman* (Dordrecht: D. Reidel Publishing Company, 1986).

Govier, Trudy, *Problems in Argument Analysis and Evaluation* (Dordrecht: Foris Publications, 1987).

Grant, M., *Ancient Rhetorical Theories of the Laughable* (University of Wisconsin Studies in Language and Literature, 21; Madison: University of Wisconsin Press, 1924).

Grassi, Ernesto, *Rhetoric as Philosophy: The Humanist Tradition* (University Park, PA: Pennsylvania State University Press, 1980).

—'Why Rhetoric Is Philosophy', *Philosophy & Rhetoric* 20.2 (1987), pp. 68-78.

Gronbeck, Bruce E., Thomas J. Farrell and Paul A. Soukup (eds.), *Media, Consciousness, and Culture: Explorations of Walter Ong's Thought* (Newbury Park: Sage, 1991).

Gross, Alan, *The Rhetoric of Science* (Cambridge, MA: Harvard University Press, 1990).

Group μ, *A General Rhetoric* (trans. Paul B. Burrell and Edgar M. Slotkin; Baltimore: The Johns Hopkins University Press, 1981).

Gumbrecht, Hans Ulrich, and K. Ludwig Pfeiffer (eds.), *Materialität der Kommunikation* (Frankfurt: Suhrkamp, 1988).

Guthrie, W.K.C., *The Sophists* (Cambridge: Cambridge University Press, 1971).

Gwynn, Aubrey, *Roman Education from Cicero to Quintilian* (New York: Columbia University Press, 1966).

Habermas, Jürgen, *The Theory of Communicative Action* (2 vols.; Boston: Beacon Press, 1984–87).

Hajnal, Istuan, *L'Ensignement de l'écriture aux universités mediévales* (Budapest: Academia Scientiarum Hungarica Budapestini, 2nd edn, 1959).

Harder, Bernhard D., 'The Militaristic Bias in Theories about Argumentation', *The Conrad Grebel Review* 7 (1989), pp. 1-9.

Havelock, Eric A., *The Literate Revolution in Greece and its Cultural Consequences* (Princeton, NJ: Princeton University Press, 1982).

—*The Muse Learns to Write: Reflections on Orality and Literacy from Antiquity to the Present* (New Haven: Yale University Press, 1986).

Havelock, Eric A., and Jackson P. Hershbell (eds.), *Communication Arts in the Ancient World* (New York: Hastings House, 1978).

Heim, Michael, *The Metaphysics of Virtual Reality* (New York: Oxford University Press, 1993).

—'The Technological Crisis of Rhetoric', *Philosophy & Rhetoric* 21.1 (1988), pp. 48-59.

Heldeman, K., *Antike Theorien über Entwicklung und Verfall der Redekunst* (Zetemata: Monographien zur klassischen Altertumswissenschaft, 77; Munich: C.H. Beck, 1982).

Hock, Ronald F., and Edward N. O'Neill, *The Chreia in Ancient Rhetoric. I. The Progymnasmata* (Atlanta: Scholars Press, 1986).

Horkheimer, Max, *Critical Theory: Selected Essays* (trans. Matthew J. O'Connell *et al.*; New York: Herder & Herder, 1972).

—'The Question Concerning Technology', in Paul Connerton (ed.), *Critical Sociology* (trans. J.O. Connell *et al.*; New York: Penguin Books, 1976), pp. 206-24.

Horner, Winifred B., *Rhetoric in the Classical Tradition* (New York: St Martin's Press, 1988).

Horner, Winifred B. (ed.), *The Present State of Scholarship in Historical and Contemporary Rhetoric* (New York: Columbia University Press, 1983).

Horton, Susan, *Interpreting Interpreting* (Baltimore: The Johns Hopkins University Press, 1979).

Howes, R.F. (ed.), *Historical Studies of Rhetoric and Rhetoricians* (New York: Cornell University Press, 1961).

Hunter, Diane (ed.), *Seduction and Theory: Readings of Gender, Representation, and Rhetoric* (Urbana: University of Illinois Press, 1989).

Hyde, M.J., and C.R. Smith, 'Hermeneutics and Rhetoric: A Seen but Unobserved Relationship', *Quarterly Journal of Speech* 65.4 (1979), pp. 347-63.

Ijselling, Samuel, *Rhetoric and Philosophy in Conflict: An Historic Survey* (trans. Paul Dunphy; The Hague: M. Nijhoff, 1976).

Ivie, Robert L., 'Scrutinizing Performances of Rhetorical Criticism', *Quarterly Journal of Speech* 80.3 (1994), p. 248.

Jaeger, Werner, *Paideia: The Ideals of Greek Culture* (3 vols.; trans. Gilbert Highet; New York: Oxford University Press, 1943–45).

Jameson, F., *The Political Unconscious: Narrative as a Socially Symbolic Act* (Ithaca: Cornell University Press, 1981).

Jarratt, Susan C., 'The First Sophists and Feminism: Discourses of the "Other"', *Hypatia* 5.1 (1990), pp. 27-41.

—*Rereading the Sophists: Classical Rhetoric Refigured* (Carbondale, IL: Southern Illinois University Press, 1991).

—'Speaking to the Past: Feminist Historiography in Rhetoric', *Pre/Text* 11.3–4 (1990), pp. 190-209.

Jaspers, David, *Rhetoric, Power and Community: An Exercise in Reserve* (Louisville, KY: Westminster/John Knox Press, 1993).

Johnson, Barbara, *The Critical Difference: Essays in the Contemporary Rhetoric of Reading* (Baltimore: The Johns Hopkins University Press, 1980).

Johnstone, Henry W., Jr, 'Reply', *Philosophy & Rhetoric* 20.2 (1987), pp. 129-38.

—'Some Reflections on Argumentation', 'A New Theory of Philosophical Argumentation', and 'Persuasion and Validity in Philosophy', in Maurice Natanson and Henry W. Johnstone, Jr (eds.), *Philosophy, Rhetoric and Argumentation* (University Park, PA: Pennylsvania State University Press, 1965).

Kennedy, George A., *The Art of Persuasion in Greece* (Princeton, NJ: Princeton University Press, 1963).

—*The Art of Persuasion in the Roman World* (Princeton, NJ: Princeton University Press, 1963).

—*Classical Rhetoric and its Christian and Secular Tradition from Ancient to Modern Times* (Chapel Hill: University of North Carolina Press, 1980).

—'The Earliest Rhetorical Handbooks', *American Journal of Philology* 80 (1959), pp. 169-78.

—*Greek Rhetoric under the Christian Emperors* (Princeton, NJ: Princeton University Press, 1983).

—'A Hoot in the Dark: The Evolution of General Rhetoric', *Philosophy & Rhetoric* 25.1 (1992), pp. 1-21.

—*New Testament Interpretation through Rhetorical Criticism* (Chapel Hill: University of North Carolina Press, 1984).

—'The Present State of the Study of Ancient Rhetoric', *Classical Philology* 70 (1975), pp. 278-82.

—*Quintilian* (Twayne's World Author Series, 66; New York: Twayne, 1969).

Kinneavy, James L., *Greek Rhetorical Origins of Christian Faith: An Inquiry* (New York: Oxford University Press, 1987).

Kopperschmidt, Josef, *Allgemeine Rhetorik: Einführung in die Theorie der persuasiven Kommunikation* (Sprache und Literatur, 79; Stuttgart: W. Kohlhammer, 1973).

—'Bibliographie zur Argumentationsforschung, 1966–1978', *Rhetorik* 1 (1980), pp. 153-59.

—'Quintilian DE ARGUMENTIS, Oder: Versuch einer argumentationstheoretischen Rekonstruktion der antiken Rhetorik', *Rhetorik* 2 (1981), pp. 59-74.

—*Rhetorica* (Philosophische Texte und Studien, 14; Heldesheim: Georg Olms, 1985).

—*Rhetorik* (2 vols.; Darmstadt: Wissenschaftliche Buchgesellschaft, 1990–91).

Kuhn, Thomas, *The Structure of Scientific Revolutions* (Chicago: University of Chicago Press, 2nd edn, 1970).

Kümmel, Werner, *The New Testament: The History of the Investigation of its Problems* (trans. S. McLean Gilmour and Howard C. Kee; Nashville: Abingdon Press, 1972).

Kusche, Ulrich, *Die unterlegende Religion: Das Judentum im Urteil deutscher Alttestamentler* (Studien zu Kirche und Israel, 12; Berlin: Institut Kirche und Judentum, 1991).

Lahurd, C.S., 'Rhetorical Criticism, Biblical Criticism and Literary Criticism: Issues of Methodological Pluralism', *Proceedings* 5 (1985), pp. 87-101.

Lakoff, Robin Tolmach, *Talking Power: The Politics of Language* (New York: Basic Books, 1990).

Lambrecht, Jan, 'Rhetorical Criticism and the New Testament', *Bijdrage: Tijdschrift voor Philosophie en Theologie* 50 (1989), pp. 239-53.

Landow, George, *Hypertext: The Convergence of Contemporary Critical Theory and Technology* (Baltimore: The Johns Hopkins University Press, 1992).

Lanham, Richard A., *A Handlist of Rhetorical Terms* (Berkeley: University of California Press, 2nd edn, 1991).

—*The Electronic Word: Democracy, Technology and the Arts* (Chicago: University of Chicago Press, 1993).

Larson, Magali Sarfatti, *The Rise of Professionalism: A Sociological Analysis* (Berkeley: University of California Press, 1977).

Larson, Richard L., 'Lloyd Bitzer's "Rhetorical Situation" and the Classification of Discourse: Problems and Implications', *Philosophy & Rhetoric* 3.3 (1970), pp. 165-68.

Lausberg, Heinrich, *Elemente der literarischen Rhetorik* (Munich: Max Hueber Verlag, 1967).

—*Handbuch der literarischen Rhetorik* (2 vols.; repr.; Stuttgart: Franz Steiner, 1990).

Leff, Michael C., and Fred J. Kauffeld (eds.), *Text in Context: Critical Dialogues on Significant Episodes in American Political Rhetoric* (Davis, CA: Hermagoras Press, 1989).

Lentz, Tony M., *Orality and Literacy in Hellenic Greece* (Carbondale, IL: Southern Illinois University Press, 1989).

Linsley, William A. (ed.), *Speech Criticism: Methods and Materials* (Dubuque, IA: Wm C. Brown, 1968).

Lord, Albert B., *The Singer of Tales* (New York: Atheneum, 1968).

Lyons, John, *Language, Meaning and Context* (Glasgow: Fontana Paperbacks, 1981).

Mack, Burton, *Anecdotes and Argument in New Testament Studies: The Chreia in Antiquity and Early Christianity* (Claremont, CA: Institute for Antiquity and Christianity, 1987).

—'Decoding the Scripture: Philo and the Rules of Rhetoric (Gen 4.2)', in F. Greenspahn, E. Helgert and B. Mack (eds.), *Nourished with Peace* (Chico, CA: Scholars Press, 1984).

—'Gilgamish and the Wizard of Oz', *Forum* 1.2 (1985), pp. 3-29.

—'The Kingdom That Didn't Come: A Social History of the Q Tradents', *Society of Biblical Literature Seminar Papers* (Atlanta: Scholars Press, 1989).

—*The Lost Gospel: The Book of Q and Christian Origins* (San Francisco: HarperCollins, 1993).

—*A Myth of Innocence: Mark and Christian Origins* (Philadelphia: Fortress Press, 1988).

—*Rhetoric and the New Testament* (Minneapolis: Fortress Press, 1990).

Mack, Burton, and Vernon Robbins, *Patterns of Persuasion in the Gospels* (Sonoma, CA: Polebridge Press, 1989).

Magass, W., *Hermeneutik, Rhetorik und Semiotik: Studien zur Rezeptionsgeschichte der Bibel* (Konstanz: University of Konstanz, 1985).

Mailloux, Steven, 'Hermeneutics', 'Pragmatism' and 'Reception Study', in Theresa Enos (ed.), *Encyclopedia of Rhetoric* (New York: Garland Press, forthcoming).

—'Interpretation', in Frank Lentricchia and Thomas McLaughlin (eds.), *Critical Terms for Literary Study* (Chicago: University of Chicago Press, 1989).

—'Misreading as a Historical Act: Cultural Rhetoric, Bible Politics, and Fuller's 1845 Review of Douglass's *Narrative*', in James L. Machor (ed.), *Readers in History: Nineteenth-Century American Literature and the Contexts of Response* (Baltimore: The Johns Hopkins University Press, 1993), pp. 2-31.

—'Power, Rhetoric, and Theory: Reading America Texts', in Gerhard Hoffmann (ed.), *Making Sense: The Role of the Reader in Contemporary American Fiction* (Munich: Wilhelm Fink, 1989).

—'A Pretext for Rhetoric: Dancing "Round the Revolution"', in Victor J. Vitanza (ed.), *Pre/Text: The First Decade, a Retrospective* (Pittsburgh: University of Pittsburgh Press, 1993).

—'Rhetoric Returns to Syracuse: Curricular Reform in English Studies', in Nancy Ruff and Isaiah Smithson (eds.), *English Studies/Culture Studies: Institutionalizing Dissent* (Urbana: University of Illinois Press, 1995).

—'Rhetorical Hermeneutics', *Critical Inquiry* 11 (1985), pp. 620-41.

—'Rhetorical Hermeneutics Revisited', *Text and Performance Quarterly* 11 (1991), pp. 233-48.

—*Rhetorical Power* (Ithaca, NY: Cornell University Press, 1989).

—'Rhetorically Covering Conflict: Gerald Graff as Curricular Rhetorician', in William Cain (ed.), *Teaching the Conflicts: Gerald Graff, Curricular Reform, and the Cultural Wars* (New York: Garland Press, 1994).

Malchup, Fritz, *Knowledge: Its Creation, Distribution, and Economic Significance* (2 vols.; Princeton, NJ: Princeton University Press, 1982).

Man, Paul de, 'Semiology and Rhetoric', in *idem* (ed.), *Allegories of Reading: Figural Language in Rousseau, Nietzsche, Rilke, and Proust* (New Haven: Yale University Press, 1979).

Marrou, H.I., *A History of Education in Antiquity* (trans. George Lamb; New York: New American Library, 1956).

Marty, Martin, *A Nation of Behavers* (Chicago: University of Chicago Press, 1976).

McKeon, Richard, *Rhetoric: Essays in Invention and Discovery* (Woodbridge, CT: Ox Bow Press, 1987).

McLuhan, Marshall, *The Guttenberg Galaxy: The Makings of Typographical Man* (Toronto: University of Toronto Press, 1962).

—*Understanding Media: The Extensions of Man* (New York: Signet/McGraw–Hill, 1964).

McLuhan, Marshall, and Quentin Fiore, *The Meaning Is the Message* (New York: Bantam Books, 1967).

Merod, Jim, *The Political Responsibility of the Critic* (Ithaca, NY: Cornell University Press, 1987).

Miller, J. Hillis, 'The Function of Rhetorical Study at the Present Time', in Paul Hunter *et al.*, *The State of the Discipline, 1970s–1980s* (New York: Association of Departments of English, 1979), pp. 10-18.

—'The Triumph of Theory, the Resistance to Reading, and the Question of the Material Base', *Publications of the Modern Language Association* 101.3 (1987), pp. 281-91.

Mitchell, W.J.T. (ed.), *Against Theory: Literary Studies and the New Pragmatism* (Chicago: University of Chicago Press, 1985).

—*The Politics of Interpretation* (Chicago: University of Chicago Press, 1983).

Mosdt, G., 'Rhetorik und Hermeneutik: Zur Konstitution der Neuzeitlichkeit', *Antike und Abendland* 30 (1984), pp. 62-79.

Moi, Tori, *Sexual/Textual Politics: Feminist Literary Theory* (London: Methuen, 1985).

Moore, Stephen, *Post Structuralism and the New Testament: Foucault and Derrida at the Foot of the Cross* (Philadelphia: Fortress Press, 1994).

Morris, Pam (ed.), *The Bakhtin Reader: Selected Writings of Bakhtin, Medvedev and Voloshinov* (London: Edward Arnold, 1994).

Muilenburg, J., 'After Form Criticism What?', *Journal of Biblical Literature* 88 (1969), pp. 1-18.

Murphy, James J. (ed.), 'Hermogenes's On Stasis: A Translation with an Introduction and Notes', *Speech Monographs* 31 (1964), pp. 54-63.

—*Rhetoric in the Middle Ages: A History of Rhetorical Theory from St. Augustine to the Renaissance* (Berkeley: University of California Press, 1974).

—*The Rhetorical Tradition and Modern Writing* (New York: Modern Language Association, 1982).

—*A Synoptic History of Classical Rhetoric* (Davis, CA: Hermagoras Press, 1983).

Natanson, Maurice, and Henry W. Johnstone, Jr (eds.), *Philosophy, Rhetoric and Argumentation* (University Park, PA: The Pennsylvania State University Press, 1965).

Neill, Stephen, *Interpretation of the New Testament 1861–1986* (Oxford: Oxford University Press, 2nd edn, 1988).

Nelson, John S., Allan Megill and Donald N. McCloskey (eds.), *The Rhetoric of the Human Sciences: Language and Argument in Scholastic and Public Affairs* (Madison, WI: University of Wisconsin Press, 1987).

Ohmann, Richard, *English in America: A Radical View of the Profession* (New York: Oxford University Press, 1976).

—*Politics of Letters* (Middletown, CT: Wesleyan University Press, 1987).

Oleson, Alexandra, and John Voss (eds.), *The Organization of Knowledge in Modern America, 1860–1920* (Baltimore: The Johns Hopkins University Press, 1979).

Oliver, Robert T., *History of Public Speaking in America* (Boston: Allyn & Bacon, 1965).

Ong, Walter, *Interfaces of the Word: Studies in the Evolution of Consciousness and Culture* (Ithaca, NY: Cornell University Press, 1977).

—*Orality and Literacy: The Technologizing of the Word* (London: Methuen, 1982).

—*The Presence of the Word: Some Prolegomena for Cultural and Religious History* (Minneapolis: University of Minnesota Press, 2nd edn, 1981).

—*20th Century Literary Theory* (Albany: SUNY Press, 1987).

—*Rhetoric, Romance, and Technology* (Ithaca, NY: Cornell University Press, 1971).

Palmer, F.R., *Modality and English Modals* (London: Longman, 1979).

—*Mood and Modality* (Cambridge: Cambridge University Press, 1986).

Parry, Adam (ed.), *The Making of Homeric Verse: The Collected Papers of Milman Parry* (Oxford: Clarendon Press, 1971).

Patrick, D., and A. Scult, *Rhetoric and Biblical Interpretation* (Bible and Literature Series, 26; Sheffield: Almond Press, 1990).

Patton, John, 'Causation and Creativity in Rhetorical Situations: Distinctions and Implications', *Quarterly Journal of Speech* 65.1 (1979), pp. 36-55.

Pearson, Birger A. (ed.), *The Future of Early Christianity* (Minneapolis: Fortress Press, 1991).

Perelman, Chaim, *De la metaphysique à la rhetorique* (Brussels: Editions de l'université de Bruxelles, 1986).

—*The Idea of Justice and the Problem of Argumentation* (London: Routledge & Kegan Paul, 1963).

—'La Quete du rationnel', in *Etudes de philosophie des sciences en hommage à Ferdinand Gonseth* (Neuchâtel: Edition du Griffon, 1950), pp. 135-42.

—*The New Rhetoric and the Humanities: Essays on Rhetoric and its Application* (Notre Dame, IN: University of Notre Dame Press, 1979).

—*The Realm of Rhetoric* (Notre Dame, IN: University of Notre Dame Press, 1982).

—'Sociologie de la connaissance et philosophie de la connaissance', *Revue internationale de philosophie* 4 (1950), pp. 309-17.

Perelman, Chaim, and Lucie Olbrechts-Tyteca, *The New Rhetoric: A Treatise on Argumentation* (Notre Dame, IN: University of Notre Dame Press, 1969).

Plett, Heinrich (ed.), *Rhetorik: Kritische Positionen zum Stand der Forschung* (Munich: Fink, 1977).

Pomeroy, Ralph, 'Fitness of Response in Bitzer's Concept of Rhetorical Discourse', *Georgia Speech Communication Journal* 4 (1972), pp. 42-71.

Porter, Stanley E., and Thomas H. Olbricht (eds.), *Rhetoric and the New Testament: Essays from the 1992 Heidelberg Conference* (*Journal for the Study of the New Testament*, Supplement Series, 90; Sheffield: Sheffield Academic Press, 1993).

—*The Rhetorical Analysis of Scripture: Essays from the 1995 London Conference* (*Journal for the Study of the New Testament*, Supplement Series, 146; Sheffield: Sheffield Academic Press, 1997).

Powell, Mark, *Bible and Modern Literary Criticism: A Critical Assessment and Annotated Bibliography* (New York: Greenwood Press, 1992).

Pratt, Mary Louise, *Toward a Speech Act Theory of Literary Discourse* (Bloomington: Indiana University Press, 1977).

Rabinowitz, P.J., *Before Reading: Narrative Conventions and the Politics of Interpretation* (Ithaca, NY: Cornell University Press, 1987).

Reboul, Oliver, 'Can There Be Non-Rhetorical Argumentation?', *Philosophy & Rhetoric* 21.3 (1988), pp. 220-330.

Richards, I.A., *The Philosophy of Rhetoric* (New York: Oxford University Press, 1936).

Richards, I.A., and C.K. Ogden, *The Meaning of Meaning* (New York: Harcourt, Brace and World, 1923).

Rickman, H.P., 'Rhetoric and Hermeneutic', *Philosophy & Rhetoric* 14.1 (1981), pp. 100-111.

Robbins, Vernon K., *Exploring the Texture of Texts: A Guide to Socio-Rhetorical Interpretations* (Valley Forge, PA: Trinity Press International, 1996).

—*Jesus the Teacher: A Socio-Rhetorical Interpretation of Mark* (Philadelphia: Fortress Press, 1984).

—'Picking Up the Fragments: From Crossan's Analysis to Rhetorical Analysis', *Forum* 1.2 (1985), pp. 31-64.

—'Pragmatic Relations as a Criterion for Authentic Sayings', *Forum* 1.3 (1985), pp. 35-63.

—'The Present and Future of Rhetorical Analysis', in Stanley E. Porter and Thomas H. Olbricht (eds.), *The Rhetorical Analysis of Scripture: Essays from the 1995 London*

Conference (*Journal for the Study of the New Testament*, Supplement Series, 146; Sheffield: Sheffield Academic Press, 1997), pp. 24-52.

—'Pronouncement Stories and Jesus' Blessing of the Children: A Rhetorical Approach', *Semeia* 29 (1983), pp. 43-74.

—'Pronouncement Stories from a Rhetorical Perspective', *Forum* 4.2 (1988), pp. 3-32.

—'Rhetoric and Culture: Exploring Types of Cultural Rhetoric in a Text', in Stanley E. Porter and Thomas H. Olbricht (eds.), *Rhetoric and the New Testament: Essays from the 1992 Heidelberg Conference* (*Journal for the Study of the New Testament*, Supplement Series, 90; Sheffield: Sheffield Academic Press, 1993), pp. 443-63.

—'A Rhetorical Typology for Classifying and Analyzing Pronouncement Stories', *Society of Biblical Literature Seminar Papers* (Atlanta: Scholars Press, 1984).

—'A Socio-Rhetorical Response: Contexts of Interaction and Forms of Exhortation', *Semeia* 50 (1990), pp. 261-71.

—*The Tapestry of Early Christian Discourse: Rhetoric, Society and Ideology* (London: Routledge, 1996).

—*What Is Socio-Rhetorical Criticism?* (Guides to Biblical Scholarship, New Testament Series; ed. Dan O. Via, Jr; Minneapolis: Fortress Press, forthcoming).

—'The Woman Who Touched Jesus' Garment: Socio-Rhetorical Analysis of the Synoptic Accounts', *New Testament Studies* 33.4 (1987), pp. 502-15.

Robbins, Vernon K., and John H. Patton, 'Rhetoric and Biblical Criticism', *Quarterly Journal of Speech* 66.4 (1980), pp. 327-37.

Roberts, W. Rhys, *Greek Rhetoric and Literary Criticism* (New York: Longmans, Green, 1928).

Ruether, Rosemary (ed.), *Women and Religion in America* (3 vols.; San Francisco: Harper & Row, 1981).

Russell, D.A., and N.G. Wilson (eds.), *Menandor Rhetor* (Oxford: Clarendon Press, 1981).

Russell, D.A., and M. Winterbottom (eds.), *Ancient Literary Criticism: The Principal Texts in New Translations* (Oxford: Clarendon Press, 1972).

Schilb, John, 'The History of Rhetoric and the Rhetoric of History', *Pre/Text* 7.1–2 (1986), pp. 11-35.

Schramm, Wilbur, *Men, Women, Messages and Media: Understanding Human Communication* (New York: Harper & Row, 2nd edn, 1982).

Schüssler Fiorenza, E., *The Book of Revelation: Justice and Judgment* (Philadelphia: Fortress Press, 1985).

—*Bread Not Stone: The Challenge of Feminist Biblical Interpretation* (Boston: Beacon Press, 1984).

—*But She Said: Feminist Practices of Biblical Interpretation* (Boston: Beacon Press, 1992).

—*Discipleship of Equals: A Critical Feminist Ekklesialogy of Liberation* (New York: Crossroad, 1993).

—'The Ethics of Biblical Interpretation: De-Centering Biblical Scholarship', *Journal of Biblical Literature* 107.1 (1988), pp. 3-17.

—'The Followers of the Lamb: Visionary Rhetoric and Social-Political Situation', in F. Segovia (ed.), *Discipleship in the New Testament* (Philadelphia: Fortress Press, 1984).

—*In Memory of Her: A Feminist Theological Reconstruction of Christian Origins* (New York: Crossroad, 1984).

—'Rhetorical Situation and Historical Reconstruction in I Corinthians', *New Testament Studies* 33 (1987), pp. 386-403.

—*Searching for the Scriptures* (New York: Crossroad, 1993).

Schwartz, Regina (ed.), *The Book and the Text: The Bible and Literary Theory* (Oxford: Basil Blackwell, 1990).

Scott, Robert L., 'Intentionality in the Rhetorical Process', in E.E. White (ed.), *Rhetoric in Transition* (University Park, PA: Pennsylvania State University Press, 1980), pp. 39-60.

—'On Viewing Rhetoric as Epistemic', *Central States Speech Journal* 18.1 (1967), pp. 9-16.

—'On Viewing Rhetoric as Epistemic: Ten Years Later', *Central States Speech Journal* 27.3 (1977), pp. 258-66.

Scult, Allen, 'The Relationship between Rhetoric and Hermeneutics Reconsidered', *Central States Speech Journal* 34 (1983), pp. 221-28.

Searle, John R., *Expression and Meaning: Studies in the Theory of Speech Acts* (New York: Cambridge University Press, 1979).

—*Intentionality: An Essay on the Philosophy of Mind* (New York: Cambridge University Press, 1983).

—*Minds, Brains and Science* (Cambridge, MA: Harvard University Press, 1984).

—*Speech Acts: An Essay in the Philosophy of Language* (Cambridge, 1969).

Sloan, Thomas, 'Rhetoric: Rhetoric in Literature', in *New Encyclopedia Britannica*, XV (London: Encyclopedia Britannica, 15th edn, 1975), pp. 802-803.

Smit, D.J., 'The Ethics of Interpretation—New Voices from the USA', *Scriptura* 33 (1990), pp. 16-26.

Stamps, D.L., 'Rhetorical Criticism and the Rhetoric of New Testament Criticism', *Literature & Theology* 6 (1992), pp. 268-79.

Sterne, Lawrence, *The Life and Opinions of Tristam Shandy* (New York: Penguin Books, 1998).

Swearingen, Jan, *Rhetoric and Irony: Western Literacy and Western Lies* (New York: Oxford University Press, 1991).

Todorov, T., 'Rhetorique et Hermeneutique', *Poetique* 23 (1975), pp. 289-415.

Toulmin, Stephen, *The Uses of Argument* (Cambridge: Cambridge University Press, 1958).

Vanhoye, A. (ed.), *L'Apôtre Paul: Personnalité, style et conception du ministère* (Leuven: Leuven University Press, 1986).

Vatz, Richard, 'The Myth of the Rhetorical Situation', *Philosophy & Rhetoric* 6.3 (1973), pp. 154-61.

Vickers, Brian, *Classical Rhetoric in English Poetry* (London: Macmillan, 1970).

—*In Defense of Rhetoric* (Oxford: Clarendon Press, 1988).

—'The Atrophy of Modern Rhetoric, Vico to DeMan', *Rhetorica* 6.1 (1988), pp. 21-56.

Vickers, Brian (ed.), *Rhetoric Revalued: Papers from the International Society for the History of Rhetoric* (Medieval and Renaissance Texts and Studies, 19; Brighampton, NY: Center for Medieval and Early Renaissance Studies, 1982).

Vitanza, Victor, ' "Some More" Notes Towards a "Third Sophistic" ', *Argumentation* 5.1 (1991), pp. 117-39.

—'Cackling with Tears in my Eyes; or, Some Responses to "The Gang of Three" Scott–Leff–Kennedy', *Rhetoric Review* 7.1 (1988), pp. 214-18.

—'Critical Sub/Versions of the History of Philosophical Rhetoric', *Rhetoric Review* 6.1 (1987), pp. 41-66.

—' "Notes" Toward Historiographies of Rhetoric; or Rhetorics of the Histories of Rhetorics: Traditional, Revisionary, and Sub/Versive', *Pre/Text* 8.1–2 (1987), pp. 63-125.

Voloshinov, V.N., *Marxism and the Philosophy of Language* (trans. L. Matejka and I.R. Titunik; Cambridge, MA: Harvard University Press).

Waits, Tom, 'Yesterday Is Here' (Track 7) *Frank's Wild Years* (Polygram Records, 1990).

Warner, Martin, *Philosophical Finesse: Studies in the Art of Rational Persuasion* (New York: Oxford University Press, 1989).

Warner, Martin (ed.), *The Bible as Rhetoric: Studies in Biblical Persuasion and Credibility* (Warwick Studies in Philosophy and Literature; London: Routledge, 1990).

Watson, Duane F. (ed.), *Persuasive Artistry: Studies in New Testament Rhetoric in Honor of George A. Kennedy* (*Journal for the Study of the New Testament*, Supplement Series, 50; Sheffield: Sheffield Academic Press, 1991).

White, Eugene E. (ed.), *Rhetoric in Transition: Studies in the Nature and Uses of Rhetoric* (University Park, PA: Pennsylvania State University Press, 1980).

Wilkerson, K.E., 'On Evaluating Theories of Rhetoric', *Philosophy & Rhetoric* 3.1 (1970), pp. 82-96.

Wire, Antoinette, *The Corinthian Women Prophets: A Reconstruction through Paul's Rhetoric* (Minneapolis: Fortress Press, 1990).

Wodehouse, P.G., 'Comrad Bingo', in *idem*, *The World of Jeeves* (New York: Harper & Row, 1967), pp. 171-87.

Wuellner, Wilhelm, 'The Argumentative Structure of 1 Thessalonians as Paradoxical Encomium', in Raymond F. Collins (ed.), *The Thessalonian Correspondence* (Bibliotheca ephemeridum theologicarum lovaniensium, 87; Leuven: Leuven University Press, 1990), pp. 117-36.

—'Arrangement', in Stanley E. Porter (ed.), *Handbook of Graeco-Roman Rhetoric from its Origins to A.D. 400* (Leiden: E.J. Brill, 1995).

—'Biblical Exegesis in the Light of the History and Historicity of Rhetoric and the Nature of the Rhetoric of Religion', in Stanley E. Porter and Thomas H. Olbricht (eds.), *Rhetoric and the New Testament: Essays from the 1992 Heidelberg Conference* (*Journal for the Study of the New Testament*, Supplement Series, 90; Sheffield: Sheffield Academic Press, 1993), pp. 492-512.

—'Critica Retorica', *Protestantismo* 49.3 (1994) (also published in English as 'Rhetorical Criticism in Biblical Studies', *Jian Dao: A Journal of Bible and Theology* 4 [1995], pp. 73-96).

—'Death and Rebirth of Rhetoric in Late Twentieth Century Exegesis', in Tord Fornberg and David Hellholm (eds.), *Texts and Contexts: Biblical Texts in their Textual and Situational Contexts* (Festschrift Lars Hartman; Oslo: Scandinavian University Press, 1995), pp. 917-30.

—'Der Jakobusbrief im Licht der Rhetorik und Textpragmatik', *Linguistica Biblica* 43 (1978), pp. 5-66.

—'Der vorchristliche Paulus und die Rhetorik', in Simon Lauer and Hanspeter Ernst (eds.), *Tempelkult und Tempelzerstörung (70 n.Chr.)* (Bern: Peter Lang, 1995), pp. 133-65.

—'Greek Rhetoric and Pauline Argumentation', in William R. Schoedel and Robert L. Wilkin (eds.), *Early Christian Literature and the Classical Intellectual Tradition: In Honorem Robert M. Grant* (Théologie Historique, 54; Paris: Beauchesne, 1979), pp. 177-88.

—*Hermeneutics and Rhetorics: From 'Truth and Method' to Truth and Power* (Stellenbosch, RSA: Centre for Hermeneutical Studies, 1989).

—*Paul and Rhetoric* (unpublished lectures and class notes; Berkeley, CA: Graduate Theological Union, 1994).

—'Paul as Pastor: The Function of Rhetorical Questions in First Corinthians', in A. Vanhoye (ed.), *L'Apôtre Paul: Personnalité, style et conception du ministère* (Leuven: Leuven University Press, 1986), pp. 49-77.

—'Paul's Letters in the Context of the *Teshuvot* Tradition Illustrated in Acts 15 [Apostolic Decree]', in Hayim Perelmuter (ed.), *Proceedings of the Conference on the Question of the Letters of Paul Viewed from the Perspective of the Jewish Responsa Mode* (Chicago: Catholic Theological Union, 1992).

—'Paul's Rhetoric of Argumentation in Romans: An Alternative to the Donfried-Karris Debate over Romans', *Catholic Biblical Quarterly* 38 (1976), pp. 330-51.

—'Putting Life Back into the Lazarus Story and its Reading: The Narrative of John 11 as the Narration of Faith', *Semeia* 54 (1991), pp. 171-85.

—'Reading Romans in Context' (unpublished Society for New Testament Studies Seminar Paper; Göttingen Conference, 25–27 August 1987).

—'Rhetorical Criticism and its Theory in Culture-Critical Perspective: The Narrative Rhetoric of John 11', in P.J. Hartin and J.H. Petzer (eds.), *Text and Interpretation: New Approaches in the Criticism of the New Testament* (Leiden: E.J. Brill, 1991), pp. 167-81.

—'The Rhetorical Genre of Jesus' Sermon in Luke 12.1–13.9', in Duane F. Watson (ed.), *Persuasive Artistry: Studies in New Testament Rhetoric in Honor of George A. Kennedy* (Sheffield: JSOT Press, 1991), pp. 93-118.

—'The Rhetorical Structure of Luke 12 in its Wider Context', *Neotestamentica* 22 (1989), pp. 283-310.

—'Toposforschung und Torahinterpretation bei Paulus und Jesus', *New Testament Studies* 24 (1978), pp. 463-83.

—'Where Is Rhetorical Criticism Taking Us?', *Catholic Biblical Quarterly* 49.3 (1987), pp. 448-63.

Wuellner, Wilhelm, and Hayim G. Perelmuter *et al.*, *Paul the Jew: Protocol of the 60. Colloquy of the Center for Hermeneutical Studies* (Berkeley: Center for Hermeneutical Studies, 1990).

Wuellner, Wilhelm, and the Bible and Culture Collective, 'Rhetorical Criticism', in Elizabeth Castelli, Stephen Moore, Gary Phillips and Regina Schwartz (eds.), *The Postmodern Bible* (New Haven: Yale University Press, 1995), pp. 149-86.

Wuthnow, Robert, *The Restructuring of American Religion: Society and Faith Since World War II* (Princeton, NJ: Princeton University Press, 1988).

Yoos, George E., 'Rhetoric of Appeal and Rhetoric of Response', *Philosophy & Rhetoric* 20.2 (1987), pp. 107-17.

Modern Rhetorical Methods (Selected Materials)

Amador, J.D.H., 'Re-discovering/Reinventing Rhetoric', *Scriptura* 50 (1994), pp. 1-22.

Ambrester, Roy, 'Identification Within: Kenneth Burke's View of the Unconscious', *Philosophy & Rhetoric* 7.4 (1974), pp. 205-16.

Andrews, James R., 'Confrontation at Columbia: A Case Study in Coercive Rhetoric', *Quarterly Journal of Speech* 55.1 (1969), pp. 9-16.

Austin, J.L., *How To Do Things with Words* (Oxford: Oxford University Press, 1966).

Bales, Robert, *Personality and Interpersonal Behavior* (New York: Holt, Rinehart Winston, 1970).

Barth, E.M., 'Toward a Praxis-Oriented Theory of Argumentation', in Marcelo Dascal (ed.), *Dialogue: An Interdisciplinary Approach* (Amsterdam: John Benjamin, 1985), pp. 73-86.

Baskerville, Barnet, 'The Cross and the Flag Evangelists of the Far Right', *Western Speech* 27.4 (1963), pp. 197-206.

Bass, Jeff D., 'The Rhetorical Opposition to Controversial Wars: Rhetorical Timing as a Generic Consideration', *Western Journal of Speech Communication* 43.3 (1979), pp. 180-91.

Bennett, W. Lance, 'Storytelling in Criminal Trials: A Model of Social Judgment', *Quarterly Journal of Speech* 64.1 (1978), pp. 1-22.

Berk, Ulrich, *Konstruktive Argumentationstheorie* (Stuttgart: Frommann-Holzboog, 1979).

Berlin, James, 'Postmodernism, Politics and Histories of Rhetoric', *Pre/Text* 11.3–4 (1990), pp. 170-87.

Berlo, David, 'A Model of the Communication Process', in Jane Blankenship and Robert Wihoit (eds.), *Selective Readings in Public Speaking* (Belmont, CA: Dickenson Press, 1966).

Black, Max, *Models and Metaphors: Studies in Language and Philosophy* (Ithaca, NY: Cornell University Press, 1962).

Blair, J. Anthony, and Ralph H. Johnson, 'Argumentation as Dialectical', *Argumentation* 1.1 (1987), pp. 41-56.

Blankenship, Jane, Marlene G. Fine and Leslie K. Davis, 'The 1980 Republican Primary Debates: The Transformation of Actor to Scene', *Quarterly Journal of Speech* 69.1 (1983), pp. 25-36.

Blankenship, Jane, and Barbara Sweeney, 'The Energy of Form', *Central States Speech Journal* 31.4 (1980), pp. 172-83.

Borel, Marie-Jeanne, 'Introduction', *Argumentation* 2.3 (1988), pp. 295-97.

Borel, Marie-Jeanne, J.B. Grize and D. Mieville, *Essai de logique naturelle* (Bern: Peter Lang, 1982).

Bormann, Ernest, 'Fantasy and Rhetorical Vision: The Rhetorical Criticism of Social Reality', *Quarterly Journal of Speech* 58.4 (1972), pp. 396-407.

—'Fetching Good out of Evil: A Rhetorical Use of Calamity', *Quarterly Journal of Speech* 63.2 (1977), pp. 130-39.

—*The Force of Fantasy: Restoring the American Dream* (Carbondale, IL: Southern Illinois University Press, 1985).

—'Symbolic Convergence Theory: A Communication Formulation', *Journal of Communication* 35 (1985), pp. 128-38.

Braet, Antoine, 'The Classical Doctrine of Status and the Rhetorical Theory of Argumentation', *Philosophy & Rhetoric* 20.2 (1987), pp. 79-93.

Brandt, William, *The Rhetoric of Argumentation* (New York: Bobbs–Merrill, 1970).

Brigance, W.N. (ed.), *A History and Criticism of American Public Address* (2 vols.; New York: McGraw–Hill, 1943).

Brinton, Alan, 'On Viewing Knowledge as Rhetorical', *Central States Speech Journal* 26.4 (1985), pp. 270-81.

Brockriede, Wayne, 'Arguers as Lovers', *Philosophy & Rhetoric* 5 (1972), pp. 1-11.

—'Constructs, Experience, and Argument', *Quarterly Journal of Speech* 71.2 (1985), pp. 151-63.

—'Rhetorical Criticism as Argument', *Quarterly Journal of Speech* 60.2 (1974), pp. 165-74.

Brown, Janet, 'Kenneth Burke and The Mod Donna: The Dramatistic Method Applied to Feminist Criticism', *Central States Speech Journal* 29 (1978), pp. 138-46.

Brown, Richard Harvey, 'Rhetoric and the Science of History: The Debate between Evolutionism and Empiricism as a Conflict in Metaphors', *Quarterly Journal of Speech* 72.2 (1986), pp. 148-61.

Brown, William R., 'The Holographic View of Argument', *Argumentation* 1 (1987), pp. 89-102.

Brummett, Barry, 'Burkean Scapegoating, Mortification, and Transcendence in Presidential Campaign Rhetoric', *Central States Speech Journal* 32.1 (1981), pp. 254-64.

—'Burke's Representative Anecdote as a Method in Media Criticism', *Critical Studies in Mass Communication* 1.2 (1984), pp. 164-76.

—'A Pentadic Analysis of Ideologies in Two Gay Rights Controversies', *Central States Speech Journal* 30 (1979), pp. 250-61.

—'Premillennial Apocalyptic as a Rhetorical Genre', *Central States Speech Journal* 35.2 (1984), pp. 84-93.

Bryant, Donald C., 'Rhetoric: Its Function and Scope', *Quarterly Journal of Speech* 39.1 (1953), pp. 405-406.

Burgess, Parke, 'The Rhetoric of Black Power: A Moral Demand', *Quarterly Journal of Speech* 54.2 (1968), pp. 122-33.

Burke, Edmund, 'Art—and the First Rough Draft of Living', *Modern Age* 8 (1964).

Butler, Sherry Devereau, 'The Apologia, 1971 Genre', *Southern Speech Communication Journal* 37.2 (1972), pp. 281-89.

Campbell, Anne, *Men, Women, and Aggression* (New York: Basic Books, 1993).

Campbell, Karlyn Kohrs, *Man Cannot Speak for Her* (2 vols.; New York: CT; London: Greenwood Press, 1989).

—'The Rhetoric of Women's Liberation: An Oxymoron', *Quarterly Journal of Speech* 59.1 (1973), pp. 74-86.

—'Stanton's "The Solitude of Self": A Rationale for Feminism', *Quarterly Journal of Speech* 66.3 (1980), pp. 304-12.

—'Style and Content in the Rhetoric of Early Afro-American Feminists', *Quarterly Journal of Speech* 72.4 (1986), pp. 434-45.

Campbell, Paul N., 'A Rhetorical View of Locutionary, Illocutionary and Perlocutionary Acts', *Quarterly Journal of Speech* 59.3 (1973), pp. 284-96.

Carlton, Charles, 'The Rhetoric of Death: Scaffold Confessions in Early Modern England', *Southern Speech Communication Journal* 41.1 (1983), pp. 66-79.

Carpenter, Ronald H., 'Admiral Mahan, "Narrative Fidelity", and the Japanese Attack on Pearl Harbor', *Quarterly Journal of Speech* 72.3 (1986), pp. 290-305.

—'A Stylistic Basis of Burkeian Identification', *Today's Speech* 20.1 (1972), pp. 19-24.

Carter, Kathryn, and Carole Spitzack (eds.), *Doing Research on Women's Communication: Perspectives on Theory and Method* (Norwood, NJ: Ablex, 1989).

Castelli, Elizabeth, Stephen Moore, Gary Phillips and Regina Schwartz (eds.), *The Postmodern Bible* (New Haven: Yale University Press, 1995).

Cathcart, Robert S., 'New Approaches to the Study of Movements: Defining Movements Rhetorically', *Western Speech* 36.2 (1972), pp. 82-87.

Cheney, George, 'The Rhetoric of Identification and the Study of Organizational Communication', *Quarterly Journal of Speech* 69.2 (1983), pp. 143-58.

Chesebro, James W., 'The Machiavellian Princess: Rhetorical Dramas for Women Managers', *Communication Quarterly* 30.3 (1982), pp. 165-72.
—'Rhetorical Strategies of Radicals', *Today's Speech* 21.2 (1972), pp. 37-48.
Chesebro, James W., and Caroline D. Hamsher, *Orientations to Public Communication* (Chicago: Science Research Association, 1976).
Chesebro, James W., and Jolene Koester, 'Paradoxical Views of "Homosexuality" in the Rhetoric of Social Movements', *Quarterly Journal of Speech* 66.2 (1980), pp. 127-39.
Coates, Jennifer, *The Semantics of Modal Anxiliaries* (London: Croom Helm, 1984).
—*Women, Men and Language: A Sociolinguistic Account of Gender Differences in Language* (New York: Longman, 2nd edn, 1993).
Communication 9.1 (1986), special volume entitled 'Feminist Critiques of Popular Culture'.
Communication 9.3–4 (1987), special volume entitled 'Intersections of Power: Criticism-Television-Gender'.
Communication 10.3–4 (1988), special volume entitled 'Postmodernism/Marxism/Feminism'.
Communication Quarterly 31.2 (1983), special volume entitled 'Women and Communication: An Introduction to the Issues'.
Conley, Thomas M., 'Ancient Rhetoric and Modern Genre Criticism', *Communication Quarterly* 37.4 (1979), pp. 47-53.
Cox, J. Robert, 'Perspectives on Rhetorical Criticism of Movements: Antiwar Dissent, 1964–1970', *Western Speech* 38.4 (1974), pp. 254-68.
Cox, J. Robert, and Charles A. Willard, *Advances in Argumentation Theory and Research* (Carbondale, IL: Southern Illinois University Press, 1982).
Cox, J. Robert, Malcolm Sillars, and Gregg B. Walker (eds.), *Argument and Social Practice: Proceedings of the Fourth SCA/AFA Conference on Argumentation* (Annandale, VA: Speech Communication Association, 1985).
Cragan, John F., and Donald C. Shields, *Applied Communication Research: A Dramatistic Approach* (Prospect Heights, IL: Waveland Press, 1981).
Crosswhite, James, 'Mood in Argumentation: Heidegger and the Exordium', *Philosophy & Rhetoric* 22.1 (1989), pp. 28-42.
Czitrom, Daniel J., *Media and the American Mind: From Morse to McLuhan* (Chapel Hill: University of North Carolina Press, 1982).
Danziger, Kurt, *Interpersonal Communication* (New York: Macmillan, 1977).
Deetz, Stanley L., 'Words with Things: Toward a Social Phenomenology of Language', *Quarterly Journal of Speech* 59.1 (1973), pp. 40-51.
Deming, Caren J., '*Hill Street Blues* as Narrative', *Critical Studies in Mass Communication* 2.1 (1985), pp. 1-22.
Dewey, John, *The Public and its Problems* (repr.; Chicago: Swallow Press, 1954).
Donaldson, Alice, 'Women Emerge as Political Speakers', *Speech Monographs* 18.1 (1951), pp. 54-61.·
Donfried, K.P., 'False Presuppositions in the Study of Romans', *Catholic Biblical Quarterly* 36 (1974), pp. 332-55.
Doyle, Vanderford, 'The Rhetoric of Romance: A Fantasy Theme Analysis of Barbara Cartland Novels', *Southern Speech Communication Journal* 51.1 (1985), pp. 24-48.
Durham, Weldon B., 'Kenneth Burke's Concept of Substance', *Quarterly Journal of Speech* 66.4 (1980), pp. 351-64.

Edelman, Murray, *The Symbolic Uses of Politics* (Urbana: University of Illinois Press, 1964).

Eemeren, Frans H. van, and Rob Grootendorst, *Speech Acts in Argumentative Discussions: A Theoretical Model for the Analysis of Discussions Directed towards Solving Conflicts of Opinion* (Dordrecht: Foris Publications, 1983).

Eemeren, Frans H. van, Rob Grootendorst and T. Kruiger, *Handbook of Argumentation Theory: A Critical Survey of Classical Backgrounds and Modern Studies* (Dordrecht: Foris Publications, 1987).

Ehrman, M., *The Meaning of Modals in Present-Day American English* (The Hague: Mouton, 1966).

Evans, Martha Noel, 'Hysteria and the Seduction of Theory', in Dianne Hunter (ed.), *Seduction and Theory: Readings of Gender, Representation and Rhetoric* (Urbana: University of Illinois Press, 1989), pp. 73-85.

Farrell, Thomas B., and G. Thomas Goodnight, 'Accidental Rhetoric: The Root Metaphors of Three Mile Island', *Communication Monographs* 48 (1981), pp. 271-300.

Fish, Stanley, *Doing What Comes Naturally: Change, Rhetoric and the Practice of Theory in Literary and Legal Studies* (London: Duke University Press, 1989).

—*Is There a Text in This Class?* (Cambridge, MA: Harvard University Press, 1982).

—'Interpreting the *Variorum*', in Jane P. Tompkins (ed.), *Reader-Response Criticism: From Formalism to Post-Structuralism* (Baltimore: The Johns Hopkins University Press, 1980), pp. 70-100.

Fisher, Jeanne, 'A Burkean Analysis of the Rhetorical Dimensions of Multiple Murder and Suicide', *Quarterly Journal of Speech* 60.2 (1974), pp. 175-89.

Fisher, Walter R., 'Genre: Concepts and Applications in Rhetorical Criticism', *Western Journal of Speech Communication* 44.4 (1980), pp. 288-99.

—*Human Communication as Narration: Toward a Philosophy of Reason, Value and Action* (Columbia, SC: University of South Carolina Press, 1987).

—'The Narrative Paradigm: An Elaboration', *Communication Monographs* 62.4 (1985), pp. 347-67.

—'Narrative as a Human Communication Paradigm: The Case of Public Moral Argument', *Communication Monographs* 61.1 (1984), pp. 1-22.

—'Rhetorical Fiction and the Presidency', *Quarterly Journal of Speech* 66.2 (1980), pp. 119-26.

—'Technical Logic, Rhetorical Logic, and Narrative Rationality', *Argumentation* 1.1 (1987), pp. 3-21.

—'Toward a Logic of Good Reasons', *Quarterly Journal of Speech* 64.4 (1978), pp. 376-84.

Fishman, J.A., *Advances in the Sociology of Language* (2 vols.; The Hague: Mouton, 1972).

—*The Sociology of Language: An Interdisciplinary Social Science Approach to Language in Society* (Rowley: Newbury House, 1972).

Flynn, Elizabeth A., and Patrocinio P. Schweickart (eds.), *Gender and Reading: Essays on Readers, Texts, and Contexts* (Baltimore: The Johns Hopkins University Press, 1986).

Foss, Karen A., and Sonja K. Foss, 'Incorporating the Feminist Perspective in Communication Scholarship: A Research Commentary', in Carol Spitzack and Kathryn Carter (eds.), *Doing Research on Women's Communication: Alternative Perspectives in Theory and Method* (Norwood, NJ: Albex, 1989).

Foss, Karen A., and Sonja K. Foss (eds.), *Women Speak: The Eloquence of Women's Lives* (Prospect Heights, IL: Waveland Press, 1991).

Foss, Sonja K., 'Women Priests in the Episcopal Church: A Cluster Analysis of Establishment Rhetoric', *Religious Communication Today* 7 (1984), pp. 1-11.

—'Equal Rights Amendment Controversy: Two Worlds in Conflict', *Quarterly Journal of Speech* 65.3 (1979), pp. 275-88.

Frentz, Thomas S., and Thomas B. Farrell, 'Language-Action: A Paradigm for Communication', *Quarterly Journal of Speech* 62.4 (1976), pp. 333-49.

Frentz, Thomas S., 'Rhetorical Conversation, Time, and Moral Action', *Quarterly Journal of Speech* 71.1 (1985), pp. 1-18.

—'Toward a Resolution of the Generative Semantics/Classical Theory Controversy: A Psycholinguistic Analysis of Metaphor', *Quarterly Journal of Speech* 60.2 (1974), pp. 125-33.

Gearhart, Sally Miller, 'The Womanization of Rhetoric', *Women's Studies International Quarterly* 2 (1979), pp. 195-201.

Givón, T., 'Evidentiality and Epistemic Space', *Studies in Language* 4 (1982), pp. 23-49.

Gold, Ellen Reid, 'The Grimke Sisters and the Emergence of the Women's Rights Movement', *Southern Speech Communication Journal* 46.4 (1981), pp. 341-60.

Golden, James L., 'Douglas Ehninger's Philosophy of Argument', *Argumentation* 1.1 (1987), pp. 23-40.

Goodman, Richard J., and William I. Gordon, 'The Rhetoric of Desecration', *Quarterly Journal of Speech* 57.1 (1971), pp. 23-31.

Göttert, Karl-Heinz, *Argumentation: Grundzüge ihrer Theorie im Bereich theoretischen Wissens und praktischen Handelns* (Tübingen: Max Niemeyer, 1978).

Govier, Trudy, *A Practical Study of Argument* (Belmont, CA: Wadsworth Publishing Company, 1985).

Graves, Michael P., 'Functions of Key Metaphors in Early Quaker Sermons, 1671–1700', *Quarterly Journal of Speech* 69.4 (1983), pp. 364-78.

Gregg, Richard B., 'Kenneth Burke's Prolegomena to the Study of the Rhetoric of Form', *Communication Quarterly* 26.4 (1978), pp. 3-13.

Gribbin, William, 'The Juggernaut Metaphor in American Rhetoric', *Quarterly Journal of Speech* 59.3 (1973), pp. 297-303.

Griffin, Leland M., 'A Dramatistic Theory of the Rhetoric of Movements', in William H. Rueckert (ed.), *Critical Responses to Kenneth Burke* (Minneapolis: University of Minnesota Press, 1969).

—'The Rhetorical Structure of the "New Left" Movement, Part I', *Quarterly Journal of Speech* 50.2 (1964), pp. 113-35.

—'The Rhetoric of Historical Movements', in W. Norwood Brigance (ed.), *A History and Criticism of American Public Address*, I (New York: McGraw-Hill, 1943).

Grize, J.B., *De la logique à l'argumentation* (Geneva: Droz, 1982).

Gronbeck, Bruce E., 'Narrative, Enactment, and Television Programming', *Southern Speech Communication Journal* 48.2 (1983), pp. 229-43.

—'The Rhetoric of Political Corruption: Sociolinguistic, Dialectical, and Ceremonial Processes', *Quarterly Journal of Speech* 64.2 (1978), pp. 155-72.

Gross, Alan, and William Keith (eds.), *Rhetorical Hermeneutics: Invention and Interpretation in the Age of Science* (Albany: State University of New York Press, 1997).

Haarscher, G., and L. Ingeber (eds.), *Justice et argumentation: Essais à la mémoire de Chaim Perelman* (Brussels: Editions de l'Universite de Bruxelles, 1986).

Hahn, Dan F., and Ruth M. Gonchar, 'Studying Social Movements: A Rhetorical Methodology', *Speech Teacher* 20.1 (1971), pp. 44-52.

Halliday, M.A.K., 'Functional Diversity in Language as Seen from a Consideration of Mood and Modality in English', *Foundation of Language* 4 (1970), pp. 225-42.

Hamlin, William J., and Harold J. Nichols, 'The Interest Value of Rhetorical Strategies Derived from Kenneth Burke's Pentad', *Western Speech* 32.2 (1973), pp. 97-102.

Hample, Dale, 'A Third Perspective on Argument', *Philosophy & Rhetoric* 18.1 (1985), pp. 1-22.

Hancock, Brenda Robinson, 'Affirmation by Negation in the Women's Liberation Movement', *Quarterly Journal of Speech* 58.3 (1972), pp. 264-71.

Harrell, Jackson, and Will A. Linkugel, 'On Rhetorical Genre: An Organizing Perspective', *Philosophy & Rhetoric* 2.4 (1978), pp. 262-81.

Harris, William V., *Ancient Literacy* (Cambridge, MA: Harvard University Press, 1989).

Hattenhauer, Darryl, 'The Rhetoric of Architecture: A Semiotic Approach', *Communication Quarterly* 32.1 (1984), pp. 71-77.

Hayakawa, S.I., *Language in Thought and Action* (New York: Harcourt, Brace & World, 1964).

Heath, Robert L., 'Kenneth Burke on Form', *Quarterly Journal of Speech* 65.4 (1979), pp. 132-43.

Hengel, Martin, *Jews, Greek and Barbarians: Aspects of the Hellenization of Judaism in the Pre-Christian Period* (Phildelphia: Fortess Press, 1980).

Hensley, Carl, 'Rhetorical Vision and the Persuasion of a Historical Movement: The Disciples of Christ in Nineteenth Century American Culture', *Quarterly Journal of Speech* 61.3 (1975), pp. 250-64.

Hietaranta, P.S., *In Defense of the Possibility of Sentential Tough Complements: An Exercise in Linguistic Argumentation and Methodological Criticism* (Tampere, Finland: University of Tampere, 1984).

Higham, John, 'The Matrix of Specialization', in Oleson and Voss (eds.), *The Organization of Modern Knowledge in Modern America, 1860–1920*, pp. 3-18.

Hikins, James W., and Kenneth S. Zagacki, 'Rhetoric, Objectivism, and the Doctrine of Tolerance', in Ian Angus and Lenore Langsdorf (eds.), *The Critical Turn: Rhetoric and Philosophy and Postmodern Discourse* (Carbondale, IL: Southern Illinois University, 1993), pp. 100-25.

Holland, L. Virginia, *Counterpoint: Kenneth Burke and Aristotle's Theories of Rhetoric* (New York: Philosophical Library, 1959).

Hudson, R.A., *Sociolinguistics* (London: Cambridge University Press, 1980).

Hyde, Michael J., and Craig R. Smith, 'Hermeneutics and Rhetoric: A Seen but Unobserved Relationship', *Quarterly Journal of Speech* 65.3 (1979), pp. 347-63.

Hymes, Dell, *Foundations in Sociolinguistics: An Ethnographic Approach* (Philadelphia: University of Pennsylvania Press, 1974).

—'On Communicative Competence', in J.B. Pride and Janet Holmes (eds.), *Sociolinguistics: Selected Readings* (Philadelphia: University of Pennsylvania Press, 1973).

—'Toward Ethnographies of Communication: The Analysis of Communicative Events', in Pier Paolo Giglioli (ed.), *Language and Social Context* (Baltimore: Penguin Books, 1972), pp. 21-44.

Inglehart, R.F., and M. Woodward, 'Language Conflicts and Political Community', *Comparative Studies in Society and History* 10 (1967), pp. 27-45.

Innis, Harold, *Empire and Communications* (Toronto: University of Toronto Press, 1972).

Ivie, Robert L., 'Literalizing the Metaphor of Soviet Savagery: President Truman's Plain Style', *Southern Speech Communication Journal* 51 (1986), pp. 91-105.

—'Presidential Motives for War', *Quarterly Journal of Speech* 60.3 (1974), pp. 337-45.

Jablonski, Carol J., 'Rhetoric, Paradox, and the Movement for Women's Ordination in the Roman Catholic Church', *Quarterly Journal of Speech* 74.2 (1988), pp. 164-83.

Jabusch, David M., 'The Rhetoric of Civil Rights', *Western Speech* 30.3 (1966), pp. 176-84.

Jackson, Sally, 'Structure of Conversational Argument: Pragmatic Bases for the Enthymeme', *Quarterly Journal of Speech* 66.3 (1980), pp. 251-65.

Jamieson, Kathleen Hall, 'Antecedent Genre as Rhetorical Constraint', *Quarterly Journal of Speech* 61.4 (1975), pp. 406-15.

—*Eloquence in an Electronic Age: The Transformation of Political Speechmaking* (New York: Oxford University Press, 1988).

—'Generic Constraints and the Rhetorical Situation', *Philosophy & Rhetoric* 6.3 (1973), pp. 162-70.

—'Interpretation of Natural Law in the Conflict over *Humanae Vitae*', *Quarterly Journal of Speech* 60.2 (1974), pp. 201-11.

—'The Metaphoric Cluster in the Rhetoric of Pope Paul VI and Edmund G. Brown, Jr.', *Quarterly Journal of Speech* 66.1 (1980), pp. 51-72.

Jamieson, Kathleen Hall, and Karlyn Kohrs Campbell (eds.), *Form and Genre: Shaping Rhetorical Action* (Falls Church, VA: Speech Communication Association, 1978).

Jamieson, Kathleen Hall, and Karlyn Kohrs Campbell, 'Rhetorical Hybrids: Fusions of Generic Elements', *Quarterly Journal of Speech* 68.2 (1982), pp. 146-57.

Jamison, Robert, and J. Dyck (eds.), *Rhetorik—Topik—Argumentation* (Stuttgart: Frommann-Holzboog, 1983).

Japp, Phyllis M., 'Ester or Isaiah? The Abolitionist-Feminist Rhetoric of Angelina Grimke', *Quarterly Journal of Speech* 71.3 (1983), pp. 335-48.

Jarvella, R.J. *et al.*, *Speech, Place and Action: Studies in Deixis and Related Topics* (New York: Wiley, 1982).

Johannesen, Richard L., Rennard Strickland and Ralph T. Eubanks (eds.), *Language Is Sermonic: Richard M. Weaver on the Nature of Rhetoric* (Baton Rouge: Louisiana State University Press, 1970).

Johnstone, Henry W., Jr, *Validity and Rhetoric in Philosophical Argument* (University Park, PA: The Dialogue Press of MAN AND WORLD, 1982).

Jordan, Mark, 'Ancient Philosophical Protreptic and the Problem of Persuasive Genres', *Rhetorica* 4.3 (1986), pp. 309-33.

Journal of Communication 35.4 (1985), pp. 73-171, a dedicated symposium entitled '*Homo Narrans*: Story-Telling in Mass Culture and Everyday Life'.

Karon, Louise, 'Presence in *The New Rhetoric*', *Philosophy & Rhetoric* 9.2 (1976), pp. 96-110.

Kastovsky, D., and A. Szwedek (eds.), *Linguistics across Historical and Geographical Boundaries: In Honour of Jacek Fisiak* (The Hague: Mouton, de Geute, 1986).

Keegan, Terence J., *Interpreting the Bible: A Popular Introduction to Biblical Hermeneutics* (New York: Paulist Press, 1985).

Kirk, John W., 'Kenneth Burke's Dramatistic Criticism Applied to the Theatre', *Southern Speech Communication Journal* 33.3 (1968), pp. 161-77.

Kirkwood, William G., 'Storytelling and Self-Confrontation: Parables as Communication Strategies', *Quarterly Journal of Speech* 69.1 (1983), pp. 58-74.

Klein, W., 'Argumentation und Argument', *Linguistik und Literaturwissenschaft* 38/39 (1980), pp. 9-57.

Klumpp, James F., 'Challenge of Radical Rhetoric: Radicalization at Columbia', *Western Speech* 37.3 (1973), pp. 146-56.

Kneupper, Charles W., 'Burkeian Invention: Two Contrasting Views: Dramatistic Invention: The Pentad as a Heuristic Procedure', *Rhetoric Society Quarterly* 9.2 (1979), pp. 130-36.

—'Dramatism and Argument', in G.W. Ziegelmueller and N. Rhodes (eds.), *Dimensions of Argument: Proceedings of the Second Summer Conference on Argument* (Annandale, VA: Speech Communication Association, 1981), pp. 894-904.

Knox, George, *Critical Moments: Kenneth Burke's Categories and Critiques* (Seattle: University of Washington Press, 1957).

Koch, Susan, and Stanley Deetz, 'Metaphor Analysis of Social Reality in Organizations', *Journal of Applied Communication Research* 9 (1981), pp. 1-15.

Kopperschmidt, J., 'Argumentationstheoretische Anfragen an die Rhetorik: Ein Rekonstruktionsversuch der antiken Rhetorik', in W. Haubrick (ed.), *Perspektiven der Rhetorik LiLi* 43/44 (1982), pp. 44-65.

—'Bibliographie zur Argumentationsforschung, 1966–1978', *Rhetorik* 1 (1980), pp. 153-59.

—'Quintilian DE ARGUMENTIS, Oder: Versuch einer argumentationstheoretischen Rekonstruktion der antiken Rhetorik', *Rhetorik* 2 (1981), pp. 59-74.

Korzybski, Alfred, *Science and Sanity* (Lakewood, CT: Institute of General Semantics, 1933).

Kramer, Cheris, 'Women's Speech: Separate but Unequal?' *Quarterly Journal of Speech* 60.1 (1974), pp. 14-24.

Kristova, Julia, 'Women Can Never Be Defined', in Elaine Marks and Isabelle de Courtivron (eds.), *New French Feminisms: An Anthology* (New York: Schocken Books, 1981), pp. 137-41.

Kroll, Becky Swanson, 'From Small Group to Public View: Mainstreaming the Women's Movement', *Communication Quarterly* 31 (1983), pp. 139-47.

Labov, William, *Language in the Inner City* (Philadelphia: University of Pennsylvania Press, 1973).

—*Sociolinguistic Patterns* (Philadelphia: University of Pennsylvania Press, 1973).

Lakoff, George, and Mark Johnson, *Metaphors We Live By* (Chicago: University of Chicago Press, 1980).

Leathers, Dale G., 'Fundamentalism of the Radical Right', *Southern Speech Communication Journal* 33.4 (1968), pp. 245-58.

Lee, Irving J., 'Four Ways of Looking at a Speech', *Quarterly Journal of Speech* 28.2 (1942), pp. 148-55.

—'General Semantics', *Quarterly Journal of Speech* 38.1 (1952), pp. 1-12.

Leff, Michael, 'I. Topical Invention and Metaphoric Interaction', *Southern Speech Communication Journal* 48.2 (1983), pp. 214-29.

Lewis, William F., 'Telling America's Story: Narrative Form and the Reagan Presidency', *Quarterly Journal of Speech* 73.3 (1987), pp. 280-302.

Lucas, S.E., 'The Schism in Rhetorical Scholarship', in James R. Andrews (ed.), *The Practice of Rhetorical Criticism* (New York: Longman, 1990), pp. 303-23.

Marshman, J.T., 'The Use of Narrative in Speaking', *Southern Speech Bulletin* 4.1 (1938), pp. 1-6.

McGuire, Michael, 'Mythic Rhetoric in Mein Kampf: A Structuralist Critique', *Quarterly Journal of Speech* 63.1 (1977), pp. 1-13.

McKerrow, Raymie, E., 'Critical Rhetoric and the Possibility of the Subject', in Ian Angus and Lenore Langsdorf (eds.), *The Critical Turn: Rhetoric and Philosophy in Postmodern Discourse* (Carbondale, IL: Southern Illinois University Press, 1993), pp. 51-67.

McKnight, Edward V., *The Bible and the Reader: An Introduction to Literary Criticism* (Philadelphia: Fortress Press, 1985).

Medhurst, Martin J., 'The First Amendment vs. Human Rights: A Case Study in Community Sentiment and Argument from Definition', *Western Journal of Speech Communication* 46.1 (1982), pp. 1-19.

Meyer, Michel, 'Argumentation in the Light of a Theory of Questioning', *Philosophy & Rhetoric* 15.2 (1982), pp. 81-103.

—*From Logic to Rhetoric* (Amsterdam: J. Benjamins, 1986).

—*Loqique, langage et argumentation* (Paris: Classiques Hachette, 1982).

—*Meaning and Reading a Philosophical Essay on Language and Literature* (Amsterdam: J. Benjamins, 1983).

Miller, Carolyn R., 'Genre as Social Action', *Quarterly Journal of Speech* 70.2 (1984), pp. 151-67.

Miller, Max, 'Argumentation and Cognition', in M. Hickmann (ed.), *Social and Functional Approaches to Language and Thought* (New York: Academic Press, 1986).

—'Culture and Collective Argumentation', *Argumentation* 1.2 (1987), pp. 127-54.

Minnich, Elisabeth, *Transforming Knowledge* (Philadelphia: Temple University Press, 1990).

Mumby, Dennis K., 'The Political Function of Narrative in Organizations', *Communications Monographs* 54.2 (1987), pp. 113-27.

Naess, Arne, *Communication and Argument: Elements of Applied Semantics* (London: Allen & Unwin, 1966).

Nichols, M.H. (ed.), *A History and Criticism of American Public Address*, III (London: Longmans, Green, 1955).

Ogden, C.K., and I.A. Richards, *The Meaning of Meaning* (London: Routledge & Kegan Paul, 1923).

Oravec, Christine, 'John Muir, Yosemite, and the Sublime Response: A Study in the Rhetoric of Preservationism', *Quarterly Journal of Speech* 67.3 (1981), pp. 245-58.

Ortony, Andrew (ed.), *Metaphor and Thought* (Cambridge: Cambridge University Press, 1979).

Osborn, Michael, 'Archetypal Metaphor in Rhetoric: The Light–Dark Family', *Quarterly Journal of Speech* 53.2 (1967), pp. 115-26.

—'The Evolution of Archetypal Speech in Rhetoric and Poetic', *Quarterly Journal of Speech* 63.4 (1977), pp. 347-63.

—'The Evolution of the Theory of Metaphor in Rhetoric', *Western Journal of Speech Communication* 31.2 (1967), pp. 121-31.

Osborn, Michael, and John Waite Bowers, 'Attitudinal Effects of Selected Types of Concluding Metaphors in Persuasive Speeches', *Speech Monographs* 33.2 (1966), pp. 147-55.

Osborn, Michael, and Douglas Ehninger, 'The Metaphor in Public Address', *Speech Monographs* 29.3 (1962), pp. 223-34.

Osborn, Michael, and Mark Johnson, 'Introduction: Metaphor in the Philosophical Tradition', in Mark Johnson (ed.), *Philosophical Perspectives on Metaphor* (Minneapolis: University of Minnesota Press, 1981), pp. 3-47.

Owen, William Foster, 'Thematic Metaphors in Relational Communication: A Conceptual Framework', *Western Journal of Speech Communication* 49 (1985), pp. 1-13.

Pearse, James A., 'Beyond the Narrational Frame: Interpretation and Metafiction', *Quarterly Journal of Speech* 66.1 (1980), pp. 73-84.

Perry, Steven, 'Rhetorical Functions of the Infestation Metaphor in Hitler's Rhetoric', *Central States Speech Journal* 34 (1983), pp. 229-35.

Philipsen, Gerry, *Speaking Culturally: Explorations in Social Communication* (New York: State University of New York Press, 1992).

Powers, Lloyd D., 'Chicano Rhetoric: Some Basic Concepts', *Southern Speech Communication Journal* 38.4 (1973), pp. 340-46.

Pratt, James, 'An Analysis of Three Crisis Speeches', *Western Speech* 34.3 (1970), pp. 194-202.

Purnell, Sandra E., 'Rhetoric/Rape: Communication as Inducement to Assault', *American Communication Association Bulletin* 16.1 (1976), pp. 20-21.

Rakow, Lana F., 'Gendered Technology, Gendered Practice', *Critical Studies in Mass Communication* 5.1 (1988), pp. 47-70.

Rauh, Gisa (ed.), *Essays on Deixis* (Tübingen: Günter Narr Verlag, 1983).

Reid, Loren, 'The Perils of Rhetorical Criticism', *Quarterly Journal of Speech* 30.4 (1944), pp. 416-22.

Rhodes, Jack, and Sara Newell (eds.), *Proceedings of the Summer Conference on Argumentation* (Annandale, VA: Speech Communication Association, 1980).

Richards, I.A., *The Philosophy of Rhetoric* (New York: Oxford University Press, 1936).

Ringer, Fritz K., 'The German Academic Community', in Alexandra Oleson and John Voss (eds.), *The Organization of Knowledge in Modern America, 1860–1920* (Baltimore: The Johns Hopkins University Press, 1976), pp. 409-27.

Rogers, Richard S., 'The Rhetoric of Militant Deism', *Quarterly Journal of Speech* 54.3 (1968), pp. 247-51.

Rosenfield, Lawrence W., 'A Case Study in Speech Criticism: The Nixon-Truman Analog', *Speech Monographs* 35.4 (1968), pp. 435-50.

Rowland, Robert C., 'Narrative: Made of Discourse or Paradigm?', *Communication Monographs* 54.3 (1987), pp. 264-75.

—'On Defining Argument', *Philosophy & Rhetoric* 20.2 (1987), pp. 139-59.

Rueckert, William, *Critical Responses to Kenneth Burke* (Minneapolis: University of Minnesota Press, 1969).

—*Kenneth Burke and the Drama of Human Relations* (Minneapolis: University of Minnesota Press, 1963).

Rushing, Janice Hooker, 'Mythic Evolution of "The New Frontier" in Mass Mediated Rhetoric', *Critical Studies in Mass Communication* 3 (1986), pp. 265-96.

—'Ronald Reagan's "Star Wars" Address: Mythic Containment of Technical Reasoning', *Quarterly Journal of Speech* 72.4 (1968), pp. 415-33.

Ryan, Halford Ross (ed.), *Oratorical Encounters: Selected Studies and Sources of Twentieth-Century Political Accusations and Apologies* (New York: Greenwood, 1988).

Sanders, Robert E., 'Utterances, Actions, and Rhetorical Inquiry', *Philosophy & Rhetoric* 9.2 (1978), pp. 114-33.

Savigny, Eike von, *Argumentation in der Literaturwissenschaft: Wissenschaftstheoretische Untersuchungen zu Lyrikinterpretationen* (Munich: Beck, 1976).

Schwab, Gabriel, 'Seduced by Witches: Nathaniel Hawthorne's *The Scarlet Letter* in the Context of New England Witchcraft Fictions', in Dianne Hunter (ed.), *Seduction and Theory: Readings of Gender, Representation and Rhetoric* (Urbana: University of Illinois Press, 1989), pp. 170-91.

Scott, Robert L., 'Argument as a Critical Art: Re-Forming Understanding', *Argumentation* 1.1 (1987), pp. 57-71.

—'Narrative Theory and Communication Research', *Quarterly Journal of Speech* 70.2 (1984), pp. 197-221.

—'The Tacit Dimension and Rhetoric', *Pre/Text: An Inter-Disciplinary Journal of Rhetoric* 2 (1981), pp. 115-26.

—'On Viewing Rhetoric as Epistemic', *Central States Speech Journal* 18.1 (1967), pp. 8-16.

—'On Viewing Rhetoric as Epistemic: Ten Years Later', *Central States Speech Journal* 27.4 (1976), pp. 258-66.

Scott, Robert L., and Wayne Brockriede, *The Rhetoric of Black Power* (New York: Harper & Row, 1969).

Scott, Robert L., and Donald K. Smith, 'The Rhetoric of Confrontation', *Quarterly Journal of Speech* 55.1 (1969), pp. 1-8.

Scult, Allen, 'The Relationship between Rhetoric and Hermeneutics Reconsidered', *Central States Speech Journal* 34.4 (1983), pp. 221-28.

Searle, John R., *Speech Acts: An Essay in the Philosophy of Language* (Cambridge: Cambridge University Press, 1976).

Sharf, Barbara F., 'A Rhetorical Analysis of Leadership Emergence in Small Groups', *Communication Monographs* 25.2 (1978), pp. 156-72.

Shields, Donald C., Laurinda Porter *et al.*, 'The Carter Persona: An Empirical Analysis of the Rhetorical Visions of Campaign '76', *Quarterly Journal of Speech* 63.3 (1977), pp. 258-73.

Shields, Donald C., 'Foreign Policy Communication Dramas: How Mediated Rhetoric Played in Peoria in Campaign '76', *Quarterly Journal of Speech* 63.3 (1977), pp. 274-89.

—'The White House Transcripts: Group Fantasy Events Concerning the Mass Media', *Central States Speech Journal* 27.4 (1974), pp. 272-79.

Simons, Herbert W., 'Toward a New Rhetoric', *Pennsylvania Speech Annual* 26.1 (1967), pp. 7-20.

—'Genres, Rules, and Collective Rhetorics: Applying the Requirements-Problems-Strategies Approach', *Communication Quarterly* 30.3 (1982), pp. 181-88.

Simons, Herbert W. (ed.), *Rhetoric in the Human Sciences* (London: Sage, 1989).

—*The Rhetorical Turn: Invention and Persuasion in the Conduct of Inquiry* (Chicago: University of Chicago Press, 1990).

Simons, Herbert W., and Aram A. Aghazarian (eds.), *Form, Genre, and the Study of Political Discourse* (Columbia: University of South Carolina Press, 1986).

Simons, Herbert W., James W. Chesebro, and C. Jack Orr, 'A Movement Perspective on the 1972 Presidential Campaign', *Quarterly Journal of Speech* 59.2 (1973), pp. 168-79.

—'Requirements, Problems, and Strategies: A Theory of Persuasion for Social Movements', *Quarterly Journal of Speech* 56.1 (1970).

Smith, Arthur L., *The Rhetoric of Black Revolution* (Boston: Allyn & Bacon, 1969).

Smith, Larry David, 'Narrative Styles in Network Coverage of the 1984 Nominating Conventions', *Western Journal of Speech Communication* 52.1 (1988), pp. 63-74.

Smith, Ralph R., and Russel R. Windes, 'The Innovational Movement: A Rhetorical Theory', *Quarterly Journal of Speech* 61.2 (1975), pp. 140-53.

Solomon, Martha, 'The Rhetoric of STOP ERA: Fatalistic Reaffirmation', *Southern Speech Communication Journal* 44.1 (1978), pp. 42-59.

—'Redemptive Rhetoric: The Continuity Motif in the Rhetoric of the Right to Life', *Central States Speech Journal* 31.1 (1980), pp. 52-62.

Sommerville, John, 'Language and the Cold War', *A Review of General Semantics* 23.4 (1966), pp. 425-34.

Spitzack, Carole J., 'Re-Thinking the Relationship between Power, Expression, and Research Practices', in Carol Ann Valentine and Nancy Hoar (eds.), *Women and Communicative Power: Theory, Research, and Practice* (Allandale, VA: Speech Communication Association), pp. 144-52.

Spitzack, Carol J., and Kathryn Carter, 'Women in Communication Studies: A Typology for Revision', *Quarterly Journal of Speech* 73.4 (1987), pp. 401-23.

Steeves, H. Leslie, 'Feminist Theories and Media Studies', *Critical Studies in Mass Communication* 4.2 (1987), pp. 95-135.

Stelzner, Herman G., 'Analysis by Metaphor', *Quarterly Journal of Speech* 51.1 (1965), pp. 52-61.

Strine, Mary, and Michael Pacnowsky, 'How to Read Interpretive Accounts of Organizational Life: Narrative Bases of Textual Authority', *Southern Speech Communication Journal* 50.3 (1985), pp. 283-97.

Swearingen, Jan, *Rhetoric and Irony: Western Literacy and Western Lies* (New York: Oxford University Press, 1991).

Taylor, Jacqueline, 'Documenting Performance Knowledge: Two Narrative Techniques in Grace Paley's Fiction', *Southern Speech Communication Journal* 53.1 (1987), pp. 65-79.

Thomas, David A. (ed.), *Argumentation as a Way of Knowing* (Annandale, VA: Speech Communication Association, 1980).

Thompkins, Phillip K., 'Kenneth Burke and the Inherent Characteristics of Formal Organizations: A Field Study', *Speech Monographs* 42.2 (1975), pp. 135-42.

Thonssen, L., and A.C. Baird, *Speech Criticism* (New York: Ronald, 1948).

Tirkkonen-Condit, S., *Argumentative Text Structure and Translation* (Jyväskylä: University of Jyväskylä, 1985).

Vartabedian, Robert A., 'Nixon's Vietnam Rhetoric: A Case Study of Apologia as Generic Paradox', *Southern States Communication Journal* 50.4 (1985), pp. 366-81.

Verene, Donald Phillip, 'Philosophy, Argument, and Narration', *Philosophy & Rhetoric* 22.2 (1989), pp. 141-44.

Vitanza, Victor, 'An Open Letter to my "Colligs": On Paraethics, Pararhetorics, and The Hysterial Turn', *Pre/Text* 11.3–4 (1990), pp. 238-87.

—*Negation, Subjectivity and the History of Rhetoric* (Albany: State University of New York Press, 1997).

—'Selections from "Neo-Triplicity": A Post(modern)-script, or Excursus, or Re/Inter/ View, May 1990', *Pre/Text* 11.3–4 (1990), pp. 269-70.

Wallace, Karl R., *Understanding Discourse: The Speech Act and Rhetorical Action* (Baton Rouge: Louisiana State University Press, 1970).

Walton, Douglas N., *Arguer's Position: A Pragmatic Study of Ad Hominem Attack, Criticism, Refutation, and Fallacy* (Westport, CT: Greenwood Press, 1985).

—*Topical Relevance in Argumentation* (Amsterdam: J. Benjamins, 1982).

Wander, Philip C., 'The Savage Child: The Image of the Negro in the Pro-Slavery Movement', *Southern Speech Communication Journal* 37.4 (1972), pp. 335-60.

Ware, B.L., and Wil A. Linkugel, 'They Spoke in Defense of Themselves: On the Generic Criticism of Apologia', *Quarterly Journal of Speech* 59.3 (1973), pp. 278-91.

Warnick, Barbara, 'The Narrative Paradigm: Another Story', *Quarterly Journal of Speech* 73.2 (1987), pp. 172-82.

Wartensleben, G. von, *Begriff der griechischen Chreia und Beiträge zur Geschichte ihrer Form* (Heidelberg, 1901).

Waterman, Leroy, 'Biblical Studies in a New Setting', *Journal of Biblical Literature* 66 (1947), pp. 1-14.

Weaver, Richard, *The Ethics of Rhetoric* (Chicago: Henry Regnery, 1965).

—*Ideas Have Consequences* (Chicago: University of Chicago Press, 1948).

—'Language is Sermonic', in Roger E. Nebergall (ed.), *Dimensions of Rhetorical Scholarship* (Norman: University of Oklahoma Department of Speech, 1963).

Welch, Kathleen, *The Contemporary Reception of Classical Rhetoric: Appropriations of Ancient Discourse* (Hillsdale, NJ: Lawrence Erlbaum, 1990).

Wenzel, Joseph W., 'The Rhetorical View of Argumentation: Exploring a Paradigm', *Argumentation* 1.1 (1987), pp. 73-88.

Wilder, Amos, *Theopoetic: Theology and the Religious Imagination* (Philadelphia: Fortress Press, 1976).

Wilkins, A.S., *Roman Education* (Cambridge: Cambridge University Press, 1905).

Willard, Charles A., 'A Reformulation of the Concept of Argument: The Constructivist/Interactionist Foundations of a Sociology of Argument', *Journal of the American Forensic Association* 14 (1978).

—*Argumentation and the Social Grounds of Knowledge* (Montgomery, AL: University of Alabama Press, 1983).

Wilson, Barrie A., *The Anatomy of Argument* (Lanham, MD: University Press of America, 1980).

Wood, Julia T., and Charles Conrad, 'Paradox in the Experiences of Professional Women', *Western Speech* 47.4 (1983), pp. 305-22.

Yearly, Steven, 'Argumentation, Epistemology and the Sociology of Language', *Argumentation* 2.4 (1988), pp. 351-67.

—'Textual Persuasion: The Role of Social Accounting in the Construction of Scientific Arguments', *Philosophy of Social Sciences* 11 (1981), pp. 409-35.

Yoakam, Doris G., 'Pioneer Women Orators of America', *Quarterly Journal of Speech* 23.2 (1937), pp. 251-59.

Ziegelmueller, George, and Jack Rhodes (eds.), *Dimensions of Argument: Proceedings of the Second Summer Conference on Argumentation* (Annandale, VA: Speech Communication Association, 1981).

Zortman, Bruce T., 'The Theatre of Ideology in Nazi Germany', *Quarterly Journal of Speech* 57.2 (1979), pp. 153-61.

Biblical Studies and Rhetoric: Old Testament
(Selected Materials)

Allen, L., 'Ezekiel 24.3–14: A Rhetorical Perspective', *Catholic Biblical Quarterly* 49 (1987), pp. 404-14.

—'The Value of Rhetorical Criticism in Psalm 69', *Journal of Biblical Literature* 105.4 (1986), pp. 577-98.

Berlin, Adele, 'Grammatical Aspects of Biblical Parallelism', *Hebrew Union College Annual* 50 (1979), pp. 17-43.

Boomershine, Thomas, 'The Structure of Narrative Rhetoric in Genesis 2–3', *Semeia* 18 (1980), pp. 113-29.

Bünker, Michael, 'Die rhetorische Disposition der Eleazarreden', *Kairos* 23.1–2 (1981), pp. 100-107.

Ceresko, Anthony R., 'A Rhetorical Analysis of David's "Boast" (1 Samuel 17.34–37): Some Reflections of Method', *Catholic Biblical Quarterly* 47 (1985), pp. 58-74.

Clifford, Richard J., 'The Function of Idol Passages in Second Isaiah', *Catholic Biblical Quarterly* 42 (1980), pp. 450-64.

—'Rhetorical Criticism in the Exegesis of Hebrew Poetry', in *Society of Biblical Literature Seminar Papers* (Atlanta: Scholars Press, 1980).

DeRoche, Michael, 'Structure, Rhetoric and Meaning in Hosea 4.4–10', *Vetus Testamentum* 33 (1983), pp. 185-98.

Dion, Paul, 'Strophic Boundaries and Rhetorical Structure in Psalm 31', *Eglise Th* 18.2 (1987), pp. 183-92.

Durlessor, James A., 'The Sinking of the Ship of Tyre (Ezek. 27): A Study of Rhetoric in Hebrew Allegory', *Proceedings* 7 (1987), pp. 72-93.

Fisch, Harold, *Poetry with a Purpose: Biblical Poetics and Interpretation* (Bloomington: Indiana University Press, 1988).

Fox, Michael V., 'Job 38 and God's Rhetoric', *Semeia* 19 (1981), pp. 53-61.

—'The Rhetoric of Ezekiel's Vision of the Valley of the Bones', *Hebrew Union College Annual* 51 (1980), pp. 1-15.

Gitay, Yehoshua, 'A Study of Amos' Art of Speech: A Rhetorical Analysis of Amos 3.1–15', *Catholic Biblical Quarterly* 42 (1980), pp. 293-309.

—'The Effectiveness of Isaiah's Speech', *Jewish Quarterly Review* 75.2 (1984), pp. 162-72.

Greenstein, Edward, 'Mixing Memory and Design: Reading Psalm 78', *Prooftexts* 10 (1990), pp. 197-218.

Isebell, Charles D., and Michael Jackson, 'Rhetorical Criticism and Jeremiah 7.1–8.3', *Vetus Testamentum* 30 (1980), pp. 20-26.

Koops, Robert, 'Rhetorical Questions and Implied Meaning in the Book of Job', *Bible Translator* 39 (1988), pp. 415-23.

Kselman, John S., 'Design and Structure in Hebrew Poetry', *SBL Seminar Papers*, 1980.

Kuntz, J. Kenneth, 'King Triumphant: A Rhetorical Study of Psalms 20 and 21', *Hebrew Annual Review* 10 (1987), pp. 157-76.

—'Psalm 18: A Rhetorical-Critical Analysis', *Journal for the Study of the Old Testament* 26 (1983), pp. 3-31.

Lenchak, T.A., *'Choose Life!' A Rhetorical-Critical Investigation of Deuteronomy 28,69–30,20* (Analecta Biblica, 29; Rome: Pontifical Biblical Institute, 1993).

Lewin, Ellen D., 'Arguing for Authority: A Rhetorical Study of Jeremiah 1.4–19 and 20.7–18', *Journal for the Study of the Old Testament* 32 (1985), pp. 105-19.

Lundbom, Jack R., 'The Double Curse in Jeremiah 20.14–18', *Journal of Biblical Literature* 104.4 (1985), pp. 589-600.

Magonet, Jonathan, 'The Rhetoric of God: Exodus 6.2–8', *Journal for the Study of the Old Testament* 27 (1983), pp. 56-67.

Mazor, Yair, 'Genesis 32: The Ideological Rhetoric and the Psychological Composition', *Biblica* 65.1 (1986), pp. 81-88.

—'Hosea 5.1–3: Between Compositional Rhetoric and Rhetorical Composition', *Journal for the Study of the Old Testament* 45 (1989), pp. 115-26.

Mintz, Alan, 'The Rhetoric of Lamentations and the Representation of Catastrophe', *Prooftexts* 2 (1982), pp. 1-17.

Mounin, Georges, 'Hebraic Rhetoric and Faithful Translation', *Bible Translator* 30.3 (1979), pp. 336-40.

Murray, D. F., 'The Rhetoric of Disputation: Re-examination of a Prophetic Genre', *Journal for the Study of the Old Testament* 38 (1987), pp. 95-121.

Ogden, Graham S., 'Psalm 60: Its Rhetoric, Form and Function', *Journal for the Study of the Old Testament* 31 (1985), pp. 83-94.

Paul, Shalom M., 'Amos 3.3–8: The Irresistible Sequence of Cause and Effect', *Hebrew Annual Review* 7 (1983), pp. 203-20.

Raabe, Paul R., 'The Effect of Repetition in the Suffering Servant Song [Isa 52.13–53.12]', *Journal of Biblical Literature* 103 (1984), pp. 77-81.

Smith, Jonathan Z., 'To Take Place: Jerusalem as a Focus of Ritual' (series of lectures given at Brown University, Providence, Rhode Island, March 1985).

Smith, Mark, 'Setting and Rhetoric in Psalm 23', *Journal for the Study of the Old Testament* 41 (1988), pp. 61-66.

Walsh, Jerome T., 'Jonah 2.3–10: A Rhetorical Critical Study', *Biblica* 2 (1982), pp. 219-29.

Willis, John T., 'Dialogue between Prophet and Audience as a Rhetorical Device in the Book of Jeremiah', *Journal for the Study of the Old Testament* 33 (1985), pp. 63-82.

Biblical Studies and Rhetoric: New Testament
(Selected Materials)

Aletti, Jean Noel, 'La presence d'un modèle rhetorique en Romains: Son role et son importance', *Biblica* 71.1 (1990), pp. 1-24.

—'Romans 1.18–3.20—incohérence ou cohérence de l'argumentation paulinienne?', *Biblica* 69.1 (1988), pp. 47-62.

Barrett, Charles Kingsley, 'Galatians as an "Apologetic" Letter', *Interpretation* 34 (1980), pp. 414-17.

Betz, Hans Dieter, *2 Corinthians 8 and 9* (Philadelphia: Fortress Press, 1985).

—'In Defense of the Spirit: Paul's Letter to the Galatians as a Document of Early Christian Apologetics', in Elisabeth Schüssler Fiorenza, *Aspects of Religious Propaganda in Judaism and Early Christianity* (Notre Dame, IN: University of Notre Dame Press, 1976).

336 *Academic Constraints in Rhetorical Criticism*

—'The Literary Composition and Function of Paul's Letter to the Galatians', *New Testament Studies* 21 (1975), pp. 353-79.

—'The Problem of Rhetoric and Theology According to the Apostle Paul', in A. Vanhoye (ed.), *L'Apôtre Paul: Personnalité, style et conception du ministère* (Leuven: Leuven University Press, 1986).

Black, David Alan, 'Hebrews 1.1–4: A Study in Discourse Analysis', *Western Theology Journal* 49 (1987), pp. 175-94.

—'The Pauline Love Command: Structure, Style and Ethics in Romans 12.9–21', *Filologia Neotestamentaria* 2 (1989), pp. 3-22.

Brodie, Thomas L., 'The Departure for Jerusalem (Luke 9.51–56) as a Rhetorical Imitation of Elijah's Departure for the Jordan (2 Kings 1.1–2.6)', *Biblica* 70.1 (1989), pp. 96-109.

—'Luke 7.36–50 as an Internalization of 2 Kings 4.1–37: A Study in Luke's Use of Rhetorical Imitation', *Biblica* 64.4 (1983), pp. 457-85.

Bultmann, Rudolph, *History of the Synoptic Tradition* (trans. J. Marsh; New York: Harper & Row, 1963).

Butts, James R., 'The Chreia in the Synoptic Gospels', *Biblical Theology Bulletin* 16.4 (1986), pp. 132-38.

Cameron, A., *Christianity and the Rhetoric of Empire: The Development of Christian Discourse* (Berkeley: University of California Press, 1994).

Chance, Bradley, 'Paul's Apology to the Corinthians', *Perspectives in Religious Studies* 9 (1982), pp. 145-55.

Church, F. Forrester, 'Rhetorical Structure and Design in Paul's Letter to Philemon', *Harvard Theological Review* 71 (1978), pp. 17-33.

Cosby, Michael, 'The Rhetorical Composition of Hebrews 11', *Journal of Biblical Literature* 107 (1988), pp. 257-73.

Cosgrove, Charles H., 'Arguing Like a Mere Human Being: Galatians 3.15–18 in Rhetorical Perspective', *New Testament Studies* 34.4 (1988), pp. 536-49.

Donelson, Lewis R., *Pseudepigraphy and Ethical Argument in the Pastoral Epistles* (Tübingen: J.C.B. Mohr, 1986).

Droge, Arthur J., 'Call Stories in Greek Biography and the Gospels', *Society of Biblical Literature Seminar Papers* 22 (Atlanta: Scholars Press, 1983), pp. 245-57.

Elliott, J.H., *A Home for the Homeless* (Philadelphia: Fortress Press, 1981).

Engberg-Pedersen, Troel, '1 Corinthians 11.16 and the Character of Pauline Exhortation' (unpublished paper read at the Society of Biblical Literature 1989 Annual Meeting, Anaham, CA).

Farrar, F.W., 'The Rhetoric of St. Paul', *The Expositor* 10 (1879), pp. 1-27.

Flore, B., 'Romans 9–11 and Classical Forensic Rhetoric', *Proceedings* 8 (1988), pp. 17-126.

Forbes, Christopher, 'Comparison, Self-Praise and Irony: Paul's Boasting and the Conventions of Hellenistic Rhetoric', *New Testament Studies* 32 (1986), pp. 1-30.

Funk, Robert, *The Five Gospels: The Search for the Authentic Words of Jesus* (Sonoma, CA: Polebridge Press, New York: Macmillan, 1993).

Hall, Robert G., 'Paul the Lawyer on Law', *Journal of Law and Religion* 3.2 (1985), pp. 331-97.

—'The Rhetorical Outline for Galatians: A Reconsideration', *Journal of Biblical Literature* 106 (1987), pp. 227-87.

Harnisch, Wolfgang, 'Einübung des neuen Seins: Paulische Paränese am Beispiel des Galäterbriefes', *Zeitschrift für Theologie und Kirche* 84.3 (1987), pp. 279-96.

Heiny, Stephen, 'The Motive for Metaphor: 2 Cor 2.14–4.6', *Society of Biblical Literature Seminar Papers* (Atlanta: Scholars Press, 1987).

Hester, James D., 'The Rhetorical Structure of Galatians 1: 11–2.14', *Journal of Biblical Literature* 103 (1984), pp. 223-33.

Hübner, Hans, 'Der Galäterbrief und das Verhältnis von antiker Rhetorik und Epistolographie', *Theologische Literaturzeitung* 109.4 (1984), pp. 241-50.

Hughes, Frank W., *Early Christian Rhetoric and 2 Thessalonians (Journal for the Study of the New Testament*, Supplement Series, 30; Sheffield: Almond Press, 1987).

Jewett, R., 'Following the Argument of Romans', *Word and World* 6.4 (1986), pp. 382-89.

—*The Thessalonian Correspondence: Pauline Rhetoric and Millenarian Piety* (Philadelphia: Fortress Press, 1986).

Johanson, B.C., *To All the Brethren: A Text-Linguistic and Rhetorical Approach to 1 Thessalonians* (Lund: Almquist & Wiksell, 1987).

Johnson, Luke Timothy, 'James 3.13–4.10 and the *topos peri phthamnou*', *Novum Testamentum* 25 (1983), pp. 327-47.

Kilgallen, John J., 'Acts 13.38–39: Culmination of Paul's Speech in Pisidia', *Biblica* 69.4 (1988), pp. 480-506.

—'The Function of Stephen's Speech (Acts 7.2–53)', *Biblica* 70.2 (1989), pp. 173-93.

Kirby, John T., 'The Rhetorical Situations of Revelation 1–3', *New Testament Studies* 34.2 (1988), pp. 197-207.

—'The Syntax of Romans 5.12: A Rhetorical Approach', *New Testament Studies* 33.2 (1987), pp. 283-86.

Klostermann, Erich, 'Zur Apologie des Paulus, Galater 1, 10–2,21', in *Gottes in der Orient: Festschrift für Otto Eissfeldt zu seinem 70. Geburtstag* (Berlin: Evangelische Verlagsanstalt, 1959).

Kruz, William S., 'Hellenistic Rhetoric in the Christological Proof of Luke–Acts', *Catholic Biblical Quarterly* 42 (1980), pp. 171-95.

Lampe, Peter, 'Theological Wisdom and the "Word about the Cross": The Rhetorical Scheme of 1 Cor 1– 4', *Interpretation* 44.2 (1990), pp. 117-31.

Lim, Timothy, ' "Not in persuasive words of wisdom, but in the demonstration of the Spirit and power" (1 Cor 2.1–5)', *Novum Testamentum* 29 (1987), pp. 137-49.

Lindars, Barnabas, 'The Rhetorical Structure of Hebrews', *New Testament Studies* 35.3 (1989), pp. 382-406.

Malherbe, Abraham, 'Exhortation in First Thessalonians', *Novum Testamentum* 25 (1983), pp. 238-56.

Martin, Clarice, 'A Chamberlain's Journey', *Semeia* 47 (1989), pp. 105-35.

Martin, Dale, 'Tongues of Angels and Other Status Indicators' (unpublished paper read at the Society of Biblical Literature 1989 Annual Meeting, Anahem, CA).

McDonald, James, 'Paul and the Preaching Ministry: A Reconsideration of 2 Cor 2.14–17 in its Context', *Journal for the Study of the New Testament* 17 (1983), pp. 35-50.

Mitchell, Margaret, 'Factionalism in 1 Corinthians 10' (unpublished paper read at the Society of Biblical Literature 1989 Annual Meeting, Anahem, CA).

Myers, Ched, *Binding the Strong Man* (Maryknoll, NY: Orbis Books, 1988).

Patrick, Dale, and Allen Scult, *Rhetoric and Biblical Interpretation* (Bible and Literature Series, 26: Sheffield: Almond Press, 1990).

Patte, Daniel, 'Kingdom and Children: Aphorism, Chreia, Structure', *Semeia* 29 (1983), pp. 1-130.

Plank, Karl A., *Paul and the Irony of Affliction* (Atlanta: Scholars Press, 1987).

Richard, Earl, 'Polemics, Old Testament, and Theology: A Study of 2 Corinthians 3.1–4.6', *Revue Biblique* 2 (1982), pp. 219-29.

Rudolph, Kurt, 'Early Christianity as a Religious-Historical Phenomenon', in Birger A. Pearson (ed.), *The Future of Early Christianity* (Minneapolis: Fortress Press, 1991).

Scott, Bernard Brandon, *Hear Then the Parable* (Minneapolis: Fortress Press, 1989).

Smit, Joop, 'The Letter of Paul to the Galatians: A Deliberative Speech', *New Testament Studies* 35.1 (1989), pp. 1-26.

Spencer, Aida Besançon, 'The Wise Fool (and the Foolish Wise): A Study of Irony in Paul (2 Cor 11.16–12.13)', *Novum Testamentum* 23 (1981), pp. 349-60.

Standaert, Benoit, 'La rhetorique antique et l'épître aux galates', *Foi Vie* 84.5 (1985), pp. 33-40.

Stowers, Stanley K., *The Diatribe and Paul's Letter to the Romans* (Chico, CA: Scholars Press, 1981).

—'Paul's Dialogue with a Fellow Jew in Romans 3.1–9', *Catholic Biblical Quarterly* 46 (1984), pp. 707-22.

Tannehill, Robert C., 'The Composition of Acts 3–5: Narrative Development and Echo Effect', *Society of Biblical Literature Seminar Papers* (Atlanta: Scholars Press, 1984).

Toit, A.B. du, 'Persuasion in Romans 1.1–17', *Biblische Zeitschrift* 33.2 (1989), pp. 192-209.

Vouga, François, 'La construction de l'histoire en Galates 3–4', *Zeitschrift der Neutestamentlichen Wissenschaft* 75.3–4 (1984), pp. 259-69.

Watson, D.F., '1 Corinthians 10.23–11.1 in the Light of Greco-Roman Rhetoric: The Role of Rhetorical Questions', *Journal of Biblical Literature* 108 (1989), pp. 301-18.

—'1 John 2.12–14 as Distributio, Conduplicatio, and Expolitio: A Rhetorical Understanding', *Journal for the Study of the New Testament* 35 (1989), pp. 97-110.

—*Invention, Arrangement, and Style: Rhetorical Criticism of Jude and 2 Peter* (Society of Biblical Literature Dissertation Series, 104; Atlanta: Scholars Press, 1988).

—'A Rhetorical Analysis of 2 John According to Greco-Roman Convention', *New Testament Studies* 35.1 (1989), pp. 104-130.

—'A Rhetorical Analysis of 3 John: A Study in Epistolary Rhetoric', *Catholic Biblical Quarterly* 51 (1989), pp. 478-501.

—'A Rhetorical Analysis of Philippians and its Implications for the Unity Question', *Novum Testamentum* 30 (1988), pp. 57-88.

Watt, J.G. van der, 'Colossians 1.3–12 Considered as an Exordium', *Journal of Theology for South Africa* 57 (1986), pp. 32-42.

Williams, James, 'Paraenesis, Excess, and Ethics', *Semeia* 50 (1990), pp. 163-87.

Wolthuis, Thomas R., 'Jude and the Rhetorician: A Dialogue on the Rhetorical Nature of the Epistle of Jude', *Calvin Theological Journal* 24 (1989), pp. 126-34.

Zweck, D., 'The Exordium of the Areopagus Speech, Acts 17: 22,23', *New Testament Studies* 35.1 (1989), pp. 94-103.

Rhetoric and the West: Medieval through Nineteenth Century (Selected Materials)

Alvarez, Fabio Chávez, '*Die brennende Vernunft': Studien zur Semantik der 'rationalitas' bei Hildegard von Bingen* (Mystik in Geschichte und Gegenwart, 1: Christliche Mystik, 8; Stuttgart: Frommann-Holzboog, 1991).

Ashworth, E.J., *The Tradition of Medieval Logic and Speculative Grammar, from Anselm to the End of the Seventeenth Century: A Bibliography from 1836 Onwards* (Leiden: E.J. Brill, 1978).

Auerbach, Erich, *Literatursprache und Publikum in der lateinischen Spätantike und im Mittelalter* (Bern: Francke, 1958).

Baldwin, Charles S., *Medieval Rhetoric and Poetic* (New York: Macmillan, 1928).

Barner, Wilfried, *Barockrhetorik: Untersuchungen zu ihren geschichtlichen Grundlagen* (Tübingen: Max Niemeyer, 1970).

Blair, Carole, 'Nietzsche's Lecture Notes on Rhetoric: a Translation', *Philosophy & Rhetoric* 16 (1983), pp. 94-129.

Bolgiani, Franco (ed.), *Mistica e Retorica: Studi Raccolti a Cura* (Florence: Olschki, 1977).

Bonner, Stanley, *Education in Ancient Rome* (Berkeley: University of California, 1977).

—*Roman Declamation in Late Republic and Early Empire* (Berkeley: University of California Press, 1949).

Breisach, E. (ed.), *Classical Rhetoric and Medieval Historiography* (Kalamazoo, MI: Medieval Institute Publications, Western Michigan University, 1985).

Briggs, John C., *Francis Bacon and the Rhetoric of Nature* (Cambridge, MA: Harvard University Press, 1989).

Camargo, Martin, 'Rhetoric', in D.L. Wagner (ed.), *The Seven Liberal Arts in the Middle Ages* (Bloomington: Indiana University Press, 1983), pp. 96-124.

Chevrier, G., 'Sur l'art de l'argumentation chez quelques romanistes médiévaux au XIIe siècle et au XIIIe siècle', *Archives de Philosophie du Droit* (1966), pp. 115-48.

Clark, Donald Lemen, *Rhetoric in Greco-Roman Education* (Morningside Heights, NY: Columbia University Press, 1957).

—'The Rise and Fall of Progymnasmata in Sixteenth and Seventeenth Century Grammar Schools', *Speech Monographs* 19.4 (1952), pp. 258-63.

Coletti, Vittorio, *L'Eloquence de la Chaire: Victoires et défaites du Latin entre moyen age et renaissance* (trans. Silvano Serventi; Paris: Cerf, 1987).

Conley, Thomas, *Rhetoric in the European Tradition* (repr.; Chicago: University of Chicago Press, 1994).

Dockhorn, Klaus, 'Luthers Glaubensbegriff und die Rhetorik: Zu Gerhard Ebelings Buch "Einführung in theologische Sprachlehre"', *Linguistica Biblica* 21/22 (1973), pp. 19-39.

—*Macht und Wirkung der Rhetorik: Vier Aufsätze zur Ideengeschichte der Vormoderne* (Bad Homburg: Gehlen, 1968).

Dunn, Walter Kevin, ' "To the Gentle Reader": Prefatory Rhetoric in the Renaissance' (PhD dissertation, New Haven: Yale University, 1988).

Dyck, Joachim, 'Überlegungen zur Rhetorik des 18. Jahrhunderts und ihrer Quellenlage', in Gert Ueding (ed.), *Rhetorik zwischen den Wissenschaften: Geschichte, System,*

Praxis als Probleme des 'Historischen Wörterbuchs der Rhetorik' (Tübingen: Max Niemeyer, 1991), pp. 99-101.

Enders, Jody M. 'The Rhetoric of Protestantism: Book 1 of Agrippa d'Aubigne's Les Tragiques', *Rhetorica* 3.4 (1985), pp. 285-94.

Evans, G.R., *The Language and Logic of the Bible: The Earlier Middle Ages* (Cambridge: Cambridge University Press, 1984).

—*The Language and Logic of the Bible: The Road to Reformation* (Cambridge: Cambridge University Press, 1985).

—*Old Arts and New Theology: The Beginnings of Theology as an Academic Discipline* (Oxford: Clarendon Press, 1980).

Farenga, Vincent, 'Periphrasis on the Origin of Rhetoric', *Modern Langauge Notes* 94 (1979), pp. 1033-55.

Fredborg, Karin M. (ed.), *The Latin Rhetorical Commentaries by Thierry of Chartres* (Studies and Texts, 84; Leiden: E.J. Brill, 1988).

Gilman, Sander L., Carol Blair and David J. Parent (eds.), *Friedrich Nietzsche on Rhetoric and Language* (New York: Oxford University Press, 1989).

Grassi, Ernesto, 'G.B. Vico und das Problem des modernen Denkens', *Zeitschrift für philosophische Forschung* 22.4 (1968), pp. 491-509.

Horner, W.R. (ed.), *Historical Rhetoric: An Annotated Bibliography of Selected Sources in English* (Boston: Hall, 1980).

Howell, Wilbur S., *Eighteenth-Century British Logic and Rhetoric* (Princeton, NJ: Princeton University Press, 1971).

—*Logic and Rhetoric in England, 1500-1700* (New York: Russell & Russell, 1961).

—'Sources of the Elocutionary Movement in England: 1700-1748', *Quarterly Journal of Speech* 45.1 (1959), pp. 1-18.

Jäger, Georg, 'Der Deutschunterricht auf Gymnasien 1780-1850', *Deutsche Vierteljahrsschrift für Literaturwissenschaft und Geistesgeschichte* 47.1 (1973), pp. 120-47.

Kennedy, George A., *Classical Rhetoric and its Christian and Secular Tradition from Ancient to Modern Times* (Chapel Hill: University of North Carolina Press, 1980).

—*Greek Rhetoric under the Christian Emperors* (Princeton, NJ: Princeton University Press, 1983).

Koch, J. (ed.), *Artes Liberales: Von der antiken Bildung zur Wissenschaft des Mittelalters* (Studien und Texte zur Geistesgeschichte des Mittelalters, 5; Leiden: E.J. Brill, 1976).

Lanham, Richard A., *The Motives of Eloquence: Literary Rhetoric in the Renaissance* (New Haven: Yale University Press, 1976).

Lewry, Osmund, 'Rhetoric at Paris and Oxford in the Mid-Thirteenth Century', *Rhetorica* 1.1 (1983), pp. 45-63.

Lindhardt, J., *Rhetor, Poeta, Historicus: Studien über rhetorische Erkenntnis und Lebensanschauung im italienischen Renaissancehumanismus* (Leiden: E.J. Brill, 1979).

Lutz, Eckart C., *Rhetorica divina: Mittelhochdeutsche Prologgebete und die rhetorische Kultur des Mittelalters* (Berlin: W. de Gruyter, 1984).

Margolin, Jean-Claude, 'Le moment historique d'Erasme: Eléments traditionnels et éléments novateurs de la rhétorique', in Gert Ueding (ed.), *Rhetorik zwischen den Wissenschaften: Geschichte, System, Praxis als Probleme des 'Historischen Wörterbuchs der Rhetorik'* (Tübingen: Max Niemeyer, 1991), pp. 109-18.

Meerhoff, Kees, 'Mélanchthon lecteur d'Agricola: Rhétorique et analyse textuelle', *Réforme, Humanisme, Renaissance* 30.16 (1990), pp. 5-22.

—*Rhétorique et poétique aux XVIe siècle en France: Du Bellay, Ramus et les autres* (Studies in Medieval and Reformation Thought, 36; Leiden: E.J. Brill, 1986).

Miller, J.M., M.H. Prosser and T.W. Benson, *Readings in Medieval Rhetoric* (Bloomington: Indiana University Press, 1973).

Murphy, James J., *Renaissance Eloquence: Studies in the Theory and Practice of Renaissance Rhetoric* (Berkeley: University of California Press, 1983).

—*Renaissance Rhetoric: A Microfiche Collection of Key Texts, A.D. 1455–1600 from the Bodleian Library, Oxford* (Davis, CA: Pergamon Press, 1983).

—*Rhetoric in the Middle Ages: A History of Rhetorical Theory from St. Augustine to the Renaissance* (Berkeley: University of California Press, 1974).

—'Rhetoric: Western European', in Joseph R. Strayer (ed.), *Dictionary of the Middle Ages*, X (New York: Charles Scribner's Sons, 1988), pp. 351-64.

—*A Synoptic History of Classical Rhetoric* (Davis, CA: Hermagoras Press, 1983).

Plett, Heinrich, *Rhetorik der Affekte: Englische Wirkungsästhetik im Zeitalter der Renaissance* (Tübingen: M. Niemeyer, 1975).

Reid, Ronald F., 'The Boylston Professorship of Rhetoric and Oratory, 1806–1904: A Case Study in Changing Concepts of Rhetoric and Pedagogy', *Quarterly Journal of Speech* 45.3 (1959), pp. 239-57.

Schanze, Helmut, 'Vom Manuskript zum Buch: Zur Problematik der "Neuen Rhetorik" um 1500 in Deutschland', *Rhetorica* 1.2 (1983), pp. 61-73.

—*Rhetorik: Beiträge zu ihrer Geschichte in Deutschland vom 16.–20. Jahrhundert* (Frankfurt: Fischer, 1974).

Schmidt, Helmut, ' "Rhetoric of the Spirit" versus "Ancient Rhetoric" am Beispiel der Quäkerpredigt: Ein psycholinguistischer Beitrag zur Erforschung der rhetorischen Prinzipen des frühen Quäkertums', *Poetica* 8 (1977), pp. 85-95.

Schneider, John R., *Philip Melanchthon's Rhetorical Construal of Biblical Authority: Oratio Sacra* (Texts and Studies in Religion, 51; Lewiston, NY: Edwin Mellen, 1990).

Seigel, Jerrold E., *Rhetoric and Philosophy in Renaissance Humanism* (Princeton, NJ: Princeton University Press, 1968).

Sermain, Jean Paul, 'La rhétorique à l'horizon de la lecture: L'herméneutique littéraire en France au XVIIe siècle', in Gert Ueding (ed.), *Rhetorik zwischen den Wissenschaften: Geschichte, System, Praxis als Probleme des 'Historischen Wörterbuchs der Rhetorik'* (Tübingen: Max Niemeyer, 1991), pp. 271-80.

Shuger, Debora, 'Morris Croll Flacius Illyricus, and the Origin of Anti-Ciceronianism', *Rhetorica* 3.4 (1985), pp. 269-84.

—*Sacred Rhetoric: The Christian Grand Style in the English Renaissance* (Princeton, NJ: Princeton University Press, 1988).

Sloane, Thomas O., *Donne, Milton, and the End of Rhetoric* (Berkeley: University of California Press, 1985).

Sonnino, Lee A., *A Handbook to Sixteenth Century Rhetoric* (New York: Barnes & Noble, 1968).

Sprunger, Keith L., 'Ames, Ramus, and the Method of Puritan Theology', *Harvard Theological Review* 5.98 (1966), pp. 133-51.

Stötzer, Ursula, *Deutsche Redekunst im 17. und 18. Jahrhundert* (Halle: M. Niemeyer, 1962).

Sutton, Jane, 'The Death of Rhetoric and its Rebirth in Philosophy', *Rhetorica* 4.3 (1986), pp. 203-26.

Unger, Hans-Heinrich, *Die Beziehung zwischen Musik und Rhetorik im 16.–18. Jahrhundert* (Würzburg, 1941).

Ward, John O., 'Magic and Rhetoric from Antiquity to the Renaissance: Some Ruminations', *Rhetorica* 6.1 (1988), pp. 57-118.

Waswo, Richard, *Language and Meaning in the Renaissance* (Princeton, NJ: Princeton University Press, 1987).

Weber, Donald, *Rhetoric and History in Revolutionary New England* (New York: Oxford University Press, 1988).

Welch, John (ed.), *Chiasmus in Antiquity: Structure, Analyses, Exegesis* (Hildesheim: Gerstenberg, 1981).

Zappen, James P., 'Aristotelian and Ramist Rhetoric in Thomas Hobbes's Leviathan: Pathos versus Ethos and Logos', *Rhetorica* 1.1 (1983), pp. 65-91.

Ziegler, Dewey Kiper, *In Divided and Distinguished Worlds: Religion and Rhetoric in the Writings of Sir Thomas Browne* (Cambridge, MA: Harvard University Press, 1943).

Vernacular Rhetorics (Selected Materials)

Alles, Gregory D., 'Epic Persuasion: Religion and Rhetoric in the ILIAD and Valmiki's RAMAYANA' (PhD dissertation; Chicago: University of Chicago, 1986).

Becker, C., 'Reasons for the Lack of Argumentation and Debate in the Far East', *International Journal of Intercultural Relations* 10 (1986), pp. 75-92.

Bodde, Derk, *China's First Unifier: A Study of the Ch'in Dynasty as Seen in the Life of Li Ssu* (Leiden: E.J. Brill, 1938).

Bol, Peter, *Man's Culture and Heaven's Way: Transitions in T'ang and Sung China* (forthcoming).

Braarvig, Jens, 'Dhârani and pratibhâna: memory and eloquence of the bodhisattvas', *Journal of the International Association for Buddhist Studies* 8.1 (1985), pp. 17-29.

Carlitz, Katherine, *The Rhetoric of Chin p'ing mei* (Bloomington: Indiana University Press, 1986).

Ch'en, Wang-tao, *Hsiu tz'u hsueh fah farn (An Introduction to Chinese Rhetoric and its Development)* (Shanghai Province: Shanghai Educational Press, 4th edn, 1979).

Cheng, I-shou, *Pi chiao hsiu tz'u (Comparative Rhetoric)* (Fu-chou: Fu-chien Province People's Press, 1982).

Cheng, Tien, and Tan, Chuan-chi (eds.), *Ku han yu hsiu tz'u hsueh tzu liao hui pien (Bibliography and Abstracts of Major References of Chinese Rhetoric)* (Beijing: Shang Wu Press, 1980).

Cheng, Tzu-yu, *Chung-kuo hsiu tz'u hsueh shih kao (The History of Chinese Rhetoric)* (Shanghai Province: Shanghai Educational Press, 1986).

Chi, Shao-te, *Ku han yu hsiu tz'u (Ancient Chinese Rhetoric)* (Chang-Chun: Chi-lin Literary and History Press, 1986).

Condon, John C., *With Respect to the Japanese* (Yarmouth, ME: Intercultural Press, 1984).

Condon, John C., and M. Saito (eds.), *Intercultural Encounters with Japan: Communication—Contact and Conflict* (Tokyo: Simul Press, 1974).

Cua, A.S., *Ethical Argumentation: A Study in Hsün Tzu's Moral Epistemology* (Honolulu: University of Hawaii Press, 1985).

—'Hsun Tzu's Theory of Argumentation: A Reconstruction', *Review of Metaphysics* 36 (1983), pp. 867-94.

De, S.K., *History of Sanskrit Poetics* (Calcutta: Firma K.L. Mukopadhyay, 1960).

De Bary, William *et al.* (eds.), *Neo-Confucian Education: The Formative Stage* (Berkeley: University of California Press, 1989).

DeWoskin, Kenneth, *Doctors, Diviners, and Magicians of Ancient China: Biographies of 'Fang-shih'* (New York: Columbia University Press, 1983).

Doi, L. Taksi, 'The Japanese Patterns of Communication and the Concept of AMAE', *Quarterly Journal of Speech* 59.2 (1973), pp. 180-85.

Fitzgerald, James L., 'The Great Epic of India as Religious Rhetoric: A Fresh Look at the MAHABHARATA', *Journal of the American Academy of Religion* 51 (1983), pp. 611-30.

Fork, Alfred, 'The Chinese Sophists', *Asiatic Journal of the North Branch of the Royal Chinese Society* 34 (1901–1902), pp. 1-37.

Fukusawa, Yukichi, *Fukusawa Yukichi on Education: Selected Works* (ed. and trans. Kiyooka Eiichi; Tokyo: University of Tokyo Press; New York: Columbia University Press, 1986).

Garrett, Mary Margaret, 'The Impact of Western Rhetoric in the East: Three Case Studies: Chinese Responses to the Jesuits's Argumentation during the Late Ming–Early Ch'ing', International Society for the History of Rhetoric Göttingen Meeting (July 1989).

—'The Mo-tzu and the Lu-shih ch'un-ch'iu: A Case Study of Classical Chinese Theory and Practice of Argument' (PhD dissertation; Berkeley: University of California, 1983).

—'Pathos in Classical Chinese Rhetoric' (unpublished paper, late 1980s).

—'Was Meng-tzu a Sophist? A Rhetorical Analysis and Critique of Meng-tzu 6a.1–5' (unpublished paper, late 1980s).

—'What is the Usefulness of Ancient Chinese Rhetoric for Modern Rhetorical Theory?' (unpublished paper, late 1980s).

Gerow, E., *A Glossary of Indian Figures of Speech* (The Hague: Mouton, 1971).

Gonda, J., *Remarks on Similes in Sanskrit Literature* (Leiden: E.J. Brill, 1949).

Han, Fei, *The Complete Works of Han Fei Tzu* (London: A. Probsthian, 1959).

—'The Rhetorical Tradition in China: Confucius and Mencius', *Today's Speech* 17 (1969), pp. 3-8.

Henricks, Robert, *Hsi K'ang chi: Philosophy and Argumentation in Third-Century China. The Essays of Hsi K'ang* (Princeton, NJ: Princeton University Press, 1983).

Hsu Shi, *The Development of the Logical Method in Ancient China* (Shanghai: Hsueh lin ch'u pan she, 1928).

Ishii, Satoshi, 'Thought Patterns as Modes of Rhetoric: The United States and Japan', in L.A. Samovar and R.E. Porter (eds.), *Intercultural Communication: A Reader* (Belmont, CA: Wadsworth, 4th edn, 1985), pp. 97-102.

Jenner, G., *Die poetischen Figuren der Inder von Bhamaha bis Mammata: Ihre Eigenart im Verhältnis zu den Figuren repräsentativer antiker Rhetoriker* (Hamburg: Appel, 1968).

Jensen, J. Vernon, 'Rhetorical Emphases of Taoism', *Rhetorica* 5.3 (1987), pp. 219-29.

—'Teaching East Asian Rhetoric', *Rhetoric Society Quarterly* 17.2 (1987), pp. 135-49.

Jian, K.C., 'A Study of the Influence of the Chinese Rhetorical Tradition on Current Speeches by Chinese Speakers in the Republic of China' (Masters thesis, Brookings, SD: South Dakota State University, 1985).

Kao, Karl S.Y., 'Rhetoric', in William H. Nienhauser (ed.), *The Indiana Companion to Traditional Chinese Literature* (Bloomington, IN: Indiana University Press, 1968), pp. 121-37.

—'Rhetorical Devices in the Chinese Literary Tradition', *Tamkang Review* 14.1–4 (1983–84), pp. 325-37.

Kim, Y.Y., 'Intercultural Personhood: An Integration of Eastern and Western Perspectives', in L.A. Samovar and R.E. Porter (eds.), *Intercultural Communication: A Reader* (Belmont, CA: Wadsworth, 1985), pp. 400-10.

Klopf, D., S. Ishii and R. Cambra, 'Patterns of Oral Communication among the Japanese', *Cross Currents (Japan)* 5 (1978), pp. 37-49.

Kroll, J.L., 'Disputation in Ancient Chinese Culture', *Early China* 11 (1985–86).

Leff, Michael, 'Body, Soul, and the Rhetoric of Decorum in Anandarhana's DHVANYALOKA' (unpublished paper, late 1980s).

Li, Wei-chi, *Hsiu tz'u hsueh (Rhetoric)* (Chang-sha: Hu-nan People's Press, 1986).

Lo, Pin-wang, 'Poetry and Rhetoric', in Stephen Owen (ed.), *The Poetry of Early T'ang* (New Haven: Yale University Press, 1977), pp. 138-50.

Morrison, John L., 'The Absence of a Rhetorical Tradition in Japanese Culture', *Western Journal of Speech Communication* 36 (1972), pp. 89-102.

Narayan, P., *Indian Rhetoric* (Allahabad, 1984).

Nishiyama, Kazuo, 'Interpersonal Persuasion in a Vertical Society: The Case of Japan', *Speech Monograph* 38 (1971), pp. 148-54.

Okabe, R., 'American Public Address in Japan: A Case Study in the Introduction of American Oratory through the YUBEN (Japanese monthly magazine on oratory)', in R.J. Jensen and J.C. Hemmerback (eds.), *In Search of Justice* (Amsterdam: Rodopi, 1987), pp. 52-72.

—'The Impact of Western Rhetoric in the East: The Case of Japan', International Society for the History of Rhetoric Göttingen Meeting, July 1989.

—'Yukichi Kukuzawa: A Promulgator of Western Rhetoric in Japan', *Quarterly Journal of Speech* 59.2 (1973), pp. 186-95.

Oliver, Robert T., *Communication and Culture in Ancient India and China* (Syracuse: Syracuse University Press, 1971).

—'The Confucian Rhetorical Tradition in Korea during the Yi Dynasty', *Quarterly Journal of Speech* 45.4 (1959), pp. 363-73.

—'The Rhetorical Implications of Taoism', *Quarterly Journal of Speech* 47.1 (1961), pp. 27-35.

Owada, Tateki, *Shujigaku [Rhetoric]* (Tokyo: Hakubunkan, 1894).

Palinkas, Lawrence A., 'Ethnicity, Identity and Mental Health: The Use of Rhetoric in an Immigrant Chinese Church', *Journal of Psychoanalytic Anthropology* 5 (1982), pp. 235-58.

—*Rhetoric and Religious Experience: The Discourse of Immigrant Chinese Churches* (Fairfax, VA: George Mason University Press, 1989).

Park, Myung-Seok, *Communication Style in Two Different Cultures: Korean and American* (Seoul: Han Shin Publishing, 1979).

Pollack, David, *The Fracture of Meaning: Japan's Synthesis of China from the Eighth through the Eighteenth Centuries* (Princeton, NJ: Princeton University Press, 1986).

Reding, Jean-Paul, *Les fondements philosophiques de la rhétorique chez les Sophistes grecs et chez les Sophistes chinois* (Bern: Peter Lang, 1990).

Reynolds, Beatrice K., 'Lao Tzu: Persuasion through Inaction and Non-speaking', *Communication Quarterly* 17 (1969), pp. 23-25.

Richman, Paula, 'Framed Narrative and the Dramatized Audience in a Tamil Buddhist Epic', *Asian Folk Studies* 44.1 (1985), pp. 81-103.

Society of Chinese Rhetoric (eds.), *Hsiu tz'u hsueh lun wen chi (Collected Essays on Rhetoric)* (Fukkien People's Press, 1983).

Song, Chern-hua *et al.*, *Hsien tai han yu hsiu tz'u hsueh (Modern Chinese Rhetoric)* (Chilin People's Press, 1984).

Takeshima, Matajiro, *Shujigaku (Rhetoric)* (Tokyo: Hakubunkan, 8th edn, 1903).

Ting-Toomey, Stella, 'Japanese Communication Patterns: Insider versus the Outsider Perspective', *Western Communication* 15 (1986), pp. 113-26.

Tsao, Ding-jen, 'The Persuasion of Kuei Ku Tzu' (PhD dissertation, University of Minnesota, 1985).

Waley, Arthur, *The Way and its Power: A Study of the TEO TE CHING and its Place in Chinese Thought* (New York: Grove, 1958).

Wang, Hsi-chieh, *Han yu hsiu tz'u hsueh (Chinese Rhetoric)* (Beijing Press, 1983).

Wei-ming, Tu, 'The Unity of Knowing and Acting: From a Neo-Confucian Perspective', in *Humanity and Self-Cultivation: Essays in Confucian Thought* (Berkeley: University of California Press, 1979), pp. 83-101.

Wright, Arthur F. (ed.), *Confucian Persuasion* (Stanford, CA: Stanford University Press, 1960).

Wright, Dale S., 'The Distance of Awakening: Rhetorical Practice in Classical Ch'an Buddhism', *Journal of the American Academy of Religion* 61.1 (1993), pp. 23-40.

Yum, J.O., 'The Impact of Confucianism in Interpersonal Relationships and Communication Patterns in East Asia', *Second Symposium on Communication and Society* (Dubrovnik, Yugoslavia, 1987).

Dissertations (1985–94)

Alexander, Thomas Craig, 'Paul's Final Exhortation to the Elders from Ephesus: The Rhetoric of Acts 20.17–38' (PhD dissertation, Atlanta, GA: Emory University, 1990).

Belleville, Linda Louise, 'Paul's Polemical Use of the Moses-Doxa Tradition in 2 Corinthians 3.12–18' (PhD dissertation, Toronto: University of St Michael's College, 1986).

Braun, Willi, 'The Use of Mediterranean Banquet Traditions in Luke 14.1–24' (PhD dissertation, Toronto: University of Toronto, 1993).

Bullmore, Michael Andrew, 'St. Paul's Theology of Rhetorical Style: An Examination of 1 Corinthians 2.1–5 in the Light of First Century Græco-Roman Rhetorical Culture' (PhD Dissertation, Chicago: Northwestern University, 1993).

Castelli, Elizabeth, 'Mimesis as a Discourse of Power in Paul's Letters' (PhD dissertation, Claremont, CA: Claremont Graduate School, 1987).

Dicicco, Mario Michael, 'Paul's Rhetorical Use of the Three Classical Methods of Proof in 2 Corinthians 10–13: Ethos, Pathos, Logos' (ThD dissertation, Chicago: Lutheran School of Theology, 1993).

Elliott, R. Neil, 'The Rhetoric of Romans: Argumentative Constraint and Strategy and Paul's "Dialogue with Judaism"' (PhD dissertation, Princeton, NJ: Princeton Theological Seminary, 1989).

Fitzgerald, J.T., 'Cracks in an Earthen Vessel: An Examination of the Catalogues of Hardship in the Corinthian Correspondence' (PhD dissertation, New Haven: Yale University, 1984).

Geoffrion, Timothy, 'An Investigation of the Purpose and the Political and Military Character of Philippians: Paul's Letter of Exhortation Calling Citizens of Heaven to Remain Steadfast' (ThD dissertation, Chicago: Lutheran School of Theology, 1992).

Harwell, Hugh Blake, 'Classical Rhetoric and Paul's Purpose in Philippians' (PhD dissertation, Louisville, KY: Southern Baptist Theological Seminary, 1993).

Humphries, Raymond, 'Paul's Rhetoric of Argumentation in I Corinthians 1–4' (PhD dissertation, Berkeley, CA: Graduate Theological Union, 1979).

Kwon, Jongseon, 'A Rhetorical Analysis of the Johannine Farewell Discourse' (PhD dissertation, Louisville, KY: Southern Baptist Theological Seminary, 1993).

Martin, Dale, 'Paul and the Rhetoric of Reconciliation: An Exegetical Investigation of the Language and Composition' (PhD dissertation, Chicago: University of Chicago, 1989).

Merritt, Howard Wayne, 'In "Word and Deed": A Contribution to the Understanding of Moral Integrity in Paul' (PhD dissertation, Atlanta, GA: Emory University, 1985).

Mesner, David Earl, 'The Rhetoric of Citations: Paul's Use of Scripture in Romans 9, Volumes 1 and 2' (PhD dissertation, Chicago: Northwestern University, 1991).

Meyer, Donald Galen, 'The Use of Rhetorical Technique by Luke in the Book of Acts. Volumes 1 and 2' (PhD dissertation, Minneapolis: University of Minnesota, 1987).

Mitchell, Margaret, 'Paul and the Rhetoric of Reconciliation: An Exegetical Investigation of the Language and Composition of I Corinthians' (PhD dissertation; Chicago: University of Chicago, 1990).

Morris, Joseph Anthony, 'Irony and Ethics in the Lukan Narrative World: A Narrative Rhetorical Reading of Luke 4.14–30' (PhD dissertation, Berkeley, CA: Graduate Theological Union, 1992).

Pogoloff, Stephen Mark, 'Logos and Sophia: The Rhetorical Situation of 1 Corinthians 1–4 in the Light of Greco-Roman Rhetoric' (PhD dissertation, Durham, NK: Duke University, 1990).

Robuck, Thomas Durward, 'The Christ-Hymn in Philippians: A Rhetorical Analysis of its Function in the Letter' (PhD dissertation, Fort Worth, TX: Southwestern Baptist Theological Seminary, 1987).

Saw, Insawn, 'Paul's Rhetoric in 1 Corinthians 15: An Analysis' (ThD dissertation, Chicago: Lutheran School of Theology, 1993).

Schlueter, Carol J., '1 Thessalonians 2.14–16: Polemical Hyperbole' (PhD dissertation, Hamilton, Ontario: McMaster University, 1992).

Smith, Abraham, 'The Social and Ethical Implications of the Pauline Rhetoric in 1 Thessalonians' (PhD dissertation, Nashville, TN: Vanderbilt University, 1990).

Thibeaux, Evelyn Rose, 'The Narrative Rhetoric of Luke 7.36–50: A Study of Context, Text and Interpretation' (PhD dissertation, Berkeley, CA: Graduate Theological Union, 1990).

Verbrugge, Verlyn, 'The Collection and Paul's Leadership of the Church in Corinth' (PhD dissertation, South Bend, IN: University of Notre Dame, 1988).

Vogel, Robert Allan, 'Against your Brother: Conflict Themes and the Rhetoric of the Gospel According to Matthew' (PhD dissertation, Eugene, OR: University of Oregon, 1989).

Wachob, Wesley Hiram, ' "The Rich in Faith" and "The Poor in Spirit": The Socio-Rhetorical Function of a Saying of Jesus in the Epistle of James' (PhD dissertation; Atlanta, GA: Emory University, 1993).

Watson, Duane Frederick, 'Rhetorical Criticism of Jude and 2 Peter: Its Contribution to Interpretation and Questions of Literary Integrity and Interrelationship' (PhD dissertation; Duke University, 1986).

Music and Rhetoric

Bonds, Mark, *Wordless Rhetoric: Musical Form and the Metaphor of the Oration* (Cambridge, MA: Harvard University Press, 1991).

Brandes, Heinz, *Studien zur musikalischen Figurenlehre im 16. Jahrhundert* (Berlin: Triltsch & Huther, 1935).

Buelow, George, 'Rhetoric and Music', *The New Grove* 15, pp. 793-803.

Butler, Gregory, 'Fugue and Rhetoric', *Journal of Music Theory* 21 (1977), pp. 49-109.

—'Music and Rhetoric in Early Seventeenth-Century English Sources', *The Musical Quarterly* 66 (1980), pp. 53-64.

Gurlitt, Wilibald, 'Musik und Rhetorik: Hinweise auf ihre geschichtliche Grundlageneinheit', *Helicon* 5 (1944) (reprinted in W. Gurlitt, *Musikgeschichte und Gegenwart* [ed. H.H. Eggbrecht; 2 vols.; Wiesbaden: Steiner, 1966], I, pp. 62-81).

Haik-Vantoura, Suzanne, *The Music of the Bible Revealed* (Berkeley: BIBAL Press, 1993).

Jensen, H.J., *The Muses' Concord: Literature, Music, and the Visual Arts in the Baroque Age* (Bloomington: Indiana University Press, 1976).

Kahn, Aharon, 'Music in Halachic Perspective', *Journal of Halacha and Contemporary Society* 14 (1987), pp. 7-46.

Le Coat, Gerrard, *The Rhetoric of the Arts, 1550–1650* (Bern, 1975).

Maniates, Maria Rika, *Mannerism in Italian Music and Culture, 1530–1630* (Chapel Hill, NC: University of North Carolina Press, 1978).

—'Music and Rhetoric: Faces of Cultural History in the Renaissance and Baroque', *Israel Studies in Musicology* 3 (1983), pp. 44-69.

Ruhnke, Martin, *Joachim Burmeister: Ein Beitrag zur Musiklehre um 1600* (Kassel: Bärenreiter, 1955).

Palisca, Claude V., 'A Clarification of "Musica Reservata" in Jean Taisnier's "Astrologiae", 1559', *Acta Musicologica* 31 (1959), pp. 133-61.

—'Ut Oratoria Musica: The Rhetorical Basis of Musical Mannerism', in F.W. Robinson and S.G. Nichols, Jr (eds.), *The Meaning of Mannerism* (Hanover, NH: University Press of New England, 1972), pp. 37-65.

Schering, Arnold, 'Die Lehre von den musikalischen Figuren', *Kirchenmusikalisches Jahrbuch* 21 (1908), pp. 106-14.

Schmitz, Arnold, 'Die oratorische Kunst J.S. Bachs: Grundfragen und Grundlagen', *Kongreß-Bericht Gesellschaft für Musikforschung* (Lüneburg, 1950/51; Kassel: Bärenreiter Verlag, 1951), pp. 33-49 (reprinted in Josef Kopperschmidt [ed.], *Rhetorik. I. Rhetorik als Texttheorie* [Darmstadt: Wissenschaftliche Buchgesellschaft, 1990], pp. 290-312).

Shellens, M., 'Die Bedeutung der "Katharsis" in der Musiklehre des Aristoteles', *Archiv für Philosophie* 7.2 (1957).

Unger, Hans-Heinrich, *Die Beziehung zwischen Musik und Rhetorik im 16.–18. Jahrhundert* (Würzburg, 1941).

Wessel, Frederick, 'Affektenlehre' and 'Figurenlehre', in Friedrich Blum (ed.), *Die Musik in Geschichte und Gegenwart* (Kassel, 1955).

—'The Affektenlehre in the 18th Century' (PhD dissertation, Indiana University, 1955).

INDEXES

INDEX OF REFERENCES

JOURNAL FOR THE STUDY OF THE NEW TESTAMENT
SUPPLEMENT SERIES